Red Rum

Red Rum

IVOR HERBERT'S
Full and extraordinary story of a horse of courage

WILLIAM LUSCOMBE PUBLISHER LIMITED
(In association with Mitchell Beazley)

2

First published in Great Britain by
William Luscombe Publisher Limited
Artists House
14 Manette Street
London W1V 5LB
1974

ISBN 0 86002 078 9

Designed by Florianne Henfield
Filmset in Monophoto Bembo by
Servis Filmsetting Limited, Manchester
Printed in Great Britain by
Tinling (1973) Ltd., Prescot, Lancs.

To all horses of courage
however humble
in admiration and gratitude

CONTENTS

FOREWORDS

From
Mr Noel H. Le Mare   (owner of Red Rum)

In two minutes and something over forty seconds, the winner of The Derby will be pushing his head past the post. Not until the first dozen round Tattenham Corner can you begin to dismiss those remaining behind. Even at 'the distance' it is often difficult to say which will win.

How different is the Grand National where even Red Rum's record time took something over nine minutes – jumping thirty fences, including the awe-inspiring Chair. It has been said that unless your horse is amongst the first six commencing the second circuit you have little chance.

In the following pages you will read about a horse which has surely proved to be the most gallant National 'chaser of the century.

His history is written for you by one of our finest Racing Authors. Read on.

Noel H. Le Mare

From
Mr Donald McCain   (trainer of Red Rum)

'That's super, the old horse has done it. That will really put him amongst the Greats,' I exclaimed when Ivor Herbert telephoned to tell me he wanted to write a full-length book about Red Rum.

Ivor's books always give the real atmosphere of Racing – after all he really knows the job and trained plenty of good winners himself! He knows what it feels like – all the ups and downs! There was nobody I would sooner have to write a book about Red Rum than Ivor Herbert. His writing informs – and entertains. I'm *delighted* to be given this opportunity to say how pleased I am he has written the *Full* story of *Red Rum*. May the book enjoy the sales it so richly deserves.

Don McCain

ACKNOWLEDGEMENTS

The research for this book and its compilation would have been impossible without the full co-operation of Red Rum's many connections, past and present, who gave me so freely of their time, recollections, notes, albums and photographs. Three experts in their fields, unconnected with the horse, additionally worked at speed to produce material for me: Neville Ring for his Irish researches, Laurie Payne from *Raceform* and *Chaseform*, and P. Carey of *Timeform*.

The immense details of Red Rum's racing career which comprise the appendices are reproduced from 138 photostats generously supplied by their publishers Raceform Ltd, of 55 Curzon Street, London W.1.

Raceform Up-to-Date, published by them in partnership with *Sporting Chronicle* Publications Ltd, is not only the indispensable vade-mecum for every racing follower, at home or away, but is the only official form book recognised by the Jockey Club. The combined experience and acute observance of the compilers of *Raceform, Chaseform, Raceform Up-to-Date, Raceform Note Book and Chaseform-Note Book* speak for themselves. Their hard facts and shrewd comments are republished here with their swift and friendly co-operation. The author is merely one of tens of thousands who could not have done without them.

IVOR HERBERT
Bradenham,
Buckinghamshire

1 'THE ONE GOOD HORSE . . .'

The horse worked between the blowing sand dunes and the grey sea tide. Ahead of the beat of his feet the dunlins scampered for safety and the gulls rose in a white cloud shrieking. The wind brought a steely wall of rain racing towards the horse across the broad beach. The red danger flags were blown out stiff as scarlet boards, cracking in the wind like thunder.

The horse was bent over his bit like a bow. His head was tucked into his left and his mouth was open showing his parrot-teeth in a snarl. (He was noticeably overshot.) The horse, as was his habit, led with his near-fore leg and, now that he was really galloping, the leg flicked outwards whistling through the air, the hoof thumping the ground, like a boxer again and again left-hooking. It was an action which would have gained him no rosette in the show ring, but which in a race, after a distance when the pressure was on, showed clearly to those who knew him that the great horse had really begun to fly.

When the pressure was on

His front hooves hammered the sand, so that the shock – when at such instant one small foot supported half a ton propelled over it and forward – was so great that you might think the feet would never stand it. Yet these were the feet which had in his mid-career been so crippled with a bone disease that he had only had a fifty-fifty chance of recovery.

His mane blew backwards and so did his lad's thick hair. The lad's body was short and broad, and it bobbed and bobbed above the horse's back, braced against arms and legs like ram-rods.

The horse was the joy of this lad's life and that life had had its troubles of every sort. Once, in another place, the horse had been the particular love of a stable girl, and his forced parting from her had smashed her interest in racing and, in a small way, had broken her heart.

On this lad's face now, racing across the sand, ecstasy and anxiety mixed and flickered, for the horse was triumphantly well – and thus nearly running away with him. The conflict in the lad's face reflected the still unresolved temptations of his life.

The sting of sand

The trainer stood very tall by the side of his old truck. Behind it were coupled the harrows with which he had just combed a two mile long strip of wrinkled sand, just wide enough for two horses to work upsides. An old tweed cap, greasy-peaked, was perched atop of his very large head. Bursting out around it, the hair which had given him the nickname 'Ginger' flickered grizzled in the wind. His eyes, screwed up against sea-spray and the sting of sand, watched nothing but his horse. On his face burned the glow of exultation.

For this was the horse for which he had been waiting down all those dark years when he and his wife had camped in small rooms with a few sticks of furniture, and money was so short that he was down to borrowing a fiver to pay for a horse to run. Through all those years, driving a taxi, dreaming of finding one day, somehow, for someone 'The One Good Horse' which would make his name, the trainer had spent money he did not have on horses which were cheap and old and lame and bad. He bought experience most dearly, but he stored it up against the day when the one good horse would come.

The trainer, so far from being born with a silver spoon or golden mangers, had been reared in a back street far from the open world of thoroughbred race horses and rich friends and introductions into stables. He had no background of horses whatsoever. He had no relation in even the lowest echelon of the racing industry. He was, in addition, the wrong build for the game.

Hope winking fitfully

He had glimpsed hope winking fitfully at the end of a shadowy tunnel of setbacks and disasters. He had lost faith sometimes. He had thought the distant light beckoning him on might turn out to be only the winking eye of a harlot. But he, like the horse who now rushed past him like a conquering express into the lashing wall of rain, had struggled on against the odds. For the horse had received in his life much unjust punishment. He had been subjected to sufficient pain from whip and bone disease to make him, had he been human, turn crook or layabout.

The rain passed across the sea. The horse came back walking in the frothy rim of the tide. There, in the shallows a few years earlier, horses and carts had been drawing nets for shrimps and codling: horses with torn tendons and twisted joints had become remarkably sound again. . . .

'A true professional'

The horse played with his bit and splashed his now sound hooves against the sea's surface like a child larking. The horse knew that his work was done, for he was, as his trainer said, 'a true professional'. He was relaxed now. His arrogance had melted into a jaunty content.

He sprang up, plunged down, the steep sand hills behind the Royal Birkdale Golf Course and made his way home, feet clipping the tarmac, leading the little string along the tree-lined avenues of Southport's smarter suburb. Here, where Victorian magnates had erected their red residences in ornate gardens with extensive coach-houses, mothers from flats and newly developed little homes, bustled their children off to school. Because the horse was famous now throughout the land commuters slowed to let him pass. Eyes followed his progress with awe from cars shuttling into Liverpool, where he had struggled for humble victory in his very first race, and later, achieved his glories.

In one commodious mansion in a tranquil street the horse's octogenarian owner lay abed. Slightly later rising was the sprightly old gentleman's only concession to the rigorous length of his life. It had begun in poverty in the last century. During it he had created great constructional works across the world and a fortune which he had now settled on his children. For him, as for his trainer, victory at Liverpool, *the* racecourse of the country, in the Grand National, *the* great race of the whole year, had been a dream born in adolescence. The owner always remembered his mother running a school and teaching the children to sing each day 'If at first you don't succeed, try, try, try again'.

To win the 'National

So it had been with him, with his trainer and with the horse who now turned towards the railway tracks and the poorer part of Birkdale. He waited at the level-crossing while a Liverpool train clattered past. The gates opened. He crossed and was in his humble street again. On his left lay, in a long and rather dingy row, a sweet shop and tobacconist, a pet centre, a Chinese fish-and-chip shop, a butcher, a small wholesale grocer. . . . On his right behind the bus-shelter, behind the row of parked secondhand cars belonging to his trainer and partner, lay the alley leading into his cosy stable-yard, overlooked by the backs of houses and embracing one solitary tree.

His cosy stable-yard

The trainer's wife looked up and out from her modern kitchen into the yard to watch the horse walk in. All those years when weeks were hard and months a struggle, and she had been worried sometimes close to breaking point, her husband had said – and she had not fully understood him – 'All we need is one good horse'. Now she comprehended for what he had striven. The horse had come:

The horse was Red Rum.

2 'STRANGE TO THINK WE HAD A 'NATIONAL WINNER AT ALL . . .'

Like most great steeplechasers Red Rum was conceived and born in Ireland. But his triumphs are not so much an accident of his breeding; they are a denial of it. For he was bred to be nothing more than a sprinter on the flat. He was planned to be inexpensive, of no consequence, and precocious enough to run quickly in the spring of his two-year-old season (before, in fact, his second birthday), with the chance of an owner winning something over a short distance without having to keep him too long. His prospects by blood were as far removed from winning a Grand National as are possible within all the muddled realm of racing.

The Rossenarra stud

The distinction of breeding our first postwar double Grand National winner, however unintentionally, belongs to Martyn J. McEnery. He is the owner and manager of the Rossenarra stud, near Kells in County Kilkenny, a quiet-spoken, pensive man, bespectacled, young-looking and born in December, 1930. He received no financial reward for Red Rum's triumphs, either directly (for there are, as yet, no breeders' prizes for the winners of our great steeplechases), nor indirectly: he sold Red Rum's dam the year after he sold her son, and he had already sold Red Rum's two elder sisters. When Red Rum galloped to glory McEnery had no relations left at home whose values, by their son's or brother's triumphs, would have trebled overnight.

McEnery is still drily amused and slightly bemused by the fact that he bred by accident a horse who has now joined that élite band of steeplechasing's immortals. 'Strange to think we had a Grand National winner here at all!' he says slowly. He speaks quietly, after deliberation and to the point, never luxuriating Irish-fashion in the pleasure of six words when one suffices. He is the antithesis of what strangers to Ireland conceive to be a typical Irishman. Nor does he claim with the benefit of hindsight, as is so often the ludicrous case in racing, any credit for or prescience about the subsequent glories of Red Rum.

It would be the easiest thing in the world for Martyn McEnery to declare that he always suspected his colt would turn out to be 'a grand lepper', that he had bred him with that thought half in mind, that he smelt steeple-chasing in his yearling action. Many other connections of great horses have, when history has safely rolled past, jumped on the band-waggon and blown their own trumpets. Martyn J. McEnery has never done any such thing.

'A grand lepper'

There rests, for all that, in pride of place on a coffee-table in the centre of his combined living-room and study a cigar-box adorned by a golden horseshoe. This is the 1973 award presented by Goff's Bloodstock Sales in Dublin to the vendor of that horse sold through them which, in the opinion of the Irish Racing Writers' Association, has done most to promote Irish horses internationally.

The award presented to Martyn McEnery at a reception in Dublin's Shelbourne Hotel on May 28th, 1974, was for Red Rum's first record-breaking National victory in the previous year. He was selected from nine other nominees all of whom had passed through Goff's on their paths to 1973 fame, including such notables as Captain Christy, Bula, Killiney, Conor Pass and Furry Glen.

During Red Rum's racing career in three most dissimilar training stables a number of very different people were to remark independently on the horse's 'professionalism'. They were to detect under his exceptional exuberance that seriousness of purpose, that pursuit of an end, which marks successful human beings. Few winning people are totally grave. They, like Red Rum, are happy to play about, to vent energy and to relax, so long as nothing for any length of time diverts their important course. Early environment moulds human and equine characters; it is significant that Martyn McEnery's Rossenarra stud was no charming, amateurish farm with an old Georgian house and rough fields split Irish-wise by touselled banks and tumbled walls and cheerful decrepit bedsteads. It was a newly established, efficient and professional undertaking, and Red Rum lived there for the first 16 months of his life.

Red Rum's profes-sionalism

Kells lies a dozen miles south of Kilkenny City on the road to Carrick-on-Suir. Kilkenny, a small, hilly grey town on a river is sometimes grandiloquently described as 'the Florence of Ireland'. It is certainly mediaeval, attractive, and still the home of arts and crafts. The Kilkenny Hounds sally out from kennels at Mount Juliet to harry the foxes across the eastern half of the county.

Kilkenny people

The McEnery family are very much Kilkenny people. They used to live several miles further south on the Carrick road at Rossenarra near Kilmoganny. The present stud, which now bears the name of the old McEnery property, was bought by Martyn's father Jack in 1941. In the war's darkest days no-one knew who might win and what the victors would do with property even in neutral Ireland. Even so its price now seems incredible. For Jack McEnery paid under £10 per acre; a sum of about £2,300 for 240 good acres. It was what they call in Ireland the 'out farm' and there was no house on it.

Jack McEnery was a well-known hunting man, dealing in hunters and half-breds and a leading light in the harum-scarum of the local point-to-points. They were then very much more cross-country affairs across natural obstacles than the minor racecourses of today. Martyn was only rising 11 when his father so astutely bought the new farm. He remembers going to point-to-point meetings as a boy when the family often had three and sometimes four winners in an afternoon.

Gowran Park

One of Ireland's most attractive racecourses, woody Gowran Park, lies 20 minutes' drive to the north-east of the new Rossenarra stud. Jack McEnery together with Jack Duggan and the late Major Dermot McCalmont from beautiful Mount Juliet were the triumvirate who re-suscitated Gowran Park races after the war. The silver cup for their important Thyestes steeplechase, a recognised pre-Cheltenham race for Irish Gold Cup candidates and won by many famous horses, including Arkle, was presented to the racecourse by Jack McEnery. It was originally a trophy won by him for the best half-bred hunter at Kilkenny show. Martyn remembers being handed the rosette and being told, 'Tell your father he's now won the cup outright'.

Breeder of flat-race horses

When Jack McEnery died the family's Kilmoganny property had to be sold to pay his death duties. The Government's Land Commission acquired most of the farm for re-distribution and the novelist Richard Condon (author of *The Manchurian Candidate*) now lives in the old McEnery house. By 1961 an ultra-modern house of Swedish design had been completed – red brick with a mass of external woodwork – on the 'out farm' near Kells, and in 1963, when Martyn was rising 33, he moved the stud there and settled down to establish himself as a commercial breeder of flat-race horses. Any connection with steeplechasing seemed buried for ever. . . .

The land is excellent; the countryside flat and feature-less. The soil has the desirably high limestone content, but except for those trees bordering the road and two survivors near the house, McEnery extirpated every tree. Now there are neatly railed paddocks divided by a central access passage. The stable yards are new, practical and plain. Concrete abounds. 'It is,' notes Neville Ring, the Irish racing writer, 'very much a *commercial* establishment.'

Martyn McEnery had hardly moved into his new establishment when he had to make the decision which would produce the horse Red Rum. He had been the owner since 1960 of a bay mare called Mared, a name strangely similar to that of the future owner of her famous son, Noel Le Mare. It was compounded from her sire's name, Magic Red, a sprinter who won a few races over five and six furlongs during the war.

Breeding Red Rum

She was foaled in 1958. Her mother was Quinta by the useful jumping sire Anwar, and her grandmother Batika was a daughter of the world-famous Blenheim. Mared and her mother Quinta were both bred by Mr S. J. Parr at his Athboy stud in Co. Meath. Quinta was totally undistinguished. Mared, to be blunt, was crazy.

A mad mother

At the end of her 2-year-old season in which she had run for her breeder's wife, Mared was hastily disposed of. She was put up for sale at Goff's and bought by Martyn McEnery for what must have seemed the suspiciously low figure of 240 guineas. Trained by John Oxx at The Curragh she had finished second in her first race when, quite unfancied in the Balrath Plate at Dublin's smart Phoenix Park in June, she had been beaten only half a length by the odds-on Another Phoenix. She had flattered to deceive: in none of her four subsequent races that summer did she even get into the money.

Her mother Quinta was placed on the flat three times as a 3-year-old in 1956, but had subsequently disappointed the Parrs. She had produced a full brother to Mared in 1959, called Via Con Deo who won on the flat as a 4-year-old in 1963 and was later placed hurdling in 1965. But in 1960, when Mared was running for the Parrs as a 2-year-old, her mother Quinta proved barren. The Parrs decided to sell her as well, and she died two years later after slipping twins. The Parrs were happy to cull Mared. She showed them a considerable loss when the cost of her creation, production and training were set against the 240 guineas (less sale commission and expenses) which they received from Martyn McEnery.

3 'SHE'S MAD . . . TAKE HER HOME!'

But McEnery's policy then was buying fillies out of training to race himself the following season. He liked Magic Red's speedy pedigree. The horse was by Link Boy and his grandmother was a famous brood-mare, Black Ray, who would turn out to be the ancestress of the illustrious Mill Reef.

Offspring of the highest class

There was also much to like about Mared's maternal grandmother Batika. Unlike her disappointing daughter Quinta she had also produced Mared's 'aunt' Spring Offensive (by Legend of France) who had proved a rattling good race mare in top-class staying flat races and then produced a series of offspring of the highest class. One of them, Fabergé II, ran second in the 2,000 Guineas and became the sire of the great Rheingold, winner of the Prix de l'Arc de Triomphe.

Some of these highlights lay far ahead when Martyn McEnery took cheap Mared home from the sales at Ballsbridge. But there were sufficient glinting strands in her breeding for him to weave a few small dreams during the winter of 1960–61. He resolved to send her into training not too far away near Carrick-on-Suir with 'Phonsie' O'Brien, brother of the all-conquering Vincent O'Brien.

Both the new trainer and the new owner of Mared received a nasty shock when 'Phonsie' O'Brien discovered the full horrors of Mared. He did not mince his words. He told the unhappy McEnery that Mared couldn't be held, that she was mad, that she did nothing but steam up and sweat all the time and that she was 'mad hot'.

A lunatic filly

'Take her away, Take her home', said 'Phonsie' O'Brien, and Martyn McEnery seemed lumbered with a lunatic filly and an apparently hopeless case.

He was cast down, but not defeated. He possesses an equable, methodical character. He approached his neighbour Mick Butler and enlisted his help with the problem creature. Butler, now training himself in a small way, patiently took Mared in hand. Weeks passed, and eventually he persuaded the filly to settle down sufficiently for another attempt to be made to train her.

It is one thing to allow an over-excited racehorse to relax on its own, rambling round fields, though a rider with busy heels, harsh hands and an electric backside cannot even contrive that. It is a very different matter when the animal must start to do sufficient fast work to get fit enough to run. The first gallop, sometimes even the first explosive excursion onto any grass which looks like a gallop, can knock down in minutes the steadiness built up over months.

The first gallop

McEnery had only started training himself in the previous year, and had won his first race, suitably enough at Gowran Park.★

Mared was now a well-grown filly of 16·1 hands but not, in McEnery's view, well made. McEnery bluntly remembers her as 'Very straight in front, terribly like Red Rum! I always considered,' says McEnery, 'that Red Rum was too straight in front and too light around his middle....' It is refreshing to hear from the breeder of a future wonder-horse, an unusual, honest opinion unvarnished by the gloss of hindsight.

A future wonder-horse

McEnery vividly recalls the horrors of taking Mared racing. 'In her stable, she was a rich bay in colour. But before a race she would turn black with sweat and white with froth *everywhere.*'

In her first two races for McEnery she ran, as they had feared, far too freely. She proved almost impossible to hold. Then McEnery sent her off to Galway on 2nd August, 1961, to run in the 7 furlong Mervue Maiden Stakes. He engaged Jackie Power to ride, the jockey who had been on her in her first and only promising race at the start of her previous year. The Mervue Maiden Stakes was of small consequence and worth £202. Mared's conduct before the race was crazy. She became so laced in a froth of sweat that 'We had to throw a bucket of water over her,' says McEnery, 'and then try to dry her off again *before* she even came into the paddock!'

In spite of this ominous overture Martyn backed her at 10 to 1. This time Jackie Power persuaded her to settle down for the first time in her career. Instead of racing off like a mad cat, she consented to remain with the field until they reached the bottom of the hill at Galway about a furlong and a half from home. At that instant Power let

Went clear to win

★ The horse, Graduate, was ridden by the good Australian jockey Garnie Bougoure, who bought him to race in Singapore in which stratum of racing he proved nearly top class.

the mad mare loose and 'swoosh', as McEnery recalls, she
flew like an arrow through the opposition and went clear
to win by 2 lengths. 'I had,' says McEnery quietly, 'a
little "touch" on her.'

Burning equine courage

Too often plaudits acclaim only the connections of
big race winners. The temperamental problems of the
wild filly Mared required more patience, more handling,
more sympathy than many a placid and honest contender
in a Classic. It was a small triumph on the part of Martyn
McEnery and his helpers to have won any race with the
creature at all. It is extraordinary that her son was not
equally mad, instead of turning out, after years of punishing races, to be the epitome of burning equine courage.

Mared ran but twice more and got placed third round
the swooping seaside track of tiny Tramore. Her astonishing racing career was over. Comparing her now with her
famous son, Martyn McEnery shakes his bespectacled head
in continuing amazement. 'It is just *unbelievable,*' he
declares, 'that Red Rum could go on racing for so long
without showing any signs of that temperament of his
mother's.'

He resolved, however, to breed from her. There was a
stallion literally on Mared's doorstep. Neron, 14 years old
when Mared was first covered, stood at £98 a service at
the Rossenarra stud itself. So she visited him two years in
succession, accepting his attentions without too many
tantrums and producing in 1963 and 1964 bay fillies,

Half-sisters to Red Rum

named Neared and Quintula. Both turned out for
McEnery even more unrewarding than their mother had
proved on the racecourse. Both went to the sales making
the pathetic sums of 110 guineas and 190 guineas
respectively. Neared, who never raced 'owing to injury',
as her owner Mr Christy Mooney reported to Donald
McCain, was offered to Red Rum's trainer in 1974 by Mr
Mooney, who lives near Portarlington, in County Offaly.
She had been covered by Even Say. Quintula was exported
as a yearling to Germany in 1965. There may still exist
somewhere out there another half-sister to the greatest
post-war Grand National winner by, what is more, a horse
who proved an excellent sire of jumpers.

It is the misfortune of owners of jumping sires, and the
great difficulty of jumping breeders, that most good
jumping sires are dead before they have established their
prowess. With a steeplechaser reaching his prime at nine
years old, the decision to send his dam to be covered by his
sire must have been made eleven years earlier. Since few

stallions start serving mares before they are four they will therefore be 15 years old before the first of their sons reaches his steeplechasing prime. Neron died in 1966, the year after Red Rum was born. . . .

Perhaps Red Rum's two elder half-sisters were ugly. Certainly the reputation of their crazy mother will have run before them at the sales. But the dreadful prices poor Martyn McEnery received for them were no more than their carcass value to a butcher.

For the following year he made a change of mate. Magic Red mares were doing quite well at stud (by the end of 1966 their progeny had won 73 races worth £31,675). McEnery resolved to breed for pure speed from Mared. He chose the grey stallion Quorum, who then was standing at Paddy Clarke's Balreask stud close to Dublin Airport. The stud, one of Ireland's oldest (it was founded in 1847) was a large one of 400 acres, usually stood three stallions and lay in that part of the country made famous by Arkle. Very close to Balreask were bred or reared not only Arkle, but the superlative 'chasers Golden Miller, Gregalach and, as if those were not coincidences enough, the only other dual Grand National winner of the century, Reynoldstown. The black horse, the previous double victor round Aintree in 1935 and 1936, was foaled in those parts in 1927, nearly 40 years before Red Rum.

The grey stallion Quorum

These considerations did not concern Martyn McEnery when he contacted Paddy Clarke at the Balreask Stud to book in his disappointing Mared to Quorum. He was influenced mainly by a family friendship. His father Jack had enjoyed many friendly dealings with Paddy Clarke and his father before him. Martyn had, as he says, 'only just started on my own'. Furthermore horses by Quorum had proved financially rewarding to the McEnery family. 'Every Quorum we'd sold before had made in the region of 1,500 guineas – respectable enough in those days,' says McEnery mildly.

Studying the top line of Quorum's pedigree suggested that he would produce sparkling sprinting speed. He traced back through the sprinters Vilmorin, Gold Bridge and Golden Boss. It was only way back that you came via The Boss to Orby who had won the Derby of 1907.

But Quorum had shown on the racecourse that he was slightly more than a sprinter himself. He nearly won the 2,000 Guineas, being second to the great Crepello, and he won the Sussex Stakes at Goodwood over a mile. He won £7,306 in stakes over distances from 5 furlongs up to a

More than a sprinter

mile, including the Jersey Stakes at Royal Ascot.

Red Rum's immense stamina

The extraordinary puzzle of the source of Red Rum's immense stamina has naturally cast the breeding pundits into disarray. When you worship the gods of the stud book and make your living like a Delphic priestess by interpreting the oracles of misty blood-lines, it is painful to find yourself presented with a nonsense. It is worth noting perhaps that, if you peer in deeply enough, you can disinter a little stamina from the recesses of Red Rum's sprinting pedigree. His father's mother's grandsire was the real old stayer Noble Star. But Noble Star was merely one of Red Rum's 16 great-great-grandparents. If you go that far back among anyone's ancestry you can prove the source of anything you want.

Mared was dispatched north to the Balreask Stud in the spring of 1964 for her visit to Quorum. She was successfully covered and returned in foal and with a bill for £251 12*s*., of which £198 was for Quorum's services and the balance (a fortnight's worth by 1974 levels) for her keep. Eleven months lapsed, her time duly came and on the evening of 3rd May, 1965, at 6 p.m. the foal who was to be named Red Rum was born at Rossenarra. 'Mared was the same foaling as she was racing,' Martyn McEnery drily recalls – 'All smoke and steam!'

'All smoke and steam'

A bay colt of average size was born in good shape. For the commercial breeder a colt is nearly always more valuable than a filly. There immediately follows an anxious inspection: are the tiny creature's limbs perfectly fashioned or malformed? Does it seem healthy? Will it take milk from the dam? A score of things can be wrong with, or happen to, the newly born foal. But all looked well and went well with temperamental Mared's first son in those first few hours.

McEnery was '*delighted* to get a Quorum colt, I thought my fortune was made. . . . But I was to get another rude awakening.'

4 'WHERE THE GYPSIES PULLED IN TO REST THEIR CARAVANS'

The young man who cared for Red Rum as a foal was Roddy O'Byrne from Kilmacthomas in the neighbouring county of Waterford. He was 19 at the time and learning the business of running a stud by living with the McEnerys who were family friends.

Roddy, a keen point-to-pointing man, worked hard as a studhand by day, but lived in the house at Rossenarra for a year. 'The McEnerys are marvellous people,' he says, 'and Martyn's wife is a beautiful woman.'

The O'Byrne family represent that type of landed horsemen, unusual in England but ubiquitous in Ireland, which assures the abundance of good-class Irish jumping bloodstock. He and his brother now together run the 400-acre farm which they inherited from their father. And on the farm there are usually no less than 60 horses. They breed and deal and raise and sell, and always have a number of good ones around. In 1974 their Financial News trained by young Jim Dreaper won the National Trial 'Chase at Punchestown, 'And,' says tall slim Roddy with relish, 'I look forward to his taking on Red Rum at Aintree!'

Roddy O'Byrne, born in December, 1946, went to school at Rockwell in Co. Tipperary. When he left he had itchy feet: he wanted to go off to Australia 'to do something on my own for myself. I had it in mind to learn to run stud farms in Australia.'

Irish jumping bloodstock

The plan never came about. But 'I still wanted to prove myself'. Thus he arrived with the McEnerys on the Rossenarra Stud.

Neither of the two senior members of the McEnery staff have any particular recollections of Mared's foal by Quorum. The stud groom, James Duncan, a tall quiet man in his late thirties when Red Rum was born, had already been eight years with the family. In his time the McEnerys have sold over 150 horses through Goff's. To his mind, and to that of the 'herd', Dick Butler, who had worked for

Red Rum's character

the family since 1941, there was nothing special about Red Rum's character in his baby days.

It is another strange coincidence in the Red Rum story that the first time stud groom James Duncan ever saw racing on television was that day at Liverpool when Red Rum (22 months after his birth) and his filly companion from Rossenarra ran against one another in a humble 2-year-old selling race.

'The Gypsy Field'

The stud, now a large place with 50 boxes and standing two stallions, was then much smaller. McEnery in 1965 had only two colt foals: 'The Quorum' (foals are called on studs by their sire's name) and 'The Miralgo' which subsequently was sent to England to be sold. Both colts were weaned from their mothers in the autumn and then turned out together in a field called 'The Gypsy'. McEnery explains: 'We've always kept the colts in "The Gypsy Field" ever since we came here. Long ago it was probably "the commonage" where the gypsies pulled in to rest their caravans.' In one instance at least, the dark people brought the field good luck.

Roddy O'Byrne, while learning the workings of a commercial stud, did most of the feeding of the foals. He carries his small head slightly to one side and nods it for emphasis. 'I was *amazed* at the amount those foals could eat.' Red Rum was to keep an enormous appetite all through his training.

High protein feeding

'Nuts weren't the thing in those days,' says McEnery, 'so Red Rum as a foal and a yearling was fed crushed Canadian oats.' The high protein feeding value of imported Canadian oats, their uniformity, dryness and clean bright colour from the prairie sunshine have made 'Canadians' (and 'Australians') keenly sought-after – in spite of their great expense – in nearly every high-class British racing stable and on most studs.

Roddy O'Byrne helped prepare the Rossenarra yearlings for Goff's September sales. It was the famous firm's centenary year and also that of the first running of the Irish Derby on the Curragh. In 1866 the classic was worth less than £450 to the winner. (Its value dropped subsequently to as little as £115.) But, transfused by sponsorship from the Irish Hospitals' Trust the winner of the race in 1966 collected over £52,000 and by 1974 had almost doubled that.

The descendants in business of that Mr Robert J. Goff, who had been appointed Auctioneer to the Irish Turf Club in 1866, had already sold two recent Irish Derby winners,

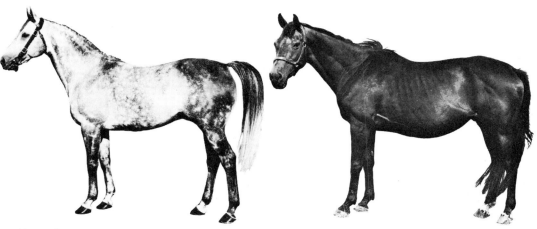

Above: Quorum, Red Rum's sire, standing at Paddy Clarke's Balreask Stud near Navan where Red Rum's dam Mared went to be covered. *Photo: John Slater*

Above: Mared, Red Rum's dam (in the summer of 1974), the once "mad crazy race mare", now many foals after Red Rum and in different ownership. *Photo: Ruth Rogers*

Left: Our hero who has inherited the colour and the bold ears of his mother without, mercifully, her temperament. There is something of Quorum in his hind-leg. *Photo: Jeremy Hoare*

Below: Shrewd-eyed, James Duncan, Stud Groom at the Rossenarra Stud, Co. Kilkenny, where Red Rum was born and reared. *Photo: Ruth Rogers*

Below: The quiet professional, Martyn McEnery, breeder and seller of Red Rum – and still faintly surprised by the horse's glories. *Photo: Ruth Rogers*

Left: Red Rum at home behind Upper Aughton Road. Like many a racehorse he chews his woodwork. *Photo: Jeremy Hoare*

Right: Sandra Kendall, who looked after her beloved "Rummy" for 4 years, started like hundreds of thousands of little girls on a pony. This is her on little "Tammy" on whom she used to ride out to Mr. Renton's famous racing stable. *Photo: Charles Wright*

Below: Sandra ("Dandra" as Bobby Renton called her) as a professional stable-girl on "Rummy" soon after he arrived as a 3-year-old off the flat. His physical development since then has been enormous.

Charles Wright, the ex-cavalryman, Head Lad to trainers Bobby Renton, Tommy Stack, and Anthony Gillam, and – through those three reigns – to Red Rum. *Photo: "The Yorkshire Post"*

"Ginger" and Beryl McCain getting married on Grand National Day, 1961. (They had got engaged on 'National Day, 1959.) The horse came from Miss Walsh's riding-stables where they met.

Above: Mrs. Lurlene Brotherton leading in her great Grand National winner Freebooter (trained by Bobby Renton) in 1950. She was to try for 22 years to find another – and sold Red Rum 7 months too soon. . . .

Left: Bobby Renton, training till he was 83 years old, got his horses out whatever the weather. Here he rides Devon Peter at Oxclose in the snow followed by Head Lad Charles Wright on Old Mull. *Photo: "The Yorkshire Post"*

Ragusa and Meadow Court, before the sales in those lovely Ballsbridge Paddocks whither Red Rum was bound.

Two months before the sales Red Rum and his Miralgo companion were brought in from 'The Gypsy' and exercised daily with plenty of walking in hand. 'All I can say about Red Rum then,' says Roddy O'Byrne, 'is that he was a *grand* horse to handle, and with a lovely temperament.'

'A *grand* horse to handle'

Knowing too well the neuroses of the mare and dreading their reproduction in her son, Martyn McEnery had been watching the colt's behaviour over the year with anxiety. It was the greatest relief to him that so far Red Rum had shown no signs of having inherited Mared's manic traits.

GOFF'S BLOODSTOCK SALES
YEARLINGS

From Rossenarra Stud.

Lot 201.

			Gold Bridge
BAY COLT	Quorum 5	Vilmorin	Queen of the Meadows
(Third produce)	(Gr. 1954)	Akimbo	Bois Roussel
(Foaled 3rd May)			Bulolo
	Mared 25	Magic Red	Link Boy
	(B. 1958)		Infra Red
		Quinta	Anwar
			Batika

MARED, **winner** and placed at three years ; also placed at two years. She has a two-year-old filly Quintula, by Neron. Own sister to Via Con Deo.
QUINTA, placed three times at three years, 1956 ; dam of the **winners Mared** (see above) and **Via Con Deo** (at four years, 1963, and placed at three years ; also placed over hurdles, 1965).
BATIKA (foaled in France) ; dam of the **winners Head Dress** (two races), **Spring Offensive** (seven races, including Desmond Stakes, Curragh, and dam of eight winners including Turbo Jet, Two Thousand Guineas Trial Stakes, etc., and £5,511, also won 11 races in U.S.A., value £86,588, including Man O'War Stakes, 1964 ; Faberge II, also second in Two Thousand Guineas, sire ; and Gallup Poll, three races in France, 1965, value £7,084), **Red Batik** (two-year-old winner in England, 1949), **W.T.**, and **Magic Black** (winner in Venezuela in 1953 and 1954), also Maiden of Orleans (dam of Blackwell, two-year-old winner in 1949 of three races ; Fulbrook, winner in 1953 and 1954 ; Maid in France, also dam of a winner, and King of France, also Mrs. Killeen, dam of winners), and Placide (placed, and dam of winners).

Stabled in Box 201.

A party of six yearlings left Rossenarra for Dublin accompanied by Roddy O'Byrne whose first experience of commercial yearling sales this would be. Red Rum's companions consisted of three fillies belonging to Martyn McEnery, including the bay nearly three months older than him by Golden Cloud out of June the Fourth whom he would meet again at Liverpool. There were also two more yearlings belonging to someone else which McEnery had been getting ready. So six youngsters were loaded into one lorry with a great deal of excitement and set off on the 80-mile journey to Dublin. They were driven from

Gowran by Matt Murphy, who now drives articulated refrigerated trucks to and from the Continent.

Morning of the sales

The living animals which he was that day taking to the capital were catalogued to come up rather too early on the middle morning of the sales, Tuesday, 20th September. The 'bay colt, (Third Produce) (Foaled 3rd May) by Quorum (Grey, 1954) out of Mared (Bay, 1958)' had been selected as the first of the Rossenarra stud's draft as Lot 201. His box, No. 201, was waiting for him. In a three-day catalogue of 549 entries the last day's offerings had to wait for their boxes until the first day's lots had left them.

Human selection exaggerates the general lottery of sales. The auctioneers, having trained noses for truffles of value and the passing scent of current fashions, have only the breeding of sales' entrants to work on when they assemble their catalogue. They do not know until the sale starts several months later, what shape the animals are, or in what condition they will be presented. So they will be in-

Importance of the vendor

fluenced by the importance of the vendor, and by whether he is an old-established client, or a new man with a lot of money who has recently purchased a large stud (and thus may be persuaded to sell here rather than at rival auctions). These types of vendors with good-sounding yearlings will be placed in better positions than the unheard-of owner with one ill-bred yearling who may never come again.

Egalitarianism does not exist in the world of racing. The slowest thoroughbred will always beat the fastest cart-horse. Opportunities are grotesquely unequal. One foal will be underfed on wretched land, his needs ignored by poor, ignorant, feckless or idle people. Another will enjoy the best of food and attention from experts with time and money. The horse's early stud days are his formative childhood. His days in training are his career. Again, some will receive all things good and helpful; others will get the kicks and ha'pence. Red Rum was to have his share of both from a wide variety of men and women.

Equal *under* the turf

The first half of the epigram may be true: Men may 'be equal *under* the turf'. But they are absolutely unequal upon it. So by breeding, birth, upbringing and training are the horses they own, and train and ride. An occasional great horse like Arkle has it good all the way; another, like Red Rum, has survived parts of his life in spite of, not because of, the hands into which he fell.

5 'I KNEW WE WERE IN FOR A DISASTER'

Luck starts very early in a yearling's life. The worst places to be drawn in most sales are the beginning or the end. Bloodstock buyers who are early birds know that most of the early lots are likely to be unpalatable worms. They wish also to test the market: to watch a dozen or so lots sold before they gauge how the economic and political events of the last few days have affected prices. By the end of the sales, buyers are surfeited. Their order-books have been filled. They are weary. Missing the last lots, they return early to homes or hotels to refresh themselves with restoring liquor and tales of horses long ago.

The auctioneers, knowing men's habits, put the apparently less attractive yearlings early and late in the day. A vicious spiral so begins: buyers believe that the auctioneers *know* that the early and late lots aren't much good. . . .

Learning from the drawbacks of the ancient system Goff's, for their yearling sales in September, 1974, instituted a brand-new procedure. They began each day much later, had an evening session after dinner – and boldly spread the plums all through their daily pudding.

Martyn McEnery's Rossenarra Stud in 1966 was only at the start of its transition from his father's old place dealing with half-breds to the important commercial undertaking it has now become. So its offerings came up very early on Tuesday: Red Rum was due only 14 lots – about 40 minutes – after the sales' ten o'clock start.

As Captain Michael Hall, that able and charming manager of Goff's for what he describes as '25 blissfully happy years', recalls, his office noted both attractive and unattractive features in Red Rum's entry. On the bonus side: his sire Quorum was enjoying a good year. Since he had started at stud in 1958 he had already sired the winners of £65,179 in 88½ races.[*] But the bloodstock world's whims are as fickle as fashion: it is what is immediately in vogue and selling well recently that most appeals. Here, too, Quorum's record was most satisfactory. In the

Red Rum's entry

---

[*] The ½ race denoting in racing parlance a dead-heat, common enough before the advent of the race-finish camera.

44 races worth £31,000

previous season of 1965 (when Red Rum had been born) 25 of Quorum's 52 runners were winners, an excellent proportion. They had won 44 races worth £31,000. During the summer of 1966 up to the start of the sales he had produced 16 individual winners of 18 races. Down in Kilkenny Martyn McEnery had been observing the progress of the horse he had selected nearly 2 years earlier with some satisfaction. Quorum could so easily have fallen out of favour.

The maternal side of Red Rum's pedigree was less attractive in September, 1966. In spite of their good statistical record the produce of Magic Red mares were now drifting out of favour. Michael Hall recalls 'they were not particularly popular, though there had once been a time when Magic Red colts – especially the greys – had been all the rage!'.

Red Alligator

Only eighteen months after Red Rum came up at the Ballsbridge sales a horse by Magic Red was to win the 1968 Grand National: Red Alligator ridden by one of Red Rum's future jockeys, Brian Fletcher. Freakish results attend the Grand National, but it did show that, against all the odds, Magic Red could produce a jumper. If Red Rum had been born two years later . . . if Red Alligator had won round Aintree two years earlier . . . with hindsight everything is easy. But there were at least a handful of people around the sales of 1966, including the author, who well knew from their own experience that the offspring of Magic Red mares made very good staying steeplechasers. Maigret (whom I trained) was one such. Muir, his full-brother in Ireland, belonging to the Willis family was another. The former, winner of six long-distance steeplechases had already proved his stamina, his jumping ability, a touch of class and – as Red Rum was to do – his marked preference for firm, fast ground, before Red Rum came up for sale. Before Red Rum was even born Maigret had won two 3-mile Irish point-to-points. But was anyone perspicacious enough to contemplate buying good-looking, cheap yearlings out of Magic Red mares to store away as future steeplechasers? They were not.

Proved his stamina

The rest of Red Rum's entry in the catalogue did not impress. There was 'not much black about it', as buyers say, meaning that there were few winning relations in the pedigree standing out in black bold-faced print. The Irish world knew about Mared's madness. She had so far bred no winner. Her two first offspring had been sold for peanuts.

Political and economic considerations that year depressed the sales. Michael Hall remembers, '1966 was a pretty disastrous year for breeders. There was a Labour Government. The credit squeeze was beginning to bite. There was the new Betting Tax. There was Capital Gains Tax. And it was a particularly bad year for the unfortunate Martyn McEnery. . . .'

The day dawned ominously. Nothing tempts out buyers like bees and adds warm fervour to their bidding fingers than a bright day. But the morning echoed the economic situation: it was grey and cold and raining. 'I was in a pessimistic mood from the start,' says McEnery.

The only possible buyer who took any real interest in Lot 201 was Pat Rohan the successful Yorkshire trainer, an Irishman by birth, son of a well-known dealer and fox-hunter in Co. Cork, and a few years younger than Martyn McEnery. He had left Ireland for Yorkshire ten years earlier to go as assistant trainer at Malton to Billy Dutton. He had taken over that good stable on Dutton's death and married his daughter. He liked sprinters. He knew McEnery. He spent some time looking at Red Rum and, McEnery remembers, 'expressed enough interest to make me more than hopeful'. When you are a seller you hang upon the murmurs, nods and becks of those who 'have your horses out'. Would they smile, wondered McEnery, when they saw how well his colt moved? Would they shake heads, purse lips if they believed that Red Rum's forelegs were too straight? Would they merely glance, grunt and pass on to someone else's offerings down the long line of boxes?

It was worse than all these things. Hardly another soul braved the wet to look at his colt at all. McEnery only recalls Tim Molony, that former great steeplechase jockey and small Leicestershire trainer, looking at Red Rum while Pat Rohan had him out in the rain. McEnery then hurried off to the auctioneer's office to place reserve prices on his horses.

It was while McEnery was away that an accident befell Red Rum. Its nature was going to be repeated later in his career, but its occurrence at the sales determined the trainer and the owner into whose hands he would first fall. In McEnery's absence Red Rum, while being led out of his box, slipped heavily. He hurt himself. Though not actually lame, he was walking a shade stiffly as he was being led around the preliminary parade ring, in full view of any other possible buyers. McEnery did not see the incident.

Neither did he see his horse's stiffness. Heartened by Rohan's early interest, he was in the auctioneer's office putting a reserve of 800 guineas on Red Rum. He put exactly the same reserve on the Golden Cloud filly whose path was going to cross Red Rum's so closely six months later.

A reserve of 800 guineas

'Well, we got into the ring,' says McEnery, 'and I knew we were in for a disaster. There was no one there.' That was hyperbole, but in sales talk 'no one' means likely bidders. Sales rings are always occupied – particularly on cold wet mornings – by old men and women nattering together, keeping snug and intending to spend no more than a quid all day and that on tea or drink and sandwiches.

'There was Pat Rohan,' McEnery says, 'but he wasn't bidding *at all!* I couldn't think why. I couldn't understand it then. Though I know now of course.'

Rohan, unaware of the colt's accident, had been back to have another look at him walking round. He saw him walking 'that little bit stiffly'. And he was put off. There is no point in 'buying trouble' in a horse. They develop enough later. It was early hours yet in the sale. There would be other colts just as attractive, better bred probably, who would walk out freely. He did not bid.

He did not bid

Bob Jeffares, a good man who sadly died well before his time in May, 1973, was the auctioneer at the time. McEnery hovered in the box behind him. The earlier lots had sold so badly and Rohan wasn't bidding and the price was stuck at a mere 400 guineas, half the minimum McEnery had decided upon half an hour earlier. At this flickering juncture in a sale the auctioneer, leaning back from the microphone which would otherwise amplify his doubts, will urgently ask the vendor – sometimes merely by an interrogatively raised eye-brow – whether he should now forget the reserve and accept the last bid. McEnery had a few seconds only to decide. Hesitation on the vendor's face will be instantly communicated to the last genuine bidder down there below. You must shake your head firmly, demonstrating you will not let your good horse go so far under his real value. Or you may sadly nod and shrug.

'Let him go'

Utterly depressed McEnery made a quick decision. He murmured to Bob Jeffares, 'Let him go'. Red Rum's reserve was cancelled. The 400 guineas bid bought the horse. McEnery was surprised to see that it had come from Tim Molony.

6 'I'LL BUY YOU A YEARLING'

For the first of four times in his astonishing career the horse
Red Rum was thus sold in a public market and available to
any passer-by. On the first two occasions anyone with the
price of a second-hand 'banger' could have taken him
home. Even on the third occasion when he had proved his
ability by winning twice, he made no more than the price
of a family car.

McEnery watched him being led out of the ring to his
left as his next lot, a Dicta Drake filly, entered from the
right and began her slow clockwise circuit. Worse was in
store for her: she failed to reach her reserve. Miserably
McEnery watched her led out unsold. Then followed his
Golden Cloud filly out of June the Fourth. Coincidentally
McEnery had placed upon her the identical reserve he had
selected for Red Rum: 800 guineas. Coincidentally the
price she reached in the bidding was exactly the 400
guineas fetched by Red Rum. Only in the world of fiction
would it seem possible that these two animals born together, who had travelled together, then been sold
together at the same place within minutes for the same
price, would finish together, dead-heating whisker to
whisker in the first race each was to contend six months
later across the Irish sea at Liverpool.

Whisker to whisker

As eleven o'clock approached in Dublin on 20th
September, 1966, the unhappy McEnery had raised a
wretched 800 guineas on two of the three yearlings he had
offered. His last chance, a Palestine filly also out of a Magic
Red mare, slightly improved the situation by selling for
975 guineas to that astute bloodstock agent the late Bertie
Kerr. The Rossenarra consignment had raised 1,775
guineas between them and McEnery had to take his Dicta
Drake filly home. From this gross amount Goff's took
'the guineas', their 5 per cent. There were also all the
travelling expenses. 'All in all,' McEnery sums up, 'a *very*
disappointing sale and I was a very disappointed man that
day.'

Roddy O'Byrne, who had cared for Red Rum for his
first year, and brought him to the sales, only to see him

'This is
scandalous'

sold for half his reserve, hated the whole day. 'I was *disgusted*,' he says eight years later, his small face flushing pink in recollected rage. He said to McEnery, 'This is scandalous! You should never have sold them!'

Martyn McEnery gave him quietly an example of the philosophy bloodstock breeders must hold. He explained that if you are breeding commercially you must sell, even at low prices, even if you were a loser on the deal, in the hope that your horses would win and that the following year buyers would therefore come back again and pay more. In McEnery's case this happened. Where he had sold for hundreds in 1966, in the years to come he was to sell for thousands.

But Michael Hall, after a quarter-century of selling horses, summed it up: 'Martyn McEnery's luck at that time was of the variety to put a less dedicated, less philosophical person out of horses for good!'

Keepers of
horses

It is too easy for the casual observer of the racing scene to notice only the rare high price and to deduce that breeders are printing money. One really bad year may erase the profit of five. And the risks when your capital is tied up into feckless horseflesh capering about fields are twenty times higher than those endured by shareholders in public companies, even in falling markets. Keepers of horses must dismiss their dreads if they are to sleep at nights. It was, as Michael Hall commented afterwards, the worst September Sales that Goffs had experienced in five years. The top price of the sale was made four hours after Red Rum was sold when the full brother to the Derby winner Larkspur made 13,000 guineas. Called Phoenix Bird he ran only five times and won just one race worth £465 15s. Red Rum costing 400 guineas had to the end of the 1973–74 season run in 78 races and earned £69,320. . . .

The buyer of McEnery's Golden Cloud filly for 400 guineas was that lively racing character Major 'Ginger' Dennistoun, a bushy-browed, darting-eyed terrier of a man, skilled in his trade, abrupt in speech and a shrewd and most successful gambler when the time arose. He rode as an amateur before the war, trained since it, won two Imperial Cups and became, through his daughter 'Tory' the father-in-law of one of steeplechasing's best benefac-

Friend to
all jockeys

tors, John Oaksey, a rider and writer of polish, and great friend to all jockeys.

The Major took his filly home to Letcombe Regis, near Wantage in Berkshire, named her Curlicue and gave her to his wife. He had it in mind that she would win early next season, perhaps first time out and that he might be able to land another nice gamble.

Tim Molony, the purchaser of Red Rum a few minutes earlier, had exactly the same intentions. But his were even more specific. A man with whom he had been long acquainted had instructed him to buy a yearling who would six months later win the 5 furlong Thursby Selling Plate, the first race at Liverpool on the Friday of the Grand National meeting. While Curlicue left Dublin for Letcombe Regis in Berkshire, Red Rum came over to the heart of England's best foxhunting country, to the little village of Wymondham, near Melton Mowbray.

Tim Molony, the first purchaser of Red Rum, had been training exactly six years when he first sat down in his small narrow study of The Manor at Wymondham to study Goff's September sales catalogue. His 47th birthday was coming up the week before the sales. He had been riding as an amateur in Ireland from 1936 until the war (he rode over 100 point-to-point winners over banks and walls), had turned professional and gone to the very summit of that hazardous tree, riding over 900 winners in his 19-year-long career, and being champion jockey five times between 1948 and 1955. Tim and his brother Martin carried off most of National Hunt racing's greatest prizes and dominated the 'chasing scene for a dashing decade.

First purchaser of Red Rum

Though he has, like all retired jockeys, thickened in thighs and quarters and shoulders since his racing days, Tim Molony still possesses the profile of a Roman centurion, with blue eyes and claret-coloured cheeks. He has had his share of life's swings and roundabouts, surviving them with the equanimity which comes less easily to the English than to the Irish, inured historically to national misfortunes. He has one daughter by his first wife, and three sons by his second, the admirable and competent Stella to whom he was married in his riding heyday back in 1951. He has no enemies on the racing scene. He has charm and is a good companion and to the callow author on his first quivering race on a proper course (at Market Rasen) the admired then Champion Jockey was helpful, heartening and highly amusing.

A good companion

One of Tim Molony's remarkable achievements was to win four consecutive Champion Hurdles. Three of these, from 1952 to 1954, were on that supreme French-bred hurdler Sir Ken, owned by the man for whom Molony had just bought Red Rum. Sir Ken had been bought and

Sir Ken trained by the redoubtable Willie Stephenson, one of only two trainers alive to have won that improbable double of the Derby and the Grand National. Sir Ken, one of the greatest hurdlers ever, won no less than 24 National Hunt races. Tim Molony rode him 19 times, one after the other, without being beaten.

Sir Ken was one of many horses owned by Manchester businessman Maurice Kingsley who became, through his admiration of Tim Molony's skills, Red Rum's first owner. Kingsley, now an elderly man of some mystery, was engaged in the textile trade and involved both in mills and in the selling of cloth. Back in the early fifties he had been introduced to Willie Stephenson as a potential patron by the bandleader Maurice Winnick. The association proved bounteous. He had horses trained by Stephenson on those soaring gallops at Royston for several brilliantly successful seasons. In that exciting spell any horse owned by Kingsley and trained by Stephenson would be dreaded by the opposition. Willie Stephenson produced over 100 winners for **Over 100** Kingsley, many the media of spectacular, even legendary **winners** gambles.

One other horse owned by Kingsley and trained by Stephenson became the connection by which Red Rum arrived with his second owner and trainer, that long-standing Yorkshire link-up of Mrs Lurlene Brotherton and Mr Bobby Renton. For it so happened in the autumn of 1958 that a 3-year-old hurdler rejoicing in the name of Dagmar Gittell had, after a preliminary outing (finishing 5th at 100/8), landed a nice gamble next time out at Haydock for Messrs Kingsley and Stephenson, winning a selling hurdle race by 6 lengths at 4 to 5 on and being bought in for 1,050 guineas. He won once more for the original combination and was then sold to Mrs Brotherton **Dagmar** to go to Renton. For this new partnership Dagmar Gittell **Gittell** did great things, and because of this satisfactory purchase it happened 10 years later that Maurice Kingsley approached Mrs Brotherton about Red Rum and murmured to her that he had for sale 'another "Dagmar"'.

Maurice Kingsley has patronised a number of trainers. At times he has been in racing with large strings; for stretches he has been out of it entirely. None of his particulars are revealed in any of the four editions of the *Directory of the Turf* (racing's comprehensive Who's Who) published between 1961 and 1974 and, alone of all the connections of Red Rum, he vouchsafed no answer to my enquiries. . . .

In racing circles Mr Kingsley has enjoyed for many

years the reputation of relishing a gamble. The success of Dagmar Gittell was one of many well-backed victories.

Soon after Tim Molony had started training on the flat, Maurice Kingsley approached him one afternoon at Pontefract races and asked him if he would look out for a horse for him. Any small trainer is delighted to be approached by a possible patron. A few brazen fellows accost likely owners – 'I've just the horse in mind for you. . . . Wouldn't the missus like to see her colours carried . . . ? Time you 'ad an 'orse agin, we was lucky once, eh . . . ?' But most trainers with pride and sensibility prefer, like a lady, to receive the approach rather than to make it.

Tim Molony knew Maurice Kingsley very well. If he could do well for him one horse might multiply into several. . . .

Molony is an excellent judge of a horse. He originally bought for 1,500 guineas Fred Winter's future great horse Pendil, and his brother Martin bought Bula for Winter in Dublin. Tim Molony had no sooner started training on the flat than he produced several two-year-old winners. These successes, following the two men's wonderful association with Sir Ken, drew Kingsley back to Tim Molony.

Pendil and Bula

'Sure,' said Tim, delighted, 'I'll be going to Dublin Sales in September. I'll buy you a yearling.'

'Right,' said Maurice Kingsley. 'Buy me one to win that two-year-old seller at Liverpool next March.' Molony's brief was short, speedy and specific.

'I'll buy you a yearling'

Kingsley particularly liked winners at Liverpool because he had a box there. It was for him a very local meeting. He told Tim to 'Spend around the four to five hundred mark', but said nothing at all about the shape, type or breeding of what he wanted. In this he showed business acumen and racing sense. If owners will say simply what they seek and what they can pay, like anyone entering a shop, they will get the best help from the trainer who is as anxious as they that the product will win. Some owners new to the game will say 'Buy me a 'National winner for four hundred quid' and be surprised at the trainer's shock or mirth. But Kingsley with experience had accurately balanced his target with his outlay. With good picking for that money the winner of a two-year-old selling race might well be bought.

'Buy me a 'National winner'

Molony had Goff's catalogue, 'so I sat down and did a bit of researching and marked off those with a pencilled cross which I thought might be cheap enough'.

Molony knew his job exactly. There were yearlings in the catalogue bred well enough to win a classic let alone a humble seller. They could make a hundred times what Kingsley wished to pay; no point in wasting time on them.

Combing a catalogue

Combing a catalogue of 500 names is tedious work, but practice makes speed. The knowledgeable eye racing over four yearlings on each double page can discard in a second those by sires too grand or too inclined to produce stayers. Molony flipped through the pages, checking the breeding, and marked down a dozen possibles for Mr Kingsley and, when he came to Lot 201, thought 'speed, pure and simple – *early* speed. Magic Red was a sprinter. Quorum was a sprinter . . .'

His deductions were perfectly sound. They would prove correct in the short run – and Molony had been instructed to plan for next March. That a horse by Quorum out of a Magic Red mare could develop into one of the greatest staying 'chasers did not occur to him. But then anything of supreme quality is a sort of freak.

Over in Dublin another expert Michael Hall had reached the same conclusion: 'One could see Red Rum maturing early and winning over 5 furlongs as a 2-year-old, but certainly it isn't *anyone's* idea of the pedigree of a National winner! It looked as though a mile would be absolutely his limit.'

'Absolutely his limit'

Molony, with his marked-up catalogue, went over to Dublin with orders all together for four yearlings including the 'Liverpool Seller' one for Maurice Kingsley. He walked down the wide grassy avenues of those Ballsbridge Sales grounds, now lamentably sold for development. He looked carefully at all the yearlings he had marked, accompanied most of the time by his brother Martin. Four good eyes are better than two. As you bustle down a row of boxes noting and marking, it's the greatest help to have with you a knowledgeable friend who can murmur behind his catalogue (as you're examining a horse's head) 'Funny sort of little lump just inside in his hock . . .'.

Noting and marking

Disappointments fall as steadily as the Irish rain. A horse whose breeding you particularly desire turns out hideous beyond the dreams of Dali. Another, whose head watches you approach with honesty and courage, discloses (when you open his box and grope in his suspiciously deep straw) to have fetlock joints inflamed like toasted tennis balls or feet turned inwards like a ruptured pigeon. Even the animal who stands in his box like a paragon may, like the backview of a stationary blonde glimpsed on a pavement, give you a nasty shock when it moves. It may waddle like a duck, mince, creep, or whirl its forelegs round like windmills.

Two things immediately struck Tim Molony about Red Rum. First: 'Good front and smashing head.' Second: 'Very good mover.'

He did notice that the colt was 'rather gassy, quite gay'. The last word has a different meaning among horsey folk than it now possesses among the pretty pouting people. 'A bit gay' from a man selling you a horse means that it is as wild as hell.

This natural exuberance led to that first accident in Red Rum's career. But Tim Molony did not see him slip and fall. He had bustled away in the rain to look at others. The Quorum yearling filled his bill. He reckoned 'I should probably get him around the 500 mark. I would have gone two or three hundred more, but I couldn't have gone further.'

Fortunately for him, and for Kingsley and the rest of our story, Molony did not observe Red Rum's stiffness in the preliminary paddock. He was inside, waiting to bid for him in his customary position: 'Under the number board where they come in'.

To his surprise (pleasure mixed with doubt: had others spotted something he'd missed?) he saw no one else bidding for the horse. Only one small, stocky person, past champion jockey, present small Leicestershire trainer, was in there nodding. Outside the rain fell greyly. Inside the colt to be called Red Rum circled the neat ring, neighing occasionally in the strange enclosure of the small amphitheatre. '400 guineas,' said Bob Jeffares, looking round vainly for any other bidder, aided in his search by the clerk in the box below him and one of Goff's attractive secretaries by his side.

Tim Molony under the number-board looked cool, but feared the sudden manifestation of a new bidder. Those seconds when it's your last bid, and the auctioneer strives to get another, drag like minutes. . . . Slap went Bob Jeffares' gavel on his desk. He looked across and gave Tim a little nod. 'Sold Mr Tim Molony 400 guineas,' he announced. 'Property of the same owner. . . .' The filly to be called Curlicue waited to come in and Major 'Ginger' Dennistoun was waiting to bid for her.

7 'OH, HE WAS GAY ALRIGHT!'

'I was delighted with him,' says Tim Molony, 'no re-
criminations.' He meant there was none of that chilled
unease which can mark the conclusion of a deal: will the
animal, so desirable when its possession was only a possibility, seem as satisfactory when it is finally yours? There
are parallels in other walks of life. . . .

Dick Morgan of Waterford and Dublin, a leading horse
transporter, sent Red Rum across the sea from Dublin to
Holyhead and thence on by road across Wales to Molony's
neat little tree-centred yard behind the main street of
Wymondham. The village lies at a meeting of five roads
and lanes within the triangle made by Melton Mowbray,
Grantham and Oakham. It is a sporting part of Leicestershire. A few miles north is the famous Garthorpe point-to-
point course. A few miles south was run in 1974 the
celebrated Melton Hunt Club cross-country ride. Molony's
Manor is cosy rather than spacious, convenient rather than
grand. Its stables occupy a corner of the main street and the
lane from the north. The house abuts the south-eastern
edge of the yard and its study looks out onto it. Red Rum's
box was the one furthest away in the north-west corner.
Various impedimenta of the Molony children, bikes and
push-cars, adorn the other entrance to the house. The yard,
full of trees, is dark.

Bought him a horse

On his return Tim telephoned Maurice Kingsley and
told him he'd bought him a horse. This is always a fraught
moment for a trainer. An owner, so expansive when he
asked you to 'look out for something', may by now have
got cold feet, a red bank balance, a big deal brewing, or
merely a moaning wife or rapacious mistress. He may
renegue, roundly denying any such commitment made in
a racecourse bar. 'Told you to buy me a horse? Never!
Said you might *look*. . . .' Or: 'Bought me a bay yearling
colt! I told you I wanted an old grey mare.' You may be
left to pay for the horse, or, if you are without funds (and
few small trainers boast big bank balances) you must find
some other patron to take over the discard double-quick
before the bill comes from the sales.

A predicament of this sort over Red Rum was going to face Tim Molony 18 months later. But, at the moment, all was well. Mr Kingsley expressed himself 'Quite pleased' and said he'd come and see him.

By the time, several months later, that Maurice Kingsley arrived at Wymondham, Red Rum was no longer a colt, but a gelding. There had been no doubts about the decision to castrate him. By no stretch of even a breeding pundit's imagination could it be said that his blood carried classic potential. It was remotely possible that he might turn out a high-class sprint handicapper, but so it is every year with several thousand yearlings and there is barely room for a score of these at stud. He was, furthermore, obstreperous. He was saucy. 'Oh, he was gay all right!' Stella Molony remembers. Best then to have him 'cut' without delay. A colt who is overfresh may do himself damage.

No one was then contemplating that the sprinting-bred yearling would ever turn into even a moderate steeplechaser, but they made fortuitously the right decision for that career. A mere handful of good steeplechasers have remained 'entire'. Only one since the war, Fortina in 1947, has won 'chasing's classic, the Cheltenham Gold Cup. None has won a postwar Grand National. Colts may hurdle happily as 3-year-olds and at 4. Hurdles are easier to jump; they are crossed at a gallop. Hurdling comes half-way between flat racing where colts predominate, and steeplechasing where they are rare. Hurdlers overall are younger than 'chasers. It is this combination of smaller obstacles and younger age which makes it possible for colts and 'full horses' to succeed over hurdles, and several win the Champion Hurdle. But it is unusual for them, older, more careful, more delicately endowed, to endure the higher hurly-burly of the steeplechase. Some people believe that it is the fear of their appendages brushing the birch tops which puts full horses off their steeplechasing stroke. But their reluctance has a less specific, more psychological cause. With the onset of middle-age is it surprising that most males prefer sunshine and the company of females to the knocks and bangs enjoyed by younger muddied oafs?

Tim Molony's decision to geld Red Rum denied our hero those particular brief pleasures of the flesh, prevented him from breeding, but concentrated his mind wonderfully and enabled him to become a superlative staying steeplechaser. The operation was swiftly done by Molony's vet from Melton Mowbray, Claude Farmer, and at the right time: in a yearling's autumn. You may geld horses

No longer a colt

Easier to jump

A superlative staying steeplechaser

later, even up to 4-year-olds, but the results are unsatis-
factory: the horses become neither one thing nor the other,
still interested but now inept and thus, like damaged men,
disappointed, disagreeable and bloody-minded.

The deed performed with a local anaesthetic is totally
painless. So long as the small cut heals normally there are
no complications. The yearling is out in the fields again
immediately, or, as in Red Rum's case, back to being
broken.

'Right from the start,' says Tim Molony, 'I put a
breaking bit in his mouth, and then a cavesson over the
bridle and we started lungeing him. I don't do a lot of
lungeing with yearlings once they know what they're
doing.' Nothing is more monotonous for horse and man
than jogging round and round in a circle at the end of a
lungeing rein. After a week a roller and side reins were put
on Red Rum's back. 'He protested and bucked,' Tim
remembers, grinning, 'but not too much.' Then they put
a saddle on and started 'driving' him.

'He
protested
and bucked'

At this point in Red Rum's career he had a stroke of luck
without which he might never have made a steeplechaser of
consequence. He had fallen into the hands of a trainer Tim
Molony, who was a great horseman, and a lad Jock Mayes,
who took time and trouble to break the yearling properly.
He might have been bought by the trainer of an under-
staffed, third-class yard, who cared little about breaking
himself and who entrusted the most important stage of a
horse's education to moronic baboons with hands as
brutal as butchers', with thumping tempers and roaring
voices. In such hellish places horses are 'broken' in days
and ridden away, ignorant and fearful and with mouths
untutored and ruined. From then on they will neither steer
properly, nor turn nor check when required. Lack of
steering, lack of brakes, lack of balance, deportment and
control may not matter too much for rubbishy little flat-
race horses, but they will render a future steeplechaser
almost useless. . . .

Tim Molony, like most good horsemen, is a great
believer in driving young horses in long reins. He runs the
reins back through the stirrup-irons on the saddle. Many
of us keep the irons from swinging about by linking them
with binder twine under the horse's girth. Like this Red
Rum was driven round the paddock, then down the lanes.
The benefits of the system are that the horse learns to
accept the feel of the saddle, the slight pressure of the
stirrup irons and the feel of the long reins along his sides

Below: Tim Molony's charming stable-yard at Wymondham — Tim and Stella's house, The Manor, in the background. We are looking out from Red Rum's box.

Bottom: Red Rum's first box in training. Outside it: trainer Tim Molony (former champion jockey) and Jock Mayes, the Head Lad, who first "backed" Red Rum.

The first race of his career. Red Rum (P. Cook up) dead-heats in a 2-year-old selling plate with Curlicue (Guest up) (*right*), the filly bred with him, sold at Dublin with him — and for exactly the same price!

Red Rum (Geoff Lewis) landing a gamble (in Maurice Kingsley's famous "Sir Ken" colours) to win the "seller" at Doncaster in March, 1968 — his penultimate race on the flat. He will soon be sold to Mrs. Brotherton

and quarters as he turns. More important than any of these things, he develops the boldness to go forward *alone*, which is counter to a thoroughbred's basic caution and gregariousness. You are yards behind him with the end of the long rein in each hand. He must pass by, with no one to lead him by the head, the terrifying straw bale, the ominous dust-bin, the parked car in which lies panting a gigantic monster.

Red Rum was good with traffic 'until he'd got some more food in him and he was a bit fresh. Then he decided he didn't like the traffic at all.'

He was backed by Molony's now Head Lad, Jock Mayes, born in Hamilton, Scotland. When Red Rum arrived, 'The Guv'nor's wife was Head Lad then,' says Mayes grinning. He came into racing because he was small and because he had an uncle in the sport already 'holding the licence for those two old ladies trainin' at Herringswell Manor 'tween Newmarket and Bury'. His uncle, after some correspondence, got him an introduction to the leading Newmarket trainer Sam Armstrong, famed producer of apprentices, and down south came wee Jock Mayes. 'After three months, Mr Armstrong decided I was too heavy at 6st 6lb and duly transferred me to Mr Waugh.' He served his time as an apprentice in Newmarket till he was 18, then went off to do four years in the RAF, ''cos my father was in it. I did signals and all that. Two and a half years in Singapore and Malaya – I loved it. Went racin' to every meeting possible.' He returned to Newmarket for 10 years till 1966 and came to Molony the year Red Rum arrived. He had only been with little flat-race horses before and found the big jumpers unpleasantly different. He is still a small light man. 'I don't really like jumpers even now. Still find 'em a bit strong for me – those great heavy heads they carry very low on the floor!'

When the moment came to back Red Rum, the yearling was led out onto the concrete wearing a breaking bridle with side-reins, and an ordinary saddle with a breast-plate. Some people first get up on a young horse inside his box. He is in familiar surroundings and there is deep straw around, in case the horse goes mad. Others, like Tim Molony, believe in getting the horse out into the open where there is more room to manoeuvre should the horse start acting the bucking bronco. Molony always fitted a breast-plate to prevent the saddle slipping backwards 'in case he went right up. The girth wouldn't be too tight,'

**Backing
Red Rum**

Mayes explains.

Over the breaking bridle was the cavesson and on it the lungeing rein – 'so's not to hurt his mouth'. Tim Molony held him very short indeed. 'The Guv'nor keeps a *very* tight hold of his head with his left hand, while he just *puts* me up, his right hand under my left knee, so I'm just *layin'* over his back, see? He keeps hold of me leg and pulls the horse round in a *tight* circle. I have one hand on the mane, and one hand behind the saddle, and I'm coaxin' the horse on and talkin' to him all the time.'

Tim Molony and Jock Mayes did this four days running with Red Rum, their average time, till they got to the next stage. This was for Mayes to swing his right leg over the saddle, so that he was at last sitting in it, rather than merely lying across it. This is the Rubicon. Up to that point you may, if the horse starts to panic, slip back a few feet on to the ground without loss of face or blood. Once you are sitting right up there on a young animal who now feels for the first time another creature bestriding him, with strange limbs hanging down either flank, explosions can erupt. Trepidations are mutually transmitted. You may feel the horse quiver under you, note his ears flicker – that first portent of alarm – see his eyes roll back, feel him start to stir beneath you, poised to leap like a lunatic into the air, lose his feet, have you off, come crashing down, break his knees. . . .

'But we've never had anything go berserk,' says Jock Mayes. 'Why? Well we've got a good man in the Guv'nor on their heads!'

Initially he kept his feet straight down out of the stirrup irons while Molony led Red Rum round in a circle. After a few days circling the yard, Molony led the bay yearling out and down a private concrete lane away from all traffic. The trouble with traffic, which lasted for years, was to start almost immediately.

8 'WE BOTH LAID DOWN ON A BANK'

The uninitiated, who suppose all racehorses are trained on regulated, multi-shared, galloping grounds like the vast expanses of Lambourn and Newmarket, would be astonished to see the thousands who do their daily work up little grass strips on the headlands of farmers' fields.

In my fortunate experience it is possible to train jumpers almost anywhere without true 'gallops', provided that you are surrounded by hills, and by farmers who will allow you occasionally to canter round their permanent grass fields. Racing's officials responsible for granting licences and permits to train would have many second thoughts (and wrongly) if they saw the rural terrain where some winners are really trained. The odd headland which is used – when Farmer Giles permits – bears little resemblance to the 'one and a half miles of first-class gallops' the applicant may have described on his form.

Training jumpers

Nor is it uncommon for small trainers seeking to impress potential patrons to drive them rapidly over their own scruffy hill to show them, like the kingdoms of the world, the beautiful but exclusive gallops owned by their rich neighbours.

There are lanes climbing the Chilterns' chalky flanks so steeply that a horse trotting up them will blow more than if he were galloped at full stretch for a mile on the flat. Hundreds of races each jumping season are lost by gormless gallop-happy trainers who, delighting in watching their old beasts daily thunder past lickety-split, leave every race at home.

But to prepare a more delicate, less developed yearling to win first time out in the spring of his 2-year-old season usually requires excellent gallops and enough 'trial cattle' to test the young horse. It is particularly to Tim Molony's credit (for as a former jumping jockey his interests could be expected to lie with chasers) that, training on farmland (and now down an old railway track) and with a small stable, he has bulls-eyed a quiverful of 2-year-old winners, fired off first time out.

To win first time out

As soon as Red Rum started going out for exercise with the rest of the Molony string he showed he was 'A

Character'. Stella Molony says grinning, 'Nearly every day he was getting into scrapes because he was so fresh and above himself. He dropped the lads many times. It was always a sort of joke: "Will he get another notch on his gun this morning?"'

Frightening but fun

'For the lads,' says Stella, 'it was frightening but fun, because everyone really loved the horse.' She did not ride him much herself, 'because he was so dangerous! He had to have a lot of work to settle him, to prevent him hurting himself when he was messing about.' As a precaution against him falling in the road after bucking, Red Rum always wore knee-boots.

It was long disputed whether Red Rum had actually dropped Jock Mayes or not. 'Well, there's a story,' Jock remembers ruefully, 'that we both laid down on a bank by the roadside, when this lorry came tearing towards us so fast. The lads said "You've either been dropped, or you pulled Red Rum down!" But there was nowhere else for us to go,' says Jock, 'so the horse got down on the bank on his side! And I did sorta slip off him, I s'pose. He got up when the lorry was gone.'

From then on in Leicestershire and later in Yorkshire Red Rum was angry about traffic. But it is typical of his character that he resents traffic rather than fears it. A few arrogant horses are like this. While timid horses cower into hedgerows the really bold horse occasionally aims a kick at a passing car, like an aristocratic of long ago booting a churlish peasant from his path.

'He'd eyes so sharp'

'He'd eyes so sharp,' says Jock Mayes, 'he'd see a tractor half a mile away up the lane and he'd whip round.'

The winter was open and mild. In December the yearling was cantering upsides with the others. Jock Mayes rode him 85 per cent of the time: 'The only time you could relax on him was when he was workin'. *Then* he was the most relaxed horse. He didn't really pull till he was a 3-year-old. When he first started to canter, he was a very, *very* smooth-actioned horse. And quick.' His wind as a youngster was always very clear.

'He wanted to go'

Tim Molony was very pleased with him. 'He was enthusiastic. He *wanted* to go.' Just before New Year's Day when Red Rum, though not yet 20 months old, became, by racing's rules, a 2-year-old, Maurice Kingsley came down to name him. He did it instantly, standing by his loose-box at the end of the line. 'Ma-*Red*,' he said in his elderly Lancashire voice, 'Quor-*Rum*. So it must be Red Rum.' Molony applied for the name. It was available. He registered it. The horse was no longer 'The Quorum Yearling', or 'the bay gelding'. He had his own official name and had become one of ten thousand registered identities on the racing scene. And now he could be entered in races.

Everyone in the yard knew that he had been bought to win 'the seller at Liverpool'. Jock Mayes grins, 'He'd been bought for this purpose! The owner had *specified* it!'

There was tremendous confidence. Even in December he was showing much better promise than Molony's other 2-year-olds, and very early in the New Year he began to gallop upsides. Now he really excelled.

Tremendous confidence

When they wanted a change of scene for faster work Molony would take four or five horses over by box to Skillington, the place belonging to that Corinthian pillar of Leicestershire foxhunting, Mrs 'Urkie' Newton. Born the Hon. Ursula Rank, she is the widow of a dashing farmer, trainer and point-to-point enthusiast, who founded the Melton Hunt Club and initiated their spectacular cross-country race. In a wet winter the ground at Skillington is always dry and perfect going. Between New Year's Day and his first race, Red Rum went over to Skillington three or four times to gallop four furlongs. He galloped in company with older horses who, Molony knew, 'could go a bit, and often with a good jumper who'd take them along well, because he was so much fitter'.

But Red Rum's programme, perfectly designed to prepare an early 2-year-old winner, contradicted in every respect the proper preparation for a potential steeplechaser. These expensive beasts remain unbroken till they are at least three years old, developing and growing usually on good Irish grass. They may have a quiet run or two as 4-year-olds, start serious racing at 5 and, on the same slow progress, reach a 'chaser's peak at 9. 'You'll ruin a decent staying 'chaser by doing *anything* with him before he's four,' has been the precept – proved year after year in practice. Until Red Rum! Until this extraordinary horse, no 'chaser of real eminence has started as he did. So far from growing for three years quietly on grass, Red Rum was broken and ridden and cantering as a *yearling*.

This extraordinary horse

Even the short careers of flat-race horses which usually end at three are thought to be harmed by racing a potentially good 3-year-old too much or too early in his 2-year-old season. Strain on the undeveloped frame damages next year's development. Furthermore, precociousness (as with people) often diminishes adult ability. A sharp early

2-year-old is often (like the young scholarship lad) burnt out by his next stage. In a horse's case he may be no good even at three. Yet here was Red Rum already breaking the basic rules of racing. He was broken at least two years too early. He was raced at least two years too soon.

Raced too soon

Red Rum's last pre-race gallop at Skillington took place during Cheltenham week. Tim Molony was so serious about his programme and so hopeful of its outcome, that he drove back specially from the scene of his riding triumphs and the merry company of a thousand racing friends to watch his 2-year-old complete his preparation. He was delighted. So were the stables. 'He was *far* better than the others,' says Jock Mayes, who intended to have his maximum bet.

Molony reported his satisfaction to Maurice Kingsley and engaged Paul Cook to ride him. Since those days Molony has generally used George Cadwaladr or 'Taffy' Thomas, but then he would shop around and chop and change according to jockeys' availability. Mayes took Red Rum up to Liverpool. 'He boxed up okay and was a good traveller. He just sweated up round his neck, just got a bit warm – took nothin' out of himself. I imagine he just wanted to get on with the job!'

A good traveller

It was Friday, 7th April and the English flat race season had been open less than a fortnight. There had been little rain. The ground had been hard at Doncaster: it was still firm beyond the Pennines at Liverpool.

A horse called Blue Spider, who had already had a run at Baldoyle (the Irish season starts earlier than ours), opened favourite. But there was heavy backing from two different quarters for the two unraced youngsters who had made their way to Dublin from the Rossenarra Stud six months earlier and were now meeting for the first time since then.

Bonds with paddock companions

It would be nice to know that they recognised each other and that some of the shrill whinneying in the saddling-boxes and paddock was due to their cries of recognition and 'How *are* you?' It is unlikely. Horses remember places most of all, then special people who have tended them. They set up very quickly strong bonds with paddock companions, bellow at parting and then, because they are both fickle and dependent, swiftly forge new links with a new friend. Common ponies are a great deal more constant than thoroughbreds.

The Golden Cloud filly which Major 'Ginger' Dennistoun had named Curlicue (it means a fantastic curl) had

been putting in some pretty fantastic work on the Major's
Berkshire gallops. He reckoned her good enough to win.
Word had leaked out already: she opened second favourite
at 4 to 1 and was backed down to 7 to 2.

But Red Rum's home prowess from remoter Leicestershire was no secret either. In the big training areas of
Berkshire, Yorkshire and Newmarket everyone knows
there's a fast 2-year-old as soon as it's done its first bit of
work. His lad's natural pride sees to that, and even the most
cautious trainer will murmur to his rivals over an evening
whisky, 'I've one who *does* go a *little* bit . . .' and droop an
eyelid.

When stable lads were indentured slaves they were
literally locked up in their quarters in remote training areas
while a big coup was being plotted and brought off.

There is a friendly pub in what was then Red Rum's little
village of Wymondham. Mr Maurice Kingsley had many
business associates in nearby Manchester. He had the
reputation of being a gambler. Molony had the reputation
of being able to bring off first-time 2-year-old winners. . . .
Red Rum, who'd never seen a racecourse or been tried on
public gallops opened third favourite at 6 to 1 till pressure
of further wagers brought him into 5's. Money for the
Irish horse and money for each of the two young Rossenarra graduates kept the price of each attractive. Tim
Molony told Maurice Kingsley in his private box that he
could have a good bet on Red Rum. 'And the Boss did!'

'I've one who
does go a
little bit . . .'

9 'HE WAS CATCHING THE FILLY SO FAST . . .'

When horses have never run before only gossip about home form suggests, till stable money confirms, that they can go a bit. The Molony and the Dennistoun camps looked askance at the money punting on each other's horses. Perhaps, thought Tim, this attractive filly of 'Ginger's' is a real flyer and faster than ours by far. He did think, however, that she looked a little backward. Major Dennistoun knew how Maurice Kingsley loved to gamble. He remembered those famous coups when Willie Stephenson trained for Kingsley. Perhaps Tim's got a really good one in Red Rum, the Major wondered. He reckoned it must have been very well galloped to be so well backed on its first appearance. The situation is that of poker. When there is no public form, hands are unseen. You hold 3's. Has the opposition, the way it's betting, got 4's?

A bit leggy

It would have carried the extraordinary coincidences of Red Rum's and Curlicue's sales and reunion too far, if they had been drawn side by side at the start of their first race. But Red Rum was best drawn, 9 of 9 runners; Curlicue in the middle, drawn 4. Paddock critics noted Red Rum as being workmanlike, but a bit leggy. They were off at two minutes past two.

'The horse *started* alright,' says Tim Molony, 'but he was a bit slow into his stride. Paul definitely gave the little horse too much to do. I was a bit worried, and I wasn't very pleased with him.' Tim Molony had had a tenner on him. So had Jock Mayes. 'My largest bet is a tenner, and that went on. And I'm sure the rest of the yard backed him, too.'

Running very greenly

Curlicue was very quickly away and into the lead. The small Irish filly, the favourite Blue Spider, cruised along at her side, comfortably on the bit. Behind them Red Rum was running very greenly in circumstances quite new to him. Young horses, however well tutored at home, are always slightly astonished by the real thing first time out. They look about them like children in some alarm. As their attention wanders they drift off a true course. Only with racing experience, as with soldiers in action, comes steadiness, concentration, complete control and instant obedience.

Red Rum had been bewildered by being suddenly asked to gallop flat out. Now at halfway Paul Cook had to sit down and start to ride him strongly. He began to improve. About 300 yards from the winning post Blue Spider led. A few strides further and she started to weaken. A furlong out Curlicue led again. At that point Red Rum suddenly found his racing legs, started to accelerate, came after the flying filly hoof over hoof – and caught her in the very last stride of the race. They crossed the winning line nose to nose. Red Rum had forced a dead-heat. He had achieved exactly one half of the objective set by Maurice Kingsley for an unknown horse the previous summer.

Found his racing legs

Tim Molony thought that, ridden differently, he would have won outright. 'He was catching the filly so fast he was ahead of her a stride past the post.'

Red Rum had, however, been hard ridden by an experienced jockey for most of his first race, driven along under strong pressure from halfway, and really pressed with whips flying in the last furlong. He had enjoyed no quiet introduction to the utterly strange business of racing. He had endured a hard race. It was to be one of many during his strange career. For most horses it would have been one of far too many, because as with people so with horses: repeated pressures and pain result in anxiety or resentment. The punished horse, knowing that sticks smite in the forefront of the battle, learns to hang back. Timidly or sullenly they drop out. They become useless.

It has astonished everyone in racing not just that Red Rum survived his hard races, but that he did so being the son of a neurotic mare. Somehow the fire in her made his will as strong as steel.

Survived his hard races

Red Rum's first contest, and strangely on the course where he was to return to world fame, had taken a mere 64.6 seconds, a fraction slower than average. The prize money was split, Mrs Dennistoun and Mr Kingsley each being enriched by £133 of 1967 money. Wagers just paid off on the odds to a half stake (the other half stake being lost in the dead heat). On the Tote to the then obtaining 4s. stake Red Rum paid out the first winning dividend of his career: 11s. 6d. to win, and 5s. 10d. place (Curlicue paid slightly better) and those clairvoyants who had achieved the forecast received £5 19s. 6d.

Both winners under the race conditions now had to be offered for sale. A convention exists among racing's

Offered for sale

brotherhood that it is bad form to bid for winners of selling races. These contests, the lowest form of racing, were originally designed as a rewarding method of disposing of stable rubbish. They have altered over the years. The temptation to run better-class, non-disposable horses in them, and to gamble on them became very strong. While it is illegal under the Rules of Racing actively to dissuade someone from bidding for your nice winner, it soon became the custom for possible bidding trainers to enquire *sotto voce* of their winning colleague 'D'you want to keep it?' If the answer was a nod, no sporting trainer would dream of bidding at the auction.

The convention about not bidding is naturally unknown to strolling players or passing pork-butchers who, hearing 'The winner will now be offered for sale . . .' are tempted to unfurl a roll of 'readies' and bid. The *claiming* of a selling race runner is even more heinous. By this antiquated custom anyone may quietly 'claim' any horse in the race by popping a note into the weighing room. Claiming in a selling race is such a racing sin that there are people whose paths cross on several racecourses every week who have not spoken to each other for years because of some monstrous claiming incident. No one – or this tale might have been very different – was wicked enough to claim either Red Rum or Curlicue.

Excellent verdict for Rossenarra

The race had been watched with delight on television by their former stud groom. Martyn McEnery was 'charmed' when he heard the result. It was in two ways an excellent verdict for the Rossenarra Stud. In the first fortnight of the season two of its progeny were now listed officially as winners.

Curlicue was first to be offered for sale. There was no bid for her. Then Jock Mayes had to lead Red Rum around. For the second time in his first two years the future great 'chaser was publicly on offer – and with dramatic irony, on the site of the Grand National. One of those who had cursorily noted him and liked him was a tall ginger-haired man, a humble permit trainer in a very small way indeed from nearby Southport, one Donald McCain. For McCain, then rising 36 and a taxi driver and used car dealer, Liverpool was already his favourite course. He had got engaged on Grand National day 1959, and gone racing. He had got married two years later on Grand National day and gone racing. Ahead in his life he would be going racing on Grand National day to the greatest of all possible tunes – all due to this workmanlike little bay gelding for whom the auctioneer was now soliciting bids.

Donald McCain was a casual bystander on Aintree
racecourse, loving its atmosphere, unknown to almost
everyone in the racing game there, dreaming dreams of
winners he might train, whose eye had been taken by the
horse who had just dead-heated for the Thursby Selling
Plate. But what good was a 2-year-flat racer to a man
without proper stables in a backstreet of Birkdale who was
struggling along part-time with the odd cheap old chaser?
McCain did not bother to watch the auction. His path
through life, and that of Red Rum did not so much cross
that April day in 1967: they lightly brushed and parted,
for a while.

10 'I'VE GOT ANOTHER "DAGMAR" FOR YOU, DEAR'

Tim Molony positioned himself so that he could catch the
auctioneer's eye lest anyone bid for his colt. Kingsley,
delighted with his winner and enriched by his wager gave
Molony no ceiling for a buying-in price. 'He was,' says
Tim, 'determined to have his horse back.'

Someone, no one yet knows who, did unsportingly bid
for Red Rum. But his depth of pocket did not match his
perspicacity. The man ran Molony up to 300 guineas at
which pittance of a price our hero was knocked down for
the second time in his short life and was safely bought in.

Another trainer, however, this time a prime veteran of   Mr Robert
his profession, who had even then been training for the   Renton
47 years since the Great War ended, had also observed
Red Rum. For Mr Robert Renton who in April, 1967, had
already passed his 79th birthday (he was born on 31st
January, 1888), Aintree was (as for young McCain) his
favourite racecourse.

But whereas McCain was a racing nobody, barely

begun on his remarkable career, the famous Mr Renton had already trained the winners of every single steeplechase round Aintree, including the Grand National with Freebooter for his special owner Mrs Brotherton. He had trained in his long career for some of the grandest and richest owners in the game. But in 1967 and still at his home, Oxclose, near Ripon in Yorkshire, he was training solely for Mrs Brotherton, and searching for another Grand National winner for her.

He knew Maurice Kingsley because of the successful deal they had both enjoyed over Dagmar Gittell nearly eight years earlier. So Bobby Renton approached Kingsley. In Tim Molony's words: 'Bobby went up to the Boss after the race and asked him if he wanted to sell Red Rum. Bobby wanted to buy him then and there.' Mr Kingsley demurred. Later perhaps, but not then. Tim Molony had assured him that the horse was 'much better than a plater'. In that case, he would certainly win again that season as a 2-year-old.

Pursuit of Red Rum

Perhaps then, and certainly at least once more before the following spring shrewd old Mr Renton persisted in his pursuit of Red Rum. On a warm summer afternoon seven years later sitting in his dark sitting-room at Oxclose with a coal fire burning, Renton remembered he had made another approach to Kingsley. He had said 'Now you've won a race, let us have him'. And Kingsley had replied, 'Not yet. I've not got my money back yet.'

Certainly Maurice Kingsley approached Mrs Brotherton at Doncaster at the spring meeting of the following year. She remembers him saying, 'I've got another "Dagmar" for you, dear. But not quite yet. I want another punt.'

With no thought for Red Rum's long-term future as a 'chaser, he was run very often as a 2-year-old. In retrospect and with a number of horses subsequently through his hands (though none of such fame) Tim Molony had the feeling, perhaps significantly, that he'd given Red Rum 'only about four races'. In fact he ran eight times from his early April start to his last appearance, wearing blinkers, again hard ridden, in the Nanpantan Nursery Handicap at Leicester on 25th September. The exertions of such a season on his young frame should have ensured that he was quite played out before he ever came to run in a steeplechase. But his connections naturally enough had no such concerns. Their minds were on more immediate, less improbable prospects. 'The Boss was very inclined to bet!' says Tim Molony wryly, 'and once you've won a seller, it's very difficult to win another. . . .'

Red Rum, this time ridden by Joe Sime, did not appear to be much fancied when he next ran, not in a seller, but in an ordinary 2-year-old race at Beverley at the end of April. As was to become his lot he was, however, briskly ridden along from halfway.

In the seven weeks before he appeared in a similar race one late evening at Teesside Park he had strengthened and improved. He was admired in the paddock. Racing's professional critics, like the sharp-eyed spotters for *Raceform*, put their praise in print. In a tiny way he had become a name to be noted. Approbation from the formbook compilers pleases any trainer: their acclaim is bestowed no more lightly than the Guide Michelin's stars. In their sense Red Rum now looked a good horse – *in his class*. And this, so far, remained the bottom league. Unfancied, ridden again by a different jockey, Larkin, he never really got into the race after (as at Aintree) rather a slow start.

Admired in the paddock

But his seven weeks' break had come at an important time. Most horses begin to 'do' as flowers grow when spring unfurls into summer. They are, despite their artificial existence, still creatures of nature. 2-year-olds are at a particularly vital stage; and Red Rum throve. He was already indicating two factors at that early age which would dominate his long career: he enjoyed firm fast ground and he preferred the warmth and dryness of the summertime to the wet chill of winter.

To the general public he seemed again unfancied when he ran next in a much smarter race at Newcastle on a still evening on 30th June. He started, in this much hotter company, an apparently rank outsider at 33 to 1. But Molony had prepared the ground well. 'The Boss had him well-backed each way!'

In the paddock before the race Red Rum showed for the first time another enduring trait of character: when he was really well, he became extremely saucy. If he'd been a schoolboy he would have rushed around cheerfully punching people and bellowing 'Yarroo!' As an over-fresh young horse, he swung his quarters, hunched his back to kick, swished his tail, crested his neck and champed on his bit. Horses in such form are a tiring 'lead-up' for their tugged and sweating lads. In the racing jargon used by *Raceform Notebook* Red Rum was 'on the best of terms with himself in the paddock'. He also had his fourth jockey in four races, George Cadwaladr. He ran a much improved race in this class to be third to the very useful winner,

He became extremely saucy

Developing the right way

Mount Athos. So far, very good. He had landed two satisfactory, if not spectacular gambles. He was developing the right way.

The form of his first race had also worked out well through Curlicue. The other young dead-heater from the Rossenarra stud had gone on to win a good stakes race very easily at classy Kempton next time out. She ran once more and again dead-heated, but this time only for fourth place and at Bath. She never ran again. 'Ginger' Dennistoun was pleased with her and fond of her. So was her breeder, Martyn McEnery who was anxious to buy her back for his stud. An obstacle appeared when the outbreak of foot and mouth disease prevented Irish buyers travelling to the Newmarket Sales. But later that year the filly was bought back on McEnery's behalf for 800 guineas, double her sale price but not dear for a good winner. So she finally returned to Rossenarra for one of the nicest existences in all the world of racing: that of a brood mare at stud. She proved a good one and continued to give satisfaction until she died aged sadly only nine in 1974.

Nursery handicaps

After Newcastle Red Rum was qualified to run in 2-year-old nursery handicaps and Tim Molony kept a sharp eye on his entries in the Racing Calendar, watching for when he was well-handicapped on a suitable track. He had won over 5 furlongs at Liverpool and been placed over 6 furlongs at Newcastle. Now Tim took a chance, against the odds of his breeding, that he would stay further as a 2-year-old. The horse had worked well enough at home and run well enough behind Mount Athos to hint that he might stay another furlong. 220 yards may not sound much, but 7 furlongs is 40 per cent further than the 5 furlongs over which he had won.

If he did so, it would be the first sign of the prodigious stamina lurking inside his growing frame. The race finally selected was the Pinley Nursery Handicap at Warwick on 28th August. This time there was yet another new jockey on the horse: D. W. Morris. Red Rum had been given the fair weight of 7st 11lb but was drawn worst of all, No. 14 of 14 runners. He opened at 7 to 1, was backed down to 6 to 1, went into the lead about 200 yards from the winning post, looked like getting caught by Parliamo, but battled

Display of courage

on with another of those displays of courage which were going to be the hallmarks of his life. He fought on, head down, neck extended, under very hard driving, to win by a neck.

Somewhere in the ruck and unfancied was another

horse who would also prove a bargain and a great success under N.H. rules: Soloning whom Fred Winter was about to buy for £500 and who would win over £13,000 in jumping stakes.

If you had suggested to anyone at Warwick that ordinary summer Monday afternoon that two of the runners in the Pinley Nursery might achieve such successes under N.H. rules, they would have thought they were being addressed by a madman. But from that humble start Soloning reached the upper echelons of the jumping world and Red Rum exceeded them.

Over in Ireland Martyn McEnery shared in the victory. Another winner bred at Rossenarra helped his name. He had also backed the horse, thanks to a meeting with Tim Molony earlier that summer. It is the custom in Ireland on a private sale, and occasionally over one at public auction, for the buyer to receive back from the seller a 'luck penny'. This may be several hundred pounds on a horse costing several thousand. It is partly buying commission, partly really to bring luck, and partly so that the vendor may truthfully brag of having sold a horse for £5,000 whereas, after he's paid out his 'luck penny' he receives net, say only £4,250 – which doesn't sound so good among the neighbours. At the time of the sale of Red Rum at Ballsbridge there had been no 'luck penny' for Tim Molony. The price McEnery had got had been too abysmal, and McEnery was as he says, 'In too foul a humour'.

Nonetheless, Molony kept him in touch with Red Rum's pleasing progress and suggested that he might well win at Warwick. Everyone was happy, and it might well have been at this point in Red Rum's career that shrewd old Bobby Renton made his second approach to Maurice Kingsley to ask him to sell him the horse, 'Now that he's won, Mr Kingsley. . . .'

Mr Kingsley was constant in his procrastination, but the jockeys on Red Rum kept on changing. At York the following week he carried Sexton in a good nursery plus a 10lb penalty for winning at Warwick. He finished 8th of 18. A fortnight later and it was the mighty Lester Piggott who bestrode him at Pontefract. This time Red Rum not only had the 'long fellow' on his back, whose power in a finish is so acute that many 2-year-olds wince in recollection, but the race was another furlong longer: 1 mile. He stayed on at his own pace to be third.

But in less than a week he was turned out to run again for the eighth time in six months. Pontefract and Piggott

A 'luck penny'

The jockeys kept changing

had occurred on 20th September. He had barely settled down at Wymondham before he was down the road to Leicester for another mile nursery on 25th September. Perhaps the great Lester, whose astute judgements of horses briefly grunted out have helped trainers the world over, suggested to Molony after Pontefract that Red Rum 'needs blinkers'. No one can recall whose idea it originally was, but for Leicester's Nanpantan Nursery (named after a village in local Charnwood Forest) our battling hero appeared disfigured in blinkers, 'the rogue's badge'.

'Needs blinkers'

Even without Red Rum it would be wrong to say that every horse wearing blinkers is a rogue. In America they wear them all colours most of the time, like girls' hats at Royal Ascot. In Britain a few horses wear them 'to aid concentration', and 'to keep their mind on the job'. Discarding such euphemisms, most horses wear them because they are either nervous or idle, lazy or duck-hearted, reluctant, rebellious or downright 'dogs' and 'thieves'.

The supposition that Red Rum after seven races and two wins as a 2–year–old could be any one of these things seems not only ludicrous but rather unpleasant. But we are now the riders in the stands. We know what lay ahead. Tim Molony at Wymondham in the late September of 1967 could have had no notion of the horse's amazing future. He believed – and he was not the last who would so believe – that Red Rum's racing performance might be improved by blinkers. And on the damn things went. He did, however, for the first time, in eight runs, not have a new jockey: D. W. Morris was back on board. Two furlongs out Red Rum was being as hard ridden as Morris knew how. Yet again severe pressure was put on the youngster. And he was carrying third top weight. He struggled grimly along on the far rails (he had been drawn unhelpfully 16 out of 17 runners) down and then up the undulating straight mile course. Three others quickened away from him in the last furlong. He finished fourth, beaten 6 lengths by the winner, a classy filly called Coonbeam, trained by a future top flat race trainer in Peter Walwyn and ridden by Scobie Breasley. Red Rum had been taking on something: the winner broke the course record.

Hard ridden yet again

Red Rum, mercifully, was retired for the season. It had been an inordinately busy one. While he had been battling on from April to September those of his age group designed for steeplechasing were enjoying a leisurely, growing summer at grass.

Retired for the season

While their days followed the prescribed pattern for producing 'chasers, developing like beefy bullocks on good land, Red Rum's had been not only energetic but pressurised. He had been subjected to hard races. While his future rivals roamed free, he had been in his box from September to September. But there was no uniformity about the distances he ran over, the type of track or the jockeys who had ridden him. In his first six months of racing Red Rum ran from 5 furlongs to 1 mile, from Warwick in the midlands up to Newcastle on the border, and endured, stoically, the different methods of seven highly contrasting jockeys in eight rides.

5 furlongs
to 1 mile

11 'AND THAT'S WHEN THE TROUBLE STARTED'

His small successes alone would not have endeared him to the yard. Lads like winners for pecuniary motives. There are presents for the lad who does the winner, for the Head Lad, and everyone else has a share in the pool. Winners inflate the *ésprit* of a yard. *This* fiver was earned by *that* horse – and thank you.

Red Rum had won one and a half small races. But he came quickly to be loved because he was already that unusual thing: a personality. He was a hazardous ride, and therefore a challenge. But whenever he bucked or sprang about all the lads knew that he did it from *joie de vivre* and not out of meanness. Some loathsome horses will plot to fling you off, lurking sullenly beneath you like a pike, lulling you into idle insecurity – only to leap, twist, drop their shoulders, explode their quarters, decant you, and sneak off sneering.

He came
quickly to
be loved

Red Rum, through all the tough surf of his life, has always managed to stay on top of the waves. Meanness, however hard his punishments, has never flickered below.

His special popularity

His special popularity was marked by his being the only horse in Wymondham to receive Christmas presents that year. One, presented by the lads, was a rubber Noddy which was 'stuck in the top of his box. It took him half a day to assassinate it,' Jock Mayes chuckles. 'He quite enjoyed it!' Alas, poor Enid. . . .

But Red Rum's two wins were not sufficient to impress his breeder. Martyn McEnery took a practical view and made a colossal mistake. He decided to get rid of Red Rum's mother. Once again he makes no excuses, is not wise after the event and does not wring his hands over might-have-beens. He says bluntly, 'Mared's stock was making very little money. And it had become essential for Goff's sales to have mares which produced stock that made a lot!'

What was more, the year after Mared produced Red Rum she was barren, unfortunately to Democratic who might well have produced something good out of her. In 1967, the year Red Rum started to race and to win she foaled a bay colt by Typhoon. This was sold cheaply for export to Italy (so her progeny ended up in both the last war's Axis countries). McEnery had her covered by Our Babu and sent her in foal to him to Goff's November Sales. On this, her second visit to Ballsbridge and only 14 months after her future famous son had been sold there, she made 600 guineas to the bid of Matt Galavan of Camolin, in McEnery's neighbouring county of Wexford.

Our Richard

Galavan had bought well. Mared rewarded him next spring with a handsome bay colt to be named Our Richard. He won a good flat race worth £603 as a 3-year-old and in the autumn of that year, 1971, and trained by Ernie Weymes he was favourite to win a £1,000 hurdle race at Ayr first time out. He finished second. Subsequently, to use the delicate euphemism which usually implies a horse has delicate legs, he has proved 'Difficult to Train'. He ran only once in the season 1972–73 and twice during 1973–74. This big, good-looking hard-pulling gelding was sold for 3,500 guineas to Anthony Gillam at Doncaster in August, 1974, as part of Mrs Brotherton's final clearance of her jumping interests.

A photograph of the horse, Red Rum's only known winning brother or sister to date, is included in the illustrations.

Since Our Richard's birth and in the hands of Mr Matt Galavan, Mared began, for a thoroughbred, an unusually long monogamous relationship with a horse lumbered with the name of Fray Bentos. She was certainly fertile. She produced by him a foal every year from 1969 to 1973 – four fillies to date and one colt (foaled in 1971). The latter was entered in Goff's one-day sale in the R.D.S. show-grounds on August 27th, 1974, as an unbroken 3-year-old, and much-heralded beforehand. However, in a gloomy day's sale (the market had started to slide in the summer of 1974) Mr Galavan's half-brother to Red Rum (like the majority of entrants) failed to sell. There is no shortage therefore of Red Rum's half-sisters, though it is doubt-ful whether purchasers will knock each other over in a frenzied rush to buy the progeny of Fray Bentos. At stud since 1966 he had sired only one winner by November, 1973, and none in that year at all. His name alone, sugges-tive of canned meat, is a deterrent in the world of horses hopefully bred to avoid that fate.

Back at Wymondham in the winter of 1967–68 all went happily with Mared's eldest son Red Rum. The lads were full of optimism about the approaching flat season. 'We hadn't *begun* to tap his potential,' declares Jock Mayes, still seething six years later over what was about to happen to his favourite.

'He was,' says Mayes, 'a great doer.' Molony feeds mostly Spillers' nuts. Red Rum got three feeds daily: 'one before first lot, fed by my Head Man at 6.30. Then one at lunchtime and one at night.' Molony added surprisingly, 'They get no mash – ever'.

'A great doer'

Jock Mayes who was then about to become Molony's Head Man, adds, 'Red Rum ate everythin' we give him. Only left once, so far as I can remember, and that was when we tried to give him a physic powder. He smelt it right away in his feed. And he left it! We didn't try it again after that. He knew what was best for him.'

I wonder whether recognition of physic powders is a magic test of a great horse. The best I ever trained, Linwell (Cheltenham Gold Cup, 1957), would never touch even a whiff of physic, either. . . . Who is to blame them? In the old days it was the barbarous custom so ruthlessly to physic horses coming in off grass, that they purged wretchedly for days. The notion was 'to clean 'em right out'. I always thought it debilitated them. Learning from Linwell I physicked my horses less and less each year until, without any ill-effects to their subsequent performance, I discarded the habit entirely. Leeches, I assured myself, are not now often used by human doctors. . . .

Red Rum enjoyed every sort of titbit: 'Everythin' and

anythin',' says Jock Mayes, 'sugar, peppermints, carrots. . . .'

New Year came and the horse became a 3-year-old. Although there was no firm plan for Red Rum to go hurdling – there was a race or two more to be won on the flat – he had already started jumping at home. This, like his **Credit due** careful breaking, stood him in the greatest stead for the **to Tim** future. It is another thing for which the credit is due to Tim **Molony** Molony. Abnormally early as yearlings, he pops his horses over two foot jumps in his circular cinder track with three jumps in the circuit. It is the best of all natural starts.

Red Rum had no ailments of any sort during his stay at Wymondham which was about to end so abruptly. 'He was always,' says Tim Molony, 'a very sound horse.'

His winter and early spring programme followed that of the previous year. As a 3-year-old he was pulling rather more strongly. To match his development he needed **Needed** proportionately extra work. There was no doubt at all at **extra work** Wymondham: Red Rum had noticeably improved through the winter. This year he was again being prepared for a first-time-out gamble, but his target came even earlier than that of 1967. The plan was that he should win Doncaster's Waterdale Selling Handicap restricted to 3-year-olds and run over 7 furlongs on the third day (27th March) of the new season.

When the weights came out Molony saw that Red Rum was set to carry 9st 2lb, very close to the top of the handicap. By now he knew very well that his horse preferred firm fast ground. When the season opened on Monday the Doncaster turf was yielding, but three days of wind had dried it out 'au point' for Red Rum for the first race of Lincoln day. Molony had got the horse as fit as if he were running for his life as well as for Mr Maurice Kingsley's money. He had engaged yet another new jockey: this time the famous Geoff Lewis had the ride.

A certainty Everyone at Doncaster seemed to 'know' that Red Rum, **to win** though carrying topweight, was a 'certainty' to win this race. It looked like another Kingsley gamble. In a field of 20 he immediately opened favourite at 9 to 2 and was backed down to 11 to 4. It was a different kettle of fish to the Liverpool coup of the previous year. This time the next favourite was right out at 8 to 1. This was the colt Duo, who in Red Rum's last race as a 2-year-old, had made up a lot of late ground at Leicester to finish $2\frac{1}{2}$ lengths behind him. Then Red Rum had carried 4lb more than Duo. Now at Doncaster he had to give him 6lb. The two fought out a desperate finish. Red Rum showed in

front a quarter of a mile from home, but Duo, racing
down the middle of the course against Red Rum's better
position on the rails, was closing on him all the way.
They were neck and neck for each striving stride of the
last two hundred yards and Red Rum, hammering on
great-heartedly, reached the post just in front by a head.

It had been a frightening last 30 seconds for his backers.
And now, for the third time in 18 months, Red Rum was
once again up for sale at public auction. There was a big
crowd around for Lincoln day. Jumping leapt large in
everyone's mind: the Grand National loomed only three
days ahead. The first day at Doncaster had included two
National Hunt races. Wasn't a well-made 3-year-old
gelding just the sort to win a little 3-year-old hurdle race
come back end, t'other side of summer? This Red Rum
might even win again on t'flat. . . . There were jumping
people about. Mr Maurice Kingsley, over from Manchester, had come up to Mrs Lurlene Brotherton, down
from nearby Kirkham Abbey, (where all her winning
racing-plates hang in the hall) to murmur 'I've another
"Dagmar" for you, dear. I just want one more punt.' And
so he had. 'Yes,' agreed Mrs Brotherton comfortably, six
years later.

The auction began. 'And that . . .' said Tim Molony
sadly, six years later in Wymondham where Red Rum
no longer was, 'And that's when the trouble started.'

Up for sale again

12 'I WAS DISGUSTED THAT HE WENT WITHOUT ME KNOWIN''

Once again, as after the previous year's seller at Liverpool it was Jock Mayes' nasty task to lead Red Rum around for sale. That rare thrill of looking after a winner, of seeing your horse out there victorious, is soon expunged after a seller by the awful dread again of losing him. Unless, as Mayes and all the stable fervently hoped, he could be once more bought in.

Doncaster Sales

Another of the dramatic ironies which festoon Red Rum's story, are the two towns where he has been for sale in England. First, Liverpool. Now Doncaster; and it would be at Doncaster again four years later in the sales ring beyond the Great North Road that another stable would see their favourite horse offered for sale against their will.

Mayes led his horse around the packed circle of people in front of Doncaster's grand weighing-room. 'I could see the guv'nor biddin' alright, but I couldna see who was the opposition. I *thought* t'was the same man that had run us up previous for the horse, but I couldna be sure. I knew the guv'nor would bid as high as possible, for this was a good horse, but when the biddin' got up towards 1,000 guineas, then I began to get really worried.'

Red Rum revolved. The auctioneer sang out his praises and the rising bids, for he was working for the racecourse on commission. Mayes had one hand on the horse's reins and his eyes on Molony's face. At such critical points in a horse's life, of which the horse himself is ignorant, the man with him, accepting the horse's dumb trust, can feel a traitor. Each time as Mayes waited for Molony to nod to the auctioneer for another bid, he thought the horse might well be lost. Each time he saw Molony nod, relief soothed him. But only momentarily. Someone out there in that moon ring of circling faces was this time really bidding for their horse. Who the hell was it? How long could the Guv'nor go on buying back the horse with Mr Kingsley's money? What had they arranged between them?

The bidding had risen to 1,000 guineas in advances of ten guineas. As the thousand was bid and passed, an extra buzz flurried through the crowd. Such levels for a seller were unusual. The bids rose now in 50 guinea jumps. 'Eleven hundred . . . and fifty? Thank you. Eleven hundred and fifty . . . Twelve? Twelve I'm bid. . . .'

At about this point Jock Mayes received the frightening impression that Mr Maurice Kingsley no longer intended to buy his horse in: 'I sorta understood it, durin' the biddin',' Jock recalls, his face still puzzling over what was then a mystery.

'At 1,400 guineas . . .' the auctioneer called, '1,400 guineas for this useful winner. . . .' His eye returned to the unknown bidder who had run Molony up all the way. 'Last chance. . . .?' The auctioneer's eyebrows were raised . . . 'At 1,400 guineas once . . . twice . . . for the last time then . . .' Slap, down came his gavel. '1,400 guineas.' A momentary pause while Red Rum's lads still doubted, then – 'Bought in.'

'This useful winner'

Two words of quick relief for Jock Mayes. He led the horse happily away through the crowd back to his box, to be washed down. Well, he was still safe in the yard, though it had cost a lot to get him back. No one then knew, of course, how cheap those 1,400 guines would prove in the end, or what a grotesque insult it would seem that such a horse could ever have been run and risked in sordid 'sellers'.

Mr Maurice Kingsley, however, thought that 1,400 guineas was too expensive. He declared to his trainer, 'I'm not having him'.

In practice the trainer usually bids on behalf of the owner. That is generally understood. Now faced with Kingsley's refusal, the unhappy Tim was in a quandary. Molony had done the bidding; Molony would carry the can.

'Alright,' Molony heard himself say, both pained and angered, 'I'll have him myself.'

'I'll have him myself'

He remembered years afterwards the instant flutter of doubt. 'I didn't know *how* I was going to pay for him! Then I thought, "It'll be alright, I'll find somebody to take him on". I *knew* I'd find somebody.' So he probably would have. In which case could Red Rum's fate possibly have led through a different chain of hands to those unlikely conquests in the National?

In the meantime Red Rum went home to Wymondham the property, not yet confirmed nor paid for, of Tim Molony, who'd ridden the winners of almost every big race bar the Grand National. He would find those 1,400 guineas for Red Rum, the selling plater, or another owner to pay for him. 'Then the next day,' Molony reflects sardonically, 'Maurice rang me up and said he'd have him.'

Brief ownership

In the 24 hours of his brief ownership, Molony had already made plans for his horse's next race. He had been so pleased with his performance at Doncaster that it was his firm intention to take Red Rum to Liverpool the very next Saturday, Grand National day, to run him in a good mile handicap, the £600 Earl of Sefton's Stakes. Two flat races in four days is strenuous; and this was the first instance of Red Rum's exceptional resilience to rapid racing. So when Mr Kingsley rang to say he'd have his horse back after all, Molony said sharply, 'Right. But I'm still going to take him to Liverpool for the Lord Sefton Stakes on Saturday.' Mr Kingsley expressed some surprise. Molony was adamant. 'And I still think he'll win.'

'With his penalty?' queried Mr Kingsley.

'Even with his 10lb penalty,' said a resolute Molony.

His very special course

So, for what would be his final flat race Red Rum made a second visit to Liverpool, his very special course. It was, furthermore, Grand National Day. And the winner of the great steeplechase off bottom weight was Red Alligator at 100 to 7 ridden by a then little-known jockey from Co. Durham, Brian Fletcher, whose path by a series of accidents would cross Red Rum's four years later; and to their mutual advantage. Watching, of course, as was his wont was Donald McCain from Southport, the permit trainer, still waiting for his 'One Good Horse'. And watching, too, was the ancient maestro Bobby Renton who had now arranged to have the horse he so much wanted.

Lester Piggott impressed

Tim Molony had for the second time persuaded mighty Lester Piggott to ride Red Rum. This great jockey picks his rides with such acumen that his choice is accepted by the masses as divine selection, and is backed accordingly. Piggott was plainly impressed by Red Rum's chances. Whatever the driving dynamo may have said about blinkers the year before, there were none on Red Rum on 30th March, 1968, when he stepped out onto Aintree two races after Red Alligator had won the 'National. Nor did Red Rum show any alarm and despondency at being once again in Piggott's iron grip.

In spite of Red Rum's severe 10lb penalty for his Doncaster win which brought him – a selling plater – up to second top weight in a reasonable handicap, he was again made favourite and started at 11 to 4. But only one other horse in the field of 21 had enjoyed the enormous benefit of a previous race that season. This was the 20 to 1 outsider Alan's Pet who, with the claiming Eccleston on top, carried 7st 8lb to Red Rum's 8st 12lb.

Red Rum beneath the pushing, driving, flourishing, coercing frame of lengthy Lester Piggott endured yet another vigorous set-to. He raced up with the leaders all the way and in the last furlong he and Alan's Pet fought it out to the post. They passed it, as he had a year before, nostril to flaring nostril. Up in the frame above a sea of applause (for he *was* the favourite and Lester's mount and he *had* shown guts) shot Red Rum's number as the winner. Piggott, too, believed he had just won as he rode back to the unsaddling enclosure.

Another vigorous set-to

Then the loudspeakers quacked: 'Correction!' Down came Red Rum's number. Up in its place went Alan's Pet's. The judge had changed his mind and reversed the placings. Tim Molony commented in the summer of '74: 'I still say the horse was never beaten at Liverpool!'

Red Rum without that 10lb penalty would have comfortably won the Sefton Stakes. It seemed a splendid augury for a profitable summer. The horse had proved what Tim Molony had always felt: that he was a good deal better than a plater. Now, too, Molony was planning ahead to the fun they would have when he could send the little horse jumping the following season. Such a balanced, gutsy horse . . . he could jump already . . . hardy too as well as handy, an ideal sort. . . .

The telephone rang at Wymondham. It was Mr Bobby Renton. He said to Tim like a bolt from the blue, 'I've bought Red Rum'.

'I've bought Red Rum'

Six years later Molony said how he felt: 'Heartbroken'. He wasn't told what Renton had paid for him. 'I think it would be £2,000 . . . Bobby Renton came down, sat on him, rode him round the paddock and asked me questions about him, what he ate, that sort of thing. And then he took him away.'

Were the yard upset to hear Red Rum had been sold?

Jock Mayes remembers glumly. 'I was *disgusted* that he went without me knowin'. It just *transpired* that the owner had sold him.'

The loss of a winning horse hurt. The loss of a popular character pained everyone. But what particularly rankled was that the deed was done with so little said.

13 'I DON'T WANT YOU TO BREAK YOUR NECK'

Red Rum's new owner and trainer, Mrs Lurlene Brotherton and Mr Bobby Renton had enjoyed a remarkable and famous association since 1945.

Six summers after they bought the horse which they hoped might win them, at last, another Grand National to follow their Freebooter's victory of 1950, they were facing one another in the small, low sitting-room at Oxclose. The window, in front of which Mrs Brotherton was sitting, commands a tidy sweep of gravel and the start of a little garden which plunges down an almost vertical slope towards the river below. The front gate, under a huddle of Wuthering Heights trees, discloses by being shut or open whether the old Master of Oxclose is at home. On my preliminary visit to see the place piloted by Anthony Gillam, Renton's next but one successor, we regarded the closed house with a touch of awe.

Master of Oxclose

Yorkshire opinion suggests that Mrs Brotherton must have paid around £3,000 for Red Rum. Tim Molony had supposed £2,000.

'£1,200,' said Bobby Renton with complete assurance, 'Mrs Brotherton paid Kingsley £1,200.' He pronounces the first syllable of her name to chime with *broth*, rather than with *brother*. Significantly, the octogenarian expert refers to her as 'Mrs Brotherton' throughout.

'Bobby paid Maurice Kingsley £1,200,' confirmed Mrs Brotherton, known to her friends as 'Muffie'. She nodded her firm chin sharply.

She refers to the once great trainer Mr Renton by the diminutive of his christian name and talks cheerfully of 'we'. Robert Renton was 86 in the summer of 1974. He was the son of a dog-collared clergyman – 'who bought Oxclose as a holiday place' and is the father of a decorated full Colonel. The trainer once had a daughter, too, who died tragically, and he had been for years a widower.

£1,200 seemed improbably little for Maurice Kingsley to take for a horse he had himself first rejected and then bought back for 1,400 guineas. It seems a loss. But he makes no comment and Red Rum's next owner and trainer are sure that is what was paid.

Bobby Renton has lived at Oxclose for over 50 years, and did all his great training from it. It stands on a very steep bank like a little cliff above the canal, beyond which lies Ripon racecourse clearly within sight and shout. Newby Hall is pointed out by Renton with pride lying in woodland further to the right. The canal is crossed by hump-backed red-brick bridges. Over these all Renton's horses would go to work on the racecourse, to jump the two schooling fences which were placed precariously close to the further bank, or to gallop 'Going between the Gates', as it was called.

'Going between the gates'

No gallop exists as they would know it in Newmarket or Lambourn, but Oxclose has yielded hundreds of winners in the 52 years Mr Robert Renton trained there. The horses worked on open pastures: 'The Hilly Fields', then further beyond, 'The Highside'. They cantered about on 'The Riverside Fields', or over 'Harry's Land' (tenanted once by a farmer called Harry Kilmington). Ripon is over 200 miles north of London and Oxclose seems away in the wilds.

From the front and garden side the house looks almost as cozy as a friendly farmstead. But the other flanks cast cold, forbidding aspects. The stable yard in which Red Rum spent four dramatic years of hope, disappointment, illness and dismissal, adjoins the backquarters of the house.

During Red Rum's four years at Oxclose he would have three completely contrasting trainers: old Bobby Renton with as much experience of jumpers as anyone alive; the young, quite inexperienced but very professional jockey, slim Tommy Stack, who was making his way up from nothing; and tall, thin Anthony Gillam, son of one Yorkshire industrialist, and maternal grandson of another.

Three contrasting trainers

He would have two constants over those years: the head lad in the little yard, old soldier Charlie Wright; and Sandra, his loving stable girl.

The once-famous stable yard is now an empty, black-creosoted, ramshackle place. Round it, like the carcasses of whales, crouch dark-grey decaying Nissen huts. Immediately behind the stable yard is a rolling field. Through a special back-window in his box – as at Wymondham coincidentally in the corner – Red Rum could enjoy a Yorkshire view of undulating grassland, straggling lines of hawthorn trees and blackthorn hedges. The small city of Ripon, unseen, unheard, where Freebooter, after his 'National was granted a civic reception, seems leagues away. Oxclose is rustic, brooding. No air of merriment stirs. The canal below the place lurks darkly, full of lost dreams and melancholy.

Yet Mr Renton's eyes glow mischievously like a goblin's. He has always been morally as well as physically fearless. Decades ago at old Bogside, where the Scottish National used to be run, he had hauled a most important titled lady – then an owner of his – scarlet-faced before the local stewards to report her for, and to make her officially recant, something she had said about him.

'Did I get the horse *vetted*?'

'Did I get the horse *vetted*?' he repeated about the Red Rum deal, as if he had misheard me.

Mrs Brotherton explained, 'Bobby always examines all his horses himself'.

This, by any standard of equine experience is extra-ordinary. I know of no other trainer who does not do every deal 'subject to veterinary examination' and then fully instructs his own vet to probe every aspect of the horse. The vet will examine and report on heart and lungs and eyes, as well as all external lumps and bumps. One celebrated practitioner, not entirely unconnected with international Three Day Event teams, seldom 'passes' a horses without a list of qualifying reservations. Another, reporting to a trainer friend who was doubtful about a possible new purchase's leg, declared exasperatedly after an hour's examination 'I tried *everything*, but I just couldn't make the blanker lame'.

Singular self-confidence

So for a trainer, however elderly and experienced, to buy a horse, particularly for a special patron, without the benefit of any professional veterinary advice, demonstrates Renton's singular self-confidence. In Red Rum's case, there was unlikely to be much wrong with a 3-year-old gelding who had survived eight races as a 2-year-old, and then come out to run two cracking good hard races within four days. Not the preparation one would desire in a future jumper, but at least it suggested the horse was not only as sound as a bell but as tough as old boots.

Renton said, 'I went to see Red Rum at Tim's. I looked him over myself. He was a beautifully *coupled* horse.' He nodded his head over the recollection. He looked very small sitting hunched right in the sofa against the dark wall, wearing an old tweed coat, cavalry twill trousers and black shoes. The fire made the room very hot on the sun-filled May afternoon, but Mr Renton wore a thick knitted waistcoat. He clasped his hands so tightly together over his knees – bent as if he were still riding – that his fingers became small white sausages. He had ridden heroically in hurdle races when he was over 70.

Once he had trained for the gold and diamond million-aire Mr Jim Joel. 'He said to me in this very room,' Renton recalled, '"Go and buy the best horse in Britain for yourself to ride. And I'll pay. For I don't want you to break your neck."'

At the pinnacle of his career there were 30 horses in Renton's Oxclose stables. When Red Rum arrived there were only eight, all Mrs Brotherton's. Renton had bought and produced some triumphant horses down the years: Freebooter, for years every good judge's beau ideal of the 'Aintree type', 'Flagrant Mac' (who won a Scottish National, as Red Rum was to do in someone else's care), Oakcliffe, Mischievous Mac, Merrycourt, Little Yid, Cushendun, Tudor Line (who was 'done' at Oxclose by a stable boy called Jimmy Fitzgerald, now a leading trainer), Cruachan, Mr Jim Joel's Glorious Twelfth and Caesar's Helm, Siracusa, Ernest, Old Mull, Chatelet, Dagmar Gittell. . . .

A great host of the winners had been Mrs Brotherton's. When she bought Red Rum in 1968 she had been trying for 18 years to find a horse to win her and Renton another Grand National. Liverpool was Renton's target, and hers, and time was running out like sand down an hour-glass.

'I liked Red Rum when I first saw him,' said Mrs Brotherton in May, 1974. Her one-time hope had just won his second Grand National and, uniquely, also the Scottish Grand National for someone else. 'He was such a taking horse, a lovely horse, but I did think he might be a bit small.' She had sold the horse – to the astonishment of the racing world – seven months too early.

Mrs 'Muffie' Brotherton, clad in a pale blue skirt to match her eyes sat alertly in the armchair in front of the window in the shadowy room at Oxclose. Talking in a direct manner, but giving away dexterously little, she clasped her hands behind her head. She possesses the authority of all mature country-based ladies cushioned by ample funds. One could see young persons quaking before her, or being exceedingly grateful to her for her kindnesses. You could recognise, too, firm basis for her reputation of having been such an attractive girl. She has pink cheeks above the pointed chin and her brows arch sharply over quick eyes. When I enquired of Mr Renton why he had finally stopped training, she sprang into the question like a protective leopardess: 'He was 83. Why *shouldn't* he

He had ridden heroically

Liverpool was Renton's target

stop? Why did *you* stop yourself?' she flashed.

'If Bobby had given up earlier,' Mrs Brotherton avowed, 'I'd have sold my horses earlier. I couldn't stand those terrible winter motor journeys, frost and fog and cold. And I said "I'll sell them".' A stern blue look defied me to doubt her: 'And I don't regret it at all.'

'I'll sell them'

But no one, not the most charitable saintly person who ever graced the racing scene, can possibly sell a horse one August and see him win the Grand National next March without regrets. Was it that she lost faith in Red Rum too soon? Or that she lost patience with the quickly changing young trainers who followed Renton at Oxclose? Or that she simply wanted 'out'? Or had she, like many ladies acting on intuition, *afterwards* found a motive to excuse an awful mistake?

14 'HIS ISN'T A STORY. IT'S A FAIRY TALE!'

Someone in the south had said to me that Mrs Brotherton was akin to that forceful character and other famous woman owner of 'chasers, the late Miss Dorothy Paget. Bar their great strings, desire for victory, and a common inclination to gamble, nothing seems further from the truth. The legendary Miss Paget loathed almost all men and kept a weird establishment of female help-mates. She changed trainers and jockeys like a weekly wash. The hospitable and gracious Mrs Brotherton ('my mother hunted from the social point of view; my father rode in point-to-points') has two children, and has stayed loyal to one jumping trainer for 30 years. I suggested that her powerful string of jumpers had been perhaps the northern equivalent of the Queen Mother's in the south?

Miss Dorothy Paget

Mrs Brotherton nodded, 'Well, until the Queen Mum went ahead we were running neck and neck with 200 winners each. . . . After Dagmar Gittell won the Topham

Trophy at Liverpool, the Queen Mother had won it another year, and she wrote a very nice letter congratulating me.'

Mrs Brotherton started racing with Mr Renton as soon as the war ended in 1945. 'My first horse was Royal Ensign. Tim Molony rode him.' Molony rode many Renton horses in those days, and still marvels at the uncanny skill of the trainer. 'Quite soon I had 12 horses, sometimes more, each season,' said Mrs Brotherton, warming her hands over past glories.

When they were looking for Freebooter, 'I hired a little 'plane, practically tied together with string – and Bobby and I flew to Ireland. We went to Dan Moore's place and Bobby rode Freebooter. Then we went off to see Klaxton.' This was a slashing 'chaser who subsequently won three successive Grand Military Gold Cups for his owner-rider David Gibson, the first in Freebooter's National year. Renton and Mrs Brotherton had certainly narrowed their choice to two top-class horses.

Looking for Freebooter

'My husband,' explained Mrs Brotherton, 'had said to me "You can spend x thousand pounds – either on one horse or several". Bobby wasn't sure between Klaxton and Freebooter. So we went back to Dan Moore's for Bobby to have a second ride. And he liked him best. But Dan Moore said, "He takes a terrible hold. He'll be no good at Aintree. . . ." But there you are.' Mrs Brotherton looked proudly and affectionately across the room at her shrewd trainer.

Her late husband, Charles Brotherton, was one of Yorkshire's most generous philanthropists. He died in 1949 after some years of failing health and partial paralysis in his right arm and leg. He reputedly gave away (he was modest and sought no glory) more than one million pounds to charities during his life, and left almost another million when he died.

Gave away £1,000,000

Lurlene, daughter of Colonel Elliot-Pyle of Kensington and Sussex, was the kindly industrialist's third wife. By her he had his first child, Anne, when he was 57. He was so exalted by his daughter's arrival that he presented his wife with a pearl necklace bought from Princess Nicholas of Greece, and all his thousands of employees with an extra pound in their 1939 pay packets saying, 'Because I'm the happiest man alive'. Additionally he set up in that year the £250,000 Charles Brotherton Trust to sponsor educational and medical charities in towns with which his huge company was connected.

He was born Charles Ratcliffe, but changed his name by deed-poll after he succeeded his uncle, the late Lord Brotherton, in 1930 in the chairmanship of the great chemical empire the latter had founded.

From his uncle he inherited the bulk of a £1,750,000 fortune. He said at Kirkham Abbey when he was 58 that he had two reasons for setting up that quarter million pound charitable trust. First, he had found so much happiness in his marriage, and in the birth of his baby daughter, and in his business success that he wanted to share it with everyone he knew. And secondly that he was 'selfish enough to want the fun of seeing for himself the good money can do'. His uncle had made most of his own philanthropic gifts so late that he did not live to see the good they did.

'The good money can do'

In his prime Charles Brotherton travelled the world on business, hunted hard and played a brisk game of tennis. Sadly, by June 1946, he was an invalid, but saying that he was 'still happy, and never happier than when I'm pushing my little daughter's pram'.

His widow still lives at Kirkham Abbey north-east of York, about 30 miles across country east of where all her great jumpers were trained by Bobby Renton. I had heard Kirkham was a beautiful place. 'Muffie' Brotherton smiled, 'I love it, and it's very comfortable and the setting's nice, but it's early Vic – not beautiful.'

Renton said, 'You'd have had a good lunch there!'

Entertains most hospitably

Mrs Brotherton entertains most hospitably. She has lots of Yorkshire friends. She gives house-parties for York races. To young officers stationed in the north of England in the early 1950's she was particularly kind. One, Captain Tim Forster, who became a trainer of renown and of his own Grand National winner Well to Do, warmly recalls those visits. 'We'd go after York races. Few of us had properly been round a leading trainer's yard before. It was a *tremendous* excitement – just after Freebooter's National – to see all these marvellous horses owned by Mrs Brotherton, Lord Rosebery and Mr Jim Joel!' They were indeed owners of a magnitude to whet the appetite of any trainer in the land.

'Bobby Renton was very quiet, very dry,' says Forster. 'He said to me "When you go to buy a young horse you want to be able to fit your bowler-hat neatly between his forelegs". I've never forgotten that – as a measure of whether it's likely to be wide enough.' It conjures up, too, in the bowler-hat, an image of a racing world which died quite suddenly in the 1950's.

Soon after Tim Forster started training on his own account, Mrs Brotherton sent him two of her horses, one of which she shared with her daughter Anne, now Mrs Anne Mears, and Master of the North Cotswold Hounds. Forster was thrilled: 'There was I, a very young trainer, getting horses from the great Mrs Brotherton! There were things in the papers about it!'

But though one of her horses, Well Packed, won for Forster at Nottingham and was placed at Birmingham, 'He went back to Mr Renton,' says Forster a trifle sadly. 'Then after a year, Mrs Brotherton wrote to me saying "Bobby Renton is cutting down".'

When Red Rum arrived at Oxclose Mrs Brotherton, though thinking him on the small side, 'Still thought he'd make a 'chaser'.

Bobby Renton chipped in: 'I said, "This is a Liverpool horse. You could run him in the National".'

'This is a Liverpool horse'

Mrs Brotherton added, correcting him, 'I said "At seven he ought to run in the National".'

Yet she sold him when he was seven. . . .

'Well, the year before I'd sold two of my horses', said Mrs Brotherton quite testily, to emphasise that the culling of Red Rum was part of a strategic policy, 'And then Red Rum was the oldest, so he had to go.'

'He won three hurdles and five 'chases when he was here,' said Bobby Renton firmly. 'Eight races.' He was right to reiterate the successes Red Rum enjoyed under his official training and then under his wing. For the money he cost, he had done well. It is just that his stakes of £3,761 earned in 4 seasons from 49 races at Oxclose, does not stand up very proudly against the £65,666 he would earn from 19 races in his first two seasons in Southport.

'I can't grumble,' said Mrs Brotherton brightly. 'Good luck to them' – meaning Red Rum's new Southport team of Noel Le Mare and 'Ginger' McCain.

'Good luck to them'

'He's been more like a pet dog there,' said Mr Renton. 'All that and the sea . . .' His voice trailed away. He might have been dreaming for the hundredth time of whether if he'd kept the horse, and kept on training . . . would he in his twilight seasons have won those two more Nationals?

'No doubt, I've been very lucky anyway,' said Mr Robert Renton briskly, gathering himself together. His wits are very much about him. He might confuse the jockeys Slack (who rode for him in the fifties) and Stack (who rode for him in the seventies), but he was as keen as mustard to find out all I knew about the swiftly rising flat-race trainer, young Barry Hills. 'I've had some beautiful horses. . . . But the labour got very difficult. And I had rheumatism. Towards the end I became rather a "soft" trainer.' He meant in the degree of work he gave his horses. He added, 'I got a bit tired of it'.

'You used to get up at 83 at crack of dawn,' said Mrs Brotherton indignant at his mild self-criticism.

'Well, I did all my own feeding,' said Renton, 'I always trained my horses "by the manger".'

He and Mrs Brotherton would always stay at the same guest-house for Cheltenham, 'Greenways'. 'Once I had the most awful rheumatism and the manager recommended his own physiotherapist. I went along one morning before racing,' Renton recounted, 'and a man in a white coat opened the door to me and asked "Have you ever tried a woman?"'

'Have you ever tried a woman?'

The old man watched me gleefully for signs of shock or mirth. 'Rather early in the morning to be offered that, I thought.' He explained, 'He meant a *masseuse*. . . .' Suddenly he chuckled with delight. His mind came looping back to Red Rum. 'His isn't a *story*,' he said. 'It's a fairy tale.'

15 'I LOVED THE HORSE FROM THE START'

Three very different people, typical of racing's contrasting strands, were working for old Mr Renton at Oxclose when Red Rum arrived from Tim Molony's in the spring of 1968. There was the sharp young Irish jockey Tommy Stack, who had just turned professional. There was Renton's head lad, Charlie Wright, a local man who had served in the Yorkshire Hussars during the war and was then 55. And there was the young stable girl Sandra, also from nearby Ripon, who had been riding with Renton's string since she was $13\frac{1}{2}$ and playing truant from school on her beloved little pony 'Tammy'.

Sandra Kendall as she then was, first saw Red Rum in his box at Oxclose. 'I loved the horse from the start. I loved his head – so full of character. So full of life, he was, and yet so kind.'

'I loved the horse'

But she had been hearing about the horse for some time before he finally arrived. 'I knew Mr Renton was very interested in him, because he came back from Doncaster races and told us he'd seen this horse and had been trying to buy him out of a seller.'

Was the inscrutable Bobby Renton then, the mysterious bidder who had done the not-done thing at Doncaster and run up Tim Molony in the bidding? Such was Sandra's impression. Mr Renton does not say.

Sandra added, 'Then Mr Renton said he'd had to pay a bigger price for it and thought he'd got it.' Bigger? The mystery thickens. Sandra continued, 'He was very excited. Next morning he told us "I've got him!". He loved the horse.'

'I've got him'

So it seems the deal was done with Maurice Kingsley as swiftly as that. In the astute world of business, articles are often not bought until the buyer has already 'pre-sold' them.

Bobby Renton wasted no time on the new acquisition for which he had been straining for so long. He allotted Red Rum to young Sandra because he had just given away one of the three horses she had been 'doing', St Willie, to Mrs Brotherton's daughter Anne.

Such is the lottery of a racing stable. One lad or girl may by ill-luck 'do' three bad horses and suffer financially by getting no presents for winners, and suffer in morale by tending animals who constantly, publicly fail. Yet there are lads like Fred Winter's Vincent Brooks, known as 'The luckiest lad in racing', because he 'does' the two stars Pendil and Bula. A lad in a tiny yard behind a used-car shop in a street in Birkdale may now have usurped that title for having 'done', against all odds, the double Grand National winner Red Rum.

Lottery of a racing stable

In a happy fairy tale Sandra, who first schooled her 'Rummy,' who 'did' him for four years, who rode him out more than 1,000 times, would have been the one who took him to Aintree for his triumphs.

As it was, she drew him by accident. St Willie had gone lame and been sent hunting. Very well, Sandra should make up her three with Mrs Brotherton's new horse, this 3-year-old off the flat.

The morning after Red Rum arrived Sandra rode him out in the back paddock immediately behind the stables. It was here on her first day of paid work for Mr Renton as a girl of 15 that she had taken her first fall. 'A horse reared over on top of me over the little hurdles.' She always schooled all 'her own horses', meaning in stable-lad jargon, the horses she 'did'. 'Several fell with me over fences and hurdles,' said Mrs Sandra Miles cheerfully six years later and securely married in her bright comfortable house in a smart street on Ripon's outskirts. What happened to Red Rum finished the joys of racing for her for ever.

'Pop him over the hurdle!'

'So the first morning I rode him out in the paddock. Gosh! I've sat on some horses, but by jove – he bucked, he kicked, he did everything but stand on his head! In fact I think he did that, too! I didn't know *what* to think. Then Mr Renton calls out "Pop him over the hurdle!" So I did. He just *flew* it – never even hesitated. He was great. But I had a job to pull him up.' Sandra's eyes glow with the thrill of it. 'I really got used to him. Touch wood, he never dropped me once.'

Girls do really love horses. Sometimes with a very special horse, a girl can love the horse to the exclusion of all else. That spring morning in the paddock Sandra and Red Rum instantly clicked. Sandra had a steady boy friend, older than she, who for years wanted to marry her. But that came about only when, four long and loving years later, 'Rummy' (pronounced in Sandra's Yorkshire voice as 'roomy') was dispatched from Oxclose to be sold.

Nicknamed her 'Dandra'

From little Sandra's schoolgirl start old Mr Renton nicknamed her 'Dandra' and called her nothing else. Her brother Walter worked for Renton and drove the horse-box. 'He was a brilliant rider and good with horses,' says Sandra. 'But he never rode as a jockey under Rules, 'cos Mrs Brotherton didn't agree with it.'

This may sound tyrannical, and certainly indicates the control Mrs Brotherton exercised over Oxclose, but it is good racing sense. If the horse-box driver also rides in races, who the devil is to bring the horses home if he gets laid out in a grisly fall?

When Sandra was 14 she was sneaking days off school to go racing with her brother in the horse-box. She even used to lead the horses round. 'One day at Manchester we had three winners and ever since then Mr Renton and

Mrs Brotherton took me all over the place! Then, when I left school, Mr Renton badly wanted me to work there. I loved horses and my parents knew I loved them.'

'I loved horses'

Like the parents of a hundred thousand horse-mad children, Mr and Mrs Kendall, though living in a town and quite disinterested themselves, indulged their children. Walter had a horse which he sold when he went to work for Renton. Sandra had little Tammy on whom she rode out with his racehorses. The pony was bought by her brother for Sandra's 13th birthday and was only put down at the age of 18 in the spring of 1974, with chronic laminitis.

Sandra started with Mr Renton at £4.50 a week. 'He liked to start you low. Then the next week he gave me £6.50. We had a good home life though: we never gave mother anything, but lived at home and we biked to work. I had six ponies at home, and I had to do them before I went up to work and after I'd finished.' The length and labours of her days would be strenuous for a grown man. For an ex-schoolgirl of 15 they were Herculean. But such is the passion of girls for horses.

Early in her stable girl's life she had the first inkling of the pain of parting with a horse. The girl or lad tends a horse all day, sometimes for years, feeding him, tending him like a maid or valet, caring for him like a nurse in sickness and in health, riding him out on biting winter mornings in the dark, and on spring days when riding is a joy. They take the horse racing, sharing the trepidation of the journey out, and the occasional triumph and general disappoint-ments on long journeys back. They get to know their horse far more intimately than anyone else can know him. Affection, even for awkward horses, is inevitable. Love, in many cases, blooms.

When riding is a joy

Yet the absentee owner who foots the bills and sees his horse for perhaps 90 minutes in a year, decides absolutely to sell the horse – either at a profit or to cut a loss. And the stable lad or lass suffers the parting.

Sandra's first winner as a stable girl subsequently went under, struggling to give two stone away to a lightweight in a handicap. 'And then they sold him and that broke my heart. Next they gave me Dagmar Gittell.'

After his initial success on leaving Maurice Kingsley for Mrs Brotherton this precursor of Red Rum had disappointed for several seasons. 'Nobody else wanted to do him,' said Sandra. 'Because he was a *devil*. And he could hardly win bad sellers! Then I looked after him and he won

no end of races, including the Topham at Liverpool.'
That was March, 1962, the year of Kilmore's National,
six years before Sandra took over Red Rum.

'We mucked out first'

Renton's routine when Red Rum arrived was for the
staff to start at 8 o'clock. 'We mucked out first,' said
Sandra, 'then rode out First Lot. Then groomed. Then rode
out Second Lot. Then it was lunchtime. We rode out every
single day whatever the weather.'

After a horse's lad, it is the Head Lad who has most to
do with his care. In a busy stable the trainer is so often
away racing or at sales that he may spend no more than a
couple of minutes a day really looking at any one horse.
The good Head Lad is around the place from pitch-dark
dawns to moonlit nights, acting something between a
matron and a sergeant-major. Red Rum enjoyed at
Oxclose the care of the old-fashioned type of Head Lad,
the sort no longer being born or moulded but who (when
I first came into racing) were greatly sought after. 'Never
make a *racing* lad your Head Lad,' several senior trainers
counselled me. 'Get, if you can, the old huntin' type of
stud groom – much more reliable sort of fella in ev'ry
way, y'know. And doesn't think he knows all about
racin'.'

Charles Wright

Bobby Renton's head lad Charles Wright was Yorkshire
born, in Masham, and lived in Ripon. By November, 1974,
he would – had the stables been still going – have done 27
years at Oxclose. He started from an advertisement in the
local paper, as Mr Renton's groom-gardener-handyman.
The job sounds now a peculiar jumble. But before the war
most countrymen knew a little bit about horses as well as
gardens. Wright still has a close-cropped military look
and preserves in a crumbling age more than mere vestiges
of the military virtues: neatness, loyalty, obedience,
responsibility. But the stables at Oxclose are empty and
tumbling down. Charles Wright preserves a beautiful
album full of photographs of all those Renton winners in
the past, of himself and his officers in the Yorkshire
Yeomanry, mounted, going off to war on their brave
horses in the days when Britain too was a place of consequence, valour and success.

Life was tough at Oxclose. 'The apprentices got ten
bob a week and their grub.' But Charlie Wright progressed till he was doing a racehorse 'Flagrant Mac', and
then one day after the old head lad, Jim Laurence, retired,
Mr Renton said to Charlie, 'Just take over things till I
get someone else.' Wright added, 'He advertised the

job, but he didn't get any suitable replies'. So Charlie
started on £8 a week plus a cottage. 'Money was always
very poor till Mr Gillam took over.' He added fairly, 'But
we did have free potatoes and milk till Mr Renton closed
the farm.'

'I'm one of those,' said Charlie Wright 'who like
their horses fed *one hour* before exercise. So I cycled to work
leaving Ripon at six.'

But he had been inured to tough conditions and unusual
comrades in the war. In 1939 he had travelled with his
cavalry troop-horses across France to Marseilles, on to
Cyprus, then to Haifa and finally to Egypt. 'At the outbreak of war the Government commandeered all the
hunters they needed under eight years old. The officers
picked out the good ones for themselves.'

But Lance-Corporal Wright was by the Suez Canal
'puttin' the horses to harness and trainin' the Arabs who
couldn't speak English how to drive 'em. We were loadin'
carts of bully-beef by the Canal – two ton loads – each
horse could pull a ton.'

Then, it being the army, he was sent from the desert
heat immediately to sleep in tents above Scotland's snow-
line with Norwegian officers (who spoke little English
either) in case the British army should invade Scandinavia.
'We cut out snowblocks to build walls for our horses under
a tarpaulin.' They tramped about in snow shoes – 'Not
even allowed outside to have a sluice – 'case it left a black
mark which Jerry could see from the air.'

After his 'demob', he had a spell with an officer whose
batman he had once been, but whose wife he found 'a bit
bombastic. In suchlike jobs you usually get on with the
one and not with the other!' Back in Yorkshire and at a
loose end, he followed the advertisement to the house,
found it 'a bit tatty, needing paint, but Mr Renton said,
"Start tomorrow".' So he did, as gardener-handyman,
rising to be Head Lad to Mr Renton, Tommy Stack and
Anthony Gillam and in charge of Red Rum all the time.

But even when the horse arrived at Oxclose the
establishment was running down. There were far fewer
gallops than there had been in the good old days when there
had been horses specially to roll and harrow them –
'tractors ruin the terrain', explained Charles Wright. 'We
had a good gallop in the middle – over the river, but when
Mr Renton sold the land, the agreement to the gallops
ended. Then we'd only a little gallop – just like a footpath
through the gates. . . .'

Inured to
tough
conditions

'Start
tomorrow'

'A hardy devil'

He thought of Red Rum when he arrived – 'He was pretty light. But he'd eat anything and he was a hardy devil.' Wright reflected, 'Best thing about Mr Renton was he'd never stint his horses on food'. When Charlie Wright was feeding Red Rum in training he gave him: '6.30 a.m. one bowl of oats with chop'. (Chaff as it's sometimes called: hay cut up fine with a chaff-cutter to give bulk to hard feeds). 'After work – one bowl of crushed oats. Midday – two bowls of crushed oats and chop. Then at night two heaped bowls of crushed oats and one bowl of whole oats – oh, he'd have a massive amount of grub!'

A gargantuan appetite

Even on top of this extraordinarily heavy diet, Sandra would from time to time sneak a bit extra for her 'Rummy'. He is a horse with a gargantuan appetite.

Charlie Wright considered Mr Renton carefully and said with simple praise, 'He knows his horses all right'. It is the highest accolade one horse-master gives to another. 'To know' means fully to understand. And that takes a special talent and a lifetime. Then Wright added with a sort of wary admiration: 'He was a cunning old fox, he was.' Noticing my surprise, he added, pregnant with rustic meaning, 'Still waters run deep, and the devil lives at the bottom.'

16 'HE WAS MURDEROUS AT TIMES'

'The cunning old fox' lost no time in getting 'the hardy devil' into action. Charlie Wright's old buff army notebook, in which, in his round and careful hand, he noted all his horses' programmes, shows that Red Rum was 'brought into steady work in May, 1968'. Once more our hero was toiling while his rivals relaxed. He had now had no summer at grass since he left Rossenarra as a yearling. But Mr Renton, aware behind his back perhaps, of time's wingéd chariot hurrying near, intended to run the horse in 3-year-old hurdle races very early in the coming season.

On the principle of starting at the top, he aimed for the season's first meeting at Cheltenham. This would not be the course most trainers would choose to introduce a flat-race horse to the difficult art of contested jumping at speed. No flight of hurdles at Cheltenham is really on the level. The gradients on the course are extreme, requiring the ability to jump while climbing hills and, which is infinitely harder, to jump downhill, under pressure towards the end of a race. The good Cheltenham horse must be an extremely well-balanced, well-schooled, active horse, quick to correct his length of stride as he both climbs and dives over the different flights. Jumping uphill his forelegs meet the ground sooner than he anticipates; jumping downhill he finds his foothold falling away with the impetus of his leap carrying him forward over his feet, much like missing a step on a staircase.

Mrs Brotherton and Mr Renton, however, liked racing at Cheltenham. Unlike many other northern trainers Bobby Renton had achieved more than his share of victories there, and he and Mrs Brotherton enjoyed their visits to the attractive spa. Moreover, they had been advised by Tim Molony of Red Rum's distinct preference for firm fast ground, which would be a rarity in mid-season. Molony had told Renton too that Red Rum had been jumping since a yearling. And Mr Renton had watched Sandra and 'Rummy' fly over those baby hurdles in the back paddock the day after he had arrived.

Sandra had the roughest of rides getting him ready.

Starting at the top . . . Cheltenham

'He was *murderous* at times'

'Even trotting out with the other horses he'd buck and fool around. You could hardly go on the roads – he was *murderous* at times. He'd go into buses and all sorts! He'd never go past a car without he'd kick out at it. It took three whole seasons before he'd settle down.'

Fortunately there were fewer cars and better-mannered motorists on the lanes round Oxclose, than in Britain's crammed south-east. Even so Red Rum was extremely lucky not to get killed in Yorkshire. He sometimes only just avoided the breaking of those legs. . . .

'Several times he kicked a car,' said Sandra. 'Though the motorists never bothered: I think they thought it was their fault for going past! We used to stop them, then I'd rush "Rummy" into any gateway I could find. We knew the roads and where the gaps were, so he was never hurt.'

But Red Rum was as dangerous to Sandra – though the ground was softer – when it came to cantering. 'He'd *never* stop bucking. He was never on four legs! We always had running martingales on, no matter what horse we rode. We tried "Rummy" once in a rubber snaffle, but he didn't like that. He used to throw his head all over the place. So he had just an ordinary plain ring snaffle.

'A *soft* mouth'

'He had a *soft* mouth, though he pulled,' Sandra explained, moving her hands gently to demonstrate not the brute force of ham-fists, but the flexed wrist and give-and-take whereby, like playing fishes, a rider of 8 stone may stop a horse weighing half a ton. 'He'd never tear away or anything. You just had to be very careful about his mouth.'

Sandra believed that, despite all these explosions and convulsions underneath her, she had never even 'lost a pedal'.

'No, I think he's the sort of horse that, once you get used to him, you get the *feel* of him. You just balance your hands on his neck and let him buck all he wants to. He'd buck even jumping hurdles. As soon as he touched ground,

'He'd buck like mad'

he'd buck like mad.'

It was the custom at Oxclose, as in the majority of stables, for the horses to be dismounted after work and led home to let them relax. But this proved impossible with Red Rum.

'Lead him out!' exclaimed Sandra, recollecting in her married tranquillity and motherhood the violence of those Oxclose mornings. 'Oh dear! Oh dear! He was *terrible*. He'd buck and rear and roll. You'd never come across another horse like him. He'd rear and roll and get a leg over the reins – well, that was it! So you couldn't lead him home after he'd galloped, at least not for the first two seasons he was with us. You'd have to ride him right back into the yard and right up to his box before you got off him.

'He was full of character,' said Sandra. 'And for a stranger to get on him – he knew right away. There was hardly anyone who'd ride him, even Tommy Stack.'

'He was full of character'

Tommy Stack had arrived at Oxclose from Ireland the same summer in which Red Rum was born. He had come from Ireland as an unpaid amateur with one little suitcase to work for nothing in the hope that he might one day become a jockey. He had enjoyed quick success as an amateur, had turned professional, but was still working as a stable lad when Red Rum arrived, 'doing his two' and considered to be not yet good enough to ride him in a race.

Six years later, Stack had become one of the star jockeys at the table's top. He painfully remembered Red Rum's arrival. 'I *hated* riding him out. He never stopped bucking and kicking. I remember one day after I'd had a fall and my back was really sore – *ow*! I had the most *terrible* ride out on him.'

Tommy added: 'Really no one rode him except Sandra. There'd be big trouble from Sandra if she saw anyone else riding her "Rummy"!'

Sandra recalled with justifiable pride, 'If I was off work Mr Renton used to keep him in his box!'

After his initial pop over the baby hurdles, Sandra schooled Red Rum with other horses three times over the big hurdles before he was sent on the long haul down to Cheltenham. 'I always schooled him,' said Sandra, 'and Mr Renton always liked him in front in case he hurt himself.' She meant jumping into the heels of the leading horse who wasn't as quick as he was, or falling over something in front that had blundered. 'He just *flew* over them – really fast!'

Over the big hurdles

Bobby Renton had decided upon a jockey. 'Josh' Gifford had ridden Dagmar Gittell to win the Topham for Mrs Brotherton and himself. He had inherited from Fred Winter the plum role of stable jockey to Ryan Price and he was making great leaps up the jockeys' table in which that season he would finish sixth.

When a trainer does not retain a stable-jockey but, as young Tommy Stack would discover to his loss, shops around outside, then an association of ideas often leads to the choice of jockey. Renton thought 'Mrs Brotherton . . . Dagmar . . . Gifford', and booked him.

'Josh' recalled afterwards, 'Mr Renton said Red Rum

Needed
'very hard
riding'

was a good young horse, but that he needed "very hard riding". And,' Gifford recalled ruefully six years afterwards, 'I'm afraid I gave him a very hard race indeed.' He is yet another professional amazed by Red Rum's ability to survive the punitive rigours of his racing.

The ground was good and fast with a small field of ten: ideal conditions for a first outing had the course not been Cheltenham and the jockey had not been ordered to give Red Rum a hard race. He jumped so well he led from the second flight of hurdles to about halfway. He came to the last hurdle with the favourite Acastus (who had already enjoyed the experience of winning a hurdle race) but could not quicken up Cheltenham's severe climb to the post. He was second, beaten four lengths, by a previous winner, and in good time. He collected the first portion of the massive fund of prize money he was going to accumulate under National Hunt Rules – £69,320 by the end of the 1973/74 season. In his first race he earned £90, enough to pay jockey Gifford, the horse-box from Oxclose and back and his keep at Renton's for a fortnight. Mrs Brotherton and Mr Renton were satisfied. For Sandra and her brother Walter, driving Red Rum the long way home to Yorkshire, pleasure in the young horse's promise was streaked with sorrow at the punishing ride he had suffered. She said, 'I think Tommy Stack told Josh Gifford that "Rummy" was lazy. He had a very hard race. He had stripes on him that lasted *weeks*. And he didn't much care for Cheltenham after that.'

Learning a
new craft

Next time, however, Sandra was absolutely livid. The pattern of multiple jockey changes which had been Red Rum's lot as a 2-year-old (seven different jockeys in his eight races) was now to be repeated as he was learning a new craft over hurdles. He was going to have another long hard season – too long, too hard for a 'baby' some would say. He was in action without a previous summer's holiday from September, 1968, until the end of May, 1969. He ran in ten races and additionally travelled to Ascot to be declared for a race but withdrawn.

It is helpful for a young flat-race horse to grow accustomed to the same pilot. He receives the same 'aids' and the jockey can report on progress or deterioration, and any new tendencies. Red Rum did not enjoy those advantages when he was flat racing.

But it is five times more important for a young hurdler trying to pick up the art of jumping at speed, when tired, when pressurised, when in a group, when blinded by

backsides and flying mud, when slipping, when 'wrong', to
have the same man on top. No two jockeys 'press the
buttons' exactly the same. With an experienced horse, the
good jockey swiftly senses the type of jumper he is and can
go along with him. But the inexperienced novice is not yet
a type. He needs guidance. He relies. And with each
different jockey a horse is trying to learn each time what the
new man on top is trying to tell him, instead of learning the
smooth, economic way of getting on with his job.

He needs
guidance

All good jumping stables retain a jockey. Most good
ones have a secondary stable jockey who will be educating
the young horses when the star jockey is either riding elsewhere or on something more fancied. The stable team will
keep continuity of schooling at home.

But outside jockeys no longer drove to remote Oxclose.
And in Red Rum's first jumping season he was ridden by
J. Gifford, A. Turnell, J. Cook, T. S. Murphy, J. Doyle, and
P. Broderick. In the first two years of his racing he had
perforce to make do with fourteen different jockeys. Was
it purely coincidence, the time of year, or the fact that by
the spring he had finally learned, that it was his last jockey
Paddy Broderick who won on him finally thrice in a row?

As had been said by many experts who know something
about Red Rum's story: 'The horse did it in spite of all!'

'The horse
did it in
spite of all!'

After 'Rummy''s second race at pleasant Market Rasen
an enraged Sandra gave his jockey a piece of her mind. 'By
Jove,' she flashed out at little Andy Turnell as he came in
on the horse, 'I hope to God you never ride my horse
again!' Sandra said afterwards, 'I'm not saying what else I
said.' She was still embarrassed six years later about her
explosion. But she justified it: 'He was last turning into the
straight and he just sat there and expected the horse to win!
And the horses were good that he was against. He came
from *nowhere*, and the poor horse had a hard race for
nothing!'

It is hard for a stable lad or girl to watch, as they may believe, (and usually from a poor vantage point), their horse's chances getting lost. Few will be as forthright as Sandra. Their chances of conveying their views to the trainer, too, are slim. Perhaps a grimace may be made on the gallops one morning, when they ask 'Who's ridin' my 'oss on Saturday, Sir?' and the Guv'nor says 'Bloggins'. But the lad cannot pick whose hands and mind will give – in his opinion – his horse the best chance of winning.

A jumping error Red Rum had started second favourite at Market Rasen after his promising Cheltenham start. He finished fourth, beaten 16 lengths. In fairness to Turnell, then a much greener pilot than the stylish self-assured jockey he has now become, *Chaseform* observers noted that the horse made a jumping error just as Turnell started his challenge.

But more significant than the manner in which Red Rum had been ridden was the state of the going: he had come across the sort of ground which he had clearly shown Molony he detested, consequently disappointing Mr Renton and Mrs Brotherton. But the warning was not heeded.

He improved next time at Nottingham where the going was good. The winner at Market Rasen, Francophile, now finished second, but Red Rum was third and only three lengths behind him – an improvement of thirteen lengths, with Francophile carrying a 7lb penalty. Red Rum's **Making up ground towards the end** running basically followed the Market Rasen pattern: he was making up ground towards the end. Unless a horse is being stopped by a dishonest trainer late progress in a race generally shows that stamina is the horse's strong suit. It is therefore better to have such a horse up with the leaders all the way. There is patently no point in holding him up for a final quick burst of acceleration. Nothing can make a horse quicken. Good riding may preserve to the right moment that little final squirt of speed. Good training can make the speed hold out a little longer. But no more.

Red Rum was already showing that, in conflict with his breeding, he possessed much more stamina than speed. The

Nottingham winner was none other than Soloning, Fred Winter's cheap buy who had run behind Red Rum in that Warwick flat race. He had already won one hurdle and been second in his other start, so he had made a far better beginning as a jumper than our hero. He ended the season with five victories compared with Red Rum's three.

It is significant that Soloning was ridden in every race that season, bar one, by Fred Winter's then stable jockey, Bobby Beasley. And he was ridden in the other – which he won too – by Winter's second stable jockey, Richard Pitman. . . . Soloning on the flat was much inferior to Red Rum.

It was soft ground again at Doncaster when Red Rum with his fourth jockey change in four hurdle races started favourite, and finished third. He had, however, come up against a cracker: Fred Rimell's Coral Diver, a future top-class hurdler making his first jump race a winning one.

Up against a cracker

Red Rum was now sensibly given a long break through deep winter. He did not run between November and March. And so by way of Wetherby and more soft ground and another new jockey, the claiming lad John Doyle, and another disappointment (6th), to the place with which he will always be linked – Liverpool.

There, running two days before Highland Wedding's Grand National, and on good fast ground, Red Rum with his fifth jockey switch found Paddy Broderick in the saddle. So far Red Rum was certainly turning out to be no juvenile star. He was easy to back in the important £1,000 4-year-old Lancashire Hurdle.

He ran, as *Chaseform Notebook* dashingly put it, 'a cracking race'. The winner was the brilliant young hurdler Clever Scot trained by that able Welsh businessman, barrister and former motor-racing driver, Colin Davies. His owner was the unusual and grandiloquent Mr Henry Alper, who was lucky enough to own that good Champion Hurdler, Persian War, whom he circulated among a bevy of trainers. Davies had schooled Clever Scot to a fine polish.

'A cracking race'

There were nine flights of hurdles in Liverpool's very sharp two-mile hurdle track instead of the usual eight. A scintillating hurdler may gain two lengths a flight over his more ordinary and plodding rivals. This is the basic, mathematical reason why flat-race form and hurdle-race form do not equate. At Liverpool particularly, round those dog-track bends on the hurdle track, a horse who can jump hurdles like lightning and make lengths at each flight, may bowl away in front and mock his pursuers. So Clever Scot

Brian Fletcher

treated Red Rum, who doggedly chased him round the bends, jumping adequately for Paddy Broderick, but losing a little at each leap to the flying feet in front. The winner was ridden by Brian Fletcher whose victory in the previous year's National had brought him to the notice of other trainers and owners. He was enjoying, as a result, almost as good a season as his best-ever of 77 winners in 1967–68. That year he was in eighth place on the list between Stan Mellor (7th) and Ron Barry (9th). Not possessing eyes in the back of his head, he saw nothing that day in the race of his future partner, Red Rum.

Fashions for jockeys cruelly come and go. A few bad races in succession, a fall which puts you not just out of action but out of trainers' minds, and the winning jockey of yesteryear is soon a semi-forgotten man. A trainer, remembering him out of loyalty and satisfaction may suggest him to an owner. The owner disturbed from an office conference or television viewing will repeat incredulously, 'Put up Bloggins on my good young horse! You must be barking mad! Feller hasn't ridden a winner for bloody years. Nerve's gone they say. He's bust. Or bonkers. Bankrupt. Bent. Maybe all four.'

The dreadful slanders perpetrated by grandstand watchers and television viewers about that heroic band risking their necks out here are worse than the cruellest things ever said about politicians.

A winning connection

Both Paddy Broderick, who first forged a winning connection with Red Rum over jumps, and Brian Fletcher, who later did the same more famously, are based in Co. Durham, near Bishop Auckland. Broderick, eight years older than Fletcher, came from Ireland and had enjoyed his best season one year earlier than Fletcher in 1966–67, when he rode 50 winners. For all those early successes, his popularity waned. At the end of the 1973–74 season this good horseman, who started Red Rum on his winning career as a jumper, was down to nine winners from 138 rides.

Nor, surprisingly, can Brian Fletcher, for all his three Grand National victories, be called a popular jockey. Even in the season 1973–74, when Red Rum won his second Grand National and the Scottish 'National, Fletcher's final results – 30 winners – fell far short of his best. His remoteness, as we shall see, may not help. . . .

'He won three on the trot'

In the spring of 1969 the gallant Paddy Broderick had 'clicked' for the season's last rides on Red Rum. Sandra was positively delighted. 'He won three on the trot! Wetherby,

Above: His box
(furthest left) at
Oxclose near Ripon
where he lived for
4 years with 3
different trainers.

Below: Mrs. Lurlene
Brotherton, his owner
for 4 years, flanked
by his second trainer,
octogenarian Bobby
Renton, and his
fourth trainer, young
Anthony Gillam, in
the field where Red
Rum first jumped
hurdles.

Moments from his Grand National double. Top row 1973. Bottom three rows 1974. Note: in the third row his one mistake, pitching on landing; in the fourth row Fletcher waving back at the crowd's clamorous ovation and "Red's" faithful retinue leaping up to greet him. *Photo: "Tophams Limited 1973 Grand National" "The Walton Group 1974 Grand National" by kind permission of British Movietone News*

Above: Tommy Stack, the jockey, who, until the spring of 1974, had ridden the most winners on Red Rum. *Photo: Kenneth Bright*
Below: Red Rum, as a 4-year-old, going out for his first race of the 1969/70 season. He's ridden by canny-looking Tommy Stack, who was briefly his third trainer. *Photo: John Grant*

Nottingham and Teesside! At Wetherby he just *cantered* home – nothing in sight – you'd have thought it was first time round! At Nottingham, only a week later, he was bucking so much going down that Paddy Broderick thought he'd never get him to the post. And he nearly dropped him after jumping the first hurdle!' (Giving one of those bucks) 'We thought he'd done too much, because he went off in front – Paddy couldn't hold him, he was so well – he was third coming to the bend and we thought he was going to be beaten. But then he just flew past them all – trotted in – no trouble at all.'

'We thought he'd done too much'

The good ground and the warmth of April and confidence in Broderick all combined to do the trick. Ten days after Nottingham he was off to Teesside, still in the highest of spirits and proof already that he was a horse who not only flourished in the spring but who at that period of the year could stand races very close together.

'At Teesside,' said Sandra, 'there were all these good young hurdlers, Explicit and all those.'

Lads leading up their horses overhear conversations as they are being saddled. 'Mr Shedden said at Teesside – "He'll never beat my Explicit",' Sandra recalled with glee. Shedden once upon a time had been Bobby Renton's Head Lad – for ten years back in 1925 – and has been one of Mrs Brotherton's flat-race trainers for years. When two trainers have horses for the same patron, rivalry is needle-sharp.

'He'll never beat my my Explicit'

'"Rummy" was last turning into the straight, and he just flew past the lot. Nothing could stop him!' So it may have seemed in Sandra's rosy memories. But Red Rum had had a struggle. He got home only by a neck from another previous winner, Rigton Prince. The vaunted Explicit, belonging to Lancashire pig-breeder Stan Wareing (who comes into Red Rum's story later) finished fourth, nearly nine lengths behind.

This particular victory, the last of Red Rum's treble, confused more than Sandra in recollection. Against all the pattern of his racing before and since it was gained on soft 'patchy' ground (which otherwise he hates) and he came from last to first, being ridden for speed, as if he had been a sprinter.

Bobby Renton was subsequently going to be harshly criticised from many authoritative quarters for his placing and running of Red Rum. The horse's former handlers at Wymondham would express themselves astonished by Renton's continual subjection of the horse the following season to ground he detested. But at Teesside on 25th April, 1969, Red Rum had beaten a very good field on soft ground. That result rightly lingered on in Renton's mind.

Red Rum ran once more that season, a month later, when he would have been better off enjoying the best of the grass. He was sent up to Ayr, scene of his future triumph in the Scottish Grand National. His running there, too, can only in retrospect have confused his trainer.

Planning a campaign

When you are planning a campaign for a horse, your choice of race will be compounded of impressions built up over the past. You begin to *feel* the horse prefers left-handed tracks to right, flat ones to hilly ones, spring to winter, fast going to soft. A pattern is shaken out of the kaleidoscope. If some pieces do not fit, you check with *Chaseform*. And there, confusingly for the future, were the facts. Red Rum had won well on the soft at Teesside. Now at Ayr the ground was firm and he ran poorly. Broderick was hard at him from soon after half-way, but he did not improve his position from the back of the field.

With benefit of hindsight it is easy to see the wrong factor was diagnosed. Sandra commented, 'They blamed Paddy Broderick, but I don't think it was him. The horse had had too much. He just wasn't himself, I knew that. He'd come straight off the flat the year before to run over hurdles. Now he knew the summer grass was there. . . .'

18 'YOU MUST BE MAD TO KEEP RUNNING THE LITTLE HORSE'

The next year was the year of the cough. The virus, as it has come to be called, has both short-term and long-term effects. A sick horse cannot run to form. And if he is run when he is sick, his wind may be so damaged as to ruin him as a racehorse for ever.

In the season of 1969–70 when Red Rum had the cough he ran no less than fourteen times. It is not surprising that he failed to win. It is not surprising that he struggled round eleven times unplaced. What is astonishing is that the horse's spirit, running in going which he plainly loathed and being subjected to punishing races, was not extinguished.

Eleven times unplaced

But his understandably miserable performances of that dire season had a side-effect which shaped his destiny: they planted in Mrs Brotherton's mind and in Mr Renton's the seeds of dissatisfaction. They began to feel that this was a moderate horse. They could not conceive that now he would ever be a good one. He was a disappointment: he would be no better – at best – than a middle-class northern handicapper. He emerged in their minds as a horse who might well be got rid of.

Sandra recalled: 'That season every horse in the yard had a virus, a bad cough. "Rummy" was really coughing. His throat was swollen and he was really bad with it.'

'Rummy' was really coughing

The virus was rampant. Anthony Gillam, who would be Red Rum's fourth trainer, was then training a handful of his own horses under a permit at nearby Roecliffe. He recalled: 'I ran Royal Charity at Perth and he should have won, but he came back coughing. Well, so did Bobby Renton's. Renton's horses weren't right all that year. I don't think he had a winner, including Red Rum and he ran fourteen times!'

Back at Wymondham, Tim Molony and head lad Jock Mayes, followed Red Rum's constant failures with increasing gloom. 'I didn't think very much of Bobby Renton for running that horse in the heavy,' says Tim

'He *hates* it'   Molony politely. 'I told him "You must be mad to keep running the little horse on the soft ground. He *hates* it."'

Poor Red Rum had even started the season unhappily, for he had not flourished at all when out at grass. 'I don't think he'd ever *known* grass,' Sandra suggested afterwards. 'He was turned out with a lot of horses in the field behind the stables. They were always playing together, so they didn't really get down to earth. Mind you,' said Sandra, gleefully, 'I always used to go out and give him a bucket of corn every night.'

Charlie Wright's neat old army notebook carefully records '*Red Rum brought into work, July 19th, 1969*'. Five years later, the last two of which she had spent entirely cut off from racing, Mrs Sandra Miles remembered that exact date which, even for a girl who loved a horse, is surprising.

No longer a novice   As in 1968, Red Rum began the season at Cheltenham and at the same meeting. No longer a novice, he had to run in an all-aged handicap. This provided the first official assessment of his ability: in a weight range extending from 10 stone up to 12st 7lb Red Rum was given a mere 10st 7lb. The handicapper certainly did not recognise in him much sign of merit.

Although Red Rum was trained only a few miles as the crows flew over flat land and river from Anthony Gillam's little place at Roecliffe, this was the first time Gillam had noticed him. But this was due to proximity rather than any distinction. Red Rum made no show of any sort. He was ridden by Renton's new stable jockey, Tommy Stack, who had now satisfied the Guv'nor (he was still working as a lad) that he was good enough to ride more of his horses.

Anthony Gillam had a runner, Royal Charity, in the very next race. He therefore took some note of his neighbour's 4-year-old. Gillam's horse won. It was Royal Charity's second win of that early season. After the first, Anthony's father, had agreed to let him give up working in the family business to train for himself. This move, and these early successes would place the young man in a position later to take over Renton's stables and the training of Red Rum.

Royal Charity   Royal Charity was Gillam's first winner under Rules, though he had enjoyed some success with point-to-pointers, including Royal Charity, a horse he and his mother had bought inexpensively at Ascot sales.* Gillam

---

* Anthony Gillam comments, 'By coincidence Tim Molony had bought the horse and we gave him a "profit". Surely further proof of what a good judge Tim is.'

rode him at Market Rasen – 'I wasn't *anywhere!* so I put him in this condition race at Southwell. He got in with all the allowances, so I couldn't do the weight.'

'Oddly enough,' says Gillam, 'though I'd always had a betting account with Ladbrokes I never used it, and on the very day of Southwell they wrote me a very rude letter, saying the account was a waste of time. So, just for fun, I had £5 to win and £10 place. Royal Charity won at 50 to 1 and I collected about £370!'

'Royal Charity won at 50 to 1'

That day at Cheltenham Gillam, though knowing very well what the famous Mr Renton looked like, had never addressed a word to his elderly neighbour. His own horse that day was ridden by the same young claiming jockey John Doyle, who had won on him at Southwell. It was at Doyle's father's Wetherby stables that young Gillam had worked holidays and weekends, riding out and mucking out and then going racing or hunting afterwards. 'I owe Tony Doyle a great deal for all his help then,' says Gillam.

John Doyle's two victories for Gillam on Royal Charity drew him to Bobby Renton's notice, and as he wanted a claiming lad at Oxclose, he retained him for that disastrous failure of a season. 'Poor John Doyle got a lot of the blame,' said Gillam afterwards. 'And I think quite unfairly.'

But young Doyle was only one of five more jockeys who had pushed and shoved Red Rum round over 30 miles of hurdle races in going he loathed while burdened by the debilitating, and potentially damaging legacy of the cough. There was Tommy Stack, John Doyle, Paddy Broderick again, Roy Edwards and Barry Brogan before Red Rum was retired in May, 1970, after a blinkered failure over three miles up at Ayr. By then he had experienced in his short but hard-pressed racing career twenty different jockeys of all sorts. They shared one thing though, which hurt our hero at the time and could have ruined him for ever: they all subjected him, under trainer's orders, to hard races.

Twenty different jockeys

19 'COULD I COME TO WORK FOR YOU FREE . . . ?'

Tommy Stack

The jockey who rode Red Rum most frequently that dreadful season was the keen young man from the remote beauties of Co. Kerry, Tommy Stack, who was later briefly to train him. Irish-born jockeys usually dominate our steeplechasing scene, though for every Tim Molony and Bryan Marshall we have had our Fred Winters. At the end of the 1973–74 season one Irishman, big Ron Barry, topped the table, and another, just behind English Richard Pitman, was third: Tommy Stack.

Most Irish jockeys spring naturally from a background of hunting, point-to-pointing and racing. It is only in a story as unusual as Red Rum's that his third trainer and stable jockey should have had a most unlikely start. Mr Thomas Brendan Stack, born November 15th, 1945, worked in Dublin's fair city as a clerk in an insurance office. His mother, totally disapproving of anything to do with racing, had wanted him to be either a vet or a priest. The order of priority was given to me by Stack with a grin.

Stack's father had a 160-acre dairy farm in Kerry which Tommy's elder brother has now taken over. His sister married a butcher in Co. Limerick who, through some cattle dealing with old Mr Renton, possessed that single tenuous contact with the English racing scene which Tommy Stack exploited.

Down the primrose paths of racing

Unusual for an Irish farmer's son, Tommy hardly even hunted as a boy. He was sent away, aged twelve, to Mungret College, in County Limerick 'to be taught by the Jesuits. But there I met two racing people: the future jockey Barry Brogan and the future trainer Bobby Barry who married one of Lord Harrington's daughters.' The dark, mercurial, unfortunate Barry Brogan, sometimes superlative, sometimes nerve-shattered, was the young man who led clerk Stack from the straight way of an insurance office down the primrose paths of racing.

In the jockeys' world of shared dangers and shared changing-rooms, shared holidays and ambulances, shared hospitals and parties, the characters of the gladiators are well known to one another. Two jumping jockeys have so far had the greatest influence on Red Rum – Tommy Stack and Brian Fletcher. Except in one trait, a cautious reluctance to spend money, they are in everything else direct opposites. Stack is shrewd, careful, business-like, calculating and ambitious. He is cool and assured in manner. Several beautiful and talented girls appear to adore him, despite his nonchalance and the business-like tempo of his life. He had quite easily more rides – in races – than any other jockey during the season 1973–74: 458 rides for his 76 winners, compared with Pitman's 316 rides for his 79 winners. Stack earns big money. He breeds horses – he bred and profitably sold the highclass flatracer Brook – and he makes money. He salts it away. 'Stack's worth a fortune,' other jockeys say. They laugh, 'Old Stacky never spends any money', but he is greatly admired by his colleagues.

458 rides

Barry Brogan, his oldest racing friend, recounted with delight, 'When Tommy first came to England he bought a little, very old black Austin for thirty or forty quid. He ran it for two and a half years – thousands and thousands of miles – and then he sold it for £70. That's really typical of Stacky!'

Against his family's objections the schoolboy Stack hankered to get into the horse world. 'One way seemed to me was to join the Irish army and get into the army equitation team and go show jumping round the world!' But he was not accepted at his interview in a Dublin barracks.

'So I went home and helped out on the farm,' said Stack, 'till it became necessary for me to go off and earn a living.' He and Brogan were not only school chums: they went on holidays together. 'Oh, Ballybunion!' exlaimed Brogan of the famous holiday resort. 'What girls there were! And what "cracks" we had down there. . . .'

But the Phoenix Assurance Company at £7 a week for a junior clerk and a small flat shared between five in Drumcondra Road, Dublin, was Stack's next move. 'We'd a lot of fun, but no money. Some days we went without food entirely.'

The pipes of the horse-world continued to call him softly. He would go off to Barry Brogan's father at weekends to ride out. 'He could,' said Brogan, 'hardly ride at all, but he was willing to learn, and prepared to have a go at anything.'

Prepared to have a go

'I knew nothing about riding,' says Stack frankly now, 'but I was very keen to model myself on a combination of Pat Taaffe and Bobby Beasley. Taaffe sat over fences better than anyone I've ever known. And Beasley was *the* stylist. Even as a little lad I thought this. I'd go home to jump things on my little pony with the *style* of Beasley, but sitting as if I was Pat Taaffe!'

Jimmy Brogan

Barry's father, Jimmy Brogan, was a short, stout man. There was a place at the end of his gallops where his horses, having worked, pulled up and walked round while he watched to see how much they were blowing. One morning as the horses – one of them ridden as usual by his son young Barry – pulled up, Mr Brogan took a packet of cigarettes out of his pocket. He was about to light one, when his face went purple and he fell over, dead.

'I'd only seen one other dead man before,' said Barry Brogan, 'and that was a stranger at a distance in a car crash. . . . Someone galloped away to fetch a priest. But it was too late. My father had died that moment in front of us all.'

The traumatic shock of that morning must have caused many of the reverberations that afterwards undermined young Brogan's equanimity and career. There were hopeful signs in the summer of 1974 that he was on the road back again.

Suddenly the trainer

On the instant of his father's death there were still the horses to be trained. They had still to be fed, worked, entered and raced. He stepped that morning into his father's boots. Tommy Stack thus found himself at weekends riding out with his old schoolfriend now suddenly the trainer. Brogan's owners now opposed him risking his neck by schooling bad jumpers. He had one such, 'a great big clumsy brute of a horse called Irish Steel', says Brogan. 'It'd fall over anything. So more as a joke than anything I asked Tommy Stack one morning, "Why don't you have a go and school this horse?" I thought Irish Steel would bury him! But Stacky had the guts to get up and have a go. And the horse jumped really well for him – better than he had for anyone else. And I thought then "Tommy Stack might really make a jockey!"' It takes one to spot one. . . .

A few months later Barry Brogan had to sack his Head Lad. His stable had three runners over in Liverpool at the National meeting and he would have to be away all week. So he asked Tommy Stack if he'd take a week off from his insurance office and come up and act as Head Lad.

Stack was not only delighted to come. After the week he loved the work so much that he resolved to pack in the insurance job. 'I gave them a month's notice. My mother was furious. "You're making a great mistake giving up this good job," she said, and it was true that I'd just had a rise. But I felt I must cut loose.' Barry's mother, Mrs Brogan, also told him that it was the height of folly to embark on a riding career 'which would very likely end in nothing'.

'The chances of getting to be a top jockey,' Mrs Brogan warned Tommy Stack 'are the same as winning the football pools.'

But 19-year-old Tommy sat down with a copy of *Horses in Training* and selected ten different English trainers simply because they listed a large number of horses. He knew none of them and indeed nothing about them. He wrote the same letter to each. He explained that he was so keen to get into racing that he wondered if he 'could come to work for you free, just for the chance of getting a ride, and the possibility of becoming a jockey'.

Of the ten leading trainers the lad had so addressed only one had the time, courtesy and kindness to bother to reply. Captain Neville Crump wrote back. But he regretted that he couldn't help him.

Tommy was disheartened. Then his brother-in-law, the butcher from Limerick, said he would write to Mr Renton of Ripon to whom he sold cattle. Bobby Renton telephoned Barry Brogan whose name Tommy had given as a reference. By good chance Tommy was in Brogan's house at the time, 'Barry did me a great favour', says Stack smiling, 'he told Mr Renton I could ride quite well.'

Bobby Renton arranged to interview Tommy Stack in the Hibernian Hotel in Dublin – 'I found Mr Renton a very charming old gentleman,' and the arrangements were made. Tommy Stack's father gave him £50, saying gruffly, 'When this runs out I expect you'll have to come back.'

Like a Kerry Dick Whittington, Tommy set off on his first visit to England and his first entry into those weighing rooms he hoped might be paved with gold.

With what was left after paying his fare, and carrying one small suitcase, young Mr Tommy Stack, future leading jockey, arrived to work for nothing at Oxclose near Ripon on 13th July, 1965. He was immediately pitched into the deep end.

Getting to be a top jockey

A Kerry Dick Whittington

20 'OH, WE'LL JUST HAVE TO RUN THE BRUTE!'

Like most new ventures, Tommy Stack's start at Oxclose under the elderly Mr Renton was a mixture of high hopes and early disappointments. 'I remember,' Sandra Kendall recalled, 'the day Tommy came. He only had the clothes he had on, and Bobby Renton bought him an old bicycle!' The stables were so shorthanded that they were taking a third lot out in the afternoon, a time in normal stables when the horses rest and the staff have three hours off. Stack had no sooner arrived than he was riding out. But he impressed Bobby Renton from the start. If he had slightly codded his way into the job, the end justified the means. He was given his first ride – naturally for Mrs Brotherton – as early as September at Newcastle. Four rides later Mr T. Stack, the unpaid amateur, rode this horse a winner – the first of his life and the start of hundreds on the way to the jockeys' championship.

Stack's first winner

'I remember,' Sandra said, 'I took his first winner away to Newcastle: New Money, he was called, a great little horse.'

Sandra watched Tommy Stack develop. 'He was very keen when he came. He still is. He's as cool as a cucumber – a businessman. But he's a good lad. And a very good jockey on certain horses.'

Sandra considered that Tommy Stack never really got on with Red Rum, 'because I think he got at him too early in a race – never kidded him on. I should say "Rummy" needs a quiet jockey like Brian Fletcher. He'd never forgive Josh Gifford for that good hiding he gave him at Cheltenham – those three stripes on him. . . . Anyone who's quiet can ride "Rummy" well. . . .' She reflected on all those races Stack had ridden the horse and added justly, 'I think Tommy rode him one of the best, although he didn't get on with him!'

Mr T. Stack stayed an amateur for two seasons and was then instructed by the authorities, reasonably enough, to turn professional. He was still a humble paid-lad 'doing his two' horses at Oxclose and getting the odd spare ride when Red Rum (who had been born the summer Stack left

Ireland) arrived. Stack was already restless. He had discovered too late that Bobby Renton was not a trainer who 'made' jockeys. He had hoped that, after his good start as an amateur, Mr Renton would give him more and more chances on his stable's horses. This gives a broader, more enduring benefit to a young jockey than simply the granting of opportunities and the giving of experience. It demonstrates to the racing world that the trainer has real faith in his young jockey. In such a way did Ryan Price 'make' Fred Winter, in spite of all the future maestro's early tumbles and blunders. To hold a jockey's licence and to work as a lad in the yard, and then not to get rides on the horses, is tantamount to the trainer declaring that the jockey isn't good enough – yet so it was with Mr Renton. He continued to shop around for different jockeys and left Stack in the wings. Stack was not just a passive witness, as when Josh Gifford gave Red Rum that first hard race over hurdles at Cheltenham; he also had to engage other jockeys. He himself booked Barry Brogan for a ride on Red Rum. Brogan remembered the horse well: 'A *big* "little horse". Always happy and giving a buck and a jump. A real character. He was super over hurdles and always jumped well.'

During the dreadful season of 1969–70 Stack rode Red Rum most of the time. 'He ran fourteen times without winning,' said Stack. 'I wasn't impressed. After a bit we all thought he was ungenuine.' The notion now seems to be so ludicrous that the astonishment showed in my face, 'Yes, we did,' Stack said. 'After all, fourteen times nowhere. So they tried him in blinkers.' Wearing these, Red Rum and Stack were second at Catterick on New Year's Eve. Much more significantly, the ground that day was not heavy, nor holding, but good. . . . *Chaseform Note-Book's* modest prognostication has a nice ring, read in the light of his future triumphs of maximum stamina. Of this two-mile hurdle race performance, it commented, '*A longer trip would probably suit him better . . .*'.

Otherwise it was, with the relics of the cough, more jockey changes, more soft ground, blinkers on and blinkers off, a change to three miles, a depressing business. . . . 'He did,' says Stack looking back, 'definitely seem to be running without interest.'

It was at that point, the nadir of his career so far, that our hero's spirit came closest to breaking point. Another month or two like this and even he would probably have been crushed.

Stack was already restless

'A big "little horse"'

Running without interest

Red Rum must have felt the greatest relief when his season was finally permitted to end in May and he could at last relax unmolested at grass. 'This time,' said Sandra, 'he did very well. He came up really big.' *Brought into steady work 16th July, 1970,'* reads Charlie Wright's notebook.

Sandra suggested, 'With him being raced so young, he hadn't grown into himself before. Nor was he getting better with age – bigger and bolder like a stallion. That was the year he was going to start in novice 'chases.'

Schooling fences

Red Rum's first school over Renton's fences by the canal was a disaster. The two obstacles were no longer well-built, nor were they well-sited, being jumped away from home (every horse does things more boldly homeward bound) and having their left flanks exposed to a vacant belt of grass and then the gaping canal. Most horses duck out left rather than right (a legacy of riders generally carrying sticks in their right hands) so that schooling fences are best built with their left wings against a hedge. And facing homewards, too. . . . There was no reason for Mr Renton in the last years of over half-a-century of training to rebuild or resite his two broken-down schooling fences. Plenty of other horses had done their schooling there before Red Rum.

Stack recalled the morning. 'He was due to run in a novice 'chase in October, so a few days before we tried to school him.' This might seem leaving it a trifle late. . . . 'However,' Stack went on, 'the two fences were only little bush things, very low, but he just *scraped* over the first one, and he'd already begun to refuse as soon as he saw the second one, a little open ditch! The second time we schooled him he was even worse. Bobby Renton groaned, "Oh, we'll just have to run the brute!"'

He was *brilliant*

What Tommy Stack did not know was that after this shambles Sandra schooled Red Rum the following day. She remembers, 'The first day he was very bad with Tommy. He never hardly took off over the first and he refused the open ditch. But the ground *was* very boggy. Next day Mr Renton says, "Put Dandra up" and we schooled him again and he was *brilliant*. He never looked back. Tommy never did get on with him.'

If Tommy Stack did not 'get on with him', it was mainly because the horse really did not impress him. For all that, as he pointed out with real delight in the summer of 1974, 'I've ridden Red Rum as many winners as Brian Fletcher has, I'm sure.'

But his early experiences on Red Rum, pushing and scrubbing him along in those hurdle-races and generally getting nowhere, convinced him the horse was very moderate. The judgement lingers on, making what Red Rum subsequently did incredible to Stack. So it is when plain dull schoolgirls are suddenly heard of luring husbands away from other homes, wild sirens of delight, and when stupid schoolboys are said to have become tycoons. You see the caterpillar still where others glimpse the butterfly. Red Rum's metamorphosis between York-shire and Lancashire was as great as that, and Tommy Stack – in spite of riding the different Red Rum for Donald McCain – still finds the change incomprehensible.

The different Red Rum

The lads and lasses 'doing' horses see their charges through rose-coloured glasses. They may grumble them-selves at the horses, as mothers berate their children, but woe betide outside critics. For Sandra the season of 1970–71 was proof positive that her 'Rummy' was a good one. 'Winning those *three* novice 'chases and except, for the once, never out of the first four all season! You must have thought then that this horse was something quite ex-ceptional. They knew this.' The use of the somewhat sinister sounding *'they'* in relation to doings at Oxclose, invariably means Mrs Lurlene Brotherton and Mr Bobby Renton. Sandra concluded, exasperatedly, 'This is why I *can't* understand why she wanted to sell him.'

Stack, more objectively, conferred qualified praise. He had not been particularly nervous he said, after that fiasco of a 'school', about riding Red Rum in his first steeplechase. Jockeys depend more on the judgements of colleagues they respect than on any glowing reports from the stable. Thus Stack recalled that his friend Stan Murphy (gravely injured in a motor accident in Ireland in 1974) had told him after riding Red Rum over hurdles – 'This horse will make a good 'chaser.' The opinion of Murphy registered and lingered on.

Riding Red Rum over hurdles

Mr Renton 'ran the brute' as he put it, at Teesside. Tommy Stack said, 'I thought after that school that the horse might well refuse the first! But he was good. He jumped like a cat. We finished third. The next time we ran him at Doncaster – big fences at Doncaster – in a two-mile condition 'chase, and he beat a high-class horse called Orient War – a horse with a touch of class.'

Stack did not go overboard. He summed Red Rum up sensibly: 'We thought then the horse would make a good "North Country" horse.' This is racing shorthand for the equivalent of football's Division 2. The standard of racing in the north is markedly lower, perhaps 10lb on average, than at Cheltenham, Newbury, Sandown or Ascot. As Arthur Stephenson consistently proves with his hundreds of winners a season nearly all north of the Trent, races up there are easier to pick up; the average North Country winner does not sally southwards.

Red Rum won that season

Red Rum won that season at Doncaster, Sedgefield and Ayr, over two miles, three miles and two and a half miles respectively. He came south three times: to Cheltenham in November (third of four finishers on yielding ground. Soloning was second) and again in March to run in the two and a half mile Mildmay of Flete steeplechase. The ground was so heavy that fences were omitted. He was never in the hunt and finished fourth of six finishers, beaten nearly 25 lengths. 'A good class race,' commented Stack, 'and the going was all against him.'

His other southern attempt was at Newbury in February eight days after he had rather luckily won his first handicap at Ayr. The favourite Bandarole went lame on the run-in while fighting it out, and Red Rum went on to win his third race of the season by half a length. He was made favourite to win Newbury's Compton 'Chase. It was the day of Cala Mesquida's Schweppes Gold Trophy.

Doping to stop horses winning occurs far less frequently than it did a decade ago. Improved security – good on most racecourses, fair in most trainers' own stables – has made it harder for the felon to get in and offer the hungry horse the heavily barbiturated sugar-lump. But the favourite in any race remains a tempting target if it is your business to 'lay' horses. There are plenty of avaricious people who will sell something valueless to the mugs born every minute – and it is a feature of racing that it embraces some of the sharpest as well as some of the stupidest people. If you are a bookmaker and know that the favourite *cannot* win because he has been 'got at', you have a licence to print your own money for that race. Financially, but quite amorally, it is 'good thinking' to spend a few hundreds to 'buy' someone to stop the favourite. Dopers can still occasionally penetrate.

A tempting target

There is just a possibility that Red Rum might have been 'got at' by some stranger that day at Newbury. Certainly his adoring Sandra would happily have broken the neck of anyone trying to harm her 'Rummy'. Moreover, she was very strong. The stable legend is that she was a Judo Black Belt. She laughs about that. 'No, I'm just strong.

Any tearaway I could hold. It's all the bad pullers I was given to ride. My brother's just as strong as me, but he couldn't hold some of them.'

One day all the lads at Oxclose bet her a pound that she couldn't pick up a 12-stone sack of corn and carry it up to the top of the barn. She flicked it up on to her shoulders and whipped up the steps.

Sandra would have as quickly disposed of any intending malefactor she caught at Newbury. But she reported, 'Something was wrong that day, definitely. "Rummy" didn't jump well. He was like a drunken horse. Tommy said he was got at. Tommy said he was like a drunkard. He told Mr Renton. I said to Mr Renton "He was bucking and kicking before the race and he slipped on the tarmac. Perhaps that shook him up, I don't know." But he was definitely wrong that day.'

The 'bucking and kicking' sounds most unlike a drugged horse. At the yearling sales he had made himself lame by slipping over. Later, in McCain's care, taking on Crisp again at Doncaster in the autumn of 1973 he was going to hurt himself before the race doing the same thing. It is worth noting (but without attaching too much significance to it) that though he started favourite he eased a little in the betting from 3 to 1 out to 7 to 2, and that the winner (but a very lucky one) was well-backed from 7 to 1 down to 11 to 2. *Chaseform Notebook* which had given Red Rum a rave notice for his previous Ayr victory . . . 'plucky individual . . . gave his all to gain the upper hand . . .' commented darkly on Newbury: 'Proved disappointing. He dropped right out of the race a mile from home and there seemed no valid excuse.'

If he was doped that day, only the perpetrators know, and neither the doer of the deed nor those who paid him are likely to announce it.

Thirteen days later Red Rum ran again up at Teesside. 'We felt,' said Sandra, 'that maybe he'd had too much after that Newbury race. Then he went, less than three weeks later, on the soft going at Cheltenham. He doesn't like Cheltenham and he hated the soft going. He had a hell of a race.'

The recollection of seeing her 'Rummy' struggle round at Cheltenham provoked Mrs Sandra Miles into a rage three years later. 'Mrs Brotherton,' she burst out, 'was a difficult woman to please. If she came into the yard and saw "Rummy" bucking – he used to buck in his box when he was well – she'd say "What on earth is he bucking for?

Can't you shut him up?'' Shut him up!' repeated Sandra, bewildered, as if her pet dog had been booted into his kennel. Sandra was nearly crying.

For Bobby Renton, more than fifty years a trainer, Red Rum was one of thousands of horses through his hands. He had fallen a great way short of his best winners. The old trainer had warmed both hands upon the fire of life. It was sinking. Was he now criticising himself for not having recognised the spark inside Red Rum? For not having been able, as 'Ginger' McCain was to do, to fan that spark into a blaze?

The last laugh?

Mrs Brotherton, too, has had many better winners in her colours than Red Rum. Yet his character seems not to have meant much to her, and that is strange for a woman owner who knows about horses. She seems to have tried to ignore Red Rum, and even to have been annoyed by him. Did she suspect then that much more lay in him than would come out at Oxclose? Did she take his bucking and kicking as a sort of mockery? Did she suspect that the horse might have the most triumphant last laugh?

21 'HE LOOKED AS IF HE WAS HATING IT ALL THE WAY'

Tommy Stack

With the exception of Red Rum's race at Wetherby on Boxing Day when Macer Gifford rode him, Tommy Stack rode him in all his other twelve races that first steeplechasing season. The keen man from Co. Kerry was really making his name. He was getting rides all over the north of England and would end up the season with around 50 winners. He won on Red Rum three times, one novice 'chase, the good condition race at Doncaster, and the lucky handicap at Ayr. He was also third on him six times: at Teesside, Cheltenham, Wetherby in November (Macer

Gifford was third on him in the £2,000 handicap on Boxing Day), at Teesside in February, Wetherby in March, and at Perth, his last race of another busy season, on 20th May.

The blinkers were not put on Red Rum that season. He ended it half-way up the low-class staying handicaps (11st 2lb at Perth when third of four) and towards the bottom of the better-class three-mile 'chases (10st 6lb at Wetherby when fifth of 8). He was finishing, on going he liked, in the spring and early summer of 1971, about 5 to 10 lengths behind the winner, plugging on, without being able to accelerate and win.

Plugging on

Discounting Sandra's loving bias, Red Rum's performances in his first season over fences ended up distinctly lower-middle class. After the mysterious Newbury flop, he did not live up to the considerable promise he showed against Orient War at Doncaster and when he was third next time out at Wetherby in a high-class Wills Premier 'Chase qualifier – 'Ran splendidly', applauded Chaseform Notebook.

In that race tall Mr Anthony Gillam finished fifth, well behind Tommy Stack on Red Rum. Next time at Sedgefield, Anthony Gillam on his Fooasaboot (trained by Jimmy Fitzgerald) was again riding in the same race as Tommy Stack. By now the contrasting pair, the lanky Yorkshire-born amateur and owner-trainer and the little professional jockey from Co. Kerry, two years his senior, were not only the firmest of friends: they were living in the same house.

Contrasting pair

Anthony Gillam, then a bachelor, was living in Ivy Farm, Roecliffe, an attractive cottage looking out on to one of the prettiest village greens in Britain. There is a friendly pub with an elderly but very spry Yorkshire head-waiter, stooping but still garbed in black tails and a white bow tie. On the green a Ladies XI regularly plays cricket on summer evenings. A cozy line of six boxes converted from the original cowshed and a few paddocks on the lane to Boroughbridge made Ivy Farm an ideal base for a young man anxious to train and ride his own horses. This was the course on which Gillam was now set, and which would, by a series of coincidences, result in his becoming very soon yet another trainer of Red Rum.

The smallholding at Roecliffe had once been part of Anthony Gillam's grandfather's Copgrove Estate, and had been bought from the estate with a Trust Fund which came to Anthony when he became 21 in July, 1968. His

Major Holliday grandfather was one of the largest and most successful owner-breeders in modern racing history, that fierce, but much respected millionaire, the late Major Lionel Holliday. In addition to his Yorkshire and Irish studs the Major owned his own training stables in Newmarket, called Lagrange where a series of private trainers administered his wishes and his massive string. By reputation a difficult man and a sharp dismisser of the inefficient, his judgement both of men and bloodstock was first class. Nearly all his private trainers left him to do great things on their own, the last being Major Dick Hern, now one of Britain's finest flat race trainers but who, on his appointment by Holliday, was barely known in racing circles.

Major Holliday's daughter married another foxhunting Yorkshire industrialist and their son, Anthony, grew up in well-to-do, horsey, but strict surroundings. His parents have a stud in Co. Limerick and live there for part of the year. Their Yorkshire home is Healaugh Old Hall, near Tadcaster, and it was from here that Anthony hunted as a boy and later worked at weekends with Tony Doyle, the **Hooked on** trainer at nearby Wetherby. He was hooked on racing **racing** from his schooldays. But his parents did not permit him to embark on it lightly or wantonly. Anthony was put to work on the shop floor of one of his father's factories, punching his card, like everyone else. 'I used to get to the factory early, like most people did, to sit in the lavatories and read the paper! They used to read the *Daily Mirror* and I read *The Sporting Chronicle*.'

He had been hoping for some time that his parents might let him start point-to-pointing when he noticed in *Horse and Hound* an advertisement for the next Doncaster Sales. They would include a couple of big young horses sent up by an owner of Willie Stephenson's. 'I don't know why it is,' said Anthony Gillam, 'but all our family have a fancy for big horses. So I said to both my parents – which was quite brave actually, because my father wasn't the sort of chap you could say those things to – I said "Don't you think these two sound super?" Hint! Hint! And "Isn't it time I was allowed to start point-to-pointing?" They just laughed and said "You don't really think you're capable of point-to-pointing yet, do you?" And I said, "No, of course not."'

Doncaster Sales 'The sales were on a Thursday,' Gillam went on, 'and on the Friday morning there was I early in the factory reading *The Sporting Chronicle* round those lavatories. I opened the page at the Doncaster Sales to see what prices the two had made. I couldn't believe my eyes! Here was this horse by Manet out of Grecian Command *"sold Gillam 950 gns"*. I didn't know what to do with myself the rest of the day. In the evening I rushed home and asked my mother "Here, did I read right?" She was terribly cool and played it down. "Yes," she said, "but you don't think it's for you?" Eventually I was allowed to see him and he was the most glorious big horse. . . .'

'I couldn't believe my eyes'

There are as many ways into the kingdom of racing as there are holes in a sieve, and though young Anthony Gillam, the businessman's son, did not have to pass through the eye of a needle, he had to work quite hard for his admission. He progressed steadily from riding in point-to-points to winning point-to-points, to riding under rules, then training under a Permit, to winning with Royal Charity and thus coming across Tommy Stack.

'One spring Tommy just turned up one night at Ivy Farm,' said Gillam. 'He was then living in digs in the bungalow at Oxclose. We saw more and more of each other and went racing together. Then in the summer of 1970 four of us went on holiday together in Corfu and had a tremendous time. When we came back I said to Tommy, "Look, instead of living over at Oxclose in that rough old place, why don't you come and live at Ivy Farm?" Which he duly did.'

They rode together in races, the professional almost invariably finishing in front of the amateur. Then at Sedgefield on 5th December, 1970 Gillam found himself again, as at Wetherby in November, riding in a race against Tommy Stack on Red Rum. Gillam was on his own horse, Foosaboot, and as they galloped round three miles of Sedgefield on that darkening December afternoon Gillam had his first real close-up of Red Rum in action. 'He looked as if he was hating it all the way,' Gillam recalled. 'I saw Tommy Stack sitting there and scrubbing him along. Red Rum had his ears laid right back as if he was loathing it all. And I was just cruising. I thought "that's one horse I *will* beat!". Then he came past me and I thought "Well, he can't keep *that* up". But they just went away from me, laughing, and won.' That was the picture of Red Rum he held in his mind for years. A smallish horse, evidently lazy or reluctant, being scrubbed along by a hard-working jockey. Gillam had had a close-up of Red Rum, but that was the impression the future Grand National winner gave in those days to all northern racegoers.

Two insults were added to the injury of being beaten in

The professional and the amateur

'He can't keep *that* up'

the Sedgefield race. *Chaseform Notebook* reported baldly on Fooasaboot – 'He needs really strong handling,' and Tommy teased Anthony after the race: 'It took me all week to persuade Bobby Renton to *run* the horse here, for he and Mrs Brotherton don't like coming to Sedgefield.'

Gillam commented with irony, 'Well, thank you very much indeed – and with you living with me at the time – very kind.'

Stack, through his butcher brother-in-law, made the link with Renton. Gillam, in the factory, learns he's got his start in racing. The two young men meet. Through their friendship the unfortunate Anthony Gillam was about to be drawn into the most distressing chapter of Red Rum's adventures, in his last, dramatic, season at Oxclose.

22 'I'D BITTEN OFF MORE THAN I COULD CHEW'

Red Rum was the joker in the pack. If he had maintained the promise of the first half of his first steeplechasing season, eighty-three-year-old Mr Renton would probably have postponed what was for him a most unfortunate decision.

Taking over the stable

But one late morning at Oxclose Renton asked Tommy Stack to come in to see him in the house at lunchtime. Stack went into the sitting-room wondering what was so important as to be unmentionable out in the stable yard or on the gallops. The old man said abruptly, 'I'm going to give up training. It's all getting too much for me.'

Stack was astonished. Bobby Renton seemed to have been a trainer as long as steeplechasing had mattered in Britain. He had grown into as permanent a part of the scene as an old oak. But he explained to Stack that he was bored with the travelling and with the paperwork. He asked directly, 'Would you be interested in taking over the stable?'

Tommy Stack boggled. It was less than six years since he had arrived at Oxclose, an ex-insurance clerk, knowing nothing of racing. He had now made his name as a jockey, but training was an entirely different kettle of fish. It needed years of pupilage and experience. Many senior jockeys fail every season to make a successful change from riding to training. What seem at first sight to be similar branches of one profession are soon harshly revealed as requiring very different qualities. And Tommy Stack was not yet 26.

Stack was not yet 26

Renton said persuasively, 'I'm sure Mrs Brotherton would leave the horses with you. . . .' He had without doubt already discussed the matter at length with his old friend and had obtained her assurance. Without her horses there would be really nothing left at Oxclose to be trained.

Young Stack still hesitated. There was a domestic complication too. He was no longer living with Anthony Gillam at Ivy Farm, but much further away on a farm near Tadcaster belonging to Gillam's parents. They had liked him and his then girl friend so much that they had offered them a vacant smallholding, Wighill Lane Farm, Healaugh, where Stack, without the same girl friend, was still happily ensconced years later in the summer of 1974. Anthony Gillam, too, was making a move. He was engaged to be married to the very attractive Miss 'Pandie' Howie, daughter of Major and Mrs John Howie, and they would be living nearby at Wheatlands Farm, slightly closer to Ripon and Oxclose.

Stack asked Renton for a week to think over the proposition and went away shrewdly to weigh the pros and cons. 'It was,' commented Anthony Gillam, 'a hell of a decision for him to make.'

As it turned out, Tommy Stack made the wrong one. He went back to Mr Renton and said, 'Yes'. It looked at first as if it was going to be all right. He took over the staff, including head lad Charlie Wright and Sandra. He paid their wages and he paid old Mr Renton a lease for the yard and the gallops. In return he collected the training fees. 'I quite liked it,' he said afterwards. 'I wasn't too worried about it and it was nice to be the boss.'

He started with a winner and he trained two more winners during the first three months of the season. But when Anthony Gillam returned from his honeymoon early in October he could tell immediately that Stack had by no means settled into his new life. 'Things weren't at all the same as when I left. Tommy was very unhappy,

Started with a winner

because he wasn't getting half the amount of rides. He'd ridden 50 winners the season before and now the rides were dwindling because he was training.'

Stack, never one to mess about when complications threaten his ambitions, had realised his error. 'With all the travelling there is in England,' he said, comparing it with Irish racing, 'you can't both ride and train.' So he went directly into Oxclose and said to Renton, 'I'm sorry, I can't do both. And I'm going on riding, so I'll have to stop training.'

Red Rum — easy to train

He had found Red Rum 'a very easy horse to train and a very good "doer". But his form was only middling.' The horse had come up from grass slightly later than usual on 1st August, 1971 when Tommy Stack got his brief trainer's licence. He ran twice in October, ridden by his trainer, at Southwell and Kelso, finishing fourth and fifth. Tommy thought him 'thoroughly disappointing'. He declared, 'I don't think he's trying'. So he decided to put the blinkers on him again for his race at Newcastle, a three-mile high-class contest, on 6th November. Quite unfancied, he ran a very much better race and finished second, beaten four lengths by the useful Slave's Dream, who had led throughout.

This was his last race when trained by Tommy Stack, and his trainer-jockey made a reasonable but wrong deduction. He was sure that the blinkers had done the trick. But there were three other less obvious factors. First, the ground on Newcastle's 'chase course was, surprisingly for November, just as Red Rum liked it: firm. Secondly, he had missed Sandra during October. Thirdly and far worse, something was going wrong with him.

'A mad-head, no mouth!'

His beloved Sandra had been off work after a horrible smash during his first two disappointing races. She thinks that her 'Rummy' missed her badly. She had been riding a horse of Mr Renton's called Naughty Story – 'he was a mad-head, no mouth!' said Sandra succinctly.

Tommy Stack said to her, 'You ride him, nobody else will'. They set off over the hump-backed bridge across the land in the loop of the canal to gallop on Ripon racecourse, for they were by then acutely short of anywhere to work the horses. The manager of the racecourse came out and said 'You shouldn't be on the course!'. But Tommy told Sandra to set off galloping.

'I don't think,' she said, 'that I've ever been so fast in my life. Round the bend his feet went from him completely. He skidded round and round and round on his side. I went into the railings and smashed my collar-bone and all my muscles. Finally I got up and walked back. Tommy said "You'll be alright". But I went to hospital and I was off three and a half weeks and I shouldn't have come back then. But Mr Renton said to me "if you're not coming back, we're going to take Red Rum out of training".'

When Sandra got out to Oxclose again she saw to her horror what had happened. 'Red Rum was a shadow – an absolute shadow. I've never seen the horse look so rough. He'd gone to *nothing*.'

'Red Rum was a shadow'

Sandra flushed with recollected fury, 'I turned to Tommy and I said "I'm leaving". He said "Don't be so daft".

'The horse was sour. He was heartbroken. But I coddled him up and we built him up. And he won for me at Catterick.'

Red Rum's new trainer, Anthony Gillam, does not agree with Sandra's view. He comments, 'The horse was perfectly well when I took over in November, and Sandra was already back at work!'

Red Rum at Catterick on 11th December, 1971 was Anthony Gillam's first victory as a public trainer, for the stable had suddenly changed into his hands. When Tommy Stack had informed Renton that he couldn't go on training, he told Anthony of his decision.

'What are you going to do?' asked Anthony. 'What will *they* do?' Tommy didn't know.

In Anthony Gillam's mind over the last few months a thought had been growing. He says now that it never occurred to him when he started point-to-pointing that he would end up a public trainer. He may not have recognised the intention, but the steps he had taken, suggest that it was at the root of all his decisions. He had progressed from point-to-pointing to proper racing with some success but only privately and for himself. The next step up in the racing game had to be to become a public trainer, to have patrons, to grow. . . .

Anthony Gillam — public trainer

He heard himself hesitantly ask Tommy Stack, 'Do you think they would even consider *me* training?'

Tommy said he would ask them. Afterwards Anthony Gillam recalled with surprise (for he is modest) and gratification (for it seemed a great honour) and with sadness (for it had been an error) that Tommy came back with the verdict: 'They'd be delighted.'

Three years later Gillam said, 'I wish in retrospect I'd never done it. I'd bitten off more than I could chew.'

From eight horses of his own close by (about which no one could blame him if he blundered) he had now taken over eight more in someone else's stable. Oxclose was twenty minutes' drive away in the opposite direction from Wheatlands Farm, as his own horses which were still at Ivy Farm, Roecliffe. The new horses, furthermore, were owned by a lady of formidable racing experience and stabled on the doorstep and in the private yard of one of the cleverest jumping trainers of all time.

Gillam had stuck his head into a hornets' nest. He comments mildly, 'I did find it difficult living here and training there. . . .'

He took over the staff as it stood: 'Charles, the head man, Sandra of course, and four lads. And Red Rum. But he wasn't the main attraction. I didn't rate him very highly. The talking horse was Polar Bear. He'd run in only four novice hurdles trained by Denys Smith and he'd won three of them! Polar Bear was the attraction of the job. He might well have run in the Arkle 'Chase at Cheltenham next spring, he looked that good.' Gillam added sadly, 'But he was a disappointment'.

Polar Bear

He also caused the first difficulties between the owner and the new trainer. Gillam reported, 'Tommy had built Polar Bear up so well that I just *couldn't* get him fit. But Mrs Brotherton kept wanting him to run. Then come January 1st Mrs Brotherton said "He's going novice 'chasing. We'll run him." But we'd had a lot of frost and bad ground and I had only got about one and a half schools into him. I knew he shouldn't run. Tommy knew he shouldn't run. But she insisted. And of course he came to the open ditch and went head over heels. . . .'

Young Anthony Gillam did not find it easy to train for Mrs Brotherton or to understand her attitudes towards her horses. She found him – not surprisingly for he was roughly a quarter of Mr Renton's age – less wise and experienced than her trainer of 30 years' standing. Mr Renton, moreover, was still living on the place. Some★ of the horses he had trained remained in his own boxes. The staff whom he had engaged and paid were still there. The horses belonged to his very old friend and special patron. The new trainer lived miles away. In those circumstances it was absolutely natural, though not necessarily helpful to young Gillam, that old Mr Renton was very much around.

★ Gillam comments, 'She had a clear-out at Doncaster Sales when I took over, which left me with only three horses of hers with which I won six races.'

Worse, by far, and more specifically, there were also almost immediate doubts about Red Rum. The third factor, after the blinkers at Newcastle and the absence of Sandra, had secretly started to work against him. Something was going wrong with Red Rum's feet.

What was starting invisibly would threaten not only Red Rum's future racing career, but even his ability to walk about without pain. The dreaded bone disease of pedalosteitis had begun.

The dreaded bone disease

23 'VERY FEW HORSES, I'M AFRAID, GET OVER IT'

It has been one of racing's best-kept secrets that the famous horse was ever a sufferer from what, in loose terms, is the equivalent of arthritis of the main pedal bone of the foot. The force and shock which this bone must endure is immense: at instants when galloping and jumping half a ton of horse strikes the ground at speeds between 30 and 40 m.p.h. The first main brunt is borne by the foot. Pictures of dummies being flung through car windscreens on 30 m.p.h. impacts reflect the violence involved. . . .'

One would expect the career of a human athlete or football player to be finished if he developed arthritis in his feet. He would be hobbling about on sticks. Yet Red Rum went on racing. And he had other complications, too: ossification of a cartilage, arthritic growths, the emergence of a spur on the bone and so on in dread array. With the full help of Red Rum's professional advisors, official reports from the horse's veterinary surgeon and physiotherapist follow on page 119.

Red Rum went on racing

The gravity of Red Rum's affliction may be summed up in the reactions of three prominent equine vets in the south

'What a horse!'

of England when I told them about it. One said, 'Impossible. The horse could never have gone on racing.' The other said, 'My God! He's finished then. How awful!' And, when I explained the period of pedalosteitis had occurred *before* the first of his Grand National victories, he shook his head in awe. 'What a horse,' he said reverently. The third remarked, 'If you had been writing fiction, no one would have believed you. . . .'

But then, as old Mr Renton sagely said, Red Rum's story is a sort of fairytale.

Beginning to feel his feet

'In my opinion,' said Anthony Gillam, 'the very first time I ran him, he was beginning to feel his feet. Even though it was soft ground at Haydock he came back with a bit of heat in his off-fore. He wasn't lame, but the heat had come up into the joint. At first I just hosed the foot and joint like mad. Then Bobby Renton gave his advice which was "Slap on clay and cow dung and lots of Stockholm Tar. Try to cool him down that way".'

Red Rum's first two races that season had also puzzled his jockey and his then trainer, Tommy Stack. 'Tommy had bunged a lot of work into him,' said Gillam. 'He couldn't understand why he hadn't done better. So that's why he put the blinkers on him at Newcastle.'

Sandra commented on the three trainers' different methods. 'Mr Renton left it to us more or less, when he was getting old. He used to watch us, but he'd let us do what we wanted. Tommy used to take notice of me with Red Rum – no doubt about that, but he couldn't get out of his head that the horse needed bags of work. Anthony Gillam was very good. He used to ask, "Well, what do *you* think, Sandra?"'

Red Rum runs moderately

Gillam would not have run the horse at Haydock on 1st December had he been a weather diviner. But the forecast was for the going to be good. It rained all day and became soft. Red Rum then ran moderately which, in those circumstances, Gillam could understand. The winner was the same horse, Red Sweeney, of Gordon Richards' who had beaten Red Rum in his second race that season at Kelso on firm going. At Haydock Red Rum ran by comparison at least 10lb worse. That could be the ground, Gillam thought. What was mysterious was the heat in the foot and the joint. A trainer would expect this from jarring on hard ground, or bruising from a stone pressed into sole or frog or heel by hard ground. But why the heat after the soft turf at Haydock? Could it be from some inflammation starting from his fetlock joint which was creeping downwards? Heat from a point of strain may move either way. But if the heat sprang from a strain of the joint why wasn't he lame?

In Gillam's position two external influences were at work. Mrs Brotherton, judging from her pressure over Polar Bear, was not likely to consent to his wasting time. And Mr Renton from his vast experience did not seem unduly worried: 'Clay and cow dung and carry on.'

So because Red Rum had blown quite heavily after the Haydock race, as horses do when they are in pain as well as when they are unfit, Anthony Gillam assumed, as Tommy Stack had, that the horse was still unfit and that he needed an inordinate amount of strenuous galloping or racing. This would not be the treatment doctors would prescribe for arthritis – once they had recognised it. And equine patients cannot talk. So Gillam kept Red Rum hard at it and ran him again ten days later.

Horses are born to confuse us, as Red Rum did next time out at Catterick. If there was anything wrong with the foot, he would surely, on firmer, faster, more painful ground, run even worse.

No one had yet allowed for the horse's courage. Rather the reverse. Tommy Stack had doubted it. But time was going to show that all those races, struggling on to finish 5th or 6th in mud he loathed, under goading boot and thwacking stick were the product of bravery over disability. So now he overcame the pain in his feet. Galloping three miles one furlong and eighty yards in the Charles Vickery Memorial Cup, a valuable race, Red Rum blinkered and driven along as hard as Tommy Stack could manage, took up the running going to the third last fence and hung on to win by a length. He earned Mrs Brotherton £930.70p. 'Mrs Brotherton came, which was very nice,' said Anthony Gillam, pleased that his owner had watched his first victory as a public trainer. 'She doesn't often go racing.'

Tommy Stack had special reasons for happiness. He had cast off the weight of being a trainer. All the anxieties were now young Gillam's. As if to celebrate the lightness of his spirit he rode a treble in a row at Catterick on December 11th, two outside rides for Shedden in the 1 o'clock and the 1.30, then Red Rum at 2. A splendid day for a jockey.

The trainer's worries, however, begin again as soon as the jockey gets off. The rider may be carefree till the next day's racing. The trainer has immediate worries about his horses. For Anthony Gillam the pleasure of victory did not

There was that heat there again extend into the evening. 'Red Rum came back level in his action,' said Gillam, 'but there was that heat there again. And I didn't know now if it was in his foot or in his joint.'

A trainer, however old and experienced, who starts to have doubts about one of his horse's health and soundness, becomes aware – even from the kindest and most patient owners – of pressure. He feels obliged either to find out what is wrong and to cure it, or to run the horse. At £30 a week racehorses are not for looking at.

Moreover, by winning at Catterick Red Rum seemed publicly to have removed the need for caution. Whatever a trainer's doubts – and Anthony Gillam's were now increasing – you cannot tell the owner that you are seriously worried about the horse, if the animal comes out and runs and wins. So Anthony ran Red Rum again at Catterick on 22nd December. The ground was suitably firm, except that now, unknown to his trainer, the firmness was hurting his foot. 'It was,' said Gillam, 'a similar sort of race to the one he'd just won there.' In fact, the class was not quite so good. 'He should have won,' Gillam said. He finished third, *Chaseform Notebook* commenting 'Found the pace a little too fast from three out'. So it must have seemed.

Running in pain From what we now know it is almost certain that his off-fore was beginning to hurt Red Rum more and more from each concussion landing after every fence. In the last half mile or so the pain, even for a horse of courage, became a little much. 'I didn't tumble to anything,' Gillam unhappily admitted two and a half years later. 'We ran him without blinkers. But Tommy said that didn't make any difference: that wasn't why he was beaten.'

Both trainer and jockey knew then that something was going wrong with the horse. But what was it?

The result of his next race seemed to confuse the issue even further. Because the ground at Catterick was generally firmer that winter than anywhere else in the North, Anthony Gillam kept entering him there. He had won the Charles Vickery on 11th December, been beaten into third place in a less valuable race on 22nd December, and now reappeared there in another well-endowed contest, the Zetland Handicap 'Chase worth £651 on New Year's Day, 1972. It would be his fourth race in a month. Tommy Stack energetically drove Red Rum on from start to finish in the four-horse race over the same 3 miles 300 yards of his two previous races there. He won by 7 lengths and a distance. In three runs at Catterick in three weeks he had earned £1,622.30. He had paid the cost of all his keep for a year. For a heavy tax payer his tax-free earnings were particularly valuable. His two victories in Yorkshire in valuable races would help considerably to establish his young trainer in his first few months as a professional. They were two more hard-earned steps up the ladder of Tommy Stack's climb to the top.

But Red Rum came back from Catterick definitely lame. He showed it plainly the next day. He stayed really lame for several bad days on end.

Red Rum lame

There was in the yard at Oxclose at that time a certain Yorkshire physiotherapist of renown who was treating one of Gillam's horses for shoulder trouble and another for back trouble. Gillam, now deeply anxious, asked if the physiotherapist could help him diagnose what was wrong with Red Rum. The gentleman, who lives not 100 miles from the Yorkshire town of Richmond and who on ethical grounds must be called merely Mr A, very properly said that he should first be called in by a qualified veterinary surgeon. He recommended a man with whom he had often worked. So it was that a certain Scots vet living not 100 miles from the Border town of Hawick arrived on the scene at Anthony Gillam's request.

The vet took X-rays of Red Rum's feet and, after he had examined them, said, 'I'm very sorry to say that he has chronic pedalosteitis in his off-fore.' He added glumly, 'Very few horses, I'm afraid, get over it.'

24 'HE'S STILL FEELING HIS OFF-FORE'

PEDAL: (L. pedalis/pes, foot) Of the foot. p. Bone (pronounced peedal, syn. 3rd phalanx) Bone inside hoof. p. osteitis/ostitis Inflamed p. bone causing pain and lameness. Diagnosis: on X-ray examination. Treatment: rest, shoeing with pad underneath sole, possibly neurectomy. *Outlook: unfavourable.*

OSTEITIS/OSTITIS: Inflamed bone. Most common cause is fracture, qv.★

The racehorse is heir to a thousand ills and accidents. His chances of survival depend on the combined wisdom, patience and solicitude of the trainer, his professional advisers and his staff. Red Rum was thrice lucky. He had an anxious, conscientious, young trainer who bothered, and who was keen to call in the best advice. He had in the vet from Hawick a man who combined experience with advanced views. He had in nearby Richmond a leading equine physiotherapist. And he had the love of his stable girl Sandra.

Treatment that cured Red Rum

Without this united care and treatment the future Grand National winner would have become a cripple. As it was, the horse remained quite lame for nearly two long months. Anthony Gillam remembered the outline of the treatment which appears below (with the permission of the two practitioners' respective professional societies) as their two official reports.

'The vet said "Put him on a course of cortisone, intramuscular, to relieve the pain". We kept that going for six weeks. The vet arranged that Mr A would come three times a week to give him ultrasonic treatment round the coronet band. He also told us to "put special Swedish hoof-pads on him".'

These 'pads' are made from a mixture resembling putty which comes in a small tub. You add a 'thinner' to it, mix

★ Taken from *The Horse's Health from A to Z* by Peter D. Rossdale and Susan M. Wreford and published by David & Charles.

it, and paint it right over the sole of the hoof and the frog.
You then put a piece of thick plaster over it. Finally you get
the blacksmith to reshoe the foot through the plastic pad
and the rubbery Swedish mould.

'Our blacksmith,' said Gillam, 'was awfully good about
it, because there was a lot to nail through, and he did think
at first that it was rather a new-fangled idea!'

Sandra said, '"Rummy" had terrible feet, shallow feet.
I used to put Stockholm Tar on them three times a day.
They got better with the treatment.'

Gillam remembered, 'After about six weeks the foot-
pads rotted – slightly Sandra's fault, because she was
determined to put Stockholm Tar on his feet and the brush
penetrated the pads and rather rotted them: it didn't
matter. They were still doing the job.'

Sandra said, 'Red Rum was petrified of the vets, but they
did a lot of good. They said they would completely cure
him.

Petrified of
vets

The veterinary surgeon from Hawick reports as follows:

During Nov./Dec. 1971 the horse was observed to be
intermittently slightly lame. The condition gradually
became more apparent over this period of time. There
was no evidence of tendon ligament or other soft tissue
involvement. Searching of the affected foot revealed dry
corns which were pared out without any improvement
in action. The wall of the hoof had become brittle and
by January, 1972, heat was present in the region of the
heels and the area sensitive to pressure. The hoof was
markedly smaller than its opposite fellow, and contrac-
tion was occurring at the heels of the off fore, and the
horse was untrainable.

X-ray of the affected part revealed pedalosteitis to be
present, localized osteophytic formation on the lateral
aspects on the angles of the pedal bone and also ossification of the lower part of the lateral cartilages, and the
presence of a spur on the proximal border of the lateral
angle of the bone, were observed. No lesions, fortunately, were to be seen on the navicular bone.

The trainer was advised that physiotherapy was the best
line of treatment and not to rest the horse but to give
him long slow exercise daily on the level roads and soft
going. The horse was to be let down on his heels and
hoof pads were applied to both fore-feet. To alleviate
pain a supplementary course of cortico-steroid therapy
was administered over a period of six weeks.

Long slow
exercise
daily

Ultra-sonic treatment was prescribed to retard ossification and to assist absorption of the spur and microwave
to assist in the pedal circulation.

Mr A, the physiotherapist, reports as follows:

I saw the horse in November, 1971, in conjunction with
the veterinary surgeon.
Various forms of pallitive treatment for soft tissue
lesions were tried with success.
We jointly saw the horse again in January, 1972. Because
of persistent heat the feet were X-rayed.
This confirmed the veterinary surgeon's fears and he
passed the horse over to me for an intensive course of
physiotherapy.
Having previously dealt with similar cases using a
combination of the normal treatment for gout and
osteoarthritis I followed this pattern using ultrasonic,
microwave and interferential therapy.

The 'long slow exercise daily' prescribed by the vet was
in the careful hands of Miss Sandra Kendall. Anthony
Gillam gives her full credit. 'If he'd gone out with the
others he'd have gone berserk, he was so fresh. So for two
months Sandra hacked him quietly round the fields, quite
on his own.'

'He came   So daily as winter reluctantly gave ground to spring
right'   Sandra and her 'Rummy' rambled round the fields and
quiet lanes together for hours. He loved that. I used to
round up bullocks on him – anything like that. I used to go
all over the place.'
'Eventually,' said Anthony Gillam, 'he came right.'
The vet from Hawick reported:

A prognosis was given that there was every reason for
optimism and that he would eventually be able to give
his normal performance when returned to work free
from pain. By mid-February the condition was much
improved and the horse recommenced training.

And the physiotherapist reported:

The veterinary surgeon re-examined the horse and
recommended full training to be resumed.

Gillam had Red Rum shod in light steel shoes – 'I always
race my horses in light steel plates, so we don't have to

Winter's morning between the sea and the sandhills. *Photo: Gerry Cranham*

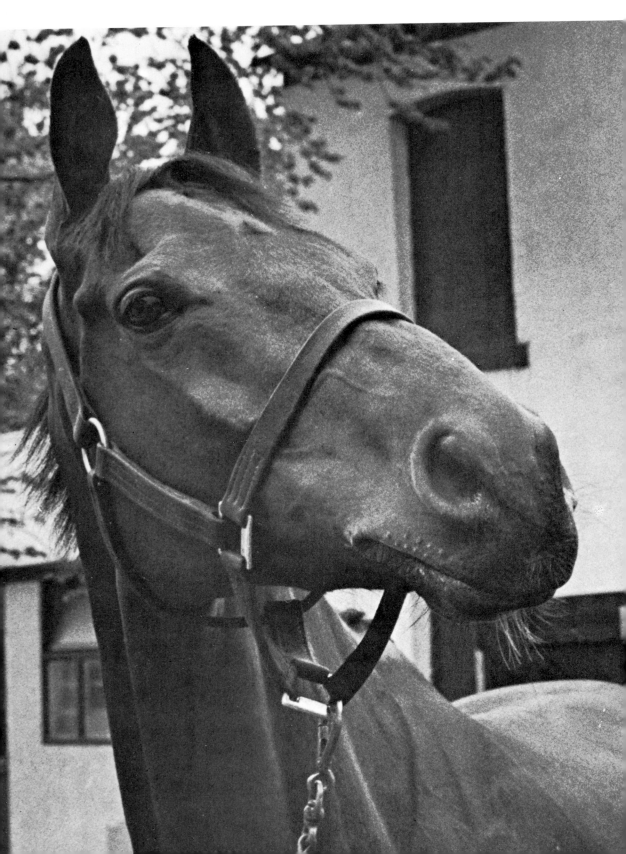

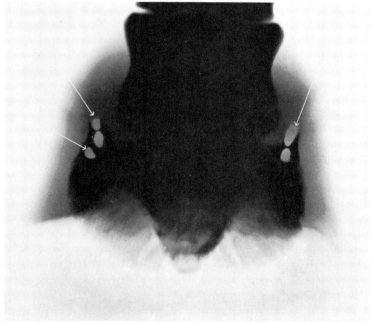

Left: Intelligence, courage and great resolution. *Photo: Jeremy Hoare*

Top: The foot so nearly permanently crippled by pedalosteitis.

Above: X-Ray, supplied by his vet, showing pedalosteitis and osteophytic formation.

Noel Le Mare
accompanied by Mrs.
Doris Solomon
receiving his
Racehorse of the
Year Award (Summer
1974).

keep changing them as you do with aluminium plates'. Over both soles they nailed a protective leather-pad between shoe and hoof.

Shod in light steel shoes

He ran the horse again at Catterick on 6th March, 1972, and for the first time in his life Red Rum hit the deck. He was lying third, and being ridden along when David French (D. Atkins) who was leading, fell at the 14th fence and Red Rum, unable to avoid the sprawling body, tumbled over him.

Tommy Stack was very disappointed. He reported to Gillam, 'In no way would I have won.'

Gillam recalled, 'Tommy was very depressed. At that point he finally lost faith in the horse. It was a bad race and he was favourite and he should have trotted up. I said to Tommy, "Don't worry. It's not your fault. I don't think the horse is right." He was sound, but he just wasn't striding out.'

Gillam thought he had given the horse enough work to run him – 'but as it turned out, nowhere near enough to do himself justice. I would have given him lots more time,' said Gillam. 'But Mrs Brotherton was very keen to run him. If he'd been mine, I don't think he'd have run again that season. But that's a fault of mine. I'm too easy with horses.'

If Red Rum had not run again that season after his lameness he would either have stayed on with Gillam or he would have been sold for very little money. There would be few buyers the next August for a horse which had not run since January. The racing world and his wife would have known there was something gravely wrong with him. Who could have bought him?

After Catterick Gillam had the trainer's unenviable task of telephoning the bad news to the owner. Mrs Brotherton took it extremely well. She said, 'He was probably short of work. Better luck next time.'

But the Catterick accident had wrecked the plans for 'next time'. It had been the intention to imitate Dagmar Gittell and win the Topham Trophy with him round Liverpool. Earlier that season Tim Molony had come up to Gillam and said so himself. But now they felt they could not take to Liverpool for a first cut at those huge fences a horse who had just got knocked over. Furthermore, Stack reported after Catterick, 'He's lost all his speed'. Jockey and trainer conferred. 'We knew he stayed,' said Gillam, 'so we agreed to go for the Scottish National.'

'He's lost all his speed'

Tommy Stack had, however, no retainer from Gillam's

small stable: he simply had an arrangement that he would ride when he could. The Olivers from Hawick – Ken, 'the benign bishop' and co-founder of Doncaster Bloodstock Sales and his able and charming wife Rhona, now offered Stack the ride in the Scottish National on their grand mare Young Ash Leaf. Tommy accepted.

Mrs Brotherton suggested Josh Gifford's younger brother Macer. Macer therefore rode Red Rum at Nottingham in his next race. Macer commented in the paddock, 'He *is* a tubby little fellow, isn't he?' Gillam said, 'Well, yes, and I'm afraid the ground won't suit you either.' Nor would the distance: it was only 2 miles 6 furlongs.

Confidence grows

The horse finished third to Nom de Guerre who had beaten him 30 lengths in their first race that season. This time, and on the same terms Red Rum was only $2\frac{1}{2}$ lengths behind. Gillam recalls 'Macer felt that if he had kicked on hard from four out we might have won'. Confidence may have ebbed in Stack's mind; in Gillam's its tide was strongly turning. He felt the horse was on the way back. This was going to make the coming parting that much more painful.

In his last race before the Scottish National he ran such a good race at Wetherby in a £3,000 race against three really good horses, Ballysagert, who won, Jomon (2nd) and Supermaster (4th) that even Tommy Stack was impressed that Red Rum finished a close-up third; beaten 2 lengths and $1\frac{1}{2}$ lengths. 'He ran a hell of a race,' said Gillam 'and on soft ground too. I was thrilled to bits and I thought we *must* have a chance in the Scottish National with only 9st 7lb.' Well, yes, as the historians may drily note, for two years later he was to win it, a mere 21 days after winning his second English Grand National, carrying a 6lb penalty to make it 11st 13lb. . . .

Tommy Stack impressed

Unfortunately an airport strike stopped Macer Gifford flying up to Ayr. 'So I seemed stuck with no jockey,' said Gillam. 'But Martin Blackshaw made sure I saw him! He could do 9st 8lb without wasting, but he had only ridden in a few 'chases because he was fresh off the flat. He *rode* the horse beautifully. The only thing was that I said "Stay close up and kick on from the *top* bend" but he must have misunderstood me, for he kicked on from the *bottom* bend and so tried to lead for all the last circuit.' Red Rum led to three fences from home and stayed on well to finish 5th about $7\frac{1}{2}$ lengths behind Quick Reply. Slave's Dream and Esban were 2nd and third. Tommy Stack, well back on Young Ash Leaf, was impressed by Red Rum's running.

Mrs Brotherton watched the race on the television.
'She played hell!' said Gillam. 'She said "If *only* he hadn't
made so much *use* of him – " I defended the boy. We'd set
off being laughed at: "What are you taking that useless
horse up to the Scottish National for?" sort of thing. And
we finished up leading over the third last, and bloody
nearly wiping their eye!'

The judgement of two people who had observed Red
Rum's running in this race now affected his future. The
Scottish vet from Hawick watched his ex-patient all the
way and noted quite clearly that in the last three-quarters of
a mile, the horse kept changing legs. Plainly he was still
feeling his foot. He observed, what was more, that over the
last four or five fences Red Rum was jumping to the left
every time, towards the rails (which is most unusual) and
thus away from that damaged off-fore. He said to Gillam,
'He's still feeling his off-fore, I'm afraid,' and Gillam told
Mrs Brotherton. Her gloom increased: there was still grave
doubt about her horse's recovery. . . .

Trainer Donald McCain in his third season as a public
trainer and still looking for his 'One Good Horse', had also
watched the race. Knowing nothing of Red Rum's mid-
season bone disease and being not too impressed by his
jockey's tactics at Ayr, he made a strong mental note about
the horse he'd first seen win a seller at Liverpool five years
earlier. This, he thought, is a real stayer, a possible Grand
National horse. If he was ever for sale, he thought, I'll
mention him to Mr Le Mare. . . .

Red Rum ran only once more for Mrs Brotherton,
Anthony Gillam and Sandra. Gillam says with his splendid
honesty, 'I made a serious mistake by running him a
fortnight later at Market Rasen. He was over the top. So
he ran really badly behind rotten horses and finished fourth.
He really did collapse.'

A blow of a more dreadful nature was now suspended
over the stables. Mrs Brotherton had made her mind up.
She was about to issue her edict.

Donald
McCain . . .
'one good
horse'

25 'THE BEST PROPORTIONED HORSE YOU'LL EVER SEE'

One May day Mrs Brotherton told Anthony Gillam, 'I'm going to sell Red Rum'.

Gillam was horrified.

Mrs Brotherton said calmly, 'I've got to sell him, because he's the oldest'. Her other horses at Oxclose were either younger and thus with apparently more potential or had leg trouble and were therefore unsaleable.

The knell of doom

To Sandra the news tolled like the knell of doom. 'Mr Gillam came and told me "I've got some bad news for you, Sandra. She's thinking of selling Red Rum." I just went potty,' Sandra exclaimed. 'I thought it was the last horse on *earth* they'd ever sell!'

She burst out at Anthony Gillam. 'That's it then, I'm going.'

Gillam said, 'He might not go'. Sandra looked puzzled. Hope flickered. Anthony explained, '*I* might buy him. I'll try.'

Gillam recalled, 'Every time I saw Mrs Brotherton during the summer I worked on her. Originally he was only going to have a 3,000 guinea reserve at the sales. During June and July I was trying to get her to raise it to 5,000 guineas. I thought I'd be nearly safe there. And I did have two buddies and we'd agreed we'd try to go into the horse together. Of course, we hadn't much money, and after a certain point we'd be beaten.'

Decision to sell

Certainly the worry about Red Rum's feet was a contributing factor in Mrs Brotherton's final decision to sell. As her son David Brotherton understood it, looking back with a friend in 1974 over the fateful decision, ensuring that Red Rum got right might mean months more of expensive treatment: 'Thousands of pounds' were somewhat loosely mentioned.

Gillam himself placed 'a hell of a lot of significance' on what the Hawick vet had reported after watching the Scottish National, but Mrs Brotherton, said Gillam was 'rather unsympathetic. She didn't understand all of what was going on about the foot trouble. As far as she's concerned,' said Gillam, 'vets are sometimes eyewash! She thinks Bobby Renton's old-fashioned remedies marvellous. But she thinks vets' bills are terribly expensive.' Gillam adds, 'However, this treatment proved to be a triumph for modern veterinary methods.'

She would not be alone. Vets' fees soar like inflated balloons. For some it is a matter of a quick glance at a horse's leg; squeeze – squeeze; tch-tch; 'poultice, Good Morning' – and that's four guineas plus VAT plus mileage! One southern vet places upon the bonnet of his car a ticking clock, so that the trainer can both hear and see the golden guineas ticking away.

Like coalminers and express-train-drivers, equine veterinary surgeons have soared up the incomes league and up the social scale. They are no longer garbed as labourers, gumbooted, in old cords and patched coats. The top men can justifiably purr up in Jaguars in flannel suits dictating notes on tape recorders and calling their office on radiotelephones. These things have to be paid for by racehorse owners. . . .

'Quite frankly,' said Anthony Gillam, 'I didn't give Mrs Brotherton half the bills I had for Red Rum! I paid them myself.'

Ironically, the horse did better that summer at grass than he had ever done. Something kept telling Gillam that Red Rum was at last coming to himself. He kept front shoes on him in the field and kept his hooves well rubbed with Cornucrescine to promote new growth. When Red Rum came off grass at the start of July he looked magnificent. Much more important, when he started trotting along the roads he was absolutely sound. The doubts of the Scots vet rang in Gillam's mind, but the horse seemed cured. Gillam wanted to buy him, and he had these two friends with whom to share him. He asked the vet 'Do you think he will stay right?' and got an uncertain answer. 'It's 50-50, and if I was you,' advised the vet, 'I wouldn't spend too much money on him.'

Gillam concurred. 'Of course he was right. And I hadn't the money anyway. I did say he might be a National horse. But I never *dreamed* he'd be such an exceptional one. . . .'

To sell a horse at a fair price you must either send him to the sales with a vet's certificate, which gives a professional opinion of his soundness, or you must warrant the horse sound. Vets are growing very chary about signing certificates of soundness. They fear legal comebacks. Several partnerships now refuse to issue any. At Doncaster

Coming to himself

a horse sold either with a 'clean and unqualified veterinary certificate' or 'subject to re-examination' can be examined by a panel of vets in the sales paddocks at the request of the buyer (who pays £11) as soon as the horse is sold. The sale is contingent upon the horse passing the panel.

Completely sound

In Red Rum's case he was thoroughly examined at Oxclose, found to be completely sound, and his V.S. Certificate was announced when his entry was made for the sales.

The horse was entered in Doncaster's good August sales, their 'Great Annual York Race Sales', probably the best market in the British Isles for both made and prospective National Hunt horses. Because Mrs Brotherton was a well-known vendor, she drew an excellent place in the catalogue. The auctioneers in their offices in Hawick prepared Red Rum's particulars with their customary care. (See below.) But they omitted from their printed copy one important piece of information and strong selling point. Red

Qualified for the Grand National

Rum had qualified himself for the Grand National, as one or two keen prospective buyers, like sharp-eyed Ginger McCain, could work out for themselves by going through the form-book and checking the value of his races won.

THE FOLLOWING THREE LOTS, PROPERTY OF MRS L. BROTHERTON, FORM HER ANNUAL CONSIGNMENT OF HORSES IN TRAINING AT THIS SALE

FROM OXCLOSE STABLES
THE PROPERTY OF MRS L. BROTHERTON

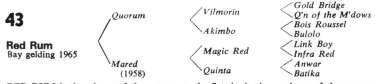

43

Red Rum
Bay gelding 1965

			Gold Bridge
	Vilmorin		Q'n of the M'dows
Quorum			Bois Roussel
	Akimbo		Bulolo
			Link Boy
	Magic Red		Infra Red
Mared			Anwar
(1958)	Quinta		Batika

RED RUM is the **winner** of three races on the flat; he is also a **winner** of three races over hurdles and placed six times. He started steeplechasing in 1970-71 season and to date is the **winner** of five steeplechases including in 1971-72 season, Zetland Handicap Chase, Catterick, £651, and Charles Vickery Memorial Cup Handicap Chase, Catterick, £930, also placed four times including third in Wetherby Handicap Chase, beaten 3½ lengths, to Ballysagert and Jomon, and on his penultimate outing placed fifth in Scottish Grand National, beaten under eight lengths to Quick Reply. V.S. Certificate at sale.

MARED, **winner** and placed at three years; also placed at two years. Dam of **Red Rum** (see above) and **Our Richard** (winner of Danure Handicap and placed at three years, also placed at two years).

QUINTA, placed three times at three years, 1956. Dam of the winners **Mared** (see above) and **Via Con Deo** (at four years, 1963, and placed at three years; also placed over hurdles, 1965).

BATIKA (foaled in France). Dam of the winners **Head Dress** (two races), **Spring Offensive** (seven races including Desmond Stakes, Curragh and dam of eight winners including Turbo Jet, 2000 Gns. Trial Stakes, etc., and £5511, also 11 races in U.S.A., value £56,588, including Man O'War Stakes, 1964; Faberge II, also second in 2000 Gns., sire, and Gallup Poll, three races in France, 1965, value £7084, also won a race in U.S.A. in 1966, value £16,932), **Red Batik** (two-year-old winner in England, 1949), **W.T.** and **Magic Black** (winner in Venezuela in 1953 and 1954), also Maiden of Orleans (dam of winners including Blackwell, Fullbrook, Maid in France and King of France).

But neither the sales catalogue nor the advertisements said that Red Rum was so qualified.

Nobody came to Oxclose to look at Red Rum before the sale and only a few people bothered to ring Gillam up about him. 'And they were only people who were curious, like Guy Cunard. I never had anybody sincerely interested.'

Gillam, like any trainer in danger of losing a horse he wanted to keep, found himself in an invidious position. He is a straight man and could not therefore even suggest to enquirers that there might have been anything gravely wrong with the horse during the previous winter. He had, moreover, to enthuse, against his own interests, about the horse's health and prospects.

An invidious position

The fact that Red Rum had not run for over two months would have looked more suspicious to the complete ignoramus than to the man who knew something. It was the usual case of a little knowledge being dangerous: those who knew a little about Red Rum had heard he hated soft ground, so they assumed he had not run in January and February for this excellent reason. Nor was it a question of his not having run since, a fact which would have deterred anyone. He might not have shone on his last race from Oxclose at Market Rasen, but he had finished fourth and sound. And a great number of people, Ginger McCain included, without the inside knowledge and thus the sharpened observation of the Scottish vet, had watched his Scottish National at Ayr on television, and thought how well he'd run. He *seemed* a hard, tough, sound horse.

Finished fourth and sound

Army training, which teaches the frequent senselessness of orders from on high, is good practice for modern state-meddling life. 'Upset?' repeated old Charlie Wright, reflecting in his potting-shed (for he was helping out in summertime in Mr Gillam's garden) on the departure of Red Rum. 'I've been in racing long enough not to get upset. You've got to get used to it, when horses have to go.'

Wright's old army notebook records, as the last entry against each of scores of his former charges, the sad order of their going: 'Sent to Mrs Mears Oct., '70 . . . Sold £900 Doncaster May, '72 . . . sent to Doncaster sales Aug., '70, sold £1,700 . . . sent hunting . . . sent to flat . . . returned to owner . . . destroyed . . . lame after work, sold July, '67 . . . sent to Stud Paddocks, Destroyed June, '72 . . . Sold Doncaster . . . sent hunting . . . Destroyed . . .'

Sandra's love for Red Rum transcended Charlie Wright's reconciled philosophy. Mr Brian Miles, now her husband, had kept the nice house in Ripon waiting for her for six and a half years. 'Brian wanted me to get married. But I never would, while Red Rum was there,' said Sandra, and so it turned out. This sort of priority may seem ludicrous to people unbitten by the horse bug. But the strength of Britain in all its horsey fields in show-jumping, Eventing, as well as in racing, is built upon people as passionate about the animals as Miss Sandra Kendall, now Mrs Miles.

The final blow

She then received the final blow. She had suffered the shock of hearing that her 'Rummy' was going to be sold. The hapless Anthony Gillam now had to approach her with even more unpleasant news.

'They're not going to let you take him to the sales,' said Gillam. He was acutely embarrassed.

Sandra exploded, 'I've taken horses to those sales, and they've had the top prices for them! They've had top prices there for *rubbishy* horses. And they won't let me take "Rummy".' She turned away.

It was her belief that another of Mrs Brotherton's flat-race trainers, 'Mick' Easterby, had influenced Mrs Brotherton's decision. She went off immediately to telephone Mr Easterby. 'I told him what I thought. He said, "Have a drink". I said "I *won't* have a drink!" I went mad at him. I said to him, "I know as soon as I put this phone down you'll go and ring her up. So the best of luck".'

Quietly digging in his garden

Sandra was not yet done. She strode off to find Mr Renton. He was quietly digging in his garden above the still waters of the dark canal. Sandra demanded, 'What's all this about?'

Bobby Renton replied, 'It's nothing to do with me. It's between the two of them.'

'Apparently I upset him,' she said two years afterwards. 'But it was the way they treated *me* after eleven years, that's what upset me. Years of hard work. I'd done them I don't know *how* many winners! But you're no better thought of. . . . This is why I cracked up. . . . I think Easterby rang Mrs Brotherton up and she rang Bobby up. So I went off down into Wales on a holiday with Brian.' Sandra blushed.

In Sandra's absence, Charles Wright, the head lad, took over Red Rum for his last week at Oxclose. On the Sunday evening before the sales, Anthony Gillam was sadly going round his horses. Bobby Renton was in the yard too. He had several times over the horse's four years at Oxclose remarked to Gillam that Red Rum was too small for a Grand National horse. That evening, however, he went into the horse's box and stood there staring agog at the bright bay. He called across the yard to young Anthony Gillam.

Old Mr Renton cried, 'Come here and look at this horse!' Gillam went into his box. Red Rum was in the straw standing, as Gillam too vividly recalls, 'just right and looking super.' The wise old trainer said to the young man with the emphasis of the elderly who, recognising the shape of something immeasurable, try to pass on some yardstick before it is too late. '*You remember him*. . . . Because this is the most perfectly balanced and best proportioned horse that you'll ever see.'

The old man looked again at the horse and turned his gnomish eyes back again towards Gillam. The horse, oblivious of his fate, turned that splendidly bold head and fearless eyes towards the tall thin young man, and the little hunched old one. He was aware, as all animals are, of tension. It shimmered in the summer evening air.

'I *know* he is,' Anthony burst out in anguish, 'so why the something something are you selling him?'

Renton wagged his old head, 'Well, Mrs Brotherton says . . .' he began.

'And it was that night I got her to put his reserve up from 3,000 to 5,000 guineas,' said Gillam. 'And at that I didn't think I'd lose him.'

26 'WHO'S McCAIN?'

From Mrs Brotherton's point of view the luck of the sales ring ran sweetly for her. Bloodstock in the summer of 1972 was a soaring market. The absurd relation between the cost of a jumper and what it might earn had not impinged on steeplechasing's supporters. Like the millions who do their weekly football pools hoping for a miracle, the thousands of jumping owners and buyers realise that one horse each year wins the Grand National. Why not one year then it could be them . . .? Money in those halcyon days was easily available.

Doncaster Bloodstock Sales which had started in 1962 were booming in their tenth year. They had turned over one million pounds in 1970 and were rising to a record of £2¾ million in 1973. Their Great Annual York Race sales reflected this glitter. The turnover in 1971 had been 170,000 guineas; at Red Rum's sale it was going nearly to double at 320,000 guineas. The delusion of the British that one flourished because one borrowed was at its craziest height.

'Just your type, I know sir'

Mrs Brotherton was a regular seller. There seemed therefore nothing suspicious about her off-loading three of her older horses. Several of her weed-outs, as Sandra said, had sold well there in the past. The third senior partner in the sales company, Harry Beeby, son of the renowned ex-trainer George Beeby, is the most polished bloodstock auctioneer now operating. No one is more adept at making the good points in each Lot sound almost irresistible and then, when he has spotted a serious bidder, mesmerising him with full conviction: 'Just your type, I know, sir,' delivered, bright-eyed and glossy-haired from a beseeching position, half-way out across his rostrum, so that it takes a hard unflatterable heart to deny Beeby that further nod which can cost you 100 guineas. That sensual combination of authority, flattery and the need for help, to which many women succumb, is equally effective in the skilled auctioneer.

As a vendor, it is one's good luck to have Harry Beeby selling your horses. Mrs Brotherton was lucky that August day in 1972. Beeby commented, 'Red Rum looked really well after the spring grass, and I believed that he would sell well, as he formed part – he was the first of the three – of Mrs Brotherton's annual consignment. For some reason,' added Harry Beeby carefully, 'her horses–in–training always attracted a lot of interest.'

Harry Beeby is a friend of Anthony Gillam. He stays with Anthony and 'Pandie' on his way south from Hawick. They had talked about Red Rum that summer after Mrs Brotherton's edict. Other people too asked Anthony if he had anything to sell. 'I'm losing my best horse,' he had replied with gloom.

A sad day for us

Red Rum was placed at peak sales time, about noon on the first day. In Sandra's absence in Wales, he went off with a lad, behaved beautifully and, said Gillam, 'Looked super. I didn't stand by his box, so I didn't see McCain or any other trainers come to look at him. I stayed away as much as I could, because it was a sad day for us. Obviously I had to be loyal to Mrs Brotherton. But I also had my personal feelings.'

Gillam was hopeful that the new reserve of 5,000 guineas which he had given to Harry Beeby would be too high for the horse to be sold and that Red Rum would return to him. He supposed that the highest bid for Red Rum would be about 4,000 guineas. He had his reserve plan, however. His two friends William Owen and David McConochie shared a good young hurdler with him called Mountain Dew who won on the first evening of that new 1972–73 season at Market Rasen just before the sales. In doing so, however, he had 'got a leg', and would be out of action. His co-owners and Anthony now resolved that, should the bidding exceed Red Rum's reserve, they would then come in and go to 5,300 guineas to try to buy him. It was as much as they could possibly afford by sharing the horse in thirds.

Gillam's reserve plan

Harry Beeby summed up his valuation. 'The horse had been in training from the very start of his 2-year-old days. Although he was only a 7-year-old, he had been in action *a very long time*. Prospective buyers might have been excused for wondering whether he had had enough racing.' There is a racing euphemism here. The implication is that the horse may be getting fed up, and that he may be no longer genuine. Tommy Stack's opinion would be quite well-known.

So much for Red Rum's drawbacks. 'On the other hand,' Beeby continued, 'he was a proven stayer and a really good jumper and he'd run a marvellous race in the Scottish Grand National that April. *And*,' Beeby added quickly, 'he was qualified for the Grand National – a point which I brought out during the auction.'

Two years later even Harry Beeby could not recall all the bidders who had had a go at Red Rum that August morning – 'But I certainly remember there was no hesitation throughout.' The bids came swiftly and he capped them, one step up, as the price ran swiftly up towards the reserve. 'I believe Jack Doyle was in at some stage,' Beeby said, referring to that flamboyant dealer who rose from being a very small trainer indeed to controlling probably the biggest turnover of any one-man-band bloodstock agency. A former patron of Doyle's remembers when years ago the former Irish rugby international was struggling along as a trainer. Twenty years later he rings Jack Doyle and is told to hang on: 'Mr Doyle is on another line to Monte Carlo . . .' Against the quiet, conservative

The bids came swiftly

Jack
Doyle

image of the established bloodstock agencies where courteous colonels were all the thing, Doyle brought show-biz push. When a horse won with whom he had been connected – nodding for it at auction in its yearling days, or telling Fred it was worth looking at – Doyle often got into the winner's enclosure and got photographed with it and the trainer. He got his credit in the caption and capitalised on it in advertisements. He has done remarkably well both for his hundreds of satisfied clients and for himself.

So Doyle bid up to his precise estimate of the horse's value. At 5,000 Red Rum was on the market and in direct danger of going. 'I know that Anthony Gillam bid,' Harry Beeby remembered, 'as he was anxious not to lose him.'

There was another bidder now, standing in his accustomed place, tweed-capped Tim Forster of the mournful mien, who had once trained for Mrs Brotherton. He had another well-to-do and mature lady owner in Mrs 'Vi' Henriques, widow of that good author Robert Henriques. Captain Forster had done very well for Mrs Henriques. His training of the bad-legged Denys Adventure to win the Arkle 'Chase at Cheltenham was a triumph of patience over weakness. She was looking for another horse. He had spotted Red Rum in the catalogue and a less honest man would now declare that he picked him out and bid for him 'because I knew he'd win the National'. Not so, Captain Tim, racing's perpetual pessimist: 'I rather thought,' he said, 'that Red Rum would be a "fun horse", which we could run on hard ground at places like Ludlow, Worcester and Devon & Exeter. . . . I *did* wonder why Mrs Brotherton was getting rid, but I thought how rare it was to find any decent 3 mile 'chaser up for sale. I went to look at him in his box. I thought that he might be a bit small, a bit "flat racey", except that he'd *done* it. . . .' He meant the 3 mile 'chasing.

Red Rum
would be a
'Fun horse'

Mrs Henriques had about £5,000 to spend on her 'fun horse' and though Tim Forster had not specifically mentioned Red Rum as a target, 'I knew at the back of my mind she'd have it.'

From the 5,000 guineas point the bidding, like duelling swords, sparked left and right between Anthony Gillam and Tim Forster. But both were quickly running out of ammunition.

Watching them with hawkish eyes was a tall man with ginger hair who had learned the auction business in the hard world of second-hand cars. He had bought a few cheap horses in his time and bid in vain for expensive ones. In a last throw for a rich old man whom he had driven in his taxi he had been empowered to bid, for him, an enormous amount. With one exception (which cost £1,500) no horse previously bought by Donald McCain of 10, Upper Aughton Road, Birkdale, Lancs, had cost more than £1,000. Now he had up to 7,000 guineas to spend to find a Grand National winner for Mr Noel Le Mare, son of a penniless missionary, who had made a fortune and was then approaching his 85th birthday. The 7,000 guineas had not been enough to buy Kippie Lodge in a previous Doncaster Sales. McCain had also failed in the past to buy for Mr Le Mare several other expensive horses which he had hoped might win a Grand National for his elderly patron. Fair Vulgan, for which Josh Gifford outbid him, was one.

> Finding a Grand National winner

He had told Mr Le Mare that he thought Red Rum would make 4 or 5,000 guineas and Le Mare had said boldly, for he trusted McCain, 'Go to 7'. McCain planned to come in at 4,000, because he believed that that was the horse's reserve price. Such was the first point of his technique. 'He went up steadyish,' said McCain, doing as he planned. 'Then at 5,000 a new bidder came in.' We know now that this was the start of the Tim Forster–Anthony Gillam duel. 'That rather worried me. New bidders don't come in at that money just to drop out again. And with only 7,000, I hadn't much margin. But the more I look at the horse going round, the more taken I am with him. And he gets better looking all the time!'

So McCain, the car-dealer, pulls a gambit he's often used successfully in the motor marts. He resolves in an instant to depth-charge the opposition by suddenly jumping the bidding upwards in a huge stride. Gillam had fallen out. Forster was weakening at 5,500 and Harry Beeby's beady eyes are fixed on McCain's face. McCain holds up one hand spread out and the thumb of his other and mouths the word 'six'.

'*Six* thousand I'm bid,' announces Harry Beeby, quite astonished, but keeping surprise well-hidden in his pale face. He looks around. But McCain's car-dealing ploy has worked: he has torpedoed his rivals. Red Rum is his. 'It did the trick. We got him. I was delighted. And scared to death! Bar the one, it was six times more than I'd spent on any other horse in my life.'

> Bought for 6,000 guineas

Red Rum is led out and back to his box, but McCain has to stay in the ring a little longer, for he has orders to buy for Mr Rimmer, another patron of his – and at much more his sort of price – a horse of Ken Oliver's called The Tunku. (He's going to win with that, too, that season.) He buys him for 940 guineas and hurries round to the stable-yard where Red Rum is standing, waiting for his next move.

Anthony Gillam desolate

Anthony Gillam is hovering, desolate in Red Rum's box. 'Ginger' McCain said with genuine sadness, 'Poor old Tony looked so sick. He looked really choked. I felt very bad about it, because I knew how I would feel if I had to lose a nice horse like him.'

Gillam asked, 'You've bought him, have you?' He asked McCain what he was going to do with him. McCain said, 'Win a few races, I hope'. Between the two of them the phrase 'a Grand National horse' emerged and hung in the air over Red Rum's bright intelligent head. McCain said, 'That's what I bought him for'. Gillam began, 'I'd always thought. . . .'

McCain remembered the sadness of the scene. 'Poor Tony was very upset about losing the horse and he said so. He said it was Mrs Brotherton's decision to sell, not his. I felt very sorry for him – a bit guilty really. He was very honest and open, and told me what he knew about the horse.'

'Don't bash him on hard ground'

Gillam recalled, 'I told McCain about his feet. I said "Don't bash him on hard ground, because I don't think he'll stand up to it".'

And McCain remembered, 'He told me everything, how far on he was in his work and so on. And off Red Rum went home.'

Friends at the sale tried in vain to cheer up the miserable Gillam. No one there knew anything about the man McCain. Gillam did not even know what he looked like till he stepped into Red Rum's box. It is any trainer's dread that a horse which leaves his yard will improve so markedly in someone else's hands that his own deficiences as a trainer will be publicly laid bare. So Gillam's friends said to him in the grey and drab-red surroundings of the sales ring, 'Who's McCain? You've nothing to worry about there. Now if he'd gone to Walwyn, you'd have had sleepless nights. . . . But McCain!' exclaimed his friends, 'He's only got a few boxes behind a garage in some town!'

Anthony Gillam, however, was not reassured. That spring watching Aintree on the television he had had what he calls 'a premonition'. He watched a horse called Glenkiln run in the Topham Trophy. 'The horse ran a stormer. And I knew that horse. He'd been with the Olivers. I was thinking of buying him at one time, but we all thought he'd got a "leg". But this McCain had bought him for a Mr Le Mare and produced him to run in that Topham and to show such tremendous form. When I saw that night who McCain had bought Red Rum for, and read the name Le Mare, it all came back to me and I had this strange premonition again.' He knew then that McCain was not just a taxi driver, but what he could do – that he *would* do – well with the horse he had just lost.

Down in Wales the unhappy Sandra on her enforced holiday bought all the papers to find out whether her 'Rummy' had been sold. When she read the awful news she said to faithful Mr Brian Miles, 'Well, Brian, we'll get married now, and I'll get out of racing.'

'We'll get married now'

The sale of Red Rum broke Sandra's heart and finished her for racehorses for ever. It seemed a long time back to the days when schoolgirl Sandra, full of hope and happiness, rode up to kindly Mr Renton's place on her little pony Tammy.

27 'MY GOD! I'VE BOUGHT A LAME HORSE!'

Red Rum crossed more than the Pennines when he left Yorkshire for Lancashire and for his fifth trainer in seven years. He moved from a drowsy yard in the country's quiet green heart to a tiny stable converted from a brewer's yard behind McCain's used-car showroom in a town's bustling side-street. The back-windows of tightly embracing houses peer down into the little cobbled oblong and its solitary tree. Half a gear-change away buses stop and traffic whines and hums. A few clickey-clicks and rumbles further and the trains from Birkdale clank across the level-crossing. Red Rum had moved to the wrong side of the tracks. The straight run of the street is completely flat and lacking in perspective. The stables lie within an amble of the sea, and some of the cold washed sea-light is reflected in the skies above Southport. Birkdale feels itself a superior suburb, but you would not expect much to be trained there except budgerigars and – in its tiny gardens – runner-beans. Nothing about the length of Upper Aughton Road suggests even the passing of a livery stable nag; the existence of steeplechasers behind the traffic seems sur-realistic.

Billy Ellison

'Rummy' had changed his Sandra for a Liverpudlian lad. Miss Sandra Kendall of Ripon had tended and loved him for four years at Oxclose. Now Billy Ellison, born on August 8th, 1945, took over. He was just twenty-seven when Red Rum arrived in the yard. Billy, square of body, square of face with that mop of square dark hair and squeezed-up naughty eyes (but he has in fact corneal ulcer trouble) has become, through Red Rum, a nationally-known figure in the racing world. He admits frankly that he was for years 'a layabout', and has had his troubles, too, with the law. His parents were, as he says, 'Ordinary working-class people. Me father's a clerk and I was born very small. At fifteen I was only 6st 12lb, so people said, "Why don't you go to be a jockey?"' Doug Smith was a childhood hero: his life looked glamorous.

Billy rode the coal-merchant's pony, and hung around the local riding school. 'They helped me write to some trainers. I went off to Ron Barnes at Norley near Warring-ton. The Head Lad there was Johnny Handes, a little Irish bloke and very helpful. The first horse I ever looked after was an old horse called North Light. I used to run down to the village with a leading rein to meet the horses coming back from exercise. Then I'd be put up on North Light and Johnny would lead me back.'

Rode in four races

Such was the manner of young Billy Ellison's riding instruction. He 'did his two', stayed five years with Barnes and rode in four races. He was second in his first race – $1\frac{1}{4}$ miles on the flat at Redcar – riding Th' Boggart. 'Never forget it – jet-black horse – butterflies in me stomach – the owner had £100 each way on us at 8 to 1. I was beaten half a length. He give me a drink afterwards. But Ron Barnes told me off. He said I should've won. One season I was there we had twenty-three winners from fourteen horses!'

Billy was smitten by his first sight of jump racing. It was at Liverpool, where he had taken a horse he did, Cold Comfort, to win the seller there on the flat, the same sort of race for which Red Rum subsequently deadheated on his first sight of the famous steeplechasing track. 'I saw

Josh Gifford win there and it seemed much more fun watching a horse go for two miles over flights of hurdles than a five furlong flat race – if you drop your race-card in a flat race by the time you pick it up it's over! I liked the class of people with the jumpers too.'

So Billy went off to work for Frank Mason, who farmed at Little Budworth, near Tarporley in Cheshire, and had been training since 1936. 'Didn't go with the intention of riding. Actually I got married there for the first time.' He was married again in 1974, after a lively interval. For five months every summer Billy worked nightly in the bar of the local Pontin's Holiday Camp.

He used to ride out for Don McCain 'for a quid a morning when I was a bit of a layabout and he was just a permit trainer'. McCain interposed, 'One morning after the end-of-season party at Pontin's – it never stops for two or three days – Billy was late for First Lot. He arrived swaying and grey. I said "Don't ride that good horse!"' 'A quid a morning'

Billy grinned wickedly. 'Best thing in the world is that beach after a hangover! First time I rode on the sands I thought 'If we get run away with here it'll take six miles to pull up.' And I broke the horse down on the beach.

'I'd kept in touch with Mr McCain, so when I was separating from my wife and wanted to get back from Cheshire to Southport – 'cos it's close by home – I went up to him at Haydock races and asked him for a job. It was 1969, the first year he had a full licence.'

Billy was not only a barman but a boxer. He won the 8st 7lb class of the Northern stable lads competition at the Piccadilly Hotel, Manchester three years running from 1970 to 1972. He fought in the national semi-finals at Chelsea Barracks and was beaten one year in the final. 'Had a tooth split at Manchester. Rode out in the cold winds on the beach and got toothache, and got beaten by a lad of Ian Balding's – very stylish lad.' Billy admires style and dresses with it.

Don McCain supported him: 'Billy *murdered* that lad in the first two rounds – then he blew up!'

Billy was doing Glenkiln, the first horse McCain bought for Mr Le Mare in the hope of winning a 'National, so the young lad saw the elderly owner (who in his youth had been a bold lad, too) several times around the yard. 'I won "The Guinea for the Lad" from "*The Racehorse*" for Glenkiln,' said Billy rightly proud of the way he turns his horses out. 'We heard the Guv'nor was going to the sale to buy another 'National horse for Mr Le Mare, owing to 'Doing' Glenkiln old "Glen" not being qualified then.' Of which dire administrative blunder more later. . . .

'I'd just finished stables and I heard the horse-box arrive and Jackie Grainger, the Head Lad, walks into the yard with Red Rum. Aye! God! He did look super! An' I thought "I'd love to do that!"'

Derek Critchley, a nice young 'claiming' lad in the yard who held a jockey's licence, had been given several rides on Golden Blue, one of Billy's horses. Critchley had brought Red Rum back from Doncaster Sales and so it seemed that he would 'do' him. Billy said slyly, 'Derek was hopin' for a few more rides on Golden Blue, so I offered him Golden Blue back for me to do Red Rum.'

Under his care won £65,666

So it was that Billy Ellison came to do a horse which in his first two seasons under his care won twelve races and was placed five times from only nineteen starts and earned £65,666 for his extremely generous owner . . . Vincent Brooks from Fred Winter's yard, nicknamed 'the luckiest lad in racing' because he does Bula and Pendil, has had his position usurped.

Billy was thrilled with his swap. 'I knew the horse had some useful form, so next day I went across the street to Steve Makin, the bookie, and got all his form-books out and studied them.' As with a company's balance-sheets and profit figures, you can read a lot into and out of the form-book. Billy Ellison is a carefree optimist, who keeps coming up, bouncing. He had just manoeuvred young Critchley into handing over this smashing new horse. He devoured Red Rum's form with soaring enthusiasm. 'It was fair old form and tho' he'd cost six times more than any other horse in the yard I couldn't understand why he was so *cheap*!'

Robin Greenway

Two days later, the first time Red Rum came out of his box, everyone in the yard thought they knew. Robin Greenway (son of McCain's vet, Ted Greenway of Little Budworth, who has kindly contributed Red Rum's vital statistics shown in Chapter 39) came to the yard to ride out. He had ridden Glenkiln an easy winner at Cartmel in an amateur race at the very end of the previous season, and was due to ride him again shortly at Hexham.

Don McCain, overjoyed by his expensive new acquisition, put Robin Greenway up on Red Rum. Trainers with new horses are like children with new toys or boys with new girls: they need their friends to admire them. They walked down through the town to the beach.

'And as soon as we start to trot out on the beach,' says

McCain, still appalled in recollection of the scene, 'Red Rum is lame. Without any doubt at all, he is going short. I thought, "My God! I've bought a lame horse!" Yet his legs were like bars of iron. I felt *sick*. I shouted "Bugger off with him into the tide then!". The others worked and cantered. Red Rum just walked about in the sea. 'And when he came out of the water,' said McCain, fixing me intently to convince me of the miracle, '*he trotted sound!* Mind you,' McCain ended cautiously, 'horses do do that – with the cold water taking out the pain – and then get worse again after. But I think the horse has never been lame since, except the day after his first 'National when he'd struck into himself.'

Walked about in the sea

McCain still winces at the narrowness of that squeak. 'We just started to go steady with him. I said, "We'll take it more quietly". We've never trotted him on the roads from then on for two reasons. One, he's a bright fellow and he could slip. The other, he might jar his feet.'

Billy chipped in, 'He doesn't *like* jogging on roads. He'd *rather* walk. He's different on the beach. Down there he'll still give a buck and a kick.'

Miles away in Scotland the clever vet who had diagnosed Red Rum's foot trouble and prescribed with the physiotherapist the right cure for it in Yorkshire, marvels at the luck by which the horse, out of all the stables in Britain, happened on one by the seaside. He says bluntly, 'Red Rum would have been *unraceable* without treatment – I'm a great believer in ultra sonics, they're the thing of the future – but I was *not* happy when I saw the horse changing feet in the Scottish National, as if they still hurt him.' He said, 'That off-fore foot is *still* contracted and shallow. So if he wasn't going to continue our treatment, where could he get something like it? In the sea. Sea water is a great thing, cooling off after exercise, stimulating the circulation. . . .'

'Sea water is a great thing'

'Ginger' McCain had not known the well-kept secret about Red Rum's generally incurable pedalosteitis, though he had made, as we shall see, several enquiries via a friend for whom jockey Stack rode. McCain remembered though, as a child, watching those broken-down old horses pulling the shrimping-carts through the tide off Southport beach and returning after two summers miraculously sound. 'All cripples and crocks,' says McCain, 'and after a couple of seasons – perfect legs!'

Mrs Brotherton's son, discussing in the summer of 1974 the equally miraculous cure of Red Rum, made the point to a friend, 'Of all the hundreds of people who could have bought him, it just happened to be a man who had only the beach to train on!'

And Mrs Sandra Miles that same summer recalled a single event when old Bobby Renton was training Red Rum, the significance of which was ignored at the time, because only in retrospect has it become pike-staff plain.

Redcar Sands'Once – and only once – when "Rummy" was at Oxclose, he went to Redcar Sands. He went with two other horses. Bobby had had a strip properly harrowed by the people on Redcar racecourse. We saddled up on the racecourse and rode down to the sands, Tommy Stack, my brother Walter and me. Mr Renton stood on the beach to watch us. We cantered two miles down, then turned to gallop the two miles back. I was in front. At first Tommy kept calling out to me several times, "Sandra! Can't you go any faster?" I shouted back "I can't! I can't!" But,' said Sandra, eyes amazed, 'When I got to the end of the gallop I was that far in front that I'd pulled up, turned round and *walked back to Mr Renton*, before the other two horses had reached him!'

Everyone had been instantly astonished by this extraordinary performance by Red Rum. It is, of course, now plain that the horse relishes galloping on sand, that he needs time to warm up (Sandra had guessed this in her criticism of some of his jockeys) and that the further he goes the more powerfully does he travel. Would 5 miles be too far for him to race? It is obvious now that he required miles more cantering first and then twice as much galloping on sand than he would ever find on ordinary gallops. It is probably true, too, that he delights in the wide spaces of the beach, that his spirit rejoices by the wild wintry sea, and that he works phenomenally well there because of it.

Soon forgottenHe never went back to the sea again during all those four years at Oxclose. It was difficult to get to Redcar sands. It took one and a half hours in Pickersgill's horse box. The amazing gallop that Red Rum had done there was soon forgotten, not to be remembered until a new season of fabulous victories had come, and the racing world was asking 'What has this man McCain, this taxi-driver, done to make Red Rum so marvellous?'

Primarily it is the beach and the sea. And if Don McCain, for whatever reason, such as the need to expand his stables, had to move Red Rum from his miles of soft sand and the cold splashing sea, then I do not believe that the horse would be as good again.

28 'I WAS ABSOLUTELY BRILLIANT WITH A CATAPULT'

The man McCain, whom hardly anyone in racing knew when he bought Red Rum, has lived nearly all his life in Birkdale. He was conceived just over the road from his present stables and born five hundred yards away. Bar his army service and jobs with horses in Cheshire, he has never moved away. Born a townsman, brought up in streets, he has yearned all his life to be a countryman. His wife Beryl surmises, 'He'd really have liked to be a gamekeeper.'

He is not sure whether his blood is originally Scots or Irish, but something in it, as often happens in the urbanised citizens of our island, yearns for nature and country things and animals. Horses are McCain's magic carpet out of the grey streets into the green fields. 'My life's ambition is to live in the country. I've always wanted to. I've never had a lot of opportunity to – getting a living – but I have a thing about badly wanting to own some land of my own.' He adds with that steely intent of purpose: 'And I will do.'

The yearning did not come directly from his parents. His father worked for forty years in the despatch department of Marshall & Snelgrove's. 'He plays about with pigeons,' said 'Ginger' affectionately, who used to race pigeons himself. Bill and Sally McCain live in Liverpool Road, Birkdale, and mind 'Ginger' and Beryl McCain's two children Joanne and Donald when needed. 'My mother,' said 'Ginger', 'still treats me like a small child.' He has two sisters (one a nursing sister at Eastbourne) and one younger brother. 'Father comes back after the war from the air force and, of course, there's another brother, sixteen years after me!'

Birkdale still enjoys the ranking of being Southport's smartest suburb – those wide and leafy avenues and richly garden-girt Victorian houses still wear slightly superior smiles. But McCain says dourly, 'Some of Birkdale's smart right enough. It's also had the muckiest slums ever.'

'Ginger', born on 21st September, 1930 – the year of Red Rum's breeder – was a schoolboy in the war. With his father away in the RAF and his mother working on munitions – 'Sometimes days, sometimes nights, obviously

McCain's magic carpet

they didn't have a lot of control. And with the war on, if you didn't go to school, they didn't chase you very hard.'

'Ginger' spent most of his schooldays with dogs. 'I've always had a whippet or decent coursing dog – Waterloo Cup's only just down the road, eight miles away. I used to go there as a boy as a beater for 7/6d a day.' He did a tremendous amount of poaching: 'Pheasants, rabbits and hares – mainly with dogs and I was absolutely brilliant with a catapult! We made our own.'

Wartime Lancashire

In wartime Lancashire horses and ponies of every sort trotted down every street. The grey roads of Birkdale clattered with tradesman's carts. 'The Cooperative Dairies had about 40 horses on the road. The laundry had two dozen horses. The dustcarts were pulled by heavy horses. The tradesmen, the butchers and bakers, had tremendously smart little outfits.' McCain's mind's eye sees those spinning wheels, the bits a-jangle, and he hears again the squeak and creak of leather harness.

His grandfather drove two horses in a cart delivering goods for a provision company. When 'Ginger' was thirteen, his grandfather had an accident, and the schoolboy played truant to do his job. 'It was the horses that attracted me. I used to ride them bareback down to the blacksmith's forge and in the summer we used to ride them round the fields.' It sounds like a picture of Edwardian England. But it was only thirty years before Red Rum won his first Grand National.

The pony never came

Young 'Ginger' longed to have a pony of his own. His grandfather was always saying, 'I'll buy you a pony.' So the boy built a shed for the pony at the bottom of the garden. The pony never came. His grandfather's promise was not kept. In McCain's voice now there lingers still the trace of an acrid tang. His face suddenly takes on its grim, forbidding, fortress look. Much of our adult motivation springs from childhood's frustration. Much of McCain's burning – and often financially crippling – desire to own horses, sprang from his grandfather's broken promise and the little empty shed waiting in vain at the bottom of the garden.

Young McCain took lots of jobs: 'milk boy on the milkcart, perch-boy in the theatre working the arc-lamps, and worked in a confectioners where I hated every minute. And I made a living fishing and poaching – which I loved.' A family friend started a riding-school and offered 'Ginger' lessons. 'I think I was only on the leading-rein once, and then I went on the beach.' So he must have had a knack.

He was very keen, and soon advanced into a good young rider, for when he was fifteen a local butcher asked 'Ginger' to ride his horses. 'Arty Edwards was his name – bald-headed fellow and a tremendous character. He had show-jumpers and did a bit of dealing.'

'Ginger' jumped Mr Edwards' horses in the cemetery behind the butcher's stables. 'He had a sharp little pony which could really stop. One day he stopped with me so quick he put me off right into a gravestone. I was knocked out dizzy, and I came round feeling a bit sick lying on the gravel by this gravestone. I can remember this "*Rest in Peace*" bit gradually looming into focus just above my head.' *'Rest in peace'*

Arty Edwards used to enter his butcher's van and hackney horse called The Colonel at all the district shows which then abounded. He had seen a hackney show-jumping, so he said to young 'Ginger', 'Here, you get up on The Colonel.' 'Ginger' said, 'The super old horse had never been sat on in his life. I climbed up and he just stood there, trembling. We got him going finally – a tremendous ride, but only trotting! He wouldn't canter.'

McCain's first sight of a racehorse was riding out with Frank Speakman's stables near Tarporley. The place remained a sort of dream. Years later he would drive his wife around that part of Cheshire, breathing it in and trying to infuse her with the delight that countryside and those horses had once granted him. He schooled an old hunter over hurdles with them on an airfield. And then quite suddenly he lost all interest in horses. He bought a motor bike and started racing it. He spent all his time in the army on motor bikes – 'I enjoyed every minute of it and thought seriously of signing on'. Lost all interest

But he left the Army when his time was up, and decided to spend the summer at home 'fiddling my time away. But they got me a job via the local labour exchange – in a wallet factory.' Sometimes a phrase uttered in kindness intending to open a door to a happy future, unintentionally becomes instead a portent of doom (if you recognise it) and a sudden glimpse of hell. If you observe it, and turn the other way, the course of your life is altered.★

★ 'Ivor,' said my chairman to me across his vast desk after my second year in the City (I was training horses before the office and re-writing my first novel during it). 'You are doing well. In forty years you will be sitting here in my place.' Uttered as a promise of delight, the words fell about me like the closing prison-house. I resolved on that instant to escape. Within weeks I had left to join a newspaper.

'A job for life'

So it happened to McCain at the wallet factory. 'Look after this job,' the man said to him, 'And you've got a job for life.'

McCain recalled, 'I thought what the hell's it got to do with him – the thought of a job for life in a wallet factory was diabolical!' He saw the gloom through that door and immediately noticed, for such is life, the opening of another. 'On the Saturday morning someone came to the house and said Frank Speakman wanted a man to work in his stables. I had my bags packed and I was gone to Tarporley that afternoon. I never gave notice to the wallet factory. I was working with horses again for £3 a week and my keep. And when I was twenty-one I got £3 10s. because I rode schooling. I did three horses in a small yard of sixteen to eighteen horses, picking up the racing side of things from the senior boys. I was as happy then as I have ever been in my life.'

Working with horses again

He was not too old at twenty-one – for he is a romantic – to have heroes to worship. 'Dick Francis and Tim Molony used to ride for us. They were so special to me. I'd been around a bit, but I still thought this was all absolutely marvellous.'

Then his weight beat him. 'I was 11st 7lb to 12 st. Too big and getting bigger. . . . So I went a mile down the road to Mrs Chambers who owned a hunting and point-to-pointing stable.'

He learned a lot there about horse management from the stud groom, old Jack Cook then over seventy, who had been stud groom to a Duke of Westminster. 'Marvellous old fellow, rather like Pickwick, very round, very red face. He always wore a black apron, breeches and a stock. "Cooky" always said he'd more or less trained Tipperary Tim, because the trainer was sick a long time.'

'I was happy enough there,' said McCain, 'For a time. . . .'

Away from racing

At this vital point in his life McCain was rising twenty-three and the course of his life was veering away from racing. He could never be a jockey. He was too heavy now even to work in racing stables as a lad. He might have jogged along in the hunting world a little longer when something happened, half way through his second season at Mrs Chambers which booted him, temporarily, out of the horse world all together. 'I got into a bit of trouble with a girl and came home and got a job working for a local taxi firm.' 'Ginger' McCain is a tall, dashing-looking fellow now. He was certainly a gay dog then.

McCain, driving his taxi, missed the horses, but he was

never bored. 'I was meeting people all the time and getting tips. I could always go out with a pound in my pocket.' Then his firm decided to close. McCain borrowed some money – 'I took the car out on HP, got a telephone, went in with a friend, and took over.'

To anyone with only a casual interest in horses McCain's sudden switch of jobs would seem certain to have put him out of the racing world for ever. But if you are as hooked on horses as some people are on more harmful things, then you simply cannot do without them. Driving a taxi, too, may seem to combine oddly with owning a racehorse, let alone training one. McCain did not think so. If he could not work with racehorses, he resolved to buy one.

Driving a taxi

So, in addition to the taxi, he now acquired his first racehorse. 'I couldn't go back to riding rubbishy horses.' The horse, Scottish Humour, was one he had 'done' at Frank Speakman's. The horse had been placed on the flat and over hurdles. He would turn out later to be a half-brother to the great Irish 'chaser Flyingbolt, who one year was challenging his stablemate Arkle. But Flyingbolt was not yet around, and his elder half-brother Scottish Humour had not only 'got a leg', but was tubed. McCain, taxi-driver, and now taxi-owner bought him from Mr Speakman for £25 to include the tube, a sweat rug and a head collar.

That was the start of McCain the trainer. And as to it being an odd job to share with taxi-driving, time would splendidly reveal that it was only by driving a taxi that McCain could meet and talk to rich men who, captive audiences, must listen to his passion for racing and perhaps echo it. One of these, he imagined dimly, might one day entrust him with his One Good Horse. It was the vaguest of lovely dreams: the rich man, the shared interest, the faith, the purchase, the winning of the Grand National. . . . He did not know that one such elderly person was really living a few furlongs away from him in a big house on the good side of the railway line, and nursing a sixty-year-long dream of winning the Grand National.

McCain the trainer

McCain had to make a beginning. No one who subsequently became a trainer of fame, can have started any lower at racing's roots than with one tubed, broken-down old racehorse in a rented stable in a unlikely street. McCain rented a box in Westbourne Road. Months passed, the horse's leg improved and McCain thought 'Why not run him?'. He applied for a Permit to train and got it. He had told himself he had wanted a racehorse to *ride*, but the wish to race one was nudging him on.

He started his racing career in officially unrecognised 'flapping' races, the way Brian Fletcher began beyond the Pennines. McCain's jockey was a local man, Jackie Grainger, now his head lad, born in Southport in 1917 and who, like 'Ginger', had been a lad at Frank Speakman's out at Tiverton, near Tarporley. With Jackie Grainger on board, Scottish Humour set out for the unauthorised race-meetings. 'They were just tracks on the outside of football fields,' says McCain, still somewhat sheepish about those activities, involvement in which technically bars you from performing under the Rules of Racing.

Jackie Grainger

The flapping races were run in heats and on a track beyond Manchester the horse and Jackie Grainger '*murdered* the opposition. Somebody started squealing about professional horses and professional jockeys. We'd had a few bob on,' says 'Ginger'. 'I was standing on the top of the gents toilet, which was a tin shed, to watch the final. Jackie wins it and never even stops. He gallops up to me and roars "Come on! Let's get off! Else we're in trouble!" I go to move. And these bloody miners are after me and the tin roof flew off the shed. . . . Somehow we got to the box and the horse into the box and off we went – never drew the money or anything.'

Jackie Grainger had been through the normal racing mill. He did fifteen years with Mr Sonny Hall at Russley Park in Wiltshire, whose academy of gentlemen-riders included Captain Neville Crump, Lord Mildmay and Major Peter Cazalet. Jackie had a few rides 'chasing and rode in India in the war when he was with the RASC – "a few winners over hurdles on hard dirt outside Calcutta!"'

Nearly killed

He looks like a charming gypsy: wrinkled face, deep twinkling eyes and a scarf knotted round his sun-tanned wind-burned neck. When he married he went out of racing, looking for more security. He was nearly killed driving a cattle-waggon in a head-on collision with another. He is still held together with five steel pins. He drove the box part-time for McCain. 'Then Don asked me to come as Head Lad.' He accepted cheerfully and went to Doncaster 'to fetch Red Rum home.' Jackie Grainger has a splendid gravelly Lancashire voice. He added sardonically, 'When I first saw Red Rum I thought he was too good lookin' to leave Mrs Brotherton's!'

Old, tubed Scottish Humour was the first of many racehorses he was going to ride work on for McCain. Frank Speakman's bad-legged reject was the first racehorse

'Ginger' McCain owned and, if you count 'flapping' round football-pitches, his first winner. The horse taught him several things of lasting value (there's no better way to start than with cheap and dicey horses – you have to be good to keep them sound), and literally by accident one essential pre-requisite about using the beach for galloping. If this accident had not befallen him, he might never have struck upon the secret of training on sand. When McCain was getting the horse ready to run under Rules a friend came to gallop him on the beach. 'In those days we didn't harrow the sand first.' McCain watched his horse galloping with those of another local permit holder. Then he saw him suddenly falter, drop right out and pull up. The horse had partially severed his tendon on a piece of broken glass left on the beach. 'He never quite came right after that,' says McCain. 'And he was a grand sort of horse and a damn good ride.'

'We didn't harrow the sand first'

From that day on McCain always harrowed a strip to clear it of dangerous débris. And so it turned out – for such is the luck of this story – that the deeply harrowed strip obviated other disadvantages of galloping on unprepared, hard, ungiving, wearying damp sand. . . .

29 'I GOT A CRUSH ON HIM WHEN HE WAS DOWN THE STABLES'

If Don McCain's training had not hit the double jackpot in 1973 and 1974 and put his name among the famous, it would have been a justifiable criticism to say that from 1952 onwards he was trying to participate in a rich man's sport without the money, the amenities, the contacts, the background, or any real hope of success. McCain, however, even when occasionally broke, went steadily on, hoping.

Additionally, because he had perforce to buy other people's rejects with money he hardly had, he found himself with problems with every horse. He had to work swiftly to cure them too, for each bowl of corn was coming painfully out of his pocket. A young man from a racing background might spend years as pupil to a grand trainer with a yard full of good, sound horses, without learning as much as McCain did in months with his equine jetsam. Nor would they have heard whistling behind them the sharp crack of poverty's whip.

Equine jetsam

McCain the taxi-driver had put in years with horses of sorts. When he won at the 'flapping' meeting Anthony Gillam was five years old, Tim Molony was champion jockey and was eight years away from starting training, and Tommy Stack was a 7-year-old in Co. Kerry. Experience McCain had, successes very few; but hope abounding. The whole edifice of steeplechasing in Britain rests upon the under-financed but optimistic and resilient shoulders of hundreds of little permit trainers like the Don McCain of the years between 1952 and 1969. Money is being spent on horses which their loving owner-trainers cannot afford. Like McCain, they are learning the hard way, striving towards some humble target like their local selling race one Bank Holiday: (total cost of three years' endeavours: £3,500; value of race £190). Like McCain, they are hoping for the One Good Horse, though only one of the hundreds once in a decade will find it. Without hope, no racing.

Beryl McCain

Like McCain, struggling owner-trainers will run into trouble from wives who believe, as Beryl McCain did, that furniture and food and somewhere to live are rather more important than buying and keeping clapped-out racehorses, everyone else's discards, who cost cruelly hard cash to keep.

Beryl met 'Ginger' when she was sixteen and says she 'Had a crush on him'. They met at the local riding school, Miss Walsh's in Southport, less than a quarter-mile from their present home between the motor show-room and the stable-yard. When Beryl left the local technical college (doing secretarial work) she got a job in an accountant's office very near Birkdale station. Outside the station sat 'Ginger' in his taxi. And so she noticed him.

'The very first time I spoke to him was in a friend's house. I said to my friend, "There's that fellow that goes down to the stables, do you dare me to say hello to him?". She said, "yes, go on". So I said "hello" and he said "hello, there", and he'll tell you now he thought "who's that cheeky young girl?" I got a crush on him when he was down the stables – all the kids used to act the fool!' Miss Kath Walsh was, says Beryl, 'A bit of a figure-head, all the children around looked up to her.'

Beryl's father, strangely enough, had been in the motor-business himself with *his* father. 'But when the war came, he panicked and sold the business and had to do ordinary factory work.'

One day Beryl was riding a friend's thoroughbred mare and 'Ginger' and his taxi-partner, Jeff Langhorn (who had once been head lad in a racing-stable), saw her go past. The friend could not afford to keep the mare herself, so Jeff and 'Ginger' offered to put the mare in training for Beryl's friend under 'Ginger''s permit. Young Beryl continued to ride her. 'I had to sit as still as a mouse on her back when she started to get filled up with corn, and she was so headstrong she'd make your hands bleed!' The mare ran unsuccessfully over hurdles and fences, but enabled Beryl to see a lot of 'Ginger'. 'We weren't engaged, and my parents were still rather against him. When he picked me up, he used to just hoot, and I'd run down the path. Oh, there were lots of trials and tribulations!' **Jeff Langhorn**

Jeff Langhorn and 'Ginger' then split up their taxi business, though they remain very close friends and neighbours. Jeff runs the grocer's shop in 'Ginger''s street. His wife, with deceptive quiet, drives her private hire car from Southport to Bournemouth and back again in a day, occasionally dropping off authors at Oxford en route.

'Ginger' took the taxis to Miss Kath Walsh's riding-stables and she became his new partner. Beryl comments, 'I was hoping to get engaged, and Ginger kept wanting to buy horses – and he didn't really have any money.'

Quite against Beryl's wishes – 'I was *cross*' – they drove one evening to a wierd house near Coventry to buy a mare – 'terribly poor' – from two strange ladies called the Misses Smith. The ladies, seeing a photograph in the paper of a mare of Don McCain's falling at Liverpool, wrote to tell him they had bred her and wondered if he'd like to buy anything else. 'But off we trooped to this farm. It was a strange place,' says Beryl shuddering, 'no electric light, no toilet, only a chamber-pot with a lantern in a freezing cold room. But they persuaded "Ginger" to buy this mare Kara Valley for fifty pounds.' **'I was *cross*'**

She was put in a stable on Duke Street, an overflow of the riding-stables. Jackie Grainger saw her 'napping' one day – 'She'll be a live wire when she gets fit,' he warned them.

Beryl was made responsible for exercising her. She was working in the Borough Architect's Office, so got up at six, bicycled to the stables, rode Kara Valley, bicycled back, worked all day at her desk, and then every evening went down to the riding school in order to see 'Ginger' who was running his taxis. Beryl pressed the idea of getting engaged. 'He wasn't very keen on the idea of marriage,' she says. Kara Valley became a portent. 'If she doesn't run well at Haydock,' declared 'Ginger' McCain with more realism than romance, 'we'll get engaged.' Horses now, as then, rule his heart. It is the major reason he is good with them.

'We'll get engaged'

Kara Valley ran poorly. 'Ginger' was as good as his proposal. 'Right,' he said, 'we'll get engaged on Grand National Day, 1959.'

'So,' says Beryl, 'We went to the 'National, and had an engagement party that evening. He had a job to get the money together to buy an engagement ring – I chose it myself, he was never any good at that sort of thing. And I said to him "when'll we get married?" He said "Two years", thinking it a long time off, "we'll get married on Grand National Day, 1961".'

This involvement with the Grand National may seem too good to be true. It is an element, of course, of what old Bobby Renton called Red Rum's 'fairy tale'. But there are two significant factors. First, it had been in McCain's mind from childhood, as it had been in Le Mare's, 'to have a go at the 'National'. The race, dominating their dreams, became the milestone of the year. Secondly – and this surprises southerners – in North-west England there *is* only one race all year and that is the Grand National. The Derby down at Epsom is ranked a distance behind.

Steve Makin

The local bookie, Steve Makin, balding with huge, high eyebrows and gapped teeth, knows that only too well. He paid out £2,600 in bets down the street the Monday after Red Rum's first 'National, and £50,000 altogether. 'He's the greatest horse in the world,' he says grinning as if he'd just come from a painful bout with the dentist. 'But I just wish he lived somewhere else. Up here, the 'National, not the Derby, is *the* race of the year.'

He adds, 'First bit of intelligence I've shown for sometime was to back him myself – £20 at 20 to 1 for the '74 'National. And,' eyes agog in June, 1974, 'I've had a lot of enquiries already about him at 10 to 1 for the '75 'National.'

Looking back on his engagement 'Ginger' recalls, 'I thought two years would be a long time, and then it slipped by, and all of a sudden you're under orders!' They'd got engaged and watched Oxo win the 'National. They got married and watched Nicolaus Silver* win it. They spent their honeymoon in Newmarket. 'Kara Valley was a brood mare by then, and she'd bred a foal,' says 'Ginger'. 'We just got more and more involved with horses. At the time we were broke. We used to live on my money and save Beryl's. But I somehow always got a horse given to me!'

Beryl's parents had not approved of her marriage – 'Dad is deaf and very hard to get through to. They didn't think "Ginger" was good enough for me – only a taxi-driver, which was no ambitious job. I didn't care, because I thought so much of him. I believed in him.'

Horses came and went. They were living in a couple of rooms on £5 a week. The flat cost £2 10s. 'We lived on 'Ginger''s odd silver that came in from taxi-ing every day.' They looked after an old horse called Home Chief, owned by a friend who held the trainer's permit, ran him at Cartmel and he won, and so became another unrecognised 'first winner' for Don McCain. After Beryl and Don had been married for eighteen months Miss Walsh decided to end the taxi partnership. 'We panicked,' says Beryl. 'We had nowhere to go. Coming back up the road from the riding-school there was this little showroom for sale, about 15 foot wide and 20 foot deep with a couple of rooms over it. They wanted £2,500 for it.'

Beryl had been saving her wages at the rate of £40 a month. She had £1,400 saved – 'no other security.' The estate agent said, 'We'll go and see the manager of the Westminster Bank in Manchester. He's a man who judges a person himself, whether he'll back you.' Beryl says, 'And he did. He thought we were sincere and would make a go of it.'

They obtained the loan and took the place (it adjoins where they now live), and started the taxi-business from there with very little furniture. 'We were working all the hours God makes,' says Beryl, 'driving those taxis, building up the clientèle . . . then "Ginger" got this enquiry about San Lorenzo . . .' Beryl sighed deeply. It had nearly meant the parting of their ways.

(* The author had been underbidder for the horse at Dublin four months earlier.)

San Lorenzo belonged to a corn merchant in Southport. He had once been a good horse winning races for Neville Crump and George Owen and owned by Major Ainscough. But he was now old, and with bad legs. He was in Ireland with Aubrey Brabazon. The corn merchant had intended to have his old horse put down, but now offered him instead to 'Ginger' McCain. Beryl said, 'We can't afford it'.

'We can't afford it'

'Ginger' said, 'Well, I'm going to have it'.

Beryl remembers, 'I tried everything, but as much as I argued – he was adamant. I remember sitting by the fire with my head in my hands and crying. I tried telling "Ginger" that if that horse came, I'd go.'

'Ginger' said bluntly, 'All right. Get your bags packed. He's on the boat.'

Beryl reflects, 'I don't think I could have left. The horse arrived. I didn't speak to 'Ginger' for a week. I wouldn't go to see the horse. He was kept in an old stable at the back of a pub.'

Eventually Beryl went to see San Lorenzo. She is a generous-hearted woman and bears no grudges. She says with real pleasure, 'He was a nice bright bay, a super animal.' He was headed – where else? – but for Don McCain's beloved Liverpool.

Thirteen hard, depressing, failing years after Mr D. M. McCain of Southport first took out his permit to train, the 14-year-old broken-down San Lorenzo turns out at Liverpool on Saturday, 2nd January, 1965.

Beryl and 'Ginger', still struggling along, are coming up to their fourth wedding anniversary.

On the evening before the race, 'Ginger' and Beryl picked up one of their regular customers, a Guinness-drinking clairvoyant called Suzy, whom they used to collect from a pub every night at twenty-past-ten. That evening Suzy said, '"Ginger", I think you're going to have a winner'.

'Ginger' declared, 'If the horse wins, Suzy, you can have free drinks all night'.

'Free drinks all night'

Beryl had been out with a friend to an Indian restaurant in Manchester and felt so desperately ill on the day of the race that she thought she would miss it.

'Ginger' had another type of problem. Normally he put an amateur up on his horses to save paying the jockey's fee. This time a professional, Robin Langley, asked McCain if he could ride old San Lorenzo in the selling 'chase. McCain borrowed a fiver from a friend in a pub to pay the fee. And San Lorenzo, disputing the lead to the 7th fence in the

Burscough Selling Handicap Steeplechase of £192 run over 2m 80 yds and off at 12.45 pm, went ahead on the flat and won, hard-ridden, by half a length.

'He trotted up,' declares McCain. And there, for posterity, is Red Rum's trainer's first official winner. The name of the race oddly foreshadowed Red Rum. It is at Burscough that he spends his summer holidays.

He trotted up

Successful trainers start in different ways. Fame has a thousand beginnings. But can any other trainer have started after thirteen years of failures with one selling 'chase winner? Would not the Average Man, beloved by doctrinaires, have years ago given up what must have seemed, after even a few seasons, a hopeless, ridiculous struggle? But McCain, like our hero, was made of tougher metal. As Noel Le Mare had been taught as a child, as Red Rum had also been learning the hard way and as 'Ginger' McCain was finally to prove, it's a question of 'Try, try, try again'.

No one, however, over those early years, was more sorely tried than young Mrs Beryl McCain.

30 'YOU'RE STARVING YOUR WIFE AND KIDS ALMOST – THAT'S HORSES FOR YOU'

Empty though the horse side proved, their motor business improved. There was a little money now to buy the odd 'banger' for resale at a profit. But a succession of bad old horses came and went, driving Beryl to distraction as 'Ginger' was driven to hope. They quarrelled. They went to sales and Beryl sat across the ring, crossing her fingers and praying 'Ginger' wouldn't get the animal for which he was bidding.

He went to Ascot sales, and rang Beryl on the way home. She said immediately, 'You've bought a horse, haven't you?' When he said, 'Yes', she put the telephone down.

He had paid 340 guineas for a huge horse called Caspian

by Crepello. He remembers the call. 'When she rang off, I muttered "Well, sod you!" And then I had to drive all the way back from Oxford thinking of the slating I was going to get.

'It's been a struggle all the time,' says Don McCain. 'Beryl's wanted a home – which she's quite entitled to. She's wanted to live comfortably. But that's all you've got,' McCain bursts out, 'if you've got nothing else.' He means the dreams. He justifies himself, 'If you're young you can stand a bit of hardship.' He justifies his pursuit of success: 'Caspian was second first time out at Ludlow and a fellow offered me £1,000 for him, and I, silly bugger, didn't take it.'

'A fellow offered me £1000 for him'

The horse never again gets placed. Beryl, against her inclinations, becomes pregnant. She was still working for the Borough Architect by day and riding out in the morning. The horses were out in rented stables on a farm. Beryl had been 'doing' the horse and towing the trailer, and at one stage when she was running a horse at Uttoxeter she stayed in very humble digs: 'I heard all these hob-nailed boots clumping up and down the stairs and there, next morning, were all these navvies with string round their pants.'

'Nobody dared talk to me about the baby. I didn't want to know. I wanted the freedom to go racing, to go on riding out.' She was five months pregnant before she saw a doctor, and when six months pregnant she was still riding. 'I found my balance was going a bit.' She rode out, too, for Mick James, an ex-jockey who had been badly smashed up. A big horse of James' ran away with the pregnant Beryl. 'This horse took off with me. I couldn't do anything. I could see this five-bar gate or some sheep-wire and a ditch and I didn't know what to head her at. She wouldn't bend. Six inches off the wire, she stopped dead and I went clean over her head and into the ditch. I was soaked through.' Apart from the wetting, she was unscathed.

Desperate days

There were other desperate days. 'Ginger' took Caspian to run at Doncaster in November. 'Beryl is seven or eight months pregnant, but she insists on coming. We take the car we used for taxi-ing and tow Caspian in a trailer. In the race he breaks down on *both* forelegs! On the way home over the Pennines there's a blizzard blowing and traffic piling up over Woodhead. I've got this trailer at the back and every time going round Woodhead, I'm not quite making it. The wheels are spinning. I couldn't see ten yards in front of me through the snow. I've got a broken-down horse in the back and I've got a heavily pregnant woman in front. And I think, 'What the *hell* am I doing this for? What the *hell's* it all for?".'

From then till Glenkiln there were terrible times. Times when, as 'Ginger' says, 'Everything had gone wrong and you're starving your wife and kids almost.' He adds, 'That's horses for you!'

'That's horses for you!'

The ray of light was still the hope that one day they'd get the 'One Good Horse'. They used to drive out to Cheshire to look at Eric Cousins' stables, to have tea and goggle at his lovely horses and dream of what it might be like. Beryl remembers, '"Ginger" used to talk about beautiful places. He said it needed only one good horse to get a place like that. I didn't understand what he meant. But he had the foresight to know. He'd seen it happen.'

McCain was still hoping to meet that someone who would give him his public chance. On several Saturday evenings he had the pleasant job of driving a charming and sprightly old gentleman from his comfortable house in Birkdale to the Prince of Wales Hotel and then to bring him home. They talked horses and racing together. 'Ginger' was desperate now to find someone to pay him to train. He had bought a horse called Cambuslang at Doncaster. Beryl was so furious she would not speak to him all the way home. 'We just hadn't the money to pay for it. But "Ginger" always seemed eventually to find the money to meet the cheque.'

It took seventeen years from 'Ginger' McCain's first permit to train for himself until 1969 when he first had official paying patrons and could apply for a Licence to train publicly. Even then his misfortunes were enough to knock a lesser man not just out of the ring, but out of the business. In his first public season he took three horses to Bangor-on-Dee. The first runner finished half way back. The second, of which they had the highest hopes, jumped only two hurdles, dropped out and had to be pulled up. (It transpired later that it had a 'soft palate'.) McCain was summoned before the stewards, who included Lord Leverhulme and Robin McAlpine, and asked – before he could run his third horse – how he could explain this flop. 'Ginger' couldn't. He 'felt sick, choked and said so'. The day had cost him so far with transport, entries and jockeys' fees about £50. He was sent out. The Stewards' Secretary said kindly to him, 'Don't worry'.

Summoned before the stewards

He went out to his jockey for his third horse, Robin Langley, told him of his abrasive encounter with the

Stewards and said 'Now for God's sake put up a good show on this one'.

And at the second fence the horse ducked out through the wing. . . .

Eric Cousins, to help 'Ginger', sent him a horse called Bardolino. 'Ginger' persuaded Mr Le Mare one Saturday evening to buy both Cambuslang and Bardolino. 'They were cheap horses,' said McCain, 'a couple of hundred pounds or something.' They were disasters. Cambuslang had a heart complaint and ran very badly at Liverpool for Mr Le Mare. Bardolino, having run second in a decent handicap, broke down so badly that he had to be put down. Cambuslang was given away. 'So I thought,' said 'Ginger' McCain cast back into outer darkness again, 'That that was Mr Le Mare gone for ever.'

'They were cheap horses'

He was sure of it. Rival trainers of experience, rivals with success, lay everywhere in wait. Rich and elderly gentlemen with a passion for racing find it remarkably easy to attract potential trainers. A horse called Busty Hill had been bought for Le Mare in Ireland. Dour Alex Kilpatrick from Collingbourne Ducis down in Wiltshire had bought Furore II for Mr Le Mare and the horse had sailed home in a 3-mile 'chase at nearby Haydock carrying top weight. 'I thought I'd had my chance,' said McCain mournfully, 'and that it had gone.'

'Ginger' still taxied Mr Le Mare

'Ginger' still taxied Mr Le Mare about and they would still chat about horses. 'But it was never suggested that I should have another horse for him.'

The unfortunate McCain, in his first year as a public trainer, achieved a solitary winner. There can have been few worse starts. Nor had earlier intimations blossomed. Mr David Rosenfield, 'a wealthy fellow', as 'Ginger' puts it, 'with some good horses with Eric Cousins had suggested that if I got a public licence he might send me a couple of horses. But he didn't'.

Worse still – and the biggest blow to any struggling trainer's budget and morale – one of his new owners removed his horses. Mr Frank Tyldesley, a builder from Llandudno, had two horses with 'Ginger' McCain. One horse 'did a tendon' the first day McCain took him schooling. The other, Ashgate, had two runs for experience. Both went home to their owner's place for their summer holidays, and never came back.

'I don't think,' says 'Ginger' frankly, 'that Mr Tyldesley had any confidence in me as a trainer. Which would be fair enough in those times.' It was five years before he won his first Grand National. The first season's one winner, was followed the next season by no winners at all. In McCain's third season he achieved two winners. It was now nearly twenty years since McCain had taken out his first permit to train. The record was worse than dismal: it seemed forlorn. But still McCain was not disheartened. He still kept on trying.

One trainer's misfortune is almost invariably another trainer's gain. McCain had now not so much a change of luck, as a peep of daylight. Opportunity belied its adage. In the shape of Mr Noel Le Mare it now knocked twice. His good horse Furore II had broken down. He was, as 'Ginger' McCain put it, 'a bit fed up'. The McCains, furthermore, had a staunch ally in Mr Le Mare's household and at his elbow. Mrs Doris Solomon and her late husband had been close friends of Mr Le Mare and his late wife. Death had diminished the foursome to a trio and now to a pair. The attractive Mrs Solomon, mother of a judge, had moved from her position on the sofa facing the Le Mares' fireplace to the vacated arm-chair facing his. She calls him with affection 'Pop'. They share, among many pleasant things like cheerful gin drinking, a mordant sense of humour, a support of things Lancastrian, and a dislike of the idle. Both admired the struggles of their taxi-driver.

A peep of daylight

Mrs Solomon used to keep in touch with the embattled McCains. She would say 'Come and have a chat with Mr Le Mare. I think he might buy another horse'.

'Ginger' kept at it. In November, 1971 he put an advertisement in the *Sporting Life* under Box 308 seeking a horse qualified for the Grand National. He got one viable reply from, coincidentally, another motor-dealer. Alfred Flannigan of Station Garage, Berwick-on-Tweed offered McCain Fair Vulgan for £5,000. It was too much.

'Ginger' kept at it

In addition, and to Beryl's agitation, 'Ginger' kept combing through the Doncaster sales catalogues. Sensing one evening Mr Le Mare's disappointment about Furore II, McCain judged the moment opportune to broach the big question once again.

Le Mare had been having a bad time with his horses. His family had clubbed together for his eightieth birthday to pay 7,000 guineas for that horse in Ireland called Busty Hill. This had been a complete flop. Furore II, for which he had given £6,000, put his foot in a hole when racing and strained a tendon so badly that the racecourse vet had prescribed his immediate destruction. Le Mare had bought a horse called Zara's Grove for £3,500 to stay in Eric

Collingwood's stable, because he got a telephone call to France (he stays regularly at the Majestic, Cannes) to tell him that the horse (who had won five races in 1969–70) would make £4,500 if sent to the sales.

'I went down to the bar in the Majestic where Doris was sitting,' Le Mare recounted, 'And said "Doris, I've bought another horse". Two fellows sitting there who belong to the faith overheard and said "*Masseltoff*".' I asked "What's that"? They said it meant "Best of luck".' Le Mare commented acidly, 'It never did much. . . .'

Lucky Streak

Later he took a fancy to a horse called Lucky Streak and told George Owen to buy it for him for 7,000 guineas. '"Ginger" comes in that night and tells me 7,000 guineas is too much. First thing next morning I get on to George Owen and say "I don't want to pay more than 5,000". George came back and said "I couldn't buy your Lucky Streak, I've bought you another". I said, "Oh hell", and put the telephone down. That was 6,000 odd. . . .

'So I said to Doris "We've finished with horses all together". Then along comes this old scout, 'Ginger'. "Oh come on, do let me buy you another horse". "Oh shut up, get out." But he nagged and nagged. . . .'

Glenkiln

'Guv'nor,' said McCain boldly, 'there's a horse coming up at Doncaster called Glenkiln and he's qualified for the Grand National.'

Mr Le Mare looked interested. 'How much would he be?'

McCain said, 'Not a lot. About 1,000.'

Le Mare considered. Mrs Solomon said warmly, 'Give "Ginger" another horse. At least he's *honest*.'

'Alright,' said old Mr Le Mare. 'If you can get him for 1,000, go and get him.'

McCain says with glee, 'So off I go to Doncaster like a scalded cat'.

As Anthony Gillam said, when he was interested in Glenkiln, racing gossip related that the horse had a suspect leg. Beryl McCain had heard that he had become his trainer Ken Oliver's hack. McCain strode into his box at Doncaster and felt his legs. 'One was definitely a fair bit warmer than the other,' said 'Ginger' McCain. 'Everybody who came in was going for this warm leg. So I thought I'd leave it for half-an-hour till the horse was walking round the outside parade ring. Out there I checked his legs again. They were perfect. So I was sure it was only body heat.'

'I checked his legs again'

'I got him for 1,000 guineas,' said McCain, 'Delighted, but worried to death, too, in case I'd bought a pup.'

McCain got home at ten next evening and immediately rang Mr Le Mare. 'I've got you that horse, sir.'

Le Mare asked, 'How much did you give?' McCain told him. Mr Le Mare slowly repeated the price, 'A thousand guineas.' He said, hammering the figure home with heavy scorn, 'It'll be a bonny bugger for one thousand guineas!'

Without Glenkiln there would have been no Red Rum. Not merely that Glenkiln's good running gave Le Mare confidence in 'Ginger' and 'Ginger' confidence in himself. But if McCain had not made a regrettable clerical blunder about Glenkiln's Grand National entry, Mr Le Mare would not have thought it necessary to seek another horse qualified for the 'National. Though a less understanding owner than the amazing Mr Le Mare would probably have given his blundering trainer the boot. . . .

For McCain, having again got his keen rich owner, having at last bought a horse which wasn't rubbish, having finally found a horse qualified for the Grand National and entered it, perpetrated a nonsense. Quite unused to the special forfeit form, he misread its intentions and, thinking he was declaring the horse to run at some special stage, in fact struck Glenkiln out of the Grand National of 1972.

Qualified for the Grand National

Of all the thousands of owners of jumpers only a hundred or so each season have horses good enough to be even entered in the Grand National. With an owner of only thirty-five, halfway through his allotted span, fury with his trainer over such a blunder would be justified. Noel Le Mare had waited fifty years to own his first race-horse. At the time of poor 'Ginger' McCain's calamity over the form the spry old gentleman was no less than eighty-five. It would require singular optimism at that age to imagine you would have many more chances of running a horse in the race you'd been dreaming about for over seventy years. . . .

'I was so worried about the paper work,' says McCain, 'that I said I'd send this form off in good time. It says on the form "Declaration to Run", but it's really declaring forfeit. When I found what I'd done I said "I can't face the Guv'nor". Beryl said "You go down and get it done now".'

'I can't face the Guv'nor'

Noel Le Mare remembered. 'Old "Ginger" came tearing down almost at midnight with his tail between his legs and said "I've made the most terrible mistake".'

'Ginger' McCain said, 'He took it like a hero. He was more disappointed for me, I think, than he was for himself. He was really genuinely sorry for me. He is the most super gentleman.'

31 'TRY, TRY, TRY AGAIN – THE HORSE IS LIKE THAT, TOO'

'The most super gentleman' was born in India on December 18th, 1887, the son of a missionary. His father's ancestors were originally French Huguenots and silk-weavers. After the Edict of Nantes (which had given the Huguenots religious liberty in 1598) was revoked by Louis XIV in 1685, the Le Mares were threatened with persecution and escaped from Catholic France. They were smuggled across the Channel and arrived in London with very little money. Later on one of their few gold pieces was stolen at the Coronation of Queen Anne.

Noel Le Mare

Like his ancestors, Noel Le Mare started with nothing, for his missionary father became a 'New Theologian', and, as Le Mare puts it in his well-endowed drawing room (mauve carpets, green walls, Grand National Cups everywhere aglitter, sun-lounge opening off left, garden behind) 'My father got the sack'. The family returned to England and the father and mother, who was a qualified teacher, started a little school in Lancashire at Fleetwood.

'But as soon as it got out that my father was a New Theologian, the parents started to take the kids away, for it was heresy in those days not to believe in the Virgin Birth.'

Before the school closed and his mother began a boarding-house little Noel with a few other children had to sing each afternoon at 4 o'clock 'If at first you don't succeed, try, try, try again'. . . . Le Mare has a resonant voice, twanged lightly with Lancashire and delivers his words with the emphasis of a minatory finger. You expect a joke or a kick at the end of each paragraph. You are often gratified. He does not show his pleasure in your reaction, but like the best of comedians and wisest of men, regards you dead-pan, eyes contemplative as a starling's over his beakish nose.

'I remembered that all my life,' says the eighty-six-year-old, neat in a white shirt sipping his gin and tonic at three in the afternoon. 'If anything went wrong I tried again. If it went wrong I tried until it went right. And that's how we got here.'

'Here' has given him a total assurance. The cockiness which must have strutted in his youth has mellowed like a fine burgundy into a round authority. He is amused by life and by most of us in it.

'Here' was reached by his creation of a world-wide construction company the shares of which, after it went public, valued his family's ownership at £5 million. Le Mare laughed. 'After the first 'National, they turned to me and said, "We believe you're a millionaire, Mr Le Mare . . .?" And I said "I'd be a bloody fool to be a millionaire at eighty-five, wouldn't I?" I don't think they understood what I meant. Of course, it's all gone amongst the family.' He nodded fondly across the fireplace at bright-eyed Mrs Doris Solomon, who allows hours of conversation to proceed with sharp attention but without any unnecessary interjections. 'This girl says about me "The world's greatest spender". And I say "Work hard, play hard. Get all the enjoyment you can out of life. When it was my own company and we weren't public I used to get *thrilled* about doing jobs".'

'We believe you're a millionaire'

Norwest Construction Company really took off in the early 1935's, building bridges, office blocks, jetties, harbours, car ferries, oil refinery bases and pipes, gasworks and private houses all across Europe. But it began after the Great War with four young men sitting round a table in a tea-house raising £250 each to finance its initial working capital.

At the start of the century Le Mare had wanted, as a boy of fourteen, to become an apprentice engineer. But it would cost £50. 'My father and mother were beautiful people, but they had no idea about money. They had no fifty quid. So I went to sea in the trawlers.'

To sea in the trawlers

From the trawlers he 'crept in at the back door of the repair shop and that's how I got my apprenticeship'. In 1906 he was working with a fitter who said to him suddenly, 'Go on son, bugger off up the main street and see what won the big race.' It was Ascetic Silver's Grand National.

'I read about it that night. I pored over the paper the next day. I read about the gambling excitement, the longest race in the world, the *hardest* race in the world. And all those strange conclusions. So many different finishes to the Grand National – more than in any other race. "By God", I determined, "I'd like to win that!"' He was eighteen. He had sixty-seven years to wait and, since the '50's when he first owned a racehorse, nearly a quarter of a century to try, try, try again.

In that Grand National week of 1906 he heard of an American millionaire in the hotel in Fleetwood. 'Every time a telegraph boy came, he gave him a sovereign.' The young Le Mare concluded – 'all Americans were millionaires' – and thought 'Good God, what *would* it be like to be a millionaire'? He resolved 'I'll work like buggery and I'll make myself one. And I'll win that race. And I'll marry a beautiful woman'.

Three ambitions

In November, 1950 he had his first winner of any consequence. He won the Prospect Hurdle at Liverpool with The Sweep trained by Alex Kilpatrick and ridden (coincidentally, because of the future Red Rum connection) by Tim Molony. He told the press then of his three ambitions of forty-five years earlier. He pointed to his wife. '*Here's* the beautiful woman.' He pointed to one of his Norwest Construction signs and said, '*There* are the millions'. He added, 'And when I win the Grand National, the Lord can take me'.

His offer returned to him with a sharp pang a few years later.

Ruby Glen

His first Grand National runner was a horse with George Owen called Ruby Glen. His ruby wedding had dawned and in the summer Owen had told him about a horse he had bought in Ireland. Le Mare forgot about it. 'I'd bought my wife diamonds, I'd bought her fur coats. What the hell was I going to do this time? I sat down and wrote her out a cheque. She looked at it and said, "This just measures up for that horse". So we went down to George, who had the sense to stuff a couple of stiff gins into us before he took us into the yard. My wife said "What do you think about it"? I said "I know damn all about a horse. It's got four legs – that's good enough for me". And we bought it. It won me a lot of races. We called it 'Ruby' because of our wedding and Glen after the name of our house here, Glenalmond. So it runs in the 'National. Here I am strutting about the paddock. . . . I went back to the seats and I see Ruby Glen walking in the parade with the others. Suddenly I remember: "Good God" I think, "If this bugger wins, I've got to go". I called out to my chauffeur, "Joe! Come here, quick. You get on the telephone to God and tell Him I've ratted on that arrangement".'

From 1911 till the end of the Great War Noel Le Mare was a merchant seaman. He was sunk with his ship in the

Mediterranean carrying troops out of Toulon – 'The Germans blew us off with guns but let us get into the lifeboats'. They were adrift two days and travelled three miles in the forty-eight hours before a Belgian ship picked them up 170 miles off Malta. 'At that rate,' says Le Mare, 'we'd just about have reached Malta now.'

When the war ended Le Mare had already resolved to start some form of construction company. He had seen out in South America the tremendous British developments and investments there and in Panama and Mexico, a 'god-send to us in the war to realise those assets', he comments now. He enjoyed himself, too, out there in bars and with what he calls 'dark beauties'.

'Dark beauties'

He is a great man still for the girls, claiming that pretty women and not winning two Grand Nationals, are the things which attract him most.

On that long ago trip to South America he went back to his ship on the last night of his shore leave and addressed himself: 'Noel, you're a bloody fool! Here you are a cog in a wheel on a ship. When the ship leaves, you leave. When 8 bells ring, you go down below. Look at the romance of building a harbour halfway across the world – and fun with the girls thrown in at night! You be a contractor.' He had set his course. 'But it took me ten ruddy years to get there.'

Like young Tommy Stack forty years later, Noel Le Mare started after the war in an insurance office. The girl he made his wife, after a few false starts, had said: 'I'll marry you if you come ashore'. Noel earned £3 per week. His wife, working in Liverpool's electricity department, heard someone asking about engineers and put his name forward. They were really asking for contractors' site-agents. Le Mare whizzed down on Sunday, chatted the man up and started at £23 per month, having first written down the terms of his employment and showed them to the representative to confirm.

He worked a couple of years for the company, laying telephone cables. He then got wind that the department were suddenly going to split their operations, letting contractors dig the trenches while the company supplied, drew and tested the cable. He said to three friends: 'Look, this is our chance, boys'. He had £40. The four men resolved to start with a £1,000 company. He borrowed the £210 balance of his £250 from a friend – 'and kept his son afterwards for thirty-five years in the office to give him employment for the thing his father did for me'.

Borrowed £210

'Four of us, all friends'

They had their first board meeting in that downstairs teahouse in Manchester. Le Mare was the secretary. 'The chief had a soft felt on, I had a soft felt, the big fat fellow had a bowler and the other chap a cap – four of us, all friends.' They registered the company. Le Mare borrowed a hut, bought some spades and shovels, hired a horse and cart, and they were in business.

They made their errors as they felt their way, under-quoting for jobs, not allowing for the local authority's reinstatement charges and often facing bills far beyond their means to pay. Le Mare's ploy then was to dispute any big account sufficiently long for his firm to earn enough on other jobs to pay it. He fought a city Corporation for $2\frac{1}{2}$ years over a matter of £750. Years later, when his fortunes had boomed he took on the Government, claiming £290,000 for the jetty he built them at Heysham, against the Ministry offer of £216,000. He fought for months all the way and finally, sitting alone in London facing eighteen men from the Ministry and the air force, he got his money.

As a boy off the trawlers Le Mare went racing at Manchester and Liverpool so long as he had 5/-. He bet in shillings. 'When I first started work, a labourer got four-pence an hour and paid half-a-crown rent a week for his house. At night he went to the vaults. The tradesmen went to the Working Men's Club, the solicitors and professional fellows went to the local hotel, and the big pots were at the Tennis Club. You knew your position and accepted it.'

But Noel Le Mare did not accept his position. 'If there's something in you, you've got to use it and develop it.' What was the something? 'To try, try, try again.' But what made him try? 'To satisfy myself. Don't give up. Never give in. The horse is like that, too. . . .'

The Sweep

He had begun owning horses with The Sweep. A friend with whom he went racing had horses with Alex Kilpatrick. 'Kilpatrick would say "Why don't you have one, Noel?".' He paid £1,500. 'I was in the money then!' He liked the name. 'It was a piebald. He was a big horse, used to tremble whilst he was being prepared. You bet I was proud of him when he ran.'

And thus via the other horses and trainers to his taxi-driver. He first saw 'Ginger' McCain in the drawing-room where he now sat sipping his gin and reminiscing. 'He'd just brought Mrs Solomon back. He used to taxi for her. Then he taxied for both of us. Then after he'd brought us home he'd have a whisky with us, and we'd have a gin and we'd have a conversation. . . .'

'Ginger' McCain interpolated, 'I used to bring Mr Le Mare home from the Prince of Wales on a Saturday night. He used to be a little bit flushed with gin and a good meal and dancing with all the girls. And we could talk horses. . . .'

Mr Le Mare said crisply, 'He worried the bloody life out of me. Every time I came home he said to me "I *would* like to train horses for you".'

So, after the first two flops and McCain out in the wilderness again, it was Glenkiln. He gets fourth twice, third four times, second once, and wins an amateur race at the very end of the season. And did not run in the 'National. . . . Three weeks before the race Noel Le Mare rang William Hill's to have £200 each way on the horse (he had run well when second at Haydock at the start of March). Hill's said, 'He's not in the race. . . .' And poor 'Ginger' McCain came tearing down at midnight to confess his blunder.

Worse than one missed opportunity was involved. The horse's Grand National qualification was running out and the race Glenkiln finally won at humble Cartmel on 29th May, 1972 did not requalify him. Thus it was that 'Ginger' came again that summer with talk of this horse Red Rum in the Doncaster sales who *was* qualified. The clouds then really flashed their silver linings, for only ten weeks after Red Rum was bought, Glenkiln by winning the £4,802 William Hill National Trial round Liverpool in October, requalified himself for ever for the 'National proper. Had he done so earlier. . . . Had Red Rum been for sale later. . . . Then neither Noel Le Mare nor 'Ginger' McCain would have bought him. Le Mare wouldn't have needed him, as he thought, 'We were aiming for the Grand National.' He exclaims with passion, 'I didn't care a damn what I did anywhere else. "*I wanted to win the National*".'

'And we could talk horses. . . .'

Silver linings

The horse who would as quickly as equinely possible fulfil Mr Le Mare's ancient ambition, established himself as 'a character' within a week of settling into McCain's snug yard. He had shown much character in his youth at Wymondham. Sandra's love of him at rural Oxclose brought it out. Now, behind the used-car showroom in Upper Aughton Road, it bloomed. Respect, affection and success wonderfully increase one's confidence. Red Rum was going to achieve all these three sweet things.

'*Different?*' He was from his arrival an object of reverence, because he had been by the standards of that little yard so enormously expensive. 'Six times the most expensive,' says little Billy Ellison, puffed up like a pouter pigeon. '"*Different*"?' he explodes. 'After riding selling platers every year on the beach I couldn't tell what *was* a good horse. But Red Rum's so different it's like getting into a big XJ after years of lil' ole bangers.'

'You couldn't tell just quietly hacking about. But about the third or fourth time I rode him in a mile gallop – really striding on down the beach – he just crept up slowly. . . .' Billy's face scrumples into delight. 'Every race he had, he came back, he got better. Now I couldn't hold one side of him galloping towards home. And he still frightens me to death riding through traffic. These silly people in cars whizzing past his backside. . . .' Billy gives those motorists who do not recognise the great horse, sharp slices of his mind.

He enjoys the passing scene When Red Rum drives, he faces backwards in his horse-box, and prefers the offside. He will not have the haynet dangling between his head and the window because he enjoys a keen inspection of the passing scene. So he tosses the haynet over and aside. There is an alarm button at the back of the box so that a lad travelling there may summon the driver in front to stop. It amuses Red Rum to press the button from time to time with his tongue and lower lip. It shows Jackie up the front that 'Red's' keeping an eye on his driving.

As tension builds up in him his lower lips flaps and twitches – 'Bangs against his upper lip', as Billy puts it, 'when he's a bit upset'. He knows immediately the difference between the blacksmith bringing ordinary work shoes and his racing plates. 'Won't even take a Polo mint,' Billy Ellison confirms, 'When he's being plated.' Recollections perhaps of past pain in those feet make him wary of the feel of the aluminium.

Head Lad Jackie Grainger pronounces 'He's a real old Christian. He's never been no trouble'. Grainger keeps to the same feeding routine – 'feed him regular at 6 a.m. even if he's going racing'. Except for nearby Haydock and Liverpool, Red Rum is sent the night before to the racecourse stables. In addition to his miles of beach galloping, and the wading in the sea, these are two other points where Red Rum's training differs from that of horses in other yards. Few racehorses get full feeds on the morning of their race. And most, unless the course is several hundred miles away, travel to the racecourse on the morning. Red Rum, furthermore, often stays the night away after racing, too, and never leaves the course before two or three hours after the last race. Most lads in other stables are in a hurry to get their horses home. Red Rum gets his late night feed at 8 p.m. 'Oats, scoop of cubes and grated carrots'.

'He's a real old Christian'

Jackie Grainger, head lad and box driver, and Billy Ellison, are a famous couple now round all the courses of northern England and Scotland. They sup the richness of racing life as it were served foaming in great tankards to be quaffed. They have composed a ballad (given on page 186) which they render on the slightest opportunity: '*O Red Rum is a racehorse*'. . . .

Jackie Grainger says: 'Most times I've seen him at the races is coming round the elbow at Liverpool. I shout "Go on Red!" and I've got a good strong voice. They reckon he can hear me. Anyway he always moves up a good few places.'

'Go on Red'

The horse's hearing is particularly acute. There may be an equine parallel with the sharp hearing and intelligence correlation doctors observe in children. The night that Jackie and Billy were down at Newbury for the 1973 Hennessy Cognac Gold Cup they were sitting in the security men's office looking out over the yard. Far away across the open space they glimpsed Red Rum's head. Jackie shouted from inside the office, 'Now Red!'.

Billy says, 'And he started to weave and jump up and down, so that I thought he'd come out over his box.' He adds lovingly, 'He hears your step anywhere and knows it.'

'In the paddock,' Jackie declares, 'he loves to be free.

He's the King! He likes his own road. You must never shout at him.'

'Racing,' muses Jackie, 'is the greatest game in the world. I could fall out with many folks, but I'll always like the horses.' His gypsy face is suddenly transfused with tenderness, that fragile thing without which no man can understand another, an animal or himself. 'Though you put in long hours,' Jackie says, 'It always seems easy work to me – not like those working in firms.' He pities those condemned to factory and office.

'I've a good team here'

'I've got a good team here,' Grainger says. 'I like a small yard with three or four lads. You can give the horses individual attention. Golden Blue started the ball rollin'. That was the first winner I had with Don. At Hexham.'

And the horse, a 9-year-old in 1974, won again on the last day of the 1973–74 season.

There is a warm ambience about the little yard. It has a good feeling of age, toil and purpose and good cheer. It belonged once to a brewery. All around live people leading active lives. The throb of the traffic and the rattle of the trains orchestrate a perimeter of bustle. Facets of Red Rum's character are mirrored in these surroundings.

'"Ginger"'s stable is so happy,' says Noel Le Mare. 'It's the happiest stable I've been near. He brings his horses back over those sandhills behind Birkdale. If I know a horse, it likes surprises. It climbs up those sandhills, thinking "What the hell's on the other side"? And in the afternoon 'Ginger''s children are playing with a football in the yard, and all the horses' heads are out, looking at what's going on. It keeps them fresh. They don't get bored. If you can get happiness in your business,' said the man who started with £40 in a teashop and created a £5 million family construction company, 'you don't need to bother about anything else.'

Le Mare had faith in McCain. 'Look here,' he affirms simply, 'I'm eighty-six. I've had a life on the trawlers, on the deep-sea ships, a life amongst navvies, a life among insurance agents and contractors and heads of businesses and Government ministers and the top people in London and all that.' Le Mare like most Lancastrians is not one whit impressed by grandeur.

'"Ginger" was solid gold'

Mr Le Mare looked back across that more than a lifespan of knowing and testing so many people. 'After that,' he says, 'it doesn't take you long to find out what sort of fellow is talking to you. It didn't take me long to find out that 'Ginger' was solid gold.'

Ginger McCain carefully prepares his harrows weighted down with old railway sleepers, watched by his two children Joanne and Donald.

Red Rum (*left*) (Billy Ellison) and his customary workhorse Glenkiln (Jackie Granger) pounding along the soft-harrowed strip. *Photo: Provincial Press Agency*

Facing the sea and the screaming gulls.

Above: Scrambling up and down the mini-Western sandhills gives Red Rum maximum exercise without hammering his once-damaged feet.

Below: A head like one from a Greek frieze. . . . And he is "parrot-mouthed" (note his overhanging top teeth). *Photo: Gerry Cranham*

Above: Red Rum leading the string on the beach the day before his second Grand National victory. *Photo: Gerry Cranham*

Far left: He's usually in front. Same tense morning. Hot favourite and about 30 hours to wait. *Photo: Gerry Cranham*

Left: Many will see in his head-carriage a powerful look of Arkle. *Photo: Gerry Cranham*

Going home after
work between the
used cars on the
forecourt, his legs still
wet and sticky from
the sea.

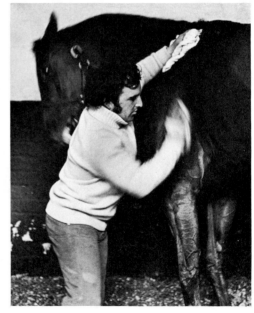

Coming home over
the railway crossing a
few yards from his
stable. He lives the
wrong side of the
tracks. . . . *Photo:
Jeremy Hoare*

When Billy "polishes
him like wood" he
both bites and kicks.
Photo: Jeremy Hoare

His first reaction when McCain rang him at 11.30 that evening after Doncaster sales to announce that he'd got Red Rum was to grumble, 'I don't like the name'. But Mrs Doris Solomon, overhearing, disagreed. 'I think it's a lovely name.' Noel Le Mare tried it backwards: MUR DER – 'so that was no good'. He asked McCain no other questions about the horse at all. 'I wouldn't bother. I have great faith in this boy.'

Beryl McCain, too, had faith in 'Ginger'. She believes in fate. When she discovered Red Rum's dam was called Mared, she was delighted: it seemed so appropriate that the horse should belong to the similarly named Le Mare. She believes in lucky places. Until September, 1972 they were 'still in this very grotty flat next-door. This property was altered over the months. Then we moved in. We'd just bought Red Rum. Then we had this great win with Glenkiln. It wouldn't have happened in the other place! We couldn't, somehow, have been successful in the other place. We couldn't have coped. It wasn't respectable enough to take owners into, it was so small and cramped. When Mr Le Mare came we used to talk to him in his car outside.'

Now there is a bright modern kitchen opening onto the yard with a dining-area behind it, where 'Ginger' will put up the screen to show friends the re-run of his Grand Nationals. Downstairs, behind the motor show-room, is his office and halfway up the stairs a splendid long sitting-room with a balcony looking down into the yard a Polo mint's pitch from Red Rum's inquisitive nose. His lovely head with those huge eyes and ears – best testament to any horse's character – is out nearly all the time, staring at the sky above the little line of boxes, then the house opposite. He cocks his head a little to one side and gazes into the heavens as if he sees something in space and is listening to strains of ethereal music.

'He has this super look,' says Beryl McCain, 'when he looks out of his box very high in the sky. I'm flattered because he knows me. Horses aren't really like dogs, who know their owners. But he recognises me. He knows my voice. When I'm at the sink I can see him looking out of his box and he sees me.' She reflects, 'After that muddy race at Catterick there was a short space when he didn't have quite that same look. . . .'

'Ginger' McCain had rightly deduced that the horse did not like mud. He resolved to run the horse early. Red Rum had completed his roadwork with Anthony Gillam and was in splendid condition at the sales. McCain, after that first dreadful shock of his lameness on the second day, took him on slowly. 'He was a bright horse to ride and he wanted some sitting on going down through the town. But he was never dirty with it'. 'Ginger' grins, 'And Billy wouldn't worry. He'd be sitting up there with a cigarette in one hand, talking about his girl friend from last night, and not thinking about what the horse was doing.' He adds, assuaging my consternation, 'We hadn't started to attach the importance to him that we do now.'

Red Rum still feels his feet

Because Red Rum still felt his feet walking on cobbles or gravel he did all his long, slow exercise walking and trotting on the beach and climbing up the towering sand-hills. Certainly, as Noel Le Mare says, that crinkled ridge of tussocky drifting dunes – a sort of mini-Western setting – soared and plunged with interest. It also afforded maximum controlled exercise. The horse was keen to spring up the slopes. Thus his back, loins, quarters, second-thighs and hocks were all being marvellously stretched and exercised every other minute. The sand was loose on the hills. It was soft so that his delicate feet were not harmed, yet he had to work his body and legs harder to climb up. At the top of each dune his front set of muscles were brought into regular play. Down he must slither on the shifting sands, still gentle to his hooves, but requiring the full stretch of tendons and muscles in fore-arms and shoulders and neck and back. He was doing that best thing for all horses: exercising without realising it, and loving the difference of it all.

When he first saw the sea, he relished it. Its vastness, its strange sound, its waves that ran baying in at him like dogs snapping at his fetlocks, never for one instant deterred him. Quite the reverse. He walked straight on in. McCain reflects, 'When I look back on the potentially good horses I've had, or the old ones that have been something, they've always gone straight into the tide without arguing. . . .' It is, of course, a demonstration of courage.

'Red Rum enjoyed it immediately'

'Red Rum enjoyed it immediately. In he went, belly-deep, then chest-deep. He relished the sea.'

He loved just as much galloping on his carefully har-rowed strip of sand. McCain's methods here, proved beyond any possible doubt by the almost magical improve-ment in Red Rum, flew in the face of all established training beliefs. It has been the conviction of trainers all my time in the sport that regular galloping on sand ruined horses. Le Mare was told by his previous trainers that 'it shortened

their step'. I have been told variously and by leading trainers that working horses frequently on beaches slowed them
down, spoiled their action, made them 'all at sea on turf
again', damaged their feet ('very dead, sand you know')
broke them down ('no give in sand'), strained their
tendons ('there's no bounce in sand'), and strained their
ligaments ('they go in too far').

All of these things may be true. The fact is that no other
leading trainer works his horses exclusively on a beach.
They go occasionally when their 'proper gallops' are too
hard in summer-drought or winter-frost, or too soft in
midwinter flood. The sand, as McCain knows, having had
to train there *faute de mieux*, remains the same. 'Boundless
and bare the lone and level sands stretch far away. . . .'

Faute de mieux

Perhaps McCain unwittingly struck upon the secret:
the continuing levelness and invariability of harrowed sand
going. Certainly he prepares it carefully. He is sure that galloping on firm, unharrowed sand, is definitely damaging.
So he weighs two spiked harrows down with two heavy
railway sleepers and pulls them very slowly indeed (a maximum 5 m.p.h.). This harrowing provides a tilth of loose
sand four inches deep. This tilth removes the initial firmness. Beneath this moist, loose working surface lies, dead
level and unpotholed, the smooth base of the old firm sand.

He harrows a two mile straight. There is therefore a strip
so long that his horses may gradually work up speed,
stretch out and as gradually pull up. The instant they come
off the harrowed strip the beat of their feet becomes
markedly louder, sharper. You can see their stride immediately shorten. Their hooves print less. Away on those
vast sands McCain carefully demonstrated the basic
essential of galloping racehorses on beaches.

Would it work as perfectly for all horses as it has for Red
Rum? Time will tell, if McCain expands his stable yet
stays by the sea. He had, until Glenkiln, a tiny stable of
very little consequence. Glenkiln, from an excellent stable,
improved. He would have gone on doing so, but working
almost daily with the flying Red Rum – in Jackie Grainger's
words – 'broke poor old Glen's heart'.

Red Rum's improvement in the hands of his fifth trainer
has been one of recent steeplechasing's greatest feats. Certainly the beach has been our hero's salvation. His feet have
been saved in their work and cooled by the sea afterwards.
The sea and the sand saved him. He loves the freedom of that
great expanse. The sea and the sand got him fit, ahead of most
of the rest of racing, for his first run for 'Ginger' McCain.

The sea and
the sand saves
Red Rum

33 'THERE WAS A BAY HORSE, RIGHT OFF THE GROUND'

Having been, as he puts it, 'a hard–up fellow' McCain is not prodigal with entries or his owners' other expenses. 'I'm getting a little out of it now, because we're becoming a lot more professional,' he says in 1974 with a modesty particularly charming after Red Rum's astonishing achievements. 'But it's not a thing that comes easily to a person who had to struggle to get a few bob together all the time.'

To save his owners expense he planned to take several horses together to Carlisle for its two–day meeting at September's end. It's a course McCain has always liked. It was only just over six weeks since Red Rum had arrived from the sales. He had been working well together with Gambling Girl. 'We'd done fairish work, without really getting after them.' The ground elsewhere on Britain's normal training grounds was very hard. But on McCain's harrowed sand gallops the going was 'absolutely super'. So they set off to Carlisle, McCain feeling 'apprehensive, having given 6,000 guineas for a horse'.

First adventure to Carlisle

When Anthony Gillam saw his ex–horse declared to run at Carlisle on going officially forecast as 'hard', he too was apprehensive. He was fond of the horse and had liked McCain very much. He had warned McCain about the horse's feet. This run, thought Gillam, might finish Red Rum for ever. As Tim Molony had watched askance when Bobby Renton was subjecting Red Rum to heavy ground, now Anthony Gillam as dubiously regarded McCain's first adventure at Carlisle. McCain had booked Tommy Stack to ride Red Rum for the very good reason, as the horse's humble new trainer immediately declared, 'that Tommy knew more about the horse than any of us'.

What was more, Tommy Stack had been instrumental in 'Ginger' McCain buying the horse at all. McCain, checking Red Rum's form before the Doncaster sales and noting how often Stack had already ridden him, went to his friend Stan Wareing, a pig farmer on an enormous scale, married to a beautiful young wife called Carol, a successful Event rider, and on whose farm with their donkey Andy, Red

Rum spends his summer holidays. Stan Wareing had horses in training with Tommy Shedden. Tommy Stack rode for him. Wareing asked Stack if Red Rum was 'all right'. Now fortunately for Mr Noel Le Mare and Donald McCain, Tommy Stack had as we know been living miles away from Oxclose for some time. The horse's pedalosteitis had not emerged during his brief training of Red Rum. He therefore knew very little about the horse's dreaded bone-disease. Had he known that Red Rum had been so gravely afflicted he must have warned Stan Wareing of it. He would have reported the veterinary opinion that, at the best, the chances of a lasting recovery were only 50/50. Stan would have telephoned 'Ginger' and 'Ginger' could not possibly have bid. The horse in those circumstances would thus have gone to Captain Tim Forster for Mrs Vi Henriques. Would that have meant another two Grand Nationals for the courteous Captain of the mournful mien who trains, on normal downland, hundreds of miles from the sand and the sea . . .?

Tommy Stack with his customary brevity and honesty reported merely, 'He's a bit footy'. Wareing related afterwards, 'I had to lean on Tommy a bit more and he then said "I think he'll be alright. Anyway I'll be delighted to ride him again".' **'He's a bit footy'**

McCain additionally had altered his policy about jockeys. In the past he had given rides to young claiming lads whom he liked. He had now concluded that this was far from being in the best interests of his horses. 'I now decided to get the best possible jockeys I could for my horses.' He therefore booked Tommy Stack for both his horses that Saturday at Carlisle.

Gambling Girl was in the first race, the eight runner first division of a novice hurdle. Nothing else had had a previous run that season and half the field, including Gambling Girl, were reported by *Chaseform* to be in varying states of backwardness. For all that, McCain's mare, always in the leading bunch, led at the 7th flight and went on to win by two lengths. She was returned at 9 to 2. The stable had backed her at 100 to 8.

Red Rum first ran for his new owner and trainer two hours later in the 3 mile handicap 'chase, remarkably well-endowed for early season Carlisle, for it was worth £622. Of the four runners, Red Rum was the scorned outsider. Gyleburn, McCain noted, was something of a Carlisle specialist. Proud King had been out already and been third. He should be fitter than Red Rum, and so should **The scorned outsider**

Lord Mostyn's owner-trained Nephin Beg★ who had already won on his previous appearance.

'He'll go well'

It was not surprising that Red Rum with his new, generally unrecognised small-town trainer, was not picked by the punters. His tall trainer, however, thought differently. Because of Gambling Girl's victory, 'Ginger' said to Tommy Stack, while chatting before the race in the paddock's centre, 'I think Red Rum is going to go well.'

Tommy looked up at McCain with one of those sharply assessing glances and retorted bluntly, 'Well, I won't beat Gyleburn.' He added helpfully, 'Don't expect too much of this horse. He always needs a couple of runs before he's anywhere near ready.' He wanted to help McCain. He had frankly been surprised at the price Red Rum had made the previous month at Doncaster. There seemed to him no likelihood of the horse improving, probably the reverse. 'Ginger' said coolly, 'I think you may be surprised'.

An unexpected success

Chaseform bestowed its 'looked well' accolade on Red Rum. He and Gyleburn (Ron Barry) duelled from three fences out, Stack felt for, and McCain watched for signs of Red Rum weakening, of blowing up. He and Gyleburn touched down together at the last – and Red Rum drew powerfully ahead to win by $\frac{3}{4}$ length. There was a murmur of surprise round the racetrack. The winner, when the outsider of four, is never exactly acclaimed.

Tommy Stack rode back into the winner's enclosure to be greeted by the overjoyed 'Ginger' and Beryl McCain. Tommy got off, stood back, studied the horse, shook his head and murmured, 'Well, I don't know what you've done to him. . . . But what a *difference*!' He was genuinely puzzled. He had driven the horse along as usual, had been surprised to find him lying up with the favourite, and had expected him to crack as he used to in his early season races.

'Ginger' McCain sleeps easy

The little stable rejoiced in its first double. 'Ginger' McCain slept easy: he had not bought a pup. Doubles even in medium-sized stables are joyful rarities. But the eight-horse yard behind the railway line now produced another double at Wetherby only ten days later. Tommy Stack was away riding at Cheltenham, so going for the best available 'Ginger' booked that charming champion 'Big Ron' Barry. They won the seller with Golden Blue (no bid for the winner) and then Red Rum took on a really high-class trio of staying steeplechasers in Ballysagert,

★ The unhappy horse died the following season during a race at Ludlow in May, 1974, collapsing when lying second.

Supermaster and Esban. They finished in that order – far behind Red Rum. He looked magnificent and won triumphantly by 12 lengths. . . .

A fortnight later on firm ground at Newcastle Red Rum beat Ballysagert again in another valuable 3 mile 'chase. Tommy Stack was back on board and hard at him for all the second time round. 'Stayed on gamely to take the lead close home,' the *Notebook* praises. Ballysagert was leading as Red Rum rose at the last to tackle him like a Trojan on the flat. Don McCain winces as he recalls that race. 'They went no pace early on, which wouldn't suit Red Rum at all. I had three owners with me that day and they'd all put a fair bit of money on him – which I didn't know about! Going to the second last, my fellow was a beaten horse and Ballysagert was going away from him. Yet on the run-in Tommy got up to win on the line, and he was going away then!'

When Stack came in, he said to 'Ginger': 'I've been *very* hard on him. You'll have to give him a break after this.'

'Ginger' went round to the other side of the horse. 'He really had had a hard race. I felt a bit sick. I would sooner have been beaten than the horse get that sort of hammering. The three owners were all ghost-white, having thought he was going to be beaten. I was a bit choked. When Red Rum was in the "Sweat Box" to test him' (a routine dope-test on winners) 'I went across to have a drink. I was worried about the horse, so I went to the stables to have a look at him.

'In the middle of the stable yard was a patch of grass. On it stood a man with his eyes popping out. There was a bay horse right off the ground, jumping and kicking. It was Billy with Red Rum. They'd just washed him off. He was so fresh and cocky you'd think he'd just come out of his box to run. Yet only fifteen minutes earlier . . .!'

Don McCain marvelled, 'I realised then that the toughness of this horse was something very, very special.' And Tommy Stack looking back on that race, declares, 'At Newcastle I really 'murdered' him. I thought he wouldn't run again for months. Yet he comes out a week later at Haydock and wins on the bit.' Stack shakes his head, astonished now by the horse's courage.

Those years of McCain failures were extinguished in a few weeks. Two doubles, three devastating victories by Red Rum and then Glenkiln turns out at Liverpool (ridden by Jimmy Bourke) to slaughter the opposition by 12 lengths in the £4,302 William Hill Grand National Trial.

The newspapers suddenly got the word about McCain and shouted it on: 'SEASIDE SCENE'S SUCCESS SECRET. . . .' 'TIDE TURNS FOR GINGER. . . .' 'THE GREMLINS RELENT AND GLENKILN WINS. . . .' 'McCAIN SWEARS BY SEASIDE TRAINING. . . .'

And in poured the telegrams: 'WOULD SOUTH-PORT AIR AND SANDS IMPROVE ME THREE STONE' wired Sam Benjamin of London. There were others like it. There had never been any before. The whole McCain training scene was greatly changing.

'Rarin' to go'

Nor was McCain just a one-horse training marvel. Red Rum's treble had not been three flashes in an early pan. More importantly, Red Rum had yet again improved at home after his gruelling Newcastle race. He was 'Rarin' to go' again. Then Red Rum knocked up four in a glorious row at nearby Haydock by easily winning, and as favourite, too, the suitably-named Southport Handicap 'Chase. He won another £684 and special paddock-sheet presented by Southport corporation. It was the first time it had ever been won by a Southport owner, and the charming Mayoress of Southport presented it to a grinning Noel Le Mare and 'Ginger' McCain embracing Mrs Doris Solomon in a male sandwich. Le Mare had said solicitously to Tommy Stack before the race, 'Now you look after yourself, young man – it's very greasy.' Tommy said, 'Don't you worry about that, Sir. This horse will look after me!'

Red Rum's fourth victory made it five wins in Tommy Stack's last five rides and put him ahead of Ron Barry in the run for the jockeys' championship. For 'Ginger' McCain's tiny stable it meant that, only three months into the season, he had won eleven races from eight horses. Upper Aughton Road had been flung onto the map. And the racing world was all a mutter: 'What was the secret of the man McCain?' 'Why should someone so long an obscure trainer suddenly start scoring?''

'RED RUM AND SEA ARE UNBEATABLE!' pronounced a *Daily Mail* headline. It was not only an accurate statement of fact but a reasonable forecast of the future.

Towards that agreed target

McCain had run Red Rum at Haydock to test how he coped with the drop-fences there, as a practice for Liverpool. The papers had not yet seen the horse as a Grand National prospect, but McCain was working steadily towards that agreed target.

The reactions of Mrs Brotherton and Mr Renton, who

had now seen their ex-horse win four decent races and about £2,500 from four starts in the few months since they sold him, cannot have been ones of joy unconfined. They said nothing at the time to Mr Le Mare or 'Ginger' McCain because they did not come across them. Nor did they know them. In retrospect, talking to me in the summer of 1974 when Red Rum's transmogrification had ceased to be a shock and become nationally accepted, they both very sportingly said they were delighted for Le Mare and McCain.

Anthony Gillam had already come up to McCain at a couple of race meetings. McCain reports: 'He kept saying "Well done" and "Great". He took it like a man – in a most super fashion. Because I know if it had been me, I would have been sick.'

A fortnight after Haydock and it was 'five in a row for Red Rum', when our hero from his fifth start for McCain won the £695 Mauchline handicap 'chase over nearly $8\frac{1}{2}$ miles at Ayr on 13th November, 1972. He won it now under top weight carrying a penalty. For the first time he was in the hands of Brian Fletcher. He was rising eight, and Fletcher from Bishop Auckland was closing the second dozen of jockeys to get on his back. His splendid association with Red Rum started, as these things do, partially by accident, but mainly by being in the right place while his rivals were in the wrong one.

Five in a row

After Haydock McCain had decided the horse should rest. 'But he came out better and better.' So he changed his mind and his plans. Thus, he could not get Tommy Stack, who was riding in the south for the highly intelligent and energetic trainer Tom Jones, who now retained him. McCain then immediately tried to get Ron Barry, but he, by his retainer with Gordon Richards, would have to ride Hurricane Rock, a fancied rival to Red Rum in the same race.

A fancied rival

Without these two, McCain wisely did not let the immediate jockey problem obscure the long-term plan.

'I thought around,' says McCain, 'with Liverpool in view, as to who might be the best person. And I thought of Brian Fletcher.' Fletcher had only ridden for McCain once before and that was at Carlisle in October when he suddenly got the offer of two rides. One, The Tunku, bought by 'Ginger' a few minutes after he bought Red Rum, fell with Fletcher when in the race with a chance. Fletcher does not say much. He had simply said to McCain after the race, 'He's all right. He'll win you races.' This was the extent of 'Ginger''s communication with Fletcher before Ayr in November, 1972.

'I thought he'd suit Red Rum'

McCain reflects, 'I thought Fletcher was possibly one of the best Liverpool jockeys. His record was pretty fair. I liked him as a horseman. He was quiet. I thought he'd suit Red Rum.'

So he did. The horse's appearance reflected not only the Scottish afternoon light but the greatest credit on his trainer. Five races in just over six weeks would convert most horses to hatstands and hay-racks. But Red Rum zoomed in by 6 lengths pursued by Ron Barry on Hurricane Rock. Quick Reply, who had won the Scottish Grand National that spring, now finished 6th of the seven runners on his seasonal reappearance, getting 3 lbs from our hero and coming in nearly 30 lengths behind him.

Now Red Rum burst out as a Grand National hope. While Brian Fletcher was undoing his sticky girths a pressman enquired 'What's the programme now?' McCain said: 'A little break and then he goes to Liverpool.' The reporter intercepted Brian to ask, 'Would this do for Liverpool?'

McCain explains, 'Brian is a very quiet fellow. He just thought about this question for a bit. Then he says quietly, "This would do for me", and walked in. We had a chat about it. He said the horse would jump Liverpool and that he'd been absolutely delighted with his ride. It was left at that.'

34 'I TOOK DAYS OFF SCHOOL TO GO FLAPPIN' IN WALES'

The press quickly seized upon this firm announcement of Red Rum's plans. 'CONSISTENT RED RUM IS NATIONAL PROSPECT,' declared *Sporting Life* and 'RED RUM EARNS A REST – AINTREE'S HIS TARGET.'

No arrangement was made then to retain Brian Fletcher for the horse, nor has there ever been one. Fletcher has in fact only visited Southport a few times on social occasions, and one of those was to parade Red Rum at Southport show in the spring of 1974. 'I had a job to stay with him,' said red-faced Fletcher, 'he was that fresh and well!'

He has no part in Red Rum's training. He has never galloped the horse at home, nor ridden him on the beach in any of his work at Southport. This is due partly to Fletcher's disinclination to get involved in the training side of horses (this sometimes worries trainers who like jockeys riding out regularly to keep themselves loosened up) and partly to McCain's disinclination to have jockeys down. Beryl McCain says '"Ginger" isn't very keen on jockeys riding work here. Whenever they've come, things haven't gone well' (Like Red Rum's first day of lameness). Beryl added, 'On grass gallops jockeys are passing trees. They get an impression of speed. But on the beach they pass nothing. They don't think they're travelling and they tend to do too much.'

'On the beach they pass nothing'

Beryl McCain says, 'Brian's very serious. He gets made a bit of fun of in the changing-room. He thinks the other jockeys are acting like schoolkids.' Beryl adds kindly, 'I think it would be better for Brian if he would act that way a bit too.'

Fletcher says, 'I've never yet ridden Red Rum on the sands because I'm a jockey that sits back and says to myself, "I've got a job to do to ride these horses. The trainer's got a job to do to place them. Therefore it's up to me to ride them and up to the trainer to train them. I never interfere,"' says Brian Fletcher gravely, 'I just turn up at the races'.

Amid the merriment of the changing-room Fletcher is

usually a loner. The other jockeys, like larking school-boys, sometimes hide his whip, or tie his tights in knots.

Brian Fletcher

Brian Fletcher lives now in a lonely little farm painted an incongruous bright blue and perched on a bleak hillside in Co. Durham. His directions had been slightly ambiguous. 'Fletcher?' asks a farmhand by the road. 'There's a reet lot o' Fletchers round here. . . . The jockey? Aye. Fest farm up t'lane on reeait'and side.' The Durham accent to which Brian Fletcher gives full rein takes a few moments for southerners to grasp. The lane along the valley is grey and very potholed. Cows moon through gaps. A long straight drive arrows up the flank of the hill to Fletcher's huddle of farm buildings. The drive is newly-fenced with criss-cross railings and divided by two cattle grids. Fletcher's friendly wife, the former Miss Barbara Moore, a nurse in Bishop Auckland, and her mother sit in the glass-fronted kitchen at the top of a steep flight of outdoor steps. Brian met Barbara in a cafeteria in town when he was working for the local trainer Denys Smith. 'She doesn't dislike horses,' says Brian, 'but she was a miner's only daughter, and a nurse, and she wasn't interested in the outdoor life.' He got engaged to her the year he rode Red Alligator to be third in the Grand National – 'The year of the pile-up.' They were married the following year in June 1968, three months after he won the race on the same horse.

I supposed his jockey's winning present had come in very handy. Fletcher scowled, 'I got the 10 per cent from the owner and nothing else.' His then fiancée, however, had been photographed at the time giving Red Alligator a grateful hug for his early wedding-present. Fletcher in an inside room and looking as if roused drowsy-eyed from heavy sleep began talking farming down a telephone with a gigantic extension. 'Cattle costin' me 120 quid apiece . . . quite good fettle . . . but I'd like to be out o' 'em at 140 quid apiece. . . .'

'You're in a different world'

He farms 52 acres and owns 35 head of cattle. 'When I'm busy a friend comes in to help.' He adds apparently inconsequentially, 'The North's not so cold as people think.' He means its people, I surmise. He dislikes the south and never wants to leave Durham. 'The atmosphere here is fabulous compared with the south. Nicer people, nicer attitudes, nicer everything! You're in a different world.'

He thought of a move south in April, 1973 when, just after his first National on Red Rum, he had a shock fall-out with Denys Smith. 'BRIAN THE NATIONAL HERO

LOSES HIS JOB' a headline shouted. He was told he wouldn't be required to ride the stables' horses. 'A complete bombshell,' Fletcher called it then, although his contract with the stable had ended in 1970, since when he has been a freelance jockey.

He lolls back looking like 'Just William' on the sofa of his opulent leather three-piece suite. Ashtrays perched on toy saddles hang over arms. The walls, painted white, sparkle with a host of horse-brasses. Furnishings are green and white. Photographs of Fletcher on innumerable winning horses jump and gallop all around. Fletcher, born May 18th, 1947, looks about sixteen. It seems incredible that he has ridden in one Grand National, let alone ridden three Grand National winners. He wears floppy moccasin slippers, brown trousers and a blue-speckled shirt. His face is rosy-red, but he is anxious about finance. When he got married and was attached to Denys Smith's stable he bought a house 400 yards away from it in Leopold Terrace, Bishop Auckland. 'Then I bought this place in 1970. It was a wreck. I've spent an awful lot of money on it.' Fletcher wags his head dolefully. He plans to buy a bigger place somewhere nearby into which to retire and 'to hang up me boots'. He has several times talked of retirement before, when depression and bone-breaks and concussion have hit him most hardly. He has suffered more than his fair share of falls, smashed his pelvis which would have stopped most people from walking on a hack, and suffered particularly bad head-injuries in a fall at Teesside. He has been, he says 'knocked out cold more times than I care to remember'.

His place is called 'Backs and Sides' Farm. 'This name used to stick in the back o' me mind. I used to think it'd be one o' the fest things I'd get changed, but it grows on you. I feel it's a shame to alter it, it's been here so long,' all delivered in rich Durham.

Brian was born and bred in Co. Durham. 'I was riding virtually before I could walk.' His father had a small dairy farm, but his main interest was training 'flapping' ponies. Brian at the age of ten was riding at these unrecognised meetings against full-grown jockeys. He raced as a schoolboy all over Britain, up at the old Edinburgh racecourse at Musselburgh, on the Border at Hawick and down in Wales. He used to cut out of school at four, 'fling me satchel down and away out to exercise the horses'. They had four or five racing all the time. 'I took days off school to go

Three
Grand
National
wins

Raced
as a
schoolboy

flappin' down in Wales.' His father loaded up the horse box and as soon as school ended away they would go to 'flap' round Westmorland.

The 'ponies' at these unrecognised meetings were usually ex-racehorses graded by size in four or five divisions between 'under 14 hands' and 'over 15.2 hands'. 'Some had won and been placed under Rules,' says Brian, 'and there were some thoroughbred mares that went flappin' that have bred winners afterwards under Rules.' He laughed mischievously over this. The courses were very sharp, whizzing round two or three fields. Denys Smith, now the local recognised trainer, had once been a 'flappin' man' himself with trotting horses. He thus knew Fletcher's father and so when Brian left school – 'I neglected my studies 'cos all I wanted to be was successful with horses – ' he went to work for Smith as a stable lad.

'It's a very hard life'

Young Brian sold some cattle and pigs to buy himself a motor-bike and on each dark morning and evening buzzed ten miles to and from Denys Smith's stables. 'It's a very hard life,' he says. 'I got £6 a week for seven days a week, startin' work at a quarter to 7, finishing at 6 o'clock with an hour and a half for dinner. If you aren't successful in the racing sphere, it's an absolute slavery.'

Brian 'did his three horses' at Smith's from the day he started, and stuck it 'because I always had this in the back of my mind that I wanted to be a steeplechase jockey'.

Denys Smith, says Brian, did not ride out with his strings, but employed two Head Lads, one in charge of the yard – 'A very tough man, but I suppose in the racing game the tougher the head lad the better' – and the other the former jockey Tommy Wyse 'who rides out both lots and works the horses.'

The delegated organisation at Holdforth Farm is unusual, but productive. Denys Smith had risen by 1974 to a 90-horse stable, the emphasis swinging steadily over the years from N.H. horses to the flat. His record is a splendidly mixed bag: a Grand National, a Lincoln, a Great Yorkshire 'Chase, a Middle Park Stakes. . . .

His first ride

Brian Fletcher found Smith 'quite a good boss' and says generously that 'Tommy Wyse taught me virtually everything I know'. After only nine months work he got his first ride in public in October, 1964 when he was only sixteen. It would be phenomenally quick progress for the average stable lad, but young Brian had those six years of race-riding experience in flapping races and was thus several seasons ahead of his school-leaving contemporaries.

In his first season he rode three winners from 24 races, in his second season four winners. 'In my third season I had 15 winners and then things began to materialise, and I got the ride on Red Alligator.'

'Materialise' is a pet word of Fletcher's. His Grand National victory on Red Alligator brought an obscure but able Durham jockey to the attention of trainers all over Britain, including 'Ginger' McCain. But Fletcher was still working for Denys Smith as a lad and not getting a retainer. Fletcher grew restless. 'Denys Smith would say to me "why did you do this? why did you do that?" and I began to think why am I stickin' this job? I was gettin' good offers from southern trainers. . . . But Tommy Wyse used to say to me that I had a good job and I would be better to stay where I was. Looking back,' says Fletcher, 'I was too loyal to Denys Smith. He really didn't appear to appreciate me at all.' He adds fairly, 'But I did have a lot of winners through him, and he started me off. . . .'

Staying, though grumbling, in the North did ensure that he was around when McCain was looking, with Stack and Barry unavailable, for a jockey for Red Rum at Ayr. The luck involved in a freelance jockey's life is two hundred times greater than that in the Grand National. More than in any other profession must he be at the right course on the right day available for the race on offer, able to do the weight and in good enough form to be acceptable to the owner. He will not have a month or so to settle in to find his feet in the job. The freelance jockey 'copping' for a chance ride will have about six minutes on a horse entirely strange to him to prove himself a hit or a miss. If he rides a stinker the trainer will probably never ask him again. If he's second or third the trainer will believe (and the owner will be convinced) that any of the horse's previous victorious partners would have won. The jockey can really only ride the winner to satisfy and there is only going to be one of those.

Fletcher was anxious to please. He was on the way to re-establishing himself after some desperate falls in the previous season. He knew nothing about McCain. 'I had been told that he sold motor-cars. That's all I knew of him. Then one day at Carlisle he asked me out of the blue to ride a novice 'chaser.'

That is generally how spare rides start. Senior jockeys and those retained by big stables do not knock each other to get chance rides for small stables on novice 'chasers. They have a lot to consider. So Fletcher came to ride Red

Victory on Red Alligator

The freelance jockey

Rum at Ayr. 'He wasn't the horse then that he is now,' he says, trying to recall the feel of him. 'He wasn't quite so fresh. Mainly I hoped he'd run well for me, because he had already won three races that season.' He meant that, more than usual in this case, he was on a hiding to nothing and riding against the odds. Tommy Stack and Ron Barry had won on Red Rum already that season. He must do at least as well and win.

'Win if you can'

For that first forging of his triumphant partnership with Red Rum, Brian Fletcher got sensibly simple orders from McCain. 'Give the horse a chance' (to settle) 'over the first two miles. Then don't be too far out of it because he stays well. Then take it up' (the running) 'three from home and win if you can.'

After that first of their victories Fletcher says, 'I was overcome with the horse. I said to McCain "This is a typical 'National horse. If you run this horse in the 'National I would love to ride him." Things materialised from there.'

From strength to strength

'Red Rum,' Fletcher affirms, 'is a much more classy individual now. He's gone from strength to strength. I don't know but what he *realises* he's done well and won the two 'Nationals. He wasn't the *character* then what he is now.'

Fletcher is something of a character himself. When at the end of the day I rose to go gathering the tape-recorders, cameras, flashlights and notebooks he watched me sardonically from his sofa. 'I hope I've not left anything behind,' I murmured. Fletcher suggested keenly, 'Like your cheque book?'

Unless the regular rider of a champion horse enjoys a very equable temperament (Arkle's Pat Taaffe was so blessed) the strain of constantly expected victories can be sorely felt. I wished Fletcher luck for next season. He exploded, 'Everybody talks about a *third* 'National! As if *two* isn't enough! People don't think about *me*! The responsibility is *here*' – he touched the tip of his shoulder and looked anguished and very vulnerable. 'The responsibility,' he exclaimed, 'is mine. . . .'

I had asked him to telephone Anthony Gillam to say I was on my way. Tardily, but kindly he did so and remarked to Gillam, 'That chap's just left. Seems to know a fair bit about racin'.' Gillam said drily, 'Well he ought to. He's trained a Gold Cup winner, you know.'

'*Eeee!*' went Fletcher down the telephone. '*Eeee!* Did he!'

Beryl McCain in her kitchen.

Billy Ellison, ex-jockey, ex-boxer, ex-bartender . . .

Owner Noel Le Mare, lad Billy Ellison and Red Rum doing his staring trick into the sky. *Photo: "Lancashire Life"*

Brian Fletcher at home.

Bob Marshall, the farrier, tending the delicate feet.

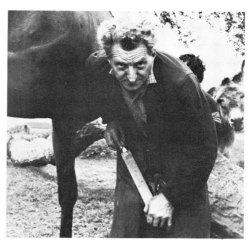

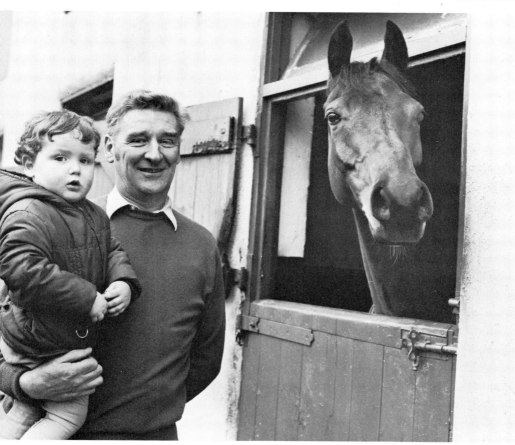

The "One Good Horse" with trainer McCain and young son Donald. *Photo: "Lancashire Life"*

At grass in the summer of '74. *Photo: Jeremy Hoare*

His summer holiday companion, Stan Wareing's donkey "Andy". *Photo: West Lancashire Press Agency*

Below: Seeing Andy off. *Photo: Jeremy Hoare*

35 'IF HE WAS A HUMAN BEING ... HE'D BE A PRIME MINISTER'

Red Rum's Ayr victory was 'Ginger' McCain's twelfth of the season. Things had never gone better. Morale in the tiny yard was ebullient. Hero-worship centred on the bright bay horse. His habits were prattled about. Two things always upset him: being plated for a race, and being bandaged before setting out. One other thing drives him berserk: being clipped. McCain and Billy groan, 'We've tried everything – the wireless on to distract him, cotton wool in his ears, so's he can't hear the buzzing. Even a hood over his head.' McCain says, 'It's when he feels the hair falling down. So Billy strokes him and I follow his hand with the clippers.' It takes no less than two weeks to finish clipping Red Rum, a task which, with a normal horse, is done in half a day. They can never clip his head.

The first autumn they tried to put a twitch on his nose to try to hold him for clipping. 'He *soon* sorted us out!' says McCain, a bit ashamed of trying this painful resort and proud of his great horse for seeing them off. 'Billy had to jump onto the manger and I was out of the door in a flash! He's a very fine-coated horse.' (And yet he survived those multiple cracks of the whip.)

'He *soon* sorted us out!'

When Billy is 'doing' him he kicks out, usually with his off-hind, and bites. 'Nips, oh aye,' exclaims Billy. 'I've had a few over the years, but I'm that little bit quicker than he is.' Red Rum does not squeal. 'Tries to,' says Billy, 'but he can't. Gives sort of groans, rather than grunts when I'm doin' him. If you knocked him about, that would really kill him.' So Billy has a rough time every evening stables. 'When he's alert he draws his bottom lip back and you can see his parrot teeth. You can polish him like a piece of wood.' Billy first sponges him all over, then dresses him over with body-brush and curry-comb, then uses a stable rubber all over for the final polish. He oils his feet as often as he can, using surprisingly (for most of us are warned against it) car sump oil.

'He's made a great difference to us going racing,' says

The Red Rum song

Billy Ellison proudly. 'People want to know you now. They're always askin' how he is.'

The 'Red Rum song' now famous in Birkdale and on northern racecourses was gradually developed by Billy and Jackie Grainger. They had heard two local singers in Southport rendering 'Old Snowball was a racehorse . . .' With the singers' help, Red Rum's devoted attendants composed this ballad which is given *fortissimo* every evening our hero is away at the races.

> O Red Rum is a racehorse
> And I wish he were mine
> He never drinks water,
> He always drinks wine.
>
> His bridle is silver,
> His mane it is gold
> And the worth of his saddle
> Has never been told.
>
> *Chorus*
> O Red Rum is a racehorse
>
> The racecourse was crowded
> And Red Rum was there,
> And the betting was heavy
> On the bay and the mare.
>
> *Chorus*
> O Red Rum . . . etc.
>
> I bet on the grey mare,
> I bet on the bay,
> If I'd bet on ole Red Rum
> I'd be a free man to-day.
>
> *Chorus*
> O Red Rum . . . etc.
>
> Away in the distance,
> Ahead of them all,
> Came a prancing and a dancing
> My noble Red Rum.
>
> O Red Rum is a racehorse
> And I wish he were mine
> He never drinks water,
> He always drinks wine.

With McCain's customary courtesy and bright enthusiasm the winning trainer dealt confidently with the
press over future plans. His horse would now have that
mid-season rest and then be prepared for Liverpool with
a couple of runs. Glenkiln was headed in the same direction **Glenkiln**
and preferred by Noel Le Mare, partly because of his **preferred**
seniority and the fact that he had bought him first (only to
be deprived of his 'National chance by that clerical mishap),
but mainly because of his wonderful performance round
Liverpool in the William Hill Grand National Trial.

While the two years younger Red Rum was knocking
up his five victories in a row, Glenkiln was failing to win
again. Red Rum did not run between Ayr on 16th November and Carlisle on 31st January. McCain had a fixed
target at which to aim, which must entail his horse resting
at some stage of the season. He was also fully aware that
Red Rum was no good on soft ground. The problem, with
February fill-dyke now greyly looming, was whether any
going other than soft or heavy would prevail before
Liverpool.

The going on Southport sands naturally remained **On**
excellent. McCain continued to work Red Rum but, as he **Southport**
puts it 'on his own, nice and quietly, and not upsides. He **sands**
thickened up with his break.' A week or so before Carlisle,
'we started to get after him a bit. But by the day he wasn't
fully wound up by a long way.'

The going at McCain's fancied Carlisle was fortunately
good. The race, though called the Cumberland Grand
National Trial handicap 'chase, was only over three miles
and was contested by a field of four. Our hero who a year
previously would have been weighted at the bottom of this
£632 handicap, now found himself sharing top weight
of 11st 9lb with Gyleburn. This was the horse which
Tommy Stack had declared caustically in September
would assuredly beat Red Rum. He had then been giving
9lb to Red Rum. Now they met at level-weights.
Gyleburn was again ridden by Ron Barry. McCain had
been pleased with Brian Fletcher's performance on Red
Rum at Ayr, but still regarded the Durham lad from Backs
and Sides Farm as having been a stop-gap there for the
absent Tommy Stack. He therefore again asked Stack if
he would ride the horse at Carlisle. Unfortunately for
Stack, and blessedly for Fletcher, Stack thought that he
would not be available. Ironically he was there, and not,
as he had expected, at the clashing Windsor meeting. As
McCain relates, 'We couldn't get Tommy, so I'd spoken

to Brian about it. Brian had asked me if I would consider him. I'd said, "Yes, if I can't get Tommy Stack".'

With the Grand National only two months away and the uncertain availability of both Stack and Ron Barry for the big race due to their stable retainers, 'Ginger' McCain thought the moment ripe to tie down Red Rum's 'National jockey. He tried Tommy Stack once more. Tommy remembers, 'I told Don McCain after Haydock that I wouldn't be able to ride Red Rum in the 'National, as I had a retainer from Tom Jones and he required me to ride Ashville.'

Like all able people McCain will always seek advice. With Glenkiln and Red Rum he had only just emerged from a world of humble horses and usually 'claiming' jockeys. He was not too sure about this retainer business. So he had a word with his experienced racing expert friend Stan Wareing, the pig producer.

'Do you think,' asked McCain, 'that we ought to offer Fletcher a retainer?'

Fletcher booked for the 'National

'Offer him nothing,' said Wareing bluntly. 'Tell him if he wants the ride he'll have to ride the horse in *all* his races prior to the 'National. Stipulate this.'

McCain accepted Wareing's advice. He spoke to Fletcher, who said 'Yes, delighted. Thank you very much'.

'And that,' says McCain grinning, 'is the only discussion we had on whether he rode the horse. And he *still* doesn't get a retainer.'

The horse after his ten-week lay off ran a thrilling Grand National trial. He went down by $1\frac{1}{2}$ lengths and a short head to Bountiful Charles (trained by the most remarkable point-to-point rider since the war, Sir Guy Cunard) and to Gyleburn (a case of good handicapping). Red Rum challenging over the last half a mile, dropped back a little going to the last fence, but came again with a rousing run on the flat and was closing swiftly on the winner.

'He literally flew'

'The Guv'nor had gone to see him,' McCain relates. 'And we were really delighted with him. He literally flew from the last and in another 30 yards we would have beaten Bountiful Charles.'

The risk of cancellations in February from fog, frost and flood is onerous. At a period when trainers of good horses are working up to Liverpool and Cheltenham the confounded whims and sulks of the British weather can drive horsemen to drink and blows. 'Ginger' McCain had given his two 'National horses plenty of engagements and he ran them both at the next Haydock meeting only seven days after Carlisle. Red Rum ran in the $3\frac{1}{2}$ mile 'National Trial worth £1,266 and Glenkiln 'whom the Guv'nor was *sure* was the best prospect for the 'National', ran the following day in a $2\frac{1}{2}$-mile handicap 'chase.

'Ginger' McCain was 'a shade disappointed' to be beaten by the unconsidered Highland Seal to whom Red Rum was trying to give 11 lbs. The victory, however, was one for an even smaller stable than McCain's, for Highland Seal was not only owned and trained but also bred by the Dening family who farm near Cullompton deep down in Devon. His victory was the stuff of which small permit trainers dream all year.

McCain noted after the race that Red Rum had markedly improved over Gyleburn who, getting 5lb from Red Rum, now finished 7 lengths behind him – an improvement of nearly a stone in our hero's form since Carlisle. 'He'd run a good race,' McCain observed, 'he'd got Proud Tarquin behind him, and Southern Lad and the 'National winner Well To Do.' 'Ginger' had also won a £5 bet with the owner of Swan-Shot, a local friend, that he'd finish in front of his – 'which we won, of course!'

'Then the Guv'nor said after the race, "Right 'Ginger', that's *your* fellow. Now tomorrow we'll see what *my* fellow can do". And Glenkiln comes out to run a cracking race to be second, too.'

Beaten by Highland Seal

The strange arrangement under which Red Rum has now won two Grand Nationals carrying his owner's second colours derives from this sporting rivalry between Noel Le Mare and 'Ginger' McCain over the two horses. Le Mare, always one for the underdog, remained loyal to the older Glenkiln in the face, and probably because of 'Ginger''s mounting enthusiasm for Red Rum. The final decision was not made until about ten days before the 'National when Le Mare again made the point that Glenkiln had won over the Liverpool fences. 'Let him have the first colours then,' said 'Ginger' McCain. 'It's your decision. Red Rum can have the second.'

Carrying his owner's second colours

Red Rum's programme was geared to include one more race, and again at handy Haydock on 3rd March for what 'Ginger' calls 'his 'National prelim'. He selected the £4,985 Greenall Whitley Handicap 'Chase run over 3 miles – 'perhaps not his best trip'. Three other factors mitigated against him: he was carrying top weight, heavy rain had turned the ground from good to soft overnight, and it was raining during the race – an element of English country life which Red Rum particularly loathes.

**On a
wet day**

Brian Fletcher declares roundly, 'On a wet day Red Rum doesn't want to go to the races. He's a miserable horse. He's a horse like a person who, on a fine day, will get his shirt off and go to work and work well. But on a wet day Red Rum curls up and he has no interest at all.' Brian thought about this for a moment and added surprisingly, 'If he was a human being I'm sure he would be Prime Minister'.

The Greenall Whitley is sponsored by the local brewery. Appositely, bright young Peter Greenall, a Cambridge undergraduate and Blue, and grandson of the head of the brewing family Lord Daresbury, rode the day's first winner owned and trained by his mother, a former point-to-point rider of dash and daring. He was not, however, cheered home by 'Ginger' McCain. The horse he just overtook at the post was 'Ginger''s The Tunku ridden by Brian Fletcher.

**Ground
against
him**

It continued to rain. In spite of the hostility of the elements, Red Rum was second to Tregarron going to the last fence. For the run-in the field switched onto the hurdle course. 'It was all cut up and heavy,' 'Ginger' McCain recalls, 'and I could see my fellow absolutely bogged down. He was *struggling* through it.' Two horses overtook him on the flat, Straight Vulgan and Red Sweeney, each carrying 16lb less than he was, and he finished fourth, beaten 7 lengths and two half-lengths. McCain declares, 'I felt a bit sick with myself for running him in that ground just before the 'National, but I was delighted with the horse. It wasn't as if he was tired and beaten. He just couldn't go through that heavy ground.'

Chaseform Notebook snapped up the point. 'Red Rum ran a great race on ground that was all against him . . .' it began and ended with the modest prognostication, 'When the ground dries up he will be winning again'. His

**Preparation
for the
'National**

next race was to be the Grand National, twenty-seven days away. Knowing Red Rum's super equine resilience his trainer was not long agitated by that hard race at Haydock. He fretted far more lest the ground failed to dry up in time for Liverpool. McCain set about a firm training programme. For the first five days after Haydock Red Rum went nowhere near the beach. He merely hacked about through the sandhills. Then he went straight back into strong work. What he did was phenomenal. Except for Thursdays and Sundays he cantered two miles every day and three days a week he was galloping over two miles afterwards. 'I really started to get after him,' said

McCain. 'For he was big and well and we started to step his feeding up.' The sort of mileage he was doing on the beach was extraordinary. 'But,' declares McCain, eyes crinkling up in his grin, 'he suddenly started to get better and better. He came on like a house on fire.'

'He came on like a house on fire'

The weather what was more, became mild, the slanting rains ceased, there was a murmur of spring warmth in the air. The spring burgeoned, too, in 'Ginger''s step. 'We got quite confident,' says McCain, 'and Glenkiln was doing well at the same time.'

The local papers fizzed with excitement over their two hometown horses. Southport has always prided itself on being quieter, less brash, more retiring than gaudy Blackpool which flashes beyond the bay. It was sufficiently retiring for many followers of steeplechasing to be quite unaware where it was. In certain broad swathes of Britain, Southport now became known because Red Rum lived in it. Glenkiln set to carry 10 st 7 lb in the National against Red Rum's 10 st 5 lb had been 40 to 1, and Red Rum 25 to 1 during the final month. Much was made of Le Mare's support for Glenkiln, for whom McCain had engaged a young jockey he fancies will be the champion very soon, christened John Joe O'Neill, now nicknamed 'Jonjo'.

'Both my horses are as fit as they can be,' McCain announced. Fletcher forecast, 'My fellow is a brilliant jumper. I'm certain he'll give me a great ride.'

'He'll give me a great ride'

Everyone who knew the McCains liked them. Everyone in Southport knew of and respected their leading citizen Noel Le Mare. His lifelong ambition to win a Grand National became common knowledge now throughout Britain as racing correspondents of national newspapers seized upon the saga of the droll octogenarian tycoon who had made it from nothing and of his warm and profitable partnership with his former taxi-driver. Le Mare had unguardedly murmured once that he must have spent about £100,000 on trying to win the Grand National and the figure was plucked out and held aloft like a jewel to be marvelled at. Reflecting afterwards, Le Mare regretted he had ever mentioned it. It made him seem, he thought, a grotesque spend-thrift. But he supposed that if one added together the capital cost of all his horses since the '50's and costed in all their keep and travelling costs and entry fees and jockeys' fees, well then it might be going on that way. But £100,000.... He shook his head slowly. And nearly all of us in the racing game would have horrid shocks adding up our costs....

'WILL DON McCAIN BRING LAURELS HOME TO BIRKDALE?'...'LE MARE HAS FINE CHANCE. ...' 'McCAIN IN CONFIDENT MOOD....' Money cascaded onto Red Rum nationwide, and deluged the local bookmakers. He would start favourite on the day.

Beryl McCain looks back in wonderment. 'I just didn't really think we were lucky enough to have a Grand National *winner*. It was "Ginger"'s ambition for many years to have a horse *run* in the race – never mind to have a winner. Secretly,' says Beryl, 'I didn't think he would win.'

Effervescent confidence

She was not borne aloft by 'Ginger''s effervescent confidence. It was that which had sustained him. For him, those long dark years were finally cast aside. All had swept marvellously forward, come what may. 'We were,' says Beryl 'both thoroughly enjoying it.' Birkdale and Southport being proud and self-possessed places had taken McCain's horses to their hearts. Had the stables been in Newmarket, Lambourn or in a large Yorkshire training centre similar excitement would not have been engendered. Cynical residents, having seen many great hopes rise and crash, would not have so enthused. But Grand National favourites don't grow on trees down Birkdale's avenues or behind its used-car sales rooms. It was a historic time in the town. The locals bragged about Red Rum. 'Ginger' McCain, once an obscure citizen, had become a leading public personality pointed out when he passed by. 'He would say,' Beryl recalls, 'that the horse had a very good chance. He was *very* confident.'

36 'THEY WERE GOING SO BLOODY FAST I COULDN'T CATCH THEM'

McCain left Red Rum's final winding-up gallop as late as the Friday, the day before the race. By the majority of trainers' standards the last long strong gallop before a major race is usually done rather earlier, often three or four days before D-day. The work immediately before the event is usually kept short and sharp. The last week running up to any big race is one of considerable strain on the trainer. In the case of an established maestro like Fred Winter, the pressure and the doubts, the urge to press on and the reluctance to risk damage, combine to pull out tensions like fraying elastic bands. In a yard before an important race the atmosphere twangs.

Two runners in the 'National

And here was Don McCain, very much the eager new boy in the big league, with two runners in the Grand National, one of them now antepost favourite and trained, what was more, most unorthodoxly on the public beach.

Some words of a man called Fred Clark, a great friend of trainer Tom Corrie's had always hung over the McCains. 'Clark,' says Beryl McCain, 'was a very knowledgeable gentleman, and the year before we bought Red Rum he spent a few months here and he said "I'll help you to get winners". "Ginger" learned a lot from him. He tried eggs and supplements and vitamins. And the horses didn't run any better. He left us saying, "You'll never have any winners as long as you've only got these beach gallops . . .".'

Beryl added simply, '"Ginger" wasn't too worried. He didn't believe him entirely.'

In the final weeks before the 1973 Grand National Beryl McCain remembers: 'I used to feel more strung up, because running a horse with a tremendous chance is always more nerve-racking than one that hasn't. We both got a bit strung up as the 'National drew closer. We were irritable.'

Poor Billy Ellison, the self-confessed former carefree layabout, was physically sick from sheer nerves most mornings in that last week. 'Billy used to get this terrible stomach trouble,' Beryl McCain remembers solicitously. She could hear the lad next door being sick most mornings before he rode out Red Rum for first lot. 'We thought it was an ulcer. And Red Rum was getting stronger and stronger every day.' This expanding, accelerating power beneath him was what so terrified the tough boxer Billy. Literally in his hands lay the hopes not just of himself but of a hundred thousand punters. Each morning Red Rum could get struck by a car, made to skid and fall on tarmac by a lorry, overreach himself slithering down a sand-dune, or run away with Billy down six miles of pounding beach.

'He frightens me to death'

'As he builds up,' says Billy, 'He frightens me to death.' He would look in every evening after stables to see whether his precious horse was all right, hadn't got colic or been cast. (He goes out most days every summer to see that Red Rum is still safe in his field at grass.) During those last weeks racing towards the 'National the strain on tough Billy Ellison became unbearable. 'The fear he might rap himself –' he mutters now still anguished. 'You wish and wish the 31st of March would come. And after his last bit of work on the last Friday – with the relief of it being over – I cried.' Trainers collect the credit, jockeys the glory, the owners the cash. All are subjected to strain. Think sometimes of the lad or girl 'doing' a famous horse. . . .

Part of Beryl and 'Ginger' McCain's popularity stems from their unaffected ingenuousness. 'For that first 'National,' Beryl admits, 'we were rather enjoying the publicity, the television cameras – we had a lot of cameras – and all that. Even on the morning of the race when I was plaiting the horse's mane, we had a camera right in his box.' The reaction of F. Winter, F. Walwyn or F. Rimell to the merest suggestion of such an intrusion would have curdled the blood of the inquirer.

Cameras out on the beach

What was even more of a strain, there were cameras out on the beach to record Red Rum's final and extraordinary gallop. It would cover that fifteen minutes when the trainer's decision, as of a general at the *moment critique* of a battle, will lead to victory or defeat. At this point in a horse's preparation, when what is left undone or done too much will by tomorrow prove irremediably wrong, most trainers would not tolerate the presence of any bystander. 'Ginger' McCain took along his great friend and confidant Stan Wareing and a television crew.

Wareing had said understandingly, 'I'll not come near him till his final gallop.' He was there with the television people early on Friday morning. Billy Ellison rode Red Rum, of course, feeling sick inside. He is no lightweight. Stripping at 10st 2lb now, he is probably riding out at 11st 7lb in clothes and with saddle, and that is plenty for a horse to hump at speed. Jackie Grainger was on Glenkiln.

McCain says, 'Red Rum and Glenkiln galloped over a mile and a half.' Red Rum, as always, led with his near-fore. As he hits top gear, he chucks his head down and, as soon as he gets into his rhythm, begins to dish with his leading foot, flicking it out-in, out-in, like a middle-weight boxer left-hooking like lightning. McCain tense, staring, watched his horses fly past against the sea. He was listening, too, sharp-eared, for the tempo of the feet hitting the scudding sand. Was it fast enough? Above the hoof-beats and the crack of the sea-breeze in the horses' sheets and against the lads' clothing, McCain strained to hear his horses' breathing. Was it a little thick? Was one of them stuffy?

'I wasn't too happy that they'd come quite a good enough pace the first time. They hadn't quickened up enough. When they came to pull up, Glenkiln stopped, but Red Rum wanted to keep on going. He started to disappear into the distance.' Billy, hanging on as if stopping a truck with steel hawsers, had his feet braced right up to Red Rum's ears.

'They came back and trotted up to us. They were both blowing a bit.' This was the instant when McCain would decide right or wrong. How much is 'a bit?'. Would one more sharp spin put them over the top? Would no more work leave them underdone for the morrow? Safer to underdo a horse. . . .

'I thought we'd run them again,' says McCain firmly. 'So the boys led them back.' They were going to gallop another 1½ miles the day before the race. Modern trainers find these exertions incredible. But the tough old trainers of yore would nod approvingly on their Elysian gallops.

'I met them in the truck about 5 furlongs out and shouted to them "Just let them *go!*". I was trying to go alongside in the truck, but they were going so bloody fast, I couldn't catch them. We were doing 45 miles an hour on the clock, and Stan Wareing's eyes were going round and round, and I wasn't *getting* to them! They'd *gone!* I was making no impression *at all!* And at last they pulled up.

'Stan thought I'd overdone it. To be quite honest,' says 'Ginger', 'I thought I had, too. I was worried about it.'

Billy Ellison and Jackie Grainger declared afterwards

that they too had both been worried for much of the last three weeks. Both had confided their anxieties to Jeff Langhorn the local grocer but former head lad: 'This 'oss,' they declared squarely, 'is gettin' too much work.'

Doubts, after that tremendous last morning's work raced through 'Ginger' McCain's head, too. The horses, Red Rum in front as usual, walked home through Birkdale, yawning itself awake. McCain drove back in his truck with a wrinkled brow. 'We came home. I had both horses sponged down and strapped right out and fed them both at lunchtime. Neither horse could get to the manger quick enough. They were fighting to get into their mangers.'

Pre-race anxiety There remained that final moment of pre-race anxiety: evening stables after a strong piece of work. This is when morning strain emerges in slight warmth and dreaded puffiness. And the McCain horses had done not an orthodox 6 furlongs to clear their winds, but two rousing $1\frac{1}{2}$ mile gallops one after the other, and the second so fast that a truck couldn't catch them going 45 m.p.h. Everyone worried during that afternoon.

'But at evening stables,' says 'Ginger', grinning again at the grand remembered relief of it, 'their legs were perfect. And both horses looked an absolute picture.' Not only were Red Rum's legs perfect – he has so far never had the slightest trouble with them – so were the feet. Since his second day at McCain's there had never been a trace of lameness. McCain was not aware that his horse had had pedalosteitis only a year before. That ignorance proved bliss. And the soft sand and the cold salt water had unknowingly effected an almost miraculous cure.

Billy Ellison had been backing Red Rum 'ever since the weights came out and I saw old Glenkiln had 2lb more. I backed him every week when I got my wages: £5 at 33 to 1, another £1 at 33's, 2 quid at 20 to 1, and so on.' **'The greatest horse in the world'** He was one of hundreds of locals, as Steve Makin the balding bookie across the street ruefully remembers. His family owns the betting shop. 'Red Rum's the greatest horse in the world,' said Makin to me wryly, 'but he's causes me an awful lot of hard work and headaches.'

Billy Ellison weighed up the risks. 'I thought that though he'd never seen Aintree' (Billy meant the fences) 'he was clever enough to keep out of trouble. He's never fallen in his life,' declared Billy, 'touch wood' – and promptly leaned across to touch the table which bore his drink.

Teetotal Tommy Stack had more experience of Red Rum's jumping than anyone else. 'He's a very light-footed horse. He gets himself right for his fences, but if you left him entirely alone he'd be over-cautious.'

'I knew he jumped well,' said Brian Fletcher, 'and wasn't too worried about him jumping at Liverpool. But when you go to Liverpool on any horse,' Fletcher declared with vehemence – 'then you've got to have 75-per-cent luck.'

'Ginger' McCain was confident about Red Rum jumping Aintree's strange fences. 'He's a *funny* horse. He's a *steady* jumper. He does nothing brilliantly. He doesn't jump like Crisp. He doesn't give the fences six inches too much or too little. He jumps and he's down and he's galloping. He'd never match a brilliant horse like Crisp at *jumping*,' McCain said realistically.

The horse's owner was a little alarmed that something might happen to Red Rum. He comforted himself by recollecting Tommy Stack's words to him that sleeting, slipping day at Haydock – 'Don't worry. The horse will look after himself.' There are some horses like that, old Mr Le Mare encouraged himself, driving to the course. Furore had been like that, his jockeys had told him. He thought about Arkle who had never been faced with the extraordinary dangers of Liverpool. 'That Arkle,' he said after Red Rum had won his two Grand Nationals and the Scottish Grand National, 'that horse Arkle was a very famous horse. But she never risked it, the Duchess never risked it at Liverpool like we've risked Red Rum.'

'The horse will look after himself'

He was patently nervous being driven to the course and someone in his car said with singular optimism, 'Never mind, Noel, if you don't win it this year, you might win it next.' Mr Le Mare retorted quickly – for everyone knew that the course was about to be sold to a strange building firm – 'I don't *want* to win next year. I want to win it *this* year while dear old Mirabel' (Aintree's popular former owner Mrs Topham) 'is still there with all her old arrangements.' Nothing would delight him more than if his horse's name could appear on Mrs Topham's gilded roll of honour, even if it would be the last of an era.

Beryl and 'Ginger' McCain were wafted across to Liverpool in a Rolls-Royce. To make their first runner in the 'National even more of a life-time's occasion, and also for that vital moral sustenance in waiting hours when friends are sorely needed, they had arranged to travel with Stan and Carol Wareing. They went out to the Wareings' house, Holly Farm, near Halsall, and because Stan is a generous host who enjoys champagne, they downed a couple of bottles. They were a party of eight: 'Ginger''s shrewd and industrious partner in their motor business Peter Cundy with his wife Marie, and the Wareings' young daughter Gilly and a schoolfriend of hers. The excitement and the champagne made their progress to the course very much a giggle and a hoot. Everyone was larking about on the way. McCain's partner Peter Cundy hardly ever went racing and, keeping business well to the fore, was introduced to Tommy Stack outside the weighing-room and promptly sold him a Datsun.

Red Rum and Glenkiln had made their own short way across to Liverpool leaving about 10.30. Our hero travelled easily and if Billy Ellison and Jackie Granger felt agitated, they showed little trace of it and went quietly about their business in the racecourse stables. The horse was allowed to settle in, to rest, to 'stale', until the more frantic moment arrived, just over an hour before the race, to get him ready. Then tension makes thumbs of fingers as you unbuckle obstinate straps and bustling lads get in each other's way and curse, and the horse, sniffing the agitation in the air, grows nervous too. Red Rum's eyes glowed. His ears cocked and flickered. His lips went snap, flap, snap, together.

In the stable yard, and then in the paddock, he was the cynosure of every racing eye.

Almost before Beryl McCain knew it she and 'Ginger' were early in the paddock's centre with Mr Le Mare and Mrs Doris Solomon watching the horses circulate inside banks of goggling eyes. Beryl explained, 'Mr Le Mare doesn't spend too long in the paddock, because he does get a little short of breath, and he doesn't want to be too short of time for getting back into the stands.'

Noel Le Mare had not conquered sixty years of commerce's tempestuous seas only to show excitement as his best chance of seizing the third of his life's triple ambitions whirled quickly closer. His friends observed him looking pale, but he hopped nimbly around and his wise eyes gazed sharply about him.

He waited until Brian Fletcher and Jonjo O'Neill came in, said to them cheerfully, 'Have a safe journey. Come back safe and sound,' which is always the sporting owner's valediction. He then set off back to the stands with Mrs Solomon. He was not, he claims, particularly excited. 'The only time I get excited,' he remarked roguishly, 'is when I go near a girl.' He was aware, however, that others might not be so calm. Because he believes that Devon Loch's controversial collapse on the run-in in ESB's 1956 'Nat-

Excitement and champagne

Cynosure of every racing eye

'Have a safe journey'

ional was due to 'an ovation too soon', he had made a plea in the *Liverpool Echo*: 'Now remember Devon Loch. Red Rum is a Liverpool horse. Half Liverpool and half South-port will be on it. For God's sake keep quiet until he's past the post.'

12 to 1 was obtainable about Red Rum on the eve of the race. 11 to 1 was forecast in the morning papers. He opened favourite at 12's and was backed down to 9 to 1 co-favourite with the mighty Australian Crisp who had opened at 14 to 1. The huge dark-brown horse had been given the maximum top-weight of 12 stone, which onerous compliment he shared with the American-owned, Irish-trained dual Cheltenham Gold Cup winner, the ill-named L'Escargot. This horse, opening at 14 to 1, was backed down to third favourite at 11 to 1, followed in the betting by Ashville, the horse for which Tommy Stack had originally had to decline the ride on Red Rum. Such are the falls of the game. Tommy Stack, Red Rum's one-time stable jockey and brief-time trainer, had no ride in the '73 'National at all. Injured in a fall at Kempton on the 10th March he would be watching his friend go by.

Red Rum 12 to 1

37 'OF ALL THINGS – TOAST AND CHAMPAGNE'

Betting was particularly heavy, unusually accurate in its selection and, for once, quite beneficial to the punters. Those who prefer the bookie-free methods of racing finance practised in the world's other major racing countries noted that William Hill's boasted of £700,000 being staked with their organisation on the race. Ladbroke's with their money-minting nationwide net of betting shops, claimed even more: $1\frac{1}{2}$ million punters had wagered more than £1 million on the race. 'Undoubtedly a record,' murmured a Ladbroke's official comfortably.

The lottery of the year

Nearly £2 million bet on one race with just a couple of betting organisations seems a maniacal amount of money for a nation somnambulating towards bankruptcy. But the British as a whole would rather gamble than work. We are the world's biggest (and so poorest) punters, the Grand National is the lottery of the year, and nowhere on the globe have there ever existed bookmakers as rich as ours.

Beryl McCain had no bet. She hardly ever does. Nor does she often watch a race with 'Ginger', particularly with Red Rum. 'We stand apart.' She went up onto the roof on her own.

'Don McCain,' said Brian Fletcher, 'did not give me any orders. I just said I was going to sit in the middle on the outside on the first circuit and hunt round. Then ride a race past the stands.'

Stay out of trouble

'Brian's plan,' said McCain, 'was to stay out of trouble on the first circuit to get the horse settled and running nicely. Then, once you're over The Chair' (just coming up to the stands) 'to sit down and ride a jockey's race. This is pretty well what he did.'

Fletcher makes another point. 'I was trying to help Jonjo, 'cos he was having his first ride round Aintree. He was on my "inner" till he fell. In all the 'Nationals I've ridden in, I always try to get a clear run on the first circuit, trying to dodge the fallers. Luck went with me.'

So did Red Rum's intelligence and his own instinct for keeping out of trouble and on his feet. He is simply that

A safe jumper

often-described but rare conveyance 'a safe jumper'. So was Arkle. So are nearly all steeplechasing stars. Without Red Rum's literally boundless stamina, even without his courage he would still be getting round and winning when the others fell. As it is, he gallops on and on, growing incredibly stronger while his ordinary rivals weaken.

'He is not in my opinion,' Brian Fletcher decides, 'a particularly brave *jumper*. He doesn't just take hold of his bit and go from A to B.' Jumping crackles with such terrifying tearaways. 'He watches what he's doing,' as Fletcher describes it. 'He sidesteps any bother, provided he has time to see it. If there's any trouble near him, he'll dodge out of it. He's a very *clever* horse. This is a horse that has *brains*.'

Brains then, and a strong sense (often quite absent in moronic horses) of self-preservation. Quickness of reflex. Observance of trouble ahead. Balance – Bobby Renton's 'beautiful proportions'. These things combine to make what he is: a natural jumper. Yet there is no vestige of

Always reckoned a careful jumper, but look at the prodigious distance he is standing off the open ditch in the 1973 Grand National.

Above: In grim
pursuit of the flagging
Crisp at the last
battered fence. . . .

Left: Celebrating the
day after the 1973
Grand National in the
"local" in Upper
Aughton Road –
always called "The
Upsteps". *Photo:
"Daily Express"*

Top: Catching the
gallant, exhausted
Australian Crisp to
win the 1973 Grand
National and smash
Golden Miller's
record time.

Above: Head Lad,
Jackie Granger
(*centre*), gripped by
Red Rum's lad, Billy
Ellison, as our hero
passes the post. (1973
Grand National).

'jumping blood' in his pedigree. Battered by man he
certainly was in some ways, but the tough school taught
him not delinquency but survival. And he was helped.
Tim Molony's little circular loose school was his kinder-
garten. Sandra Kendall, as was, schooled him on. Dozens
of different jockeys doing different things made him, as a
young man learns to cope with different bosses, utterly
self-reliant. And finally his foot stopped hurting and he
loved his supremacy on the long wide sands, and he found
in battle-scarred Brian Fletcher someone who wouldn't
badger and bother him, but let him settle.

The ground on 31st March, 1973 was exactly as Red
Rum loves it: firm. Brian Fletcher had warmed up with a
4th in the first race, the BP Shield Handicap Hurdle. Don
McCain was relieved to see him safe round and home.

Firm ground

38 runners paraded for the Grand National. It was worth
£25,486 and, 3 minutes late at 3.18 p.m., the field leapt
forward on the start of a journey of 4 miles and 856 yards
which only 17 would complete. The firmness of the ground
strongly suggested a fast pace. The jockeys had received
their customary half-heard cautionary warning against
going a mad gallop early on. No one, in fact, believed that
records were about to be broken.

Nothing accelerated steeplechasing's soaring popularity
more than its television coverage by the cool and competent BBC. Its leading racing commentator Peter O'Sullevan is a legend in his lifetime. A victorious owner himself on the highest level both on the flat and under N.H.
Rules, he knows the game from the muck-yard up to its
rich and noble patrons. His commentaries set a standard
so far unequalled. And he begins:

'They're off. And Rouge Autumn starts fast on the inside,
with Sunny Lad and Go-Pontinental moving up on the
outside with Beggar's Way, then comes Black Secret with
General Symons on his outside and Richeleau and Glenkiln. Crisp has gone right up there with Sunny Lad on the
inside, then comes Hurricane Rock, then Mill Door over
on the far side with Endless Folly, Beggar's Way and Black
Secret, and with Rouge Autumn disputing it, they come
to the first.'

'They're off!'

John Hanmer takes up the commentary:

'Black Secret over in the lead. There's a faller – Richeleau
has gone at the first – and as they go towards the second,

Grey Sombrero on the outside along with Ashville, then Glenkiln, then comes Black Secret, General Symons then Highland Seal. . . . Over the ditch and Grey Sombrero over first. There's a faller at that one – Ashville fell.'

Then shrewd Julian Wilson, beady-eyed, the intense and furrowed-brow'd skilled television interviewer, takes up the racing tale:

Towards Bechers

'And spread right across the course with Grey Sombrero the leader over that one, from Endless Folly in the centre, Black Secret towards the outside, Highland Seal just scrambled over that one. Crisp is right up there on the inside, as they race down towards the fifth. As they race down towards Bechers, it's the grey, Grey Sombrero, racing wide of the field, the clear leader from Crisp in second, Black Secret third. At Bechers – Grey Sombrero over – and *just* clears it – from Crisp in second, Black Secret third, Endless Folly fourth, Sunny Lad five, Rouge Autumn is sixth and Beggar's Way is a faller at Bechers. Over the next, with Crisp *now* the leader from Grey Sombrero, then Black Secret and Endless Folly . . . they come towards the Canal Turn. Nereo has been pulled up and Crisp is the leader from Grey Sombrero, Black Secret, Endless Folly . . . then comes Spanish Steps. Highland Seal has been pulled up as they jump the next. Crisp over it from Grey Sombrero, Black Secret. . . .

John Hanmer resumes from his vantage point:

'As they go towards the next fence it's Crisp the clear leader from Grey Sombrero, Endless Folly, Black Secret, then comes Great Noise, Sunny Lad, then Rouge Autumn, then comes Tarquin Bid, behind Tarquin Bid is Red Rum, then Spanish Steps, then Hurricane Rock and Glenkiln as they go across the Melling Road.'

We pick up Peter O'Sullevan again as they turn onto the racecourse.

Red Rum well in there

. . . 'Crisp, well clear, over from Grey Sombrero who jumps it second, Endless Folly jumps it third, then Great Noise fourth, five is Black Secret, six is Rouge Autumn, seven is Spanish Steps and eight Tarquin Bid and nine is Red Rum and ten, on the inside, is Sunny Lad as they come to the next. Crisp over in the lead and clear. . . . Red Rum well

in there' (he was 12th) 'and then comes Glenkiln. . . .
Coming to the Chair now – this is one of the biggest.
Crisp, his ears pricked, jumps it beautifully in the lead – he
just pecked a little bit, but got away with it. Grey Sombrero's gone at that one. Grey Sombrero's a faller, Glenkiln's a faller –'

Beryl McCain was staring from the top of the stand. 'I
saw Red Rum on the wide outside all the way round. I
saw Crisp. Then I saw poor "Glen" fall. We'd all got soft
spots for him, 'cos he's a super and very kind horse. He fell
at the Chair and I saw him struggle. He couldn't get up.
His leg was stuck in the bottom of the fence. Canharis
jumped over after him and clouted him on the back of the
head. He got up. He was dazed. He jumped the water
and fell in and the whole of his back legs were covered with
the water. And he pulled himself out and they caught him
by the stables. I hadn't watched Red Rum. And by the time
Glen was out of the water, they'd jumped the first fence
second time round and Crisp was still in the lead, but Red
Rum was *second!*'

Over the
Chair

'Ginger' McCain was delighted to see Brian Fletcher
really riding Red Rum along over the Chair and then the
water. They improved five or six places very rapidly.

Thus away over the Melling Road with the giant Crisp
loping along in front, turning the enormous fences into
hurdles, seeming as if he was cantering ahead of a pack of
galloping ponies.

Fletcher says: 'From the third fence on the second circuit,
from the ditch, I was chasing this horse in front of me. I
didn't know what it was. I couldn't tell it was Crisp.'

John Hanmer calls the remnants as they thunder past him:

'Crisp at the ditch, the nineteenth, he stood right back, he
jumped it well, he's right out in front still of Red Rum,
second, Rouge Autumn is third, Spanish Steps fourth,
Tarquin Bid is fifth, Great Noise is sixth, then Endless
Folly and Black Secret.'

Julian Wilson's admiration of great Crisp sends his voice
sailing:

'And Richard Pitman over that one on Crisp and what a
fantastic ride he's having! I can't remember a horse so far
ahead in the Grand National at this stage! Jumping that

second was Red Rum, then Spanish Steps on the outside of Rouge Autumn, Great Noise made a mistake there, but coming to the next . . . Crisp is over that one, safely over the one before Bechers from Red Rum. . . . Crisp comes on his own to Bechers Brook for the second time, Crisp the top weight. Richard Pitman over it in tremendous style and he's about twenty lengths clear from Red Rum in second place, behind comes Spanish Steps, then Hurricane Rock. Crisp is over the twenty-third *already*, and racing down to the Canal Turn, as Red Rum jumps the twenty-third in second place. . . . Crisp jumps the Canal Turn, clear. He's still twenty lengths clear from Red Rum in second.'

'I just thought at the Canal Turn,' says 'Ginger' McCain, 'that we'd be second and how unlucky we were to meet Crisp. . . .'

'Seeing the race afterwards,' reflects little Brian Fletcher, 'I've often said to myself that if I'd *ever* said "I'm going to be second", if I'd ever dropped my hands or eased off Red Rum for one moment, then I *would* have been second.'

Fletcher did not ease. Red Rum did not falter. Fletcher drew his whip at Anchor Bridge. He hit Red Rum twice, thrice, four times. The bay horse quickened. 'Knowing the horse would stay and jump,' says Fletcher, 'and had only 10st 5lb on his back, I never accepted he'd be second.'

John Hanmer saw the move, but Crisp was still, as Julian Wilson had shouted, a long long way ahead of Red Rum.' Hanmer called quickly, 'Crisp has got three to jump, he's well clear of Red Rum, who's made a bit of ground. Spanish Steps is third, Hurricane Rock is fourth. Over the third from home, Crisp over safely. Red Rum in second place, then Spanish Steps, Hurricane Rock just passing Spanish Steps. . . . As they go across the Melling Road, with two to jump, it's Crisp with Red Rum in second place *making* ground, but a very long gap after that to Hurricane Rock, Spanish Steps and Rouge Autumn. . . .'

Peter O'Sullevan takes up the saga of the slowly shrinking lead, Crisp conceding one stone nine pounds to his pursuer. 'It's Crisp in the lead from Red Rum, but Red Rum *still* making ground on him! Brian Fletcher on Red Rum chasing Dick Pitman on Crisp. Crisp still *well* clear with two fences left to jump in the 1973 National and this great Australian 'chaser, Crisp, with twelve stone on his back and ten stone five on the back of Red Rum, who's

chasing him and they look to have it *absolutely* to themselves. At the second last . . . Crisp is over. And clear of
Red Rum who's jumping it a long way back. In third place
is Spanish Steps then Hurricane Rock and Rouge Autumn
and L'Escargot. But coming to the final fence in the
'National now . . . and it's Crisp *still* going in great style
with twelve stone on his back. He jumps it well. Red Rum
is about fifteen lengths behind him as he jumps it. Dick
Pitman coming to the elbow now in the National. He's
got two hundred and fifty yards to run. But *Crisp is just
wandering off the true line now*. *He's beginning to lose concentration*. He's been out there on his own for so long. *And
Red Rum is making ground on him*. Still as they come to the
line, it's a furlong to run now, two hundred yards now for
Crisp, and Red Rum *still* closing on him, and Crisp is
getting *very* tired, and Red Rum is pounding after him
and Red Rum is the one who finishes the strongest. *He's
going to get up! Red Rum is going to win the 'National!* At the
line Red Rum has just *snatched* it from Crisp! *And Red Rum
is the winner!* And Crisp is second and L'Escargot is just
coming up to be third. . . .

Red Rum
fifteen
lengths
behind

Beryl McCain was alone and shaking on the top of the
stands. 'When Red Rum came back onto the racecourse I
was getting excited that he was going to be *second*. This
was fantastic. I started not being able to hold my glasses
still. Then it became worse. And he jumped the last and I
was getting very weepy and I just broke down. There was
a lady stood in front of me and she got hold of me. And she
let me put my head on her shoulder and I was crying my
heart out. She said, "Which is yours?" and I said "It's
Red Rum". She said "He's won. Are you alright?" and I
said "Yes".'

'He's
won'

'She came to me afterwards,' said Beryl McCain, 'and
asked "Do you remember me?" I said, "Thank you very
much for looking after me". She said, "I completely
understand. I was the same when my husband rode the
winner of the 'National in '69. I'm Eddie Harty's wife."'

Old Mr Le Mare was white. 'When he was catching up
on Crisp, they're all cheering and shouting and bawling,
and I just sit there and look. . . .' But another owner of
McCain's had watched him with some anxiety. 'He was
shouting and cheering. His hands were in the air. I thought
he'd have a heart attack.' McCain said afterwards, bringing
out all his loving admiration for Noel Le Mare, 'The
Guv'nor tells me his face never moved!'

'Hope your Guv'nor's all right?' a friend of 'Ginger''s gasped, running to congratulate him as the horse was mobbed by deliriously excited Jackie Grainger and Billy Ellison.

Dazed with glory

They ran at and round him hugging and slapping him, as if they would wrestle him to the ground. Red Rum was escorted in by the two police horses. Noel Le Mare, who claims he is only excited by women, got down in the unsaddling enclosure. They brought him a chair. He sat on it dazed with glory, his head a little slanted, his mouth smiling with the delight of having won something even more than the world's greatest steeplechase.

'All these people in my box,' said Mr Le Mare, 'jumping up and down like mad people!' He gave a twinkle. 'I never batted an eyelid,' he said.

It was only 67 years since Le Mare the engineer's apprentice had read about Ascetic Silver's Grand National and seen that American millionaire spinning sovereigns outside the Fleetwood Hotel. It was a normal man's lifetime since he'd made his three resolves. It seemed to him, in that euphoria of dreams come true, only a day or so back across the troubled years to McCain's first winner, San Lorenzo, here at Liverpool. Mr Le Mare had watched that race from the rails. 'The horse looked to me like a donkey amongst a lot of good animals, but he came storming in, and I lost my breath and everything to get to "Ginger".' So now when the third of his three dreams came true, he struggled back to get to 'Ginger'.

As the horse came in McCain's grin beamed over the hub-hub suitably like the Cheshire cat's: he has always loved that next-door county. There he stood all in brown with a furry collar, face alight, looking the nicest fellow in the world, murmuring 'I'm only a glorified amateur. . . .

'You can't get on top of him'

Knew my feller would tackle him all the way . . . you can't get on top of him. . . .'

Beryl recovered, not quite tear-stained but eyes enormous and shining, was there in her blue coat under her white Russian hat. The One Good Horse that 'Ginger' had been on about all these years, driving through Cheshire, pointing out the big places and the grand horses, the One Good Horse had come.

And Brian Fletcher, scarlet-faced, sweating, gap-toothed, triumphantly grinning, was trying inarticulately to recount his victory with much chopping and punching of his left hand. His mother, a charming-looking lady, all aglow had (as Brian would say) materialised suddenly at his side and had come in proudly with her son squeezed by the mounted policemen. Brian murmured some good and loving things about her, and moistness of the eyes was added to the heated damp of victory.

McCain had watched the race from the top of the County Stand. 'I thought, honestly, we were going to win it even 50 yards off going to the last.' He said immediately in praise of Crisp, 'He didn't waver till after he'd jumped the last. Red Rum went absolutely straight compared to Crisp who definitely wandered off to the left.' The huge Australian, punch-drunk with fatigue, had tottered left towards the dolls like an exhausted explorer, at the end of his tether, struggling into sight of home. 'Ginger' said, 'Crisp was magnificent. The weight bogged him down. But I couldn't see the same thing happening to Red Rum. I think he would have kept going come what may. Till he dropped. Because this is him.'

Red Rum had smashed the generally accepted Grand National record time set up by Golden Miller in 1934. (In some record books Reynoldstown carrying 11st 4lb in 1935 (the first year of his double) is credited with 9 mins 20.2 secs compared with 'The Miller's' 9.20.4 secs carrying 12st 2lb). Red Rum's time, an incredible half-a-minute quicker than the *average* time, was 9 mins 1.9 secs – a speed over the 30 biggest obstacles in Britain of nearly 29 m.p.h.

A record time

The corks came out of the champagne bottles in a fusillade on the racecourse. Fletcher and McCain agreed to pay for a case each to go into the weighing room for the jockeys and valets. McCain remarked afterwards, 'Somehow I seemed to pay for both. . . .' Charitably he put it down to the riotous moment of victory.

At last the McCain's party set off back for Birkdale.

'We were only about five minutes in front of the box,' says 'Ginger', 'and when we turned up the road I saw the road blocked. I thought there had been an accident. I saw police-cars, and there must have been four or five hundred people and the streets were jammed. The police weren't even *trying* to get people through. Everyone was at a standstill. But everybody was being marvellous about it. Then the box comes round the corner with its headlights on and all its lights flashing and the horns going. Jackie's driving and the boys are all hanging out of the cab. . . . It was *grand*.' McCain's face suddenly switches into one of sympathy. In the elation of victory he was thinking of the faller. 'But it was rather sad as well, because Glenkiln had had a desperate fall and was very, very sore.' The ramp went down, Red Rum came out and received a blast of tremendous cheering. McCain said to Billy Ellison, 'Take him up the road fifty yards for the people to see,' McCain grinned again at the delight of the greeting, then added, 'But while that's going on poor old Glenkiln slips out of the box and slides into the stable, very stiff, very sore. And he's such a good-hearted horse, that I felt very sad.'

The celebrations exploded

The celebrations exploded down the streets and into the little yard. A tide of people shouting and cheering swept over the cobbles round Red Rum's box, and then jostled into the McCains' small house. Strangers from the streets, magnetised by their new local hero, converged upon him and upon the celebratory drinks.

'Then everybody seemed to come into the house! I don't know where they came from.' 'Ginger' added, abashed, 'I'd had a couple of crates of champagne brought in before the race – got a bit carried away, I suppose. . . .' He would never have admitted such confidence before. He went on, 'They got stuck into those. Then the toast-machine got started and everybody was eating toast. Of all things, toast and champagne! The yard was crammed full. The police had a few jars too.' The rejoicing continued for an hour and a half and then McCain decided that the horses needed a rest. 'We filtered the people out quietly and some went off. The Guv'nor was having a do at the Prince of Wales so we went off there. But I didn't feel like getting too involved in a party, so about ten of us went and had a quiet meal in the dining room of the Prince of Wales. I think the Guv'nor had a bill for around £800 for champagne. I think all of Southport had free drinks on him.'

Reluctant to be a hero

But the pendulum reaction to the greatest triumph of 'Ginger' McCain's life began to swing. He is a quiet man, gratified but reluctant to be suddenly a hero. 'The dinner was a little bit of an anti-climax after it all. I would have preferred it to be *very* quiet with just a few close friends.'

He had moreover a small anxiety about Red Rum. During the race the record-breaking winner had struck into his near-fore and given himself a small, but very deep cut. The scar clearly remained fifteen months later. 'It was a nasty deep little cut,' said 'Ginger' McCain, 'and he was rather sore. We bandaged it and he stayed in his box for three days, resting.'

There was no rest on the morrow for the McCains. Noel Le Mare looked understandably, and in 'Ginger''s words, 'very peaky and very tucked up afterwards'. But on the Sunday 'Ginger''s and Beryl's house filled up again with celebrants and they decided to go down the street to their nearest pub, always know to its habitués for visible reasons as 'The Upsteps'.

It was already crowded, with a thunder of voices and collection of splendid Lancashire urban faces making 'Coronation Street' seem plastic rubbish. A rousing cheer exploded as 'Ginger''s tall frame squeezed in through the door and his now famous face beamed down on the hot, laughing throng. After a very great victory in a very great race, after defeating ill-luck and hardship, something magic attaches to the connections of the triumphant horse. Ordinary people want to touch them for luck and to record, '"Ginger" had a word wi' me this mornin''.

'Ginger' rashly shouted out 'Drinks all round twice!'. He said, 'Everybody had drinks twice and twice again and so on and we'd been at the champagne that morning, anyway. Oh, it was a *good day. . . .!*'

'Oh, it was a *good day*'

If it had not been for Red Rum's over-reach he would have gone for the Scottish National that first year in 1973. With the wound, there was no question of running him again. After three days he was ridden out again deep into the sea. It cured his over-reach. It took away the soreness. He was sound again. He accepted homage as he passed through the town. 'It's not really a horsey town,' said 'Ginger', 'but he's about the greatest celebrity Southport's ever had.'

The season ended. Noel Le Mare toweringly topped the owners' list with stakes of £34,196 won by three horses in eight races (Red Rum had won six of them). 'Ginger' McCain proved conclusively that he was no one-horse trainer by producing eight different winners of eighteen races worth £37,404. He ranked 6th in the trainers' table, finishing between the two large stables of Bob Turnell (5th) and David Barons (7th). Of Red Rum's jockeys that year, Ron Barry sailed away with the championship with 125 winners, Tommy Stack was 3rd with 71 and Brian Fletcher, now established as our hero's partner, ended up 6th with 47 winners. Of the perils of the sport there was lower down the list a poignant reminder. The late Doug Barrott, killed in action, had finished his season, and his life, with 43 winners.

Red Rum spent his first Lancashire summer half on a farm of Stan Wareing's on the flat land near Burscough, and half with a herd of other holidaying horses in a big 35-acre field which McCain rents for grazing and school-ing. Windy and flat it borders a dual-carriage way. At the first farm Red Rum was turned out with the Wareings' Andy, the original shaggy donkey, an animal unattractive in appearance and personality, resembling a scruffy don and acting like a surly-minded picket. Beauty, however, lies in Red Rum's eye. For the first week he was caught every evening, boxed up and driven back to his stables. (There are naturally no green paddocks in the middle of Birkdale.) 'But,' says 'Ginger', 'he grew more and more bloody-minded about leaving that donkey. So after the first week we just left him out day and night, and he stayed out ten weeks.'

Red Rum behaved profession-ally

He switched halfway through to the other field to join the horse-herd, with which he might well have got into trouble, as their kicking-order was already as firmly established as the Civil Service's. Red Rum behaved pro-fessionally. There was no mad galloping. He cantered off a few hundred yards, picked a new pal in a jumper called Morning Light, put his muzzle down to the warm summer grass and settled down, with his beaky parrot-mouth, to some steady, serious cropping.

McCain wastes no time roughing his horses off. 'Once we decided to do it, off come their-hind shoes and three days later they're out!'

The blacksmith, Bob Marshall, a Lancashire craftsman and character with a tremendous nose, has the vital task of keeping Red Rum's delicate feet in working order. 'They're definitely not good feet. Can't allow myself to make any little mistakes – follow me meanin'? – If there's just a bit more pressure there' (tapping the horse's hoof) 'than here. . . .' Marshall wags his head ominously. 'Look, they're still that little bit different. But they're both growin'. When he came he took a five plate – normal enough. But in 1974 after the Grand National a five plate would go nowhere near! It was at least one inch too short!' With all his years of hammering experience the blacksmith was astonished. The growth of the feet was extraordinary. It cannot be ascribed after so long to the physiotherapy and ultra-sonics and Swedish pads and Stockholm Tar of the winter and spring of 1971–72. Something had caused the hooves to grow. By growing, it seems that the pressure on those poor old bones had been eliminated.

The blacksmith says critically, 'His feet are still too flat and shallow.' Grazing, Red Rum has one foreleg, usually the near fore, extended and bent at the knee, toe touching the ground rather than the heel. But it was nothing to be alarmed about: McCain said he always grazed like that. 'The sign of a good horse? I don't know . . . well, perhaps.' And we talked of great horses we had known.

'The sign of a good horse?'

When Red Rum stands, feet together, regarding you with a champion horse's hauteur, that near-fore is definitely turned in. To be frank, the great horse is not only parrot-mouthed but pigeon-toed. It is lucky that he can fly like an eagle. . . .

Stooping over Red Rum's upturned off-fore where all the trouble had struck, the sweat trickles down the blacksmith's beaky nose. He started his craft as a 14-year-old. He was 51 when 'Rum *Red*' as he calls him, won his second Grand National. He brims with confidence and damns layabouts, free-loaders and most modern youth. Since 1948 his family have shod nothing but horses. His father started a forge in Liverpool. His elder brother had just retired from one in Birmingham. 'We only work for the animal,' said Bob Marshall aggressively, 'We don't give two blanks for the customer – they only pay us.' He glanced at McCain who was perched, waiting like a large ginger bird, on the bare fallen tree. McCain smiled. The blacksmith said to needle him, '*I* prefer light steel shoes, not aluminium. . . . Saves changin' 'em so often.'

The blacksmith does not approve either of ready-made bought-in shoes. 'We make our own. We take full precautions – follow my meanin'? – *Every* shoe we make is a brushing shoe. *Every* shoe is an over-reach shoe. . . .

'We make our own shoes'

'I don't think a farrier should be *told*,' Bob Marshall continued. 'He only has to run his hands down the legs to tell how a horse'll move. No need to have him out to see him move. You can tell from how they stand, from a *severe* looking into it.'

He thought that the exercise over sandhills, along the beach and the total absence of trotting on the roads had saved Red Rum's feet, so far, from a further onset of pedalosteitis. When the horse starts conditioning he is out for two hours, two or three days a week, and except for shoving himself up the sandhills and slithering down, he walks all the way home.

Red Rum sensible of admiration

In 1973, McCain brought Red Rum up 'a shade later than usual, towards the back-end of August'. The Grand National winner had been invited by his fellow, less-famous citizens to parade at the Southport Show. He and Glenkiln travelled together – it was 'Ginger' McCain's charming and practical idea – and they paraded all three evenings. 'He loved it. He got very fussed over. He realises he's not going racing and he loves this type of thing. But he got very full of himself – they had to take the band away,' said 'Ginger' McCain. Arkle adored adulation. So now does Red Rum. There is no doubt at all that horses of intelligence and success, from childrens' ponies to Aintree heroes, are just as sensible of admiration as people. Like mankind, they thrive on warm waves lapping them in love.

Don McCain wastes no time getting the horse cantering. When most trainers are putting in four to six weeks pounding along the roads (a percussive exercise which would cripple Red Rum) McCain has him cantering ten to fourteen days after first coming in from grass. 'But only steadily,' said 'Ginger', noting my surprise, 'And only for about 6 or 7 furlongs.'

A great number of people, and many with experience, now told McCain that winning the Grand National finished off most horses, that winning a desperate hard set-to which broke Golden Miller's record would certainly finish Red Rum, and that anyway he'd need re-schooling after jumping Aintree's weird obstacles. McCain took note of the last and least depressing of the experts' opinions and boxed Red Rum out with two lead horses to school his champion over hurdles – 'to quicken him up, as these people had said'. McCain had a hunch Red Rum might not enjoy an exercise he could now justifiably

Infra dig

consider *infra dig*. McCain made all three horses take one sweep round the field first, then the trio swept towards the first flight of schooling fences. Red Rum was upon them, had jumped them, before he realised it. Then he knew he'd been tricked and was shaking his head in fury: The mighty horse who'd sprung over Aintree's thirty mammoths, clapped on all brakes at the sight of the second tiny hurdle, declared obviously, 'And stuff you, too!' and ducked out to the side . . . McCain gave him best.

The horse knew best. He need never school again.

There was one plain and simple target that season: Liverpool again. The programme till then was sagely kept flexible: two or three runs before Christmas, 'knock him off when the ground goes, then bring him back into work, with perhaps two races before Liverpool, possibly both at Haydock,' planned 'Ginger' McCain.

His immediate intention sprang from the best of horse psychology. Red Rum, in smashing Golden Miller's 39-year-old record round Aintree had endured a very hard race indeed. Its effects could well be longer lasting than the summer. Those experts who declared that Red Rum might now be finished, might dreadfully be right. . . . Glancing back down Aintree's roll of honour it was horribly plain that of the previous six winners Well to Do, Specify, Highland Wedding and Foinavon had done little of any subsequent consequence.

McCain intended to find 'an easy contest and let him *murder* one or two bad horses. This would make him cock-a-hoop again and bring him right back. I didn't want to get him involved in another hard race too soon.' He intended to obey that best of all training adages: to run his horse in the worst company.

Red Rum came quickly into strong work, throve, seemed better than ever and, only five weeks after he came in from the fields, was entered in a race at Perth on 26th September. 'Ginger' McCain had never been there, but had it in mind that it was a humble place but a stiff galloping track. When he arrived he discovered to his dismay that it was 'a very sharp round little track, not at all suitable for an out-and-out stayer like Red Rum'. Nor were his competititors the old donkeys for which he had hoped. Proud Stone ridden by big Ron Barry and trained by his retaining stable, Gordon Richards' near Penrith, had already run and won and was strongly fancied. Even with Proud Stone's penalty Red Rum, round this un-helpful track and far from fully fit, would be giving nearly a stone to the previous winner. Getting the horse ready was full of foreboding. Would he balloon over the first few fences as some horses do fresh from Aintree? Would he run without fire? McCain believed it just possible, and very much hoped not.

'He was always going well,' McCain remembers. It was bliss for him to realise that his horse had patently suffered no after-effects of Aintree. Red Rum and Proud Stone raced together, fighting it out, over the last three fences.

Liverpool again

Racing after Aintree

They came to the last together. McCain watched his horse land safely and began to walk down off the stands as Red Rum, showing a delightfully new turn of foot, sprinted clear of the fitter Proud Stone to win by $1\frac{1}{2}$ lengths. From 'Ginger' McCain's mind a huge cloud was lifted. Liverpool had not harmed his horse. He even seemed – dare he believe it? – a better horse than ever. He and Beryl walked delightedly to the unsaddling enclosure, with spring in their toes that lovely autumn day in Scotland and with dreams in their heads of another fabulous season.

'A bit of trouble'

Thus it was that McCain was rather puzzled when Brian Fletcher said as he rode in, 'There might be a bit of trouble. . . . But we're all right.'

Gordon Richards had exchanged a quick conversation with Ron Barry in the second's enclosure. He now came past 'Ginger', squeezed his elbow and said, 'I'm sorry "Ginger", I've got to object. My people have gambled on this horse.'

McCain thought Gordon Richards might be joking. He had seen nothing to which anyone could possibly object. And he was monopolised with joy that Red Rum had 'come back'. Then he heard the announcement that the objection was for 'squeezing over the last and squeezing on the run-in'. 'Ginger' McCain exploded: 'The thought of anyone squeezing Ron was ludicrous!' He had clearly seen the two horses jumping the last fence with about four feet of daylight between them, and both jumping straight as dies.

Brian Fletcher erupted

The two jockeys went into the stewards' room. Ron Barry said afterwards that he hardly had to put his case, because Brian Fletcher had erupted that it was a disgrace that when we bring a Grand National winner here all you can think of is taking the race off him!' – and more righteous indignation to the same effect. Ron Barry stood poker-faced, trying not to laugh. He told McCain later that as soon as Brian had slapped Red Rum going to the last, Proud Stone 'hadn't wanted to know'. There was no patrol camera. The stewards upheld Barry's objection and disqualified Red Rum and placed him second. McCain commented, 'I think the stewards were very wrong'. He allowed that the horses' lines from the last fence to the post had closed together. He declared 'The track is a distorted shape, but that isn't the *horse's* responsibility!'.

McCain is far too big a man to nurse ill-will about that squeezing business. 'Big Ron' is a great friend of his. A photograph of the two horses jumping the last with room for one of his largest used-cars between them was sent to McCain after the race. Ron Barry got married to a tall and attractive blonde, Liz Young, in the summer of 1974. McCain sent him the coloured photograph mounted and framed with the sardonic caption boldly inscribed on it: 'SQUEEZE ME!'.

Most trainers of Grand National winners tend to keep them in cotton wool. They rarely appear early with the riff-raff. They emerge like leading actors making entrances when racing has become important in November, when the stage has been set, and lesser characters established, and the plot advanced. But 'Ginger' McCain is boldly unorthodox. He left Red Rum up in Perth racecourse stables, then sent him direct from there to Carlisle two days later and ran him in a 3 mile handicap 'chase the next day, 29th September. It was the programme you might consider for a hard-ground plater of no importance. But for a great 'National winner to camp out in racecourse stables, to be away from home nearly a week, to run twice in two 3-mile steeplechases within three days . . . tch, tch, tch, clicked the clever old know-all's tongues. Up shot eyebrows. Heads were wagged. If anything went amiss, 'Ginger' McCain would lose the reputation his last season had finally bestowed on him.

McCain is boldly unorthodox

None of these considerations remained long in McCain's head. He had embarked on a bold plan. On it would go. At Carlisle Red Rum was made odds-on, only Canharis being remotely fancied to beat him. Yet Red Rum was again lumbered with 12st 4lb. And 'Ginger' bursts out laughing at the remembrance of that race. 'It was just as if he'd taken that objection personally – having that race pinched off him at Perth; as if he was saying to those stewards "I'll bloody show you this time!". I've never seen a horse finish up that Carlisle hill like it. He went past the winning post – winning by 15 lengths and 15 lengths – and round the bend and just *disappeared*. I thought "Oh hell! What's happened? What's the matter with Brian?" And when Brian comes back he's laughing his socks off. Brian shouts out "I couldn't pull the bugger up after the race. He was running away with me!"

He just disappeared

'And that,' says McCain with awe,' was after three miles round a stiff track, and only three days after that other three miles up at Perth. It was just *fantastic.*'

McCain now knew without a passing cloud of doubt that his horse had again improved almost unbelievably on the previous year. McCain realised, with a feeling of awe, that Red Rum was even more than a record-breaking Grand National winner: he was something quite extra-ordinary. The North of England was buzzing now not only with Red Rum's praises, but with those of the man McCain. The subject of speculation had become an object of admiration.

Red Rum smashes course record

More was in store. A mere fortnight later, and again humping 12st 4lb, Red Rum smashes the course record at Ayr by 7 seconds to win the £1,551 Joan Mackay 3 mile handicap 'chase. He beats a high-class field including Straight Vulgan (Ron Barry) and Tartan Ace (Tommy Stack) to each of whom he gives nearly 2 stone. So his former partners, booting along behind, see our hero speeding away. Straight Vulgan was beaten a length, and was quite out-accelerated by Red Rum on the run-in. Tartan Ace finished 5th, 17 lengths behind. 'I've never seen him look quite so impressive,' says McCain marvelling at his super horse. 'He just swept up to the leaders, as they turned into the straight, like a yacht with a wet sail, and took up the running really sailing away.'

The Sporting Life, a professional paper whose serious hyperbole, reported 'They don't come with more courage than Red Rum. The Grand National hero took reporters are accurate, unemotional people, not given to Ayr's Joan Mackay handicap 'chase slicing 7 seconds off the course record. . . . He is certainly the exception to the 'National winners' – "they-dont-come-back" – rule. . . .'

Chaseform Notebook commented with a flamboyance unique that season: 'Looked magnificent . . . fantastic performance . . . truly great horse. . . .'

'Fantastic performance'

Red Rum had blundered at the last, picked up, fought back and gone on to win. The jumping error was, McCain said, 'Something he started to do that season. It's usually when he's headed the leader. He did it in the Hennessy three out and he did it in the Scottish Grand National. . . .'

'Ginger' McCain is puzzled by this "chancing" and just a little worried by it. It seems that when Red Rum suddenly has nothing to pursue his concentration slips.

The ground stayed as firm as Red Rum loves it all the early autumn of 1973, and off he went to Newcastle on the last day of October. He won the £860 3 mile handicap 'chase going away from Neville Crump's fancied San-Feliu. Captain Crump of Middleham had been a hero of Donald McCain's for years. McCain's own recent triumphs had not suggested to this modest man that he was yet in Crump's league; he glowed like a praised beginner when the red-faced stentorian Captain strode up to congratulate him. 'That must be a tremendous animal,' declared Neville Crump. 'I don't see any way in which we're ever going to beat him,' Crump warmly announced, relishing, like the sportsman he is, any great horse's performance, even if not his. 'That was a fair compliment,' remarked the uninflated 'Ginger' McCain, 'from a man like Neville Crump.'

Among the experienced journalists in Newcastle's press-room it was agreed that by now, if Red Rum were trained by a leading southern public trainer like Fred Winter or Fulke Walwyn, he would already be hailed as another Arkle. He had already begun similarly to spark the general public's imagination. His humble circumstances (so unlike Arkle's who had everything good going for him all his life) and his new chain of victories had started a flow of fanmail which was to swamp poor Beryl McCain.

McCain was delighted by the Newcastle victory for another reason. One of Red Rum's hind plates had been trodden on during the race and had been partially torn off. A piece of it had been twisted inwards like a scythe. It had been scooping away as he galloped. He had cuts on the inside of his opposite hock. Red Rum's performance under this pain was particularly impressive and was another example of his gallantry. The relief that he had not lamed himself was considerable. The horse could have been very seriously injured.

Example of gallantry

Red Rum's target remained the Grand National – if there was one. The slow minuet of 'Will she? Won't she? Will it? Won't it?' was once again lilting over Mrs Topham's threatened Aintree. McCain who thinks very little of Cheltenham compared with his beloved Liverpool, began to cast his eyes towards the south. He might well take on those southern cracks in the Hennessy Gold Cup at the month's end.

**Challenge
to Crisp**

Red Rum's next race was, however, what Donald McCain humbly calls 'a shade ambitious, a bit of stupidity on my part'. He was to challenge Crisp in a two-horse match at Doncaster over $3\frac{1}{4}$ miles for £1,763 at a meeting which clashed with the Mackeson Gold Cup down at Cheltenham. The ground was good.

Those scintillating superlatives so justly lavished on Crisp after the '73 Grand National had slightly grated on Red Rum's supporters. Several wrote protesting letters to the sporting papers about what they read as denigration of Southport's hero. Certainly he had been receiving nearly two stone from the bounding Australian colossus, but he had stayed and jumped and gone on and got him, hadn't he? And look what he'd done since: first past the post every time out. Fred Winter's mighty Crisp had whizzed round to be third in a hurdle at Worcester ('better for the race', as *Chaseform* nudgingly observed) and had then easily won a $2\frac{1}{2}$ mile chase at Newbury in record time surging ahead when Charlie Potheen, at level weights, fell just behind him at the 14th fence.

**Level
weights**

To put the matter to the test, to measure Red Rum's improvement, to silence those who said he was a handi-capper, Don McCain decided to take on Crisp at Doncaster at level weights. At Liverpool Crisp had carried 12 stone to Red Rum's 10st 5lb, giving away 23lb. Could a horse of eight years old improve this much in seven months? It seemed thoroughly unlikely. But it was ironically going to be the precise weight increase given to Red Rum for his next Grand National. . . .

A match round Doncaster was a different thing entirely. Level-weight races usually cut up to nothing, and there had only been four acceptors at the four-day stage. The public gave Red Rum no chance at all, and Sir Chester Manifold's highly versatile Australian was 11 to 4 on.

Red Rum did not improve his own chances before the race. McCain likes Billy Ellison to let the horse give a jump and a kick before he's saddled, as he had done at Newbury with Sandra in that novice 'chase years earlier. Walking round in Doncaster's deep straw undercover ring, he whipped round with Billy, slipped on the wooden boards beneath the straw and went down, feet scrabbling noisily. When he scrambled up, McCain saw to his horror that his horse was definitely going short behind. He sent him off briskly into the main parade ring. 'Get him out there where there's more room for him to fool around!' he shouted to Billy. He walked behind Red Rum frowning over his action. Red Rum's movement gradually improved. McCain deliberated: should he take him out of the race...? He considered. . . . If he did, wouldn't the world think him windy that he'd run away from Crisp? McCain hardened his heart. He said nothing, and his horse ran.

Crisp made all the running, waiting in front in a reasonably fast-run duel. Red Rum came at him under pressure to try to challenge, but Crisp sailed ahead in the last half mile, only weakening between the last two fences. He beat Red Rum a resounding eight lengths. The Grand National winner appeared out of his class.

Crisp wins

McCain is loth to make too much of Red Rum's pre-race fall and lameness. But Brian Fletcher independently agreed that something felt wrong. 'That was the only race,' Fletcher declared to me unequivocally the following summer, 'that I've known Red Rum not feel himself. Perhaps he didn't like Crisp settin' that hell of a gallop start to finish, I don't know. Crisp probably beat him on merit, but maybe Red Rum had an off-day. He just lacked the *courage* that he has normally.'

Perhaps his back hurt him. Perhaps having only one other horse – and that a black giant clear in front – hood-winked him that this was a loathed 'school' rather than a race. Perhaps he did not care to be taken along by something which he knew was quicker over the ground and quicker through the air than he was.

I ran our Gold Cup winner Linwell in two semi-matches against Crudwell. We were out-manoeuvred and out-speeded both times. In big fields in the highest class Crudwell was granted only a distant prospect of Linwell's tail. In these two minute fields Crudwell made our star look slow. I, like McCain at Doncaster, was crestfallen.

There was blue gloom in Upper Aughton Road. Beryl McCain was so upset she howled in the stables. The lads felt crushed. Their darling was not invincible. He had *not* apparently improved those 23lb. The cursed Crisp had publicly avenged the 'National and wiped their hero's eye!

Their hero was not invincible

But Crisp's leg had gone in the race. That weakening as he strode to the last fence had been pain from the strain. When Crisp got back to Lambourn he was lame. He never ran again all season. The huge horse from the other side of the world has had, so far, three marked effects on the one-time selling-plater from Kilkenny. The speed set by Crisp in the '73 'National insured that Red Rum, by catching him, would smash Golden Miller's old record. By beating Red Rum so easily at Doncaster Red Rum's relative weight would henceforward be kept down. But Crisp's Doncaster injury, which kept him out of running in the following National, let Red Rum's weight rise to the maximum. After Doncaster Red Rum would have been given at least 8lb less than Crisp. Dr Phil Bull's '*Timeform*' ratings for April, 1974 (before Red Rum had won his Scottish Grand National) made no bones about it: they awarded Crisp 173 and Red Rum 156.

They may meet again. A renewal of their rivalry was Fred Winter's purpose when at the Racehorse of the Year Dinner in the summer of 1974 he cabled – in Crisp's name – an arrogant challenge to Red Rum who was being honoured that night with the flat-race heroine Dahlia.

Hennessy Cognac Gold Cup

It was the early winter of 1973 when for the first time in the one and a half years McCain had trained him Red Rum forayed south of the Trent. Only a fortnight after his Doncaster defeat he travelled down to Newbury to run in the £7,435 Hennessy Cognac Gold Cup Handicap Chase (the famous race's new and elongated title) over $3\frac{1}{4}$ miles. Red Rum was fairly handicapped with 11st 4lb. Charlie Potheen (Ron Barry) carried a stone more (a dreadful weight in that company). Red Candle carried a stone less. The latter, trained by that interesting character, Lt. Colonel 'Ricky' Vallance at Bishop's Cannings in darkest Wiltshire, had shown some late promise in two races that season: his first outing when 4th in a £2,000 hurdle race at Chepstow – 'Strong run two out, too much to do' says *Chaseform* caustically, and still more significantly in the Mackeson Gold Cup at Cheltenham.

Red Candle

Red Candle had won the $2\frac{1}{2}$ miles Mackeson in 1972. This time at 9 to 1 he made some progress after the 11th fence but did not, as *Chaseform* would say, 'trouble the leaders'. He finished 7th. In the fortnight between that race and the Hennessy the chestnut horse had evidently pleased his patient trainer. Opening an outsider at Newbury at 20 to 1, he was backed down to 12 to 1.

Red Rum was 'particularly well', as McCain recalls, and it was on the eve of the race in the racecourse stables that he so nearly jumped over his box-door when he heard Jackie Grainger's muffled shout of '*Red*!' The ground – 'good with a little bit of give', was not exactly as he liked it, but was certainly not his detested soft. McCain savoured the parade of past Hennessy winners: 'Kirsten, Mandarin, Taxidermist, Stalbridge Colonist – how different they all looked,' he said delightedly, for he is a romantic, in love with the history of steeplechasing and all its heroes.

An enormous concourse of southern racegoers who had only watched Red Rum on television and read about his northern exploits, flocked round to examine him in the flesh. Most, expected him to be little, were surprised by his size. He has been measured for us by his veterinary surgeon, Mr E. D. Greenway at 16.2 hands with his shoes on. Arkle was 16.2$\frac{1}{8}$. A full comparison of all the measurements of both these equine supremes will be found on the next page. 'What a pity,' commented Ted Greenway of what he rates 'This really great horse' – 'we can't measure the most vital statistic of all – the size of the "engine"'.

Surprised by his size

 Perfect conformation makes horses seem small. It is the ill-made gangling creature who seems enormous by offending the eye until you walk in close to him. Beautifully made and balanced horses like Red Rum seem small at first glance, and grow bigger as you walk in closer: it is the test of good conformation. All the crowd at Newbury admired Red Rum's. Many were surprised by his extreme jauntiness.

Charlie Potheen was surprisingly made favourite: Red Rum was easy to back at 8 to 1. The big gamble was on Red Candle. Charlie Potheen, a desperate tearaway, declined to settle. By the fourth fence he was bowling away in front and led the field strongly with only one blunder until the 17th fence. Red Rum worked his passage through towards the leaders and now snatched up the running from Charlie Potheen who weakened as if shot. 'Red Rum then really rooted the third last,' McCain remembers. It was that 'error-when-leading' which McCain had anxiously noted before. Red Rum dropped back to third, then fourth, as lightly-weighted Red Candle, who had been waiting like a wolf in the rear, came racing through the struggling field and took up the running going to the second last. Colonel Vallance seemed at that instant to be assured of a richly rewarded victory.

Most of us had then discounted Red Rum's chance. But there he was again in an instant, worrying his way forward, and into the race. It was now Red Candle's turn to blunder and at the worst place: the last fence. As he scrambled over it, Red Rum came storming down on him. 'Red Rum jumped the last like a terrier!' exclaimed McCain 'He really pinged it, got back on terms with Red Candle – then it was a *super* contest! I thought we got up. Then they came in and they said we were beat. Brian thought he'd *just* got up. . . .' They waited for the photograph. Giving away a stone Red Rum had been beaten a

A gallant finish

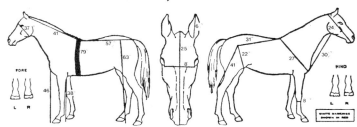

ANIMAL	COLOUR	BREED	SEX	AGE	HEIGHT
ARKLE	BAY	THOROUGHBRED	GELDING	8	16.2 1/8
	SIRE	DAM	SIRE OF DAM		
	ARCHIVE	BRIGHT CHERRY	KNIGHT OF THE GARTER		

Markings

Head:— Poll to upper lip - Front view 25½" - Side view 24½". Width between eyes 8".
Orifice of ear 6½". Circumference of jaw 37½".

Limbs:— Withers to point of shoulder 27". Point of shoulder to ground 46". Point of elbow to ground 38".
Hip to stifle 22". Hip to ground 63".
HIP TO HOCK: 41"
BONE: 8½". (Circumference below knee).

Body:— HEIGHT: 16.2 1/8 (shod).
GIRTH: 79"
Rein neck extended:- From poll to highest point of withers 41½".
Withers to root of tail following contour of spine 51½".

Remarks:— Angle of jaw to point of shoulder 30½".
Withers to hip (external angle of ileum) 31".

Date:—   23rd December, 1965.   Measurements taken five days prior to winning
King George VI Chase, Kempton.

S.M. Cosgrove. M.R.C.V.S.

Full measurements of the famous Arkle (above), winner of 3 Cheltenham Gold Cups and more than £75,000 in prize money and those of Red Rum (below) measured in July 1974.

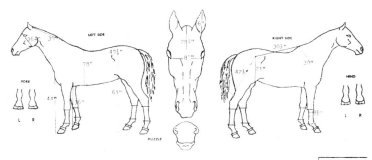

NAME	COLOUR	SEX	DATE OF BIRTH	SIRE	DAM
RED RUM	BAY	GELDING	1965	QUORUM	MARED

HEAD
LIMBS: LF, RF, LH, RH — No white markings
BODY: Nil.
ACQUIRED: Nil.

Height   - 16.2 h.h. (with shoes on).
Girth   - 78"
Bone   - 8½" (Circumference of cannon below knee).
Poll to upper lip - 29½" (Front View).
Width between eyes - 8½".
Circumference of jaw - 36½" (below eyes).
Orifice of ear - 6".
Withers to point of shoulder - 30".
Point of shoulder to ground - 44".
Point of elbow to ground - 36".
Hip (ext. angle of ileum) to stifle 21", to ground 61", to hock 42½"
Rein - neck extended - 38" (Poll to highest point of withers).
Withers to root of tail - 49½" (Following contour of spine).
Withers to hip - 30½".
(ext. angle of ileum).

(IF NO MARKINGS—THIS FACT TO BE STATED)

DATE OF EXAMINATION 17th July, 1974.   SIGNATURE of qualified Veterinary Surgeon
(Not to be the owner or trainer of the horse for which the Certificate is issued)
Stonehouse Farm,   G.R. Greenway.
Little Budworth, Cheshire.   M.R.C.V.S.

shorthead. 'It was the six inches from the tip of Red Candle's nose to the ring of the bit in his mouth,' declared 'Ginger'. 'My chappie was *reaching* for his next stride, when the other fellow had taken his.' He had been beaten, as they say in the sport, 'on the nod'. Those six inches cost £5,175 or £862.50 per inch. But that did not concern the Red Rum camp.

On the Nod

Mr Le Mare, with his customary and unpublicised generosity, presented Brian Fletcher and Don McCain with 10 per cent each of the stakes for being second. The yard were also rewarded. Billy Ellison's savings mounted. His new wife remarked to him (as the patient Mr Miles must have felt about Miss Sandra Kendall) 'You love Red Rum more than you do me'.

Billy pulled her leg, 'I do. So if he wins *two* Grand Nationals you've got problems!' By the summer of 1974 Billy had paid the deposit on two houses out of his rewards for caring for Red Rum.

But in unpecuniary ways too, the stables were genuinely thrilled by Red Rum's great run in the Hennessy. On his first visit south from Upper Aughton Road he had so nearly defeated the best of England for the biggest staying 'chase of the pre-Christmas season. Anthony Watt, a useful young 'chaser receiving 4lb from Red Rum was 6 lengths behind him. And then followed three sturdy form horses, Cuckolder (who would beat The Dikler two months later in the Great Yorkshire Chase at Doncaster), the redoubtable Duke of Alburquerque's Nereo and the persevering Spanish Steps, all of whom were plodding on while the two 'Reds' raced like tigers to the post. 'It was a great contest,' beamed the defeated McCain, and southerners who had never met the lanky man from Southport realised what northern racing people mean when they declare '"Ginger" is the nicest man in the game'.

John Oaksey came up, twinkle-eyed and grinning. 'Look at him,' he said to McCain, pointing to Red Rum. 'No point telling him he's been beaten!' McCain nodded proudly. The horse indeed believed all the cheering was for him. No one could even guess it then, not even 'Ginger' McCain in his highest hopes, but if Red Rum's nose had been six inches further forward at the end of those $3\frac{1}{4}$ miles, then he would have broken, by the season's end, the immortal Arkle's all-time record for a 'chaser of stakes won. Red Rum's fractional defeat at Newbury cost him a first prize of £7,455. When that season ended he would be lying only £4,522 behind Arkle's enormous target.

Praise from John Oaksey

Red Rum returned to Birkdale and began his midwinter rest. He would resume his Grand National preparation at Haydock, McCain planned. But the best laid schemes of jumping trainers 'Gang aft a-gley' when the weather fouls up racing.

Red Rum travelled to Haydock. It was cancelled. McCain took him on to Catterick – 'We were getting a shade desperate. We wanted to get him going'. When they reached Catterick it was sluicing icy-grey buckets from the dark sky. McCain couldn't decide whether to run. They had 12st 7lb to hump in the soft in weather he loathed. The press badgered him for an announcement. Brian Fletcher begged him not to run. Arthur Stephenson said, 'Don't run him, lad'. McCain said, 'Thank you,' and then realised Stephenson had a runner in the race himself. This was a spot of gamesmanship which made 'Ginger' chuckle: 'Arthur came up afterwards and we had a joke about it. He said "Well, you've got to try everything!".'

'You've got to try everything'

Brian Fletcher rode the winner of the second race, and although after a winner most jockeys find the going perfect, Fletcher still insisted: 'Don't run him. This is no good for him at all.'

'Right', thought McCain. 'That's it then.'

He told Jackie Grainger of his decision when they were saddling Anet's Pet to be second in the third race. Grainger wagged his head. He said 'Red's so well, you've *got* to do something with him'. McCain said, 'No, we can't run him'. But they chatted as they were saddling and then McCain found Noel Le Mare and discussed the problem again. They decided to let the horse run but to tell Fletcher to pull him up if he was struggling.

They were now embarked upon that most awkward of situations: a conflict of interests between those of the horse and those of the punters. Every horseman will rate the animal in his hands who must race if he says so, as more important than punters who have no need to bet. Equally racing men are aware of the extent to which punters' money finances the sport. When a horse is a national hero, he has a specially large band of supporters. Yet, as a national hero, he needs specially to be protected. Hovering over this dilemma fluttered the shadow of the stewards intent to see that horses run on their merits and that there are no non-triers.

All of this was clear to McCain. But only some of it to Noel Le Mare. He nodded. Then he said, '"Ginger", you must make an announcement to the public that the horse isn't really trying. I don't want them wasting their money.'

McCain tried to explain that though the intention behind such an announcement was splendidly sincere, it would be by racing's rules a public declaration of cheating. Le Mare allowed himself reluctantly to be convinced. He would still have preferred a broadcast declaration of the stables' decision; and who would disagree pragmatically that, in the spirit of the law, though not by its letter, he would have been correct? He would have been proved correct, that is, provided the horse *did* pull up. As things turned out, the cynical public would have put quite a different construction on Le Mare's helpful intentions.

It was left to a brief word from the uncertain trainer to the dubious jockey. 'Right,' said 'Ginger' to Brian in the paddock, 'Look after him and if in doubt, pull up.' Many are the good trainers who in similar circumstances have murmured the same.

Red Rum went surlily round, ears clapped right back, loathing every minute of it. To keep him out of the worst ground, Fletcher steered him round on the wide outside. Not only was he giving away over 2 stone to much of the opposition, but he was giving away distance, too, and in both directions, for he was at the back of the field until the start of the last muddy circuit. He then, still hating the conditions, began to grind his way angrily forward till he could challenge. Crump's horse Fanatic crashed through the roots of the last fence and Red Rum pounded on to win by eight lengths. Relief gave McCain a smattering of arrogance. 'I was a bit cocky, but with everything against him, it was a brilliant performance. So I thought "I'll give the press something to chew on".' He announced, 'Given the right ground and a clear run this horse *will win* the 'National.' And walked away.

His outrageously confident prediction was the more remarkable because the weights for the Grand National had appeared the previous week shooting Red Rum up the maximum 23lb to topweight of 12 stone. 'Bloody hell! That's a bit nasty!' McCain had blurted out when he heard the news. He'd expected about 11st 10lb and would have been thrilled with a few pounds less. Typically of McCain, his later reaction was one of qualified pleasure: top weight in the 'National was one hell of a compliment to his horse, and he announced this frankly. Racing's wise official handicappers armed with their new computer had stated simply that Red Rum, the record-breaker, was the best horse in the race. No horse, however, in the history of the race had ever before been so heavily penalised for winning once. The bookmakers extended the odds against Red Rum from 12 to 1 to 20 to 1, and a number of racing tipsters advised their readers even at those odds to keep their money till the day.

One more race before Aintree

After Catterick McCain reckoned his horse needed one more race. He again picked the Greenall Whitley at Haydock. The ground was soft on 2nd March, but the sun shone brightly, and after Red Rum's dour victory in Catterick's mud, McCain was hoping that the going might not now be too heavy. Red Rum was however lumbered with 12st 7lb, a wearisome burden to hump round three miles of soft ground only twenty-eight days before the Grand National. Fate decreed that he should not do so. At the very first fence Red Rum discarded 10 stone when an astonished Brian Fletcher was catapulted from his saddle by a horse suddenly crashing into him from behind.

McCain was desperate. Riderless horses are at risk. Many panic without a pilot, try to jump iron railings or concrete posts and impale themselves, gallop across tarmac car-parks, slip and break their knees, crash into cars while their eyes are on the flying field, or simply cross the other runners to bring about a débâcle of flailing legs.

Red Rum goes round alone

'We needed this race badly. Now we wouldn't have it.' He dashed into the middle of the course, and so did Beryl, to try to catch Red Rum before he injured himself galloping loose. Red Rum however coolly decided that he needed the race and if Brian wasn't going along with him, too bad; he'd have to go round alone. He resolved as usual to win, and went to the front, jumping every fence. Soon he was cutting out the work with Glanford Brigg.

Tommy Stack had been unshipped at the first, too, and he and Brian Fletcher joined McCain in the middle. 'Something hit me in the middle of the back and I went straight out the saddle,' Brian said. (It was Noble Hero, whose jockey Macer Gifford afterwards apologised).

Riderless Red Rum and Glanford Brigg keep bowling along in front. McCain, wonderfully relieved that his horse is unharmed and obviously taking care, calls out to Alan McTaggart standing in the course's centre, 'Bet you a level pound mine wins this race'. 'Done,' says the Scotsman. They come together to the last and the piloted Glanford Brigg is switched on to the new run-in to go for the winning-post. No one has given Red Rum a revised plan of the course, so thinking that Glanford Brigg is cravenly deserting the contest, Red Rum bowls on over the next open ditch and the water jump while Glanford Brigg scurries along the flat beside him to the winning-post.

'Owe you a quid,' shouts McCain to McTaggart bounding over the mud to try to catch his precious horse. 'Nonsense,' says the Scot, 'Yours jumped two more than the winner.'

Beryl McCain had watched Red Rum running loose at first with trepidation, then relief, then pride when she saw how brilliantly he was running and jumping without a jockey. As the two horses jumped the official last fence together Beryl McCain said 'You could see Red Rum's eyes as he turned to look at the other horse, thinking he'd gone wrong'. As the other runners finished, the course whirled alive with horses turning, wheeling and cantering back. Red Rum was loose in the throng, galloping about in immediate danger of crashing into the rails. Beryl ran out into the middle of the track to catch him.

Running and jumping brilliantly

'Don't be a daft bitch,' shouted 'Ginger', fearful that his wife would get bowled over into the mud by a half a ton of horse. But Beryl aimed herself at Red Rum as he came galloping past her. She shouted '*Red!*'. The horse heard her, stopped, turned, came back towards her, and she grabbed his reins safely. All was well. He had run his race without the weight.

'He came home, ate up,' said 'Ginger', 'and acted all superior: "What do I want with jockeys?" – that type of thing.' Relief that Red Rum had not been injured at Haydock made that race a subject of jokes. But McCain was unable to weigh up the benefit which that riderless 'school' had done the horse. While he had feared that 12st 7lb in the mud might prove too severe a 'National preparation, he now suspected that carrying only 2st 7lb without Fletcher to boot him along might mean that Red Rum had not had enough of a race.

The beach provided its usual superb going and Red Rum never missed a day's work in his last month. McCain had been worried by a remark Tommy Shedden had made to him when the horse ran at Catterick. Shedden had observed 'I don't think he's carrying quite the same condition over his loins, "Ginger", that he had last year.' McCain thought, 'Oh Lord! I've been too easy on him.' And he crammed the work into Red Rum. He used to stand and watch the horse every night going through those moments of calculating contemplation which every trainer knows. 'One night he'd look tremendous. Then the next you'd think he didn't. . . .' What worried 'Ginger' much more in March, 1974 was the rain continually soaking into the new-owned Liverpool racecourse. McCain fretted. Then ten days before the 'National the weather smiled again. McCain sent a friend to Liverpool to check the going. 'The turf's like silk,' came back the word. 'If we can get four or five days of good weather, it's going to be marvellous ground.' It is fortunate for Red Rum that Aintree's wonderful old turf, now so little used, is rarely heavy.

'I've been too easy on him'

But McCain wanted something faster than merely good ground, particularly this year when his horse had 12 stone to carry. 'You have to be pretty lucky to get fast ground at this time of the year. But we got it.' The drier the days, the more confident McCain grew.

McCain's confidence grows

He had backed Red Rum £50 each way at 14 to 1. He asked Noel Le Mare, 'Would you like the same bet?' The owner said, 'Please!' So McCain let him have his bet 'and never bothered backing him myself.' He has so far never had a penny on the horse any time he has run, and it is most unlikely now, with racing's superstitions in full cry, that he ever will.

McCain's yard in 1973 had consisted of only eight horses and four lads and the generous Noel Le Mare had given them £1,500 between them to celebrate his first Grand National victory. The stables had now been extended right up to the back wall to provide eighteen boxes. The little yard was crammed. Out of it the astonishing trainer would now produce no less than three Grand National runners, one sixth of his stable. In addition to Red Rum and his hardworked galloping-horse, Glenkiln, The Tunku, which he had bought cheaply at Doncaster just after Red Rum, would also be performing. Belonging to Dennis Rimmer he too had greatly improved on his past form, and had won a Wills Premier Qualifier 'Chase and a Doncaster handicap. Richard Evans would ride him, Reg Crank would be on Glenkiln, and Brian Fletcher naturally continued on Red Rum.

The three horses were in a string of nine galloping nearly two miles on Ainsdale beach on the Wednesday before the race. On the Friday before the race Red Rum galloped 6 furlongs lickety-spit. And then did it again. McCain was delighted. Corals and Mecca offered Red Rum joint favourite at 10's with L'Escargot. Ladbrokes suggested 7's Red Rum. William Hill said 8's Red Rum. Glenkiln was at 50's and The Tunku at 100 to 1. On the eve of the race the Racegoers Club organised an Aintree walk-round: a group of leading jockeys guided a party to gape at the size of Becher's, the Canal Turn, and the grisly Chair.

Superstition insisted that the McCains follow precisely the same morning's programme as that of the previous year. As tension crackled in the yard and press photographers and television camera-men crouched and clicked, flashed and flooded, buzzed and pointed, Beryl McCain again with nervous fingers carefully plaited our hero's mane. The gods of racing were being placated with the same offerings. But the horse had become a public star.

Tension crackled in the yard

'There were interviews in the yard with the press, with the BBC, with the television people,' said 'Ginger', 'then the adrenalin really got pumping when Red Rum was loaded into the box.' A local crowd had gathered in the street outside the yard as if to greet a king off to claim his throne. They set up a cheer as Red Rum walked past the used-cars and up the ramp of his horse-box. 'Ginger' and Beryl McCain got ready to drive out to Stan and Carol Wareing's. 'As we get in the car, it's the usual stuff,' said 'Ginger'. 'Stomach turning over, feeling uncomfortable, feeling that little bit niggly. . . .' Once again they were refreshed by the hospitable Wareings' champagne. Again the Rolls-Royce flying lady was festooned with ribbons. Again they larked about with the electric windows and waved wildly at passing lorry-drivers as they careered towards Aintree racecourse.

Beryl was in a state. At Haydock, when Brian had been knocked off at the first fence, she had forgotten her binoculars. Now she found she had left them in the back of Jonjo O'Neill's car. 'I had this horrible feeling that what had happened at Haydock was going to happen at Aintree if I had no binoculars. I dived into the weighing-room and asked "Can anybody lend me some?" Nobody could. Then she found Dennis Leah, a Cheshire training friend from Little Budworth where 'Ginger' had been in the old days. He was standing by the television monitor and happily lent Beryl his binoculars. 'As soon as I got the glasses,' said Beryl, 'I felt better.'

'I had this horrible feeling'

Then she tried to find the same place on the stands from

where she had watched in 1973. But she wasn't sure of the place. She moved around uncertainly. She didn't want to be with 'Ginger' for that had never been lucky. She looked round to glimpse him standing only six steps behind her with Stan Wareing. She hoped they wouldn't see her. But there was a delay getting the parade started. In it Stan Wareing squeezed through the crowd to reach her and asked, 'Are you going to stop with us?' She could barely speak now. She shook her head.

Red Rum was drifting in the betting from 8 to 1 favourite out to 11's, in the face of frenzied punting on Scout (backed from 18 to 1 to 7 to 1, favourite) and for L'Escargot (backed from 10's down to 17 to 2).

The 1974 'National plan

The race began. The start had been delayed four minutes partially by some histrionics performed by the wilful and costly Princess Camilla. Charles Dickens led almost from the start with Rough Silk, Sunny Lad, Rouge Autumn and Straight Vulgan and L'Escargot in the leading bunch. The plan was so identical to the previous year's that 'Ginger' McCain had not even discussed it with Brain Fletcher. For the first two miles, Fletcher would again 'hunt round'. For all that first circuit Beryl could not relax for a moment. She kept her fingers crossed in dread of the loose horses. 'There was one particular loose horse right in front of Brian and I thought it'd be sure to bring him down.'

The three BBC TV commentators had not read the race far enough back towards the rear to mention Red Rum before the field swept onto the racecourse in a dazzle of colour at the end of the first huge circuit. At the one before the dreaded Chair Peter O'Sullevan saw the zig-zagging threats of the loose horses.

'Red Rum going well'

'The two leaders – Pearl of Montreal and Charles Dickens – then Sunny Lad and L'Escargot and then just in behind them Spanish Steps, and then comes Rouge Autumn, San-Feliu, Straight Vulgan –' Fletcher here began his run and O'Sullevan spotted him instantly 'And right up there Red Rum going well, going strongly in the centre of the field. Coming up to The Chair now and as they do so it's Charles Dickens with a loose horse *perilously* near to him. Charles Dickens jumps it but he's *very* nearly brought down . . . but he survives all right. L'Escargot jumped it on the inside, Pearl of Montreal just in the lead and it's Pearl of Montreal as they come to the water from Charles Dickens and L'Escargot and Sunny Lad and then Vulgan Town. Then comes Spanish Steps, behind Spanish Steps is Rough Silk, then San-Feliu, and then Red Rum.

Behind them Straight Vulgan and then Norwegian Flag on the inside of Norwegian Flag is Glenkiln. . . .'

Then Beryl McCain saw the loose horse run out towards the stables and 'Ginger' McCain on the top of the stands felt not a worry at all. 'It was like a summer's day, warm beautiful weather and I was watching Brian's yellow cap bobbing along.' (Fletcher was still wearing Le Mare's second colours with the yellow cap.)

The fields raced away from the stands, onto the second circuit and John Hanmer took up the commentary:

'Almost at the seventeenth and it's Pearl of Montreal on the inside from Vulgan Town, Charles Dickens and right up with them L'Escargot is close up. All the leaders over that safely. Vulgan Town disputing it with Charles Dickens and Pearl of Montreal. Then comes Straight Vulgan. And Red Rum, last year's winner, taking *very* close order now, as they jump the eighteenth. And again all the leaders over safely except for Straight Vulgan. Straight Vulgan went at that and it's Vulgan Town from Charles Dickens, then comes Sunny Lad, L'Escargot, Red Rum, then Scout taking close order on the outside, then comes Pearl of Montreal. Glenkiln has gone at the ditch. As they go to the next fence, the 20th, it's Charles Dickens, L'Escargot and Red Rum.' The competent quick nasal chant of Julian Wilson seizes the running thread:

'Charles Dickens is the leader over that one from L'Escargot with a good pitch on the inside. Red Rum much closer now on the outside. Vulgan Town is in fourth place now. Scout's got a good pitch towards the outside as they come to the one before Bechers. And it's Charles Dickens who leads over it from L'Escargot on the inside, Red Rum on the outside, Scout is right up there. Vulgan Town is in fifth place.' At this instant Wilson's voice changes upwards. He glimpses the astonishing sight which will never be forgotten by anyone who saw it: Red Rum was cantering over the field as if they were riding-school hacks. Fletcher was standing up in his irons actually trying to restrain Red Rum from running away. The horse's sudden superiority scourged his opponents as if they were trash.

Wilson shouted:

Red Rum's superiority

'They run down towards Bechers for the second and last time, and as they do so the leader is now the 1973 winner Red Rum! Red Rum from Charles Dickens, L'Escargot, Scout, Vulgan Town as they jump Bechers. . . .'

A horse apart

At the Canal Turn Red Rum was mocking his pursuers. He was moving as if only at half-speed, bounding over the ground as if he were laughing with delight while those behind – Charles Dickens, Scout, L'Escargot, Spanish Steps, Vulgan Town, Rough Silk and Stephen's Society toiled behind him like normal racehorses under pressure in a race of their own with three and a half miles gone. . . . And Red Rum was sauntering in the sunlight. He was Billy Ellison's 'big XJ among the ole bangers'. He was that day at Liverpool a horse apart, a giant among minnows – and yet those minnows were, like L'Escargot and Spanish Steps, horses of class.

Red Rum spurned them. The quick ground he loves spun behind his dancing feet. The warm sun he needs blessed him. He swaggered. Darkness lay behind him. Those awful struggles were forgotten. He played the King at Liverpool, making the rest serfs. In many old observers' minds this was the most memorable superiority ever shown round Aintree.

With only four more of Aintree's towering but tattered fences left Red Rum was four lengths clear and still on the bridle. Fletcher explained 'I *had* to go to the front going to Becher's. I went to the front so early, 'cos if I'd restrained him any longer I'd have got myself into trouble or something.' The little jockey's pink face could hardly register the ease of his horse's forward cruise.

His only mistake

Running towards home Red Rum made his only mistake. Over-jumping, he pitched forward and for an instant looked like blundering. Fletcher sat right back, well and safely like the best of Aintree jockeys and before the forward pitch of Red Rum's neck and head were done, his other foreleg flashed forward to take the weight and keep him moving with only the briefest hiccup in his stride. It was done quick as a conjuror, and he was galloping on. 'Didn't lose any momentum at all!' exclaimed McCain. 'You *never* get the impression this horse is going to fall.'

Then, crossing the Melling Road, L'Escargot, dual winner of 'chasing's Gold Cup classic, moves forward closer, his blinkered head extending like a snake towards Red Rum, topped by the darkly sinister goggles of jockey Carberry. Will it be like last year now, the long-time leader getting hauled down in the dying seconds as a stag is pulled down by a wolf?

'I saw L'Escargot come to him,' said Beryl, 'And I thought "Oh goodness he's going well: we're going to be

The fallen greets the victor. His second Grand National, 1974, and won with flaunting ease under top weight. *Photo: Provincial Press*

Below: Pulling up after the second Grand National, Brian Fletcher and Jackie Granger beside themselves with joy. *Photo: "Sunday Express"*

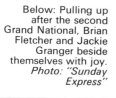

Left: Brian Fletcher raised his hand in a victory wave before the post and the "horse spurted ahead so quick Brian had to grab him!". After $4\frac{1}{2}$ miles. . . .

Perhaps the best "still" ever of the Grand National. Red Rum (No. 1), carrying top weight, sails over Becher's with Brian Fletcher sitting perfectly relaxed. *Photo: Gerry Cranham*

Below: Loading up
the box through the
used-car lot.

Bottom: Off to work.

beat''. And I looked over my shoulder to ''Ginger'' and I could see he thought the same.'

Peter O'Sullevan came in quick and strong as the gap started closing.

'It's Red Rum with L'Escargot chasing him now, the two top weights, Red Rum from L'Escargot. Red Rum for England, trying to complete that great double that hasn't been done since Reynoldstown, being pressed by L'Escargot now for Ireland. Then comes Spanish Steps improving on Charles Dickens. Then Scout, and behind them Vulgan Town and then Rough Silk. They're coming now to the second last fence in the 'National. And it's Brian Fletcher on Red Rum being pressed by Tommy Carberry on L'Escargot. The two top-weighted ones at the second last in the 'National. . . . It's Red Rum with a clear advantage there from L'Escargot who jumped it second. Then comes Charles Dickens third, and Spanish Steps. . . .'

'Ginger' watched L'Escargot and thought ''Oh Lord, that's too close for a horse of that class. He's got that Gold Cup speed and we're giving him a pound.'' But our horse seemed to sense it. He jumped the last absolutely flying.'

The gap had closed. Then Red Rum spurted like a sprinter. He sped towards the last smashed fence as bright as a bay button. He headed into a mountainous wall of acclamation.

Peter O'Sullevan's voice rose above the tumult:

Red Rum spurted like a sprinter

'This is the last fence now. It looks as though Red Rum has only got to jump it! But remember he deprived the winner of it on the flat last year. Now he's jumped it in the lead and it's *Red Rum!* This great local crowd giving him a *tremendous* ovation. Red Rum from L'Escargot, Tommy Carberry is trying to close the gap, but he's not going to. They come to the elbow. A furlong to run, he's got a big weight remember – twenty three pounds more than last year, but he's *going* to hold on. It's Red Rum from L'Escargot in second, Charles Dickens third, and Spanish Steps fourth, and racing up towards the line *and Red Rum getting the ovation of his career* – Brian Fletcher *acknowledging the cheers of the crowds* as he comes to the line! *The winner of the 'National.* L'Escargot is second, and Charles Dickens third, and fourth is Spanish Steps and then comes Rough Silk and Vulgan Town. Behind them Rouge Autumn and then the gallant Duke of Alburquerque on Nereo. . . .'

'It's Red Rum!'

'He settled it going to the last,' said 'Ginger' McCain. 'And on the run in, it was quite a joke really, Brian *putting his hand up to wave to the crowds!* Fantastic. Getting a bit cocky, too. The horse thought Brian was going to hit him. And he accelerated so bloody fast that Brian had to bring his hand quick to grab the reins. *That horse was going to run away with him,*' said 'Ginger' McCain, wide-eyed with marvelling at any horse who under 12 stone and after $4\frac{1}{2}$ miles and 30 gigantic fences could so spurt at the end of it all as to be really running away.

'He just ran home'

'He just *ran* home,' said McCain. L'Escargot, dual Cheltenham Gold Cup winner, had got to within three lengths of Red Rum racing to the last and yet on the run-in, with Brian Fletcher stopping riding to greet the crowd and then pulling up, our hero had extended the distance to 7 cock-a-hoop lengths. Behind him stretched a field as numerous as any since Fletcher had won his first 'National on Red Alligator back in 1968. 17 had completed.

'What a horse!'

'The jockey was so overjoyed' declared Noel Le Mare 'that he waved to us in the box. When he came in he just said "What a horse! What a horse! He didn't need a jockey!" Then he went on talking to David Coleman and I could have smacked Coleman's face! He said to the boy, "I think you picked up £6,000 last time. Will you get £10,000 this time?" Then he turned to me and had a few words, then to 'Ginger' who is very cryptic. Coleman asked him "What is the future for him?". And "Ginger" said "Aintree again next year. Subject to the owner's approval".'

And after the climax there was a down-beat ending of the day. McCain had his first runner on the flat in a race after the 'National. He wouldn't, he says, go round the corner to watch a flat race, but he'd drive miles to watch great chasers cross black fences together. His flat-race horse, what was more, ran disappointingly. McCain wandered off to have a drink alone. Then he felt a great urge to get away from the crowds into the quiet country that he has always loved. He walked onto the steeplechase course. Then he found himself walking further and further away. It was a beautiful late spring afternoon. The warmth of the sun on the turf over which Red Rum had raced had brought out the fresh smell of growing summer with a bouquet like a Loire wine. McCain had been flung into the skies by his horse's triumph. Now he drifted on, feeling again the quiet countryman which lives inside his bones. He heard the larks sing over Aintree and saw a hare crouch, then run with huge hindlegs and flattened ears. He walked on and on, dreaming, walking where his marvellous horse had galloped. He was, he said, 'living it all again. . .'.

He had no notion of the time. He was a mile away down the course when the last race had been run. The crowds had jostled home, leaving their refuse and their hopes. Tens of thousands of locals had left rejoicing in their hero. McCain kept strolling on round the course, thinking of all those hopes he had kept alive during two decades of dark years. He had known secretly that he would bring it off. Now that he had, it seemed incredible. . . . And he had in his pocket the key to Stan Wareing's Rolls. He came to, saw the time, strode back across the turf which had now made him doubly famous. The stands were empty.

Suddenly in the dusk his partner Peter Cundy and Stan Wareing found him: 'Where the devil have you been? We've been worried sick.'

They collected two more crates of champagne at Stan Wareing's, returned to Upper Aughton Road, continued celebrating, reached the Prince of Wales very late for a dinner of six which ended up as eighteen and at four in the morning were still carousing in Mr Le Mare's commodious residence. 'The Guv'nor was stuck in the middle of six attractive girls,' said 'Ginger' McCain proudly, 'all lit up, and thoroughly enjoying himself.'

41 'BUT HE'S BRILLIANT'

The week ensuing was one of indecision. Was Red Rum's season over? Might they run him a month later in the Whitbread Gold Cup at Sandown? Or in the Scottish 'National in three weeks? There was even some talk about the Grand Steeple de Paris. McCain had always had the intention of going to Ayr if the horse was well enough. So he seemed. A week after the Grand National he was actually leading attractive Carol Wareing's Event horse in a sharp gallop on Ainsdale beach. . . .

But no one else thought Red Rum should run again.

Brian Fletcher said no. Julian Wilson even wrote poor 'Ginger' a letter explaining that horses can't come back so quickly after the Grand National as to run well in the Scottish 'National. In an interview with Wilson, Tommy Stack had commented '"Ginger" has made no mistakes with the horse so far, I don't think we should tell him what to do with him now.' But all other pundits advised McCain that, because the two 'Nationals had never been won in the same year before, it shouldn't be tried.

The new
Red Rum

In the memories of some there lingered pictures of Red Rum in his old days struggling round on soft ground, hating it all and taking hidings. These people could not realise that the new Red Rum of the beach had entirely changed his attitude. They thought that to run him again, and over four miles at Ayr, would sour him again. 'Don't risk it,' they urged the uncertain McCain. 'Don't run him again.'

There was also what McCain calls a 'mish-mash' about whether Red Rum would have to carry a penalty. 'They were all quoting the rule book at me,' he grumbled, 'which I never read anyway, and finally they said that instead of 11st 7lb he'd better carry 11st 13lb.' This, with most people, would have been the final straw. An extra 6lb penalty would have been quite sufficient on Red Rum's back to break McCain's resolve. But just as

The
Scottish
Grand
National

Red Rum is a special horse, so is McCain a special character. They are both battlers. McCain against a flood-tide of negative advice kept to his course. He would attempt the impossible again. He would go for the Scottish 'National.

They drove to Scotland in Stan Wareing's car. Beryl McCain did not come. 'Ginger' drove. The atmosphere was rasping. 'Ginger' did not utter one word all the long miles. Red Rum had gone up earlier to settle down. They took Bob Marshall the farrier to be at hand in case he spread his racing-plates. 'Well,' says McCain drolly, 'Sugar Ray Robinson used to take his own hairdresser, so why shouldn't Red Rum take his own blacksmith?' But no horse had ever won the Grand National and the Scottish 'National in the same year. . . .

Fletcher, even on the course, was still opposed to running. 'Invariably horses that have run round Liverpool never come out the same season. It's like you having a hard day's work,' he explains. 'The next time you've got that job to do you won't put the same heart into it.'

As John Oaksey was ruefully to discover and generously to report, 'By all the rules he should have been a tired horse in need of a holiday. But to Mr Noel Le Mare's Red Rum the rules do not apply.'

Brian Fletcher admitted, 'He did look gloriously well, but he wasn't bucking and squealing.' It was his tenth race in seven months. Fletcher recalled, 'Pat Buckley leaned over to me in the parade and said, "God, that horse looks well, Brian". I said, "He's a *dead* horse. He's lost his character and charm." And throughout the race the horse wasn't as fresh. He wasn't himself.'

It was a mere two years since Red Rum owned by Mrs Brotherton and trained by Anthony Gillam had churned round this course under 9st 8lb. Now he carried 11st 13lb and started 11 to 8 favourite. Like his owner and his trainer he had come up from rags to riches. And now, like them, he would need great courage once again. Twenty-one days before and he'd danced over 30 great fences under 12 stone. He had galloped $4\frac{1}{2}$ miles. Now he must gallop four miles more.

'Ginger' McCain watched anxiously from the stands. They were walking round and round at the start for a seeming age. McCain scowled. He gnawed his lip. He dreaded that he had made a terribly wrong decision. 'Ginger''s temper frayed. Most of the other jockeys during the delay, got off their horses to rest their backs. 'Bet Brian doesn't get off,' he muttered savagely to Stan Wareing. 'Bet Brian's the only one sitting there.'

Fletcher did not dismount with the rest. But McCain agrees, that it was probably a good thing: if Fletcher had dismounted, Red Rum might have played up, and got loose. At last they start. – 'There he is right on the inside and third or fourth last all the way', says 'Ginger', 'in a position to get knocked over if anything falls'.

McCain was in a torment, for he had everything to lose and everything for which to curse himself. Unless Red Rum won it, and won easily, the critics would snap him to shreds. 'Running a double 'National winner again!' They'd shriek. 'Ignorant! Greedy! Wicked! Cruel!'

He groans now, remembering the ordeal of that race. 'He was *always* on the rails. Then they were stretching out into the straight and I really got the wind up. I knew this was where it would tell. I felt sick. He jumps the third last. He goes to tackle John Oaksey on Proud Tarquin. There's this horse on the rails running on like an express train' (it was Kildagin). 'I thought "He's going to do us". Then, slap, my fellow hits the second last. *Bump!* It's like the Hennessy.'

'The rules do not apply'

A slow start

'It's like the Hennessy'

That mistake put Oaksey and Proud Tarquin back in the race. Everyone thought – and John Oaksey snatched at the hope – that Red Rum's present weight and past exertions on top of this blunder must now really stop him.

'He's brilliant!' 'But he's *brilliant!*' shouts 'Ginger'. 'He's back into his stride and gone *whoosh* like a bullet! He more or less stuck up two fingers at Proud Tarquin. And he *just ran away from him!*'

The ovation that day at Ayr was the greatest ever given to a horse there, and some said that no more clamorous din had ever been heard on any racecourse in all Britain. 'It made the Hampden Roar,' as *The Sporting Life* succinctly put it, 'sound a mere ripple.'

Red Rum won, spurting away, by four lengths from Proud Tarquin, with Kildagin third, and Canharis fourth. He had travelled the four miles 120 yards in 8 mins 8 seconds. He had won another £7,922 to bring his colossal total under N.H. rules to £69,320 (nearly all of it earned in the last two seasons). His earnings in the 1972–73 season of £28,882 had themselves been a record, surpassing Arkle's best annual figure. Now that great sum had itself been easily overtaken. Red Rum's total for 1973–1974 season had, with the Scottish Grand National slung beneath his sporran, reached £36,779. For Le Mare and McCain who were so lucky to find both him and each other, he had so far won twelve races and been five times placed from 19 starts. Now he had done another unique thing by winning the two 'Nationals, and in three weeks. Oaksey had said before the race that Red Rum 'looked a sort of miracle'. Afterwards that highly admirable and just defeated amateur sportingly declared that 'Red Rum was assured already of immortality'.

'Away he goes' The great crowd had started bellowing for him at the second last fence. 'When Brian pulled him to the outside to go,' recalls McCain, 'I got the impression there was a slight hesitation. Then he's into top gear and away he goes.' McCain's eyes sparkle with delight.

'*What* a reception . . .' 'Ginger' breathed out. 'The owner of Proud Tarquin, Sir John Thomson, came over and said, "It's a privilege to be beaten by a horse like that". The owner of the third said something too along those lines.' Two months later and the tough Mr McCain was still blinking away emotion. 'It made me choke,' he said. 'Those good working people who came up to shake my hand, coming up and shaking, people who appreciated a good horse and who'd just come to see him win.'

'And Tommy Stack, who's ridden him all those previous races, goes past him and gives the horse three or four good old pats. And that was nice – sort of one old friend to another. Afterwards Tommy saw the lads, went over and slipped them a quid or two.'

McCain was detained by a crowd from Carlisle who seized him and bore him aloft and into their crowded coach. They were shouting 'We've come all the way from Carlisle to see this great horse of yours, and now you're going to have a drink with us.' As 'Ginger' was hoisted into the coach, a hoarse and beery cheer exploded, and two bottles were stuck into his hands. Nor could he leave the coach till the beer had been downed and he had signed every racecard. Ayr racecourse, sensible of Red Rum's historic achievement, commissioned a statue of him to stand on the field of glory. Only one other steeple-chaser (and he is dead) has been so honoured: Arkle at Cheltenham.

An historic achievement

Because Beryl (as 'Ginger' puts it) 'had the wind up, too, about the Scottish 'National', she went to Bangor-on-Dee – and watched their runner there get beaten a neck. A heaving crowd jostles into a bar there to watch the Scottish 'National on a television set. At the very front of the crowd squat several portly old ladies roosting on shooting-sticks. The crowd waits patiently. Just as they're down at the start at Ayr, a fellow pushes through the crowd at Bangor to switch the set to flat-racing at Newbury. Screams of protest rend the throng. There are shrieks of 'Lynch him!'. The old ladies set about him with their shooting-sticks. He runs bludgeoned from the bar. . . .

Such passion does Red Rum engender. His fan-mail, which had started to stream into the McCain's small house in Upper Aughton Road after his first Grand National, became a torrent after his second Grand National and a deluge after Ayr. Beryl McCain is overwhelmed. 'Letters . . .' she sighs, 'I have all the paperwork and the accounts and the children do hinder a bit, and sometimes in the evening I just don't *feel* like doing them. I joke about having to have a secretary, but it would be nice. . . .'

Red Rum's fan mail

A great spread of Red Rum's fan-mail covers my study floor as I come to the end of this attempt to chronicle part of this great horse's life. Most letters beg for photographs or shoes, send cheques, post greeting-cards. Children enclose toys and coloured postcards and postal orders. The letters come from Headmasters – 'all the world loves a *real* champion' – and from children, 'Give him a pat from me he's the greatest since Arkle'. From old disabled ladies: 'May I join the queue to have one of Red Rum's horse-shoes? I could do with some luck. . . .' From old-age pensioners in Scotland – 'I put my last 50p on Red Rum last Saturday'. From a man of 92: 'I've seen plenty of Nationals but I've never seen a finer winner'. From the sports-writer of a school magazine enclosing a written interview: '*Is Red Rum going for next year's 'National?'*. Beryl writes in '*Yes, all being well*'.

Poems, too

And poems, as Arkle had, and letters to the horse himself: 'Dear Red Rum I am six and a half . . .'. And letters from chartered accountants: 'I am sure this will create a great deal of goodwill for your future business . . .'. From Spillers Farm Feeds . . .'We would like the privilege of featuring Red Rum . . .'. From an anonymous fan scrawled on a scrap of paper inside a parcel 'Thank you for winning. Hope you like these mints'. A football fan from Leicester City sent the horse a pin-up postcard of mares at grass. 'Dear Red, sorry to say I didn't back you this year, thought you had too much pud. Very well done. Your mates across the city did us too at Villa Park, they deserved it too. Best of luck. Hope you like the picture. Leicester Lad.'

Two students wrote from a college in Spain. And Julian Wilson wrote from Fulham, 'If it were possible to eat humble pie through the post I would do so'.

The letters come from every corner of England, Scotland, Wales and Ireland. From cottages, hotels, offices, tenement blocks and manor houses. They are typed on engraved paper, scrawled on cards, printed on little ruled sheets. They start 'Dear Mr McCain', 'Dear Don', 'Dear Ginger', 'Dear Red Rum . . . I think you are a fantastic horse and your trainer must be very good. My dad backed Kildagin . . .'.

Comparison with Arkle

Arkle's fan-mail was tremendous, as I recall from being allowed by Betty and Tom Dreaper to tote a suitcase-full back from Ireland. Red Rum's has already exceeded it. He is without doubt already as popular a public hero, and as great a phenomenon in the horse world. Is he, that odious comparison, as great a horse? He would not have beaten Arkle in a Cheltenham Gold Cup. But would Arkle have stood up and stayed $4\frac{1}{2}$ miles round Aintree twice? I doubt it. His connections did not consider it. And, as Noel Le Mare so proudly says, 'Arkle was not *risked*'.

The two horses are at the pinnacles of the two highest but different trees in steeplechasing's forest: the classic park course, brilliant Cheltenham winner; and the Grand National horse representing an even longer road down racing's heritage.

But they are different, too, in much more vital ways. For Arkle it was goodness and light all his days, till his accident at Kempton. He was bred by steeplechasing people of jumping stock to be a steeplechaser. He was bought by a paragon of steeplechasing owners, Anne, Duchess of Westminster, and kept by her all his days. He was trained throughout his magnificent career by one wise man, old Tom Dreaper, one of the greatest trainers who ever cast eye upon a horse. He was ridden in almost every one of his panoply of races by a superlative steeplechasing jockey in Pat Taaffe.

He was in human terms, the silver-spooned aristocrat with every advantage from birth, who could rejoice in the best education, have the right friends and flourish in a beautifully organised career.

We have seen how wildly different has been the case of Red Rum. Bred wrong, sold cheap, handled by five trainers, ridden by nearly two dozen jockeys, moved from Ireland to Leicestershire to Yorkshire to Lancashire, racing from a 2-year-old onwards through eight seasons so far and 78 races – and most of them hard ones. He has achieved his triumphs against the odds, without advantages and very often, as McCain has said, in spite of people. He is like the man who makes it from rags: a survivor. He survived his mad mother, his sprinting father and the hard two-year-old racing which should, by all rules, have cut down his career to a couple of seasons. He survived much punishment in severe races. He survived the year of coughing. He survived one of the worst diseases in his foot. He survived because he possesses, in my experience, more toughness, more resilience, more downright, upright soaring courage than any horse I've ever been honoured to know.

And he could be said, at this point in our island story, to be an example to us all.

A survivor

Red Rum on the flat

Red Rum as a two-year-old (taken from Racehorses of 1967):
. . . third foal: cost 400 gns as a yearling: dam won over 7f: retained for 300 gns after dead-heating in seller at Liverpool in the spring: trained on well, and was successful again at Warwick in August, beating Parliamo a neck in a nursery: stays 1m: acts well on firm going: wore blinkers on last outing.
T. Molony.   Rating 84

As a three-year-old (Racehorses of 1968):
. . . fairly useful handicapper: retained for 1,400 gns after winning seller at Doncaster in March: favourite, had every chance when short-head second of 21 behind Alan's Pet carrying 10lb penalty in non-seller at Liverpool later in same week: stays 1m: appears to act on any going: sold privately after second outing, and is trained under N.H. rules by R. Renton.   Rating 88

Red Rum's jumping career

The following commentaries are extracts from the final Chasing edition of 'Timeform' for each season from 1968/69 to 1973/74.

1968/69
. . . promising young novice hurdler: placed in very useful company on more than one occasion, notably when 10 lengths runner-up to Clever Scot in Lancashire Hurdle at Liverpool: capable of winning races. R. Renton.
                                    Hurdles Rating 122

1969/70
. . . fairly moderate hurdler: looked to be regaining his good form of last season when runner-up to At Ease in handicap at Catterick in December, (tried in blinkers for first time) but has been somewhat disappointing in his last four races: stays $2\frac{1}{2}$m: acts on soft going. R. Renton.
                                    Hurdles Rating 130

1970/71
. . . fair chaser: gained the upper hand with a better jump at the last and ran on well to beat Orient War by $\frac{3}{4}$ length in novice chase at Doncaster in November: stayed on

gamely to score by 2 lengths from Choir Belle in minor event at Sedgefield the following month: led run-in when winning handicap by $\frac{1}{2}$ length from Banderole at Ayr in February: stays very well: acts on any going.
R. Renton.   Chase Rating 127
                                  Hurdles Rating 133

1971/72

. . . fair chaser: winner of two handicaps at Catterick this season, scoring by a length from Proud King and by 7 lengths from Great Noise: $2\frac{1}{2}$ lengths third to Nom de Guerre in similar event at Nottingham in March on latest outing: stays well: acts on any going: has worn blinkers but does just as well without them.
T. A. Gillam.   Chase Rating 123

1972/73

. . . useful chaser: co-favourite, climaxed a great season in which he has won no less than six races, with a game victory in Grand National at Liverpool in March, chasing clear leader Crisp from a long way out, still having 15 lengths to make up at the last but keeping on strongly to lead in last 25 yds and win going away by $\frac{3}{4}$ length, the pair finishing a long way clear: stays extremely well: acts on any going: has worn blinkers: game and consistent: sound jumper: sold out of T. A. Gillam's stable 6,000 gns Doncaster August (1972) Sales.
D. McCain.   Chase Rating 145

1973/74

This, the final Timeform of the 1973/74 season commentary, was published before Red Rum won the Scottish Grand National.

. . . very smart chaser: won six races in 1972/73, including Grand National at Liverpool: better than ever this season, and gave a magnificent performance when defying top weight in Grand National in March, jumping well, taking command before Bechers on second circuit and always looking like winning from this point, eventually scoring by 7 lengths from L'Escargot: winner at Carlisle, Ayr, Newcastle and Catterick and ran marvellous race to finish short-head second to Red Candle in Hennessy Cognac Gold Cup at Newbury earlier in season: stays extreme distances: acts on any going: has worn blinkers: most genuine and consistent: sound jumper.
D. McCain.   Chase Rating 156

How to Read the Form

THE GOING, shown at the head of each meeting, is recorded in the following stages:
Hard; Firm; Good; Yielding; Soft; Heavy.

PRIZE MONEY for the first three (certain races first four) is shown thus: £340 (£90: £40).

WEIGHTS shown are the actual weights carried. Small figures against weight denote overweight carried in lbs.
$‡^3$ $‡^5$ $‡^7$ = apprentice allowance deducted.
(7x) = including 7lb extra for win after publication of weights.

OWNER of the winner is shown in parentheses before the trainer.

THE DRAW for places at the start, when material, is shown immediately after each jockey's name.

BLINKERS: (H) following name of horse denotes hood or blinkers.

THE OFFICIAL DISTANCES between the first six horses are shown on the right-hand side immediately preceding their position at the finish.
For major races, closely contested sprints and two-year-old events, distances beyond sixth place may be shown after inspection of race-finish photographs.

RACE-TIMES are unofficial. Figures in parentheses following the times show: (1) the number of seconds either faster or slower than the standard (average) for the course distance. (2) the number of seconds slower than the record time as shown in Best Times for Courses. Standard (average) time comparisons are prefixed by either 'a' or 'b' – a (slower than standard), b (faster than standard). Record time comparisons in 2-y-o races refer to the 2-y-o record times in all cases.

THE PARADE RING
Classification of horses on looks:

v nice c = very nice colt: outstanding on looks
nice c = nice colt; very good sort
gd sort = well made: above average on looks
wl grwn = well grown: furnished to frame

w'like = workmanlike
h.d.w. = has done well improved in looks
scope = scope for development
cmpt = compact
lt-f = light-framed
unf = unfurnished: not furnished to frame
nt grwn = not grown

lw = looked very fit
bkwd = backward in condition
str = strong
swtg = sweating excessively
t = tubed
b = bandaged fore
b.hind = do. hind
H = hood or blinkers

Abbreviations

THE RUNNING
a = always
a.p. = always prom.
appr = approaching
awrdd = awarded
b.b.v = broke blood vessel
bel = below
bhd = behind
bk = back
blkd = baulked
bmpd = bumped
bnd = bend
btn = beaten
c = came
cd = could
ch = chance
chal = challenge (d)
cl = close
cld = claimed
clr = clear
ct = caught
crse = course
dist = distance (240 yds from w.p.)
drvn = driven
dsptd = disputed
dwlt = dwelt
effrt = effort
ent = entering
ev ch = every chance
f = furlong
fdd = faded
fin = finish
fnl = final
grnd = ground
hd = head
hdd = headed
hdwy = headway

hl = hill
hmpd = hampered
½-wy = half way
impd = improved
ins = inside
l = length
lckd = lacked
ld = lead
ldr = leader
lft = left
lkd = looked
m = mile
mid div = mid division
n.d = no danger
n.g.t = not go through
nk = neck
no ex = no extra pace
no imp = no impression
nrr = nearer
nrst fin = nearest at finish
nt = not
nvr = never
out = from finish
outpcd = outpaced
ol = place
press = pressure
prog = progress
prom = prominent
p.u = pulled up
qckn = quicken
r = race
rcvr = recover
rdn = ridden
rm = room
rn = ran
rng = running
r.o = ran on

rspnse = response
rt = right
r.wl = ran well
s = start
s.h = short head
shld = should
shwd = showed
s.i.s. = slowly into stride
slt = slight
sme = some
spd = speed
s.s = started slowly
st = straight
stdy = steady
stdd = steadied
str = strong
strtnd = straightened
swvd = swerved
tch = touch
th = there
thro = through
thrght = throughout
tk = took
t.n.p. = took no part
t.o = tailed off
trbld = troubled
u.p = under pressure
uphl = uphill
v = very
w = with
wd = wide
wknd = weakened
wl = well
wnr = winner
w.r.s. = whipped round start
wy = way

LIVERPOOL, Fri., Apr. 7th (Firm)
THURSBY (S) PTE (2-Y.O.) £133 ea   5f   2.0

1967

RED RUM 9-0	Cook	9	w'like: leggy: rn green: rdn ½wy: str rn fr bel dist: got up last strde	—†
CURLICUE 8-11	WGuest	4	cmpt: bkwd: led: rdn & hdd bel dist: led ins dist: ct cl hme	—†
Blue Spider 8-11	Lake	1	small: str: lw: w ldr on bit: led bel dist: sn rdn: hdd & wknd ins dist	3.3
Heala Belle 8-11	Larkin	6	lw: sn prom: wknd bel dist	8.4
Miss Moonlight 8-11	WCarson	3	small: s.l.s: nrst fin	1.5
Dunaroon 8-6‡⁵	Hetherington	7	small: nt go pce	2.6
Overula 8-7‡⁷	Eccleston	2	a.outpcd	0
Ventriloquist 9-0	LBrown		nvr bttr than mid div	0
Friars Park 9-0	Swinburn	8	leggy: scope: s.l.s: nt rcvr	0

S.P.: 11/10 BlueSpider, 7/2 CURLICUE, 5 RED RUM, 8 HealaBelle, 100/8 MissMoonlight, 20 Others. Red Rum (Mr M Kingsley) T Molony, Melton Mowbray; bt in 300 gns; Curlicue (Mrs N Dennistoun) J Dennistoun, Letcombe Regis. nt sold. 9 Rn   64.6 sec (.6)

1967

BEVERLEY, Sat., Apr. 29th (Good)
TICKTON JUVENILE STKS (2-Y.O.) £364   5f   4.0

CAPTIVATED 9-0	EHide	1	a.cl up: led bel dist: rdn thro	—1
Hodhard 9-5	Connorton	3	led aftr 1f to bel dist: rdn: r.o	1.2
Strawberry Moon 8-7	Ryan	9	led 1f: effrt & rdn bel dist: no ex	2½.3
Ness Lane 8-10	LBrown	2	gd sort: a.prom: no hdwy fr bel dist	2.4
Pastina 8-2‡5	Oldroyd	4	gd sort: leggy: lw: in tch: pushd along ½wy: no hdwy: rn green	3.5
Willshow 8-10	Skilling	11	w'like: neat: outpcd: nvr nrr	¾.6
Red Rum 8-10	Sime	5	hdwy & rdn 2f out: sn btn	0
Royal Picaroon 8-3‡7	Barnes	6	str: cmpt: bkwd: nvr wnt pce	0
Moon Probe 8-5‡5	CWilliams	10	w'like: cmpt: bkwd: rdn ½wy: nvr bttr than mid div	0
Golden Blast 8-7	Littlewood	8	n.d	0
Well Versed 8-7	Rawlinson	11	w'like: a.wl bhd	0

S.P.: 6/4 Pastina, 13/8 Hodhard, 4 CAPTIVATED, 10 RedRum, 20 Strawberry Moon, 25 NessLane, 33 Others. (Mr D Robinson) W Elsey, Malton. 11 Rn 64.3 sec (1.7 under av)

TEESSIDE PARK, Mon., June 19th (Firm)
VANE ARMS PTE (2-Y.O.) £345   6f   8.50

RED PIXIE 8-5	Etherington	11	lw: hdwy ½wy: led dist: drvn out	—1
Remraf 8-5	Bentley	8	led over 3f out: sn rdn: nt qckn fnl f	2.2
French Myth 8-1(²)‡3	Cadwaladr	9	gd sort: leggy: lw: jnd ldrs 3f out: wknd ins fnl f	3.3
Fortzeno 8-2	EHide	4	led over 2f: btn 2f out	4.4
Mi Lu 8-1(⁴)‡5	Blackshaw	5	prom tl rdn & btn over 2f out	1½.5
Vistum 8-0‡5	Oldroyd	6	lw: nvr nrr	1.6
Vianne 8-2	Buckle	10	cl up to ½wy	0
Swale Manor 8-2	Drabble	7	outpcd	0
Red Rum 8-7	Larkin	1	h.d.w: s.s: nt rcvr	0
Queen of the Moss 8-2	Skilling	3	t.o	0
Rising Water 8-5	Connorton	2	lft s: virtually t.n.p	0

S.P.: 5/2 RisingWater, 3 Remraf, 5 RED PIXIE, 7 FrenchMyth, 8 Fortzeno, 9 MiLu, 100/7 RedRum, 100/6 Vistum, 50 Others. (Mr J W Roylance) M H Easterby, Malton. 11 Rn   1m 13 (1 under av)

Red Rum has done well and furnished to his frame in the last two months but was never able to recover from a slow start.

NEWCASTLE, Fri., June 30th (Good to firm)
ANGERTON STKS (2-Y.O. C & G) £415   6f   6.45

MOUNT ATHOS 9-3	Faggotter	7	bhd: swtchd outsde dist: qcknd to ld ins fnl f	—1
Waggy 9-3	Maddock	2	jnd ldr ½wy: rdn bel dist: r.o	1.2
Red Rum 9-0	Cadwaladr	5	a.cl up: nt qckn fr bel dist	1.3
Bold Flush 8-10	Seagrave	1	lw: prom: hmpd dist: nt rcr	1.4
Bold William 8-10	Connorton	3	h: led tl wknd over 1f out	nk.5
Pickering 8-10	EHide	4	gd sort: scope: s.i.s: prom: kpt on	1.6
Carruthers 8-10	LBrown	9	lw: cl up 4f	s.h.7
Dobbin 9-0	DSmith	6	lw: cl up tl wknd over 1f out	0
Lintloch 8-7	Etherington	8	nvr trbld ldrs	0

S.P.: 6/4 MOUNT ATHOS, 7/2 Dobbin, 7 Pickering, 15/2 BoldFlush, 100/9 Waggy, 100/8 BoldWilliam,Carruthers, 33 RedRum, 50 Lintloch. (Mr A J Struthers) H Whiteman, Ayr. 9 Rn   1m 17.4 (1.4)

Red Rum, on the best of terms with himself in the paddock, showed improved ability to match his physical development during recent months. He ran a useful race, battling on well in the last two furlongs, but was not good enough to cope with the first two. He should win another race before long.

WARWICK, Mon., Aug. 28th (Firm)
PINLEY NURSERY H'CAP £467   7f   4.0

RED RUM 7-11	DWMorris	14	3rd st: led jst ins fnl f: jst hld on	—1
Parliamo 7-7‡⁵	AMurray	1	5th st: hdwy bel dist: unable qckn	nk.2
Bavard 8-1	Cheshire	10	9th st: r.o wl fnl 2f: nt rch wnr	2½.3
Rose Diana 7-10	MThomas	3	h: led ent st tl wknd ins fnl f	nk.4
Sealed 8-1	Tulk	7	4th st: no ndwy	2½.5
Up at Dawn 8-0	Greening	12	8th st: no real hdwy	s.h.6
Regal Norwich 7-11	TCarter	9	6th st: nvr plcd to chall	½.7
Mojave 7-12‡³	CWilliams	2	led: 2nd st: wknd qckly	0
Laplander 7-10(¹)	Lynch	13	dwlt s: 7th st: sn lost pl	0
Go Gipsy Go 8-9	Swinburn	5	no show	0

Also ran:—

Sara's Star 7-10(²)‡⁵	Currie	11	Soloning 7-8	Cullen	8
Yip I Addy 7-2‡⁷	Barton	6	Beat Music 6-7‡⁷	Leaver	4

S.P.: 3 Bavard, 9/2 RoseDiana, 6 RED RUM, 7 Mojave, 15/2 GoGipsyGo, 10 Sealed, 100/6 RegalNorwich,Parliamo, 20 Up at Dawn,Soloning, 25 YipIAddy, 33 Others. (Mr M Kingsley) T Molony, Melton Mowbray. 14 Rn
Red Rum, always well placed, took the lead just inside the final furlong and held on in a driving finish.

YORK, Thurs., Sept. 7th (Holding)
BISHOPTHORPE NURSERY H'CAP £598   7f   3.30

ANISEED 7-2 (⁴)‡⁵	AMurray	7	h: mde all: hld on wl	—1
Stardao 7-0(²)‡⁷	Bremner	12	hdwy & changed posn 2f out: ev ch fnl f: wknd	1½.2
Maria Helena 9-1	Durr	16	hdwy 3f out: shkn up bel dist: fin wl	s.h.3
Stonewall 7-11	RHutchinson	14	lw: hdwy 3f out: chall 2f out: nt qckn fnl f	1½.4
Galmerro 7-13	Barclay	9	lw: prom to 2f out: no hdwy	2.5
Caecilia 7-2‡³	EJohnson	5	wnt 2nd 3f out: wknd fr bel dist	2.6
Ardear 7-6	WCarson	2	hdwy 3f out: one pce	s.h.7
Red Rum 7-11‡⁵ (10x)	Sexton	3	lw: cl up 4f	½.8
The Diddler 8-12	Etherington	1	cl up 4f	0
Mi Lu 7-5	Bentley	18	lw: cl up 3f	0
Humility 7-4(¹¹)‡⁷	RichardHutchinson	6	cl up 3f: t.o	0
Psidium's Rock 7-0	Parkes	4	s.l.s: hdwy ½wy: n.d	0

Also ran:—

Caballero 7-13	Cook	13	EdwardtheSixth 7-5(²)	Cullen	15
Sea Rover 7-12	Letherby	10	Carruthers 7-3(⁷)‡⁵	Horrocks	17
Singing Pool 7-8	Sime	11	Golden Gal 7-0	McIntosh	8

S.P.: 100/30 MariaHelena, 4 Stonewall, 10 TheDiddler, 100/8 RedRum, MiLu, Caecilia, 100/7 ANISEED, Caballero, 100/6 SingingPool, 25 SeaRover, Galmerro, Stardao, Carruthers, EdwardtheSixth, 50 Others. (Lord Harrington) G Brooke, N'mkt. 18 Rn   1m 30.8 (1.8)

PONTEFRACT, Wed., Sept. 20th (Good)
MINOR NURSERY H'CAP £414   1m   4.30

STARDAO 7-5‡⁷	Bremner	4	wnt 4th st: effrt over 1f out: r.o: led ins fnl f	—1
Ardear 7-9(¹)‡³	Hetherington	6	led early: led st: r.o one pce	¾.2
Red Rum 8-5	Piggott	7	wnt 6th st: r.o one pce	4.3
Penfort 8-4	Henry	10	lw: wnt 3rd st: wknd ins fnl f	¼.4
Be Tolerant 7-10	Skilling	3	prom tl lost pl & 5th st	5.5
Up at Dawn 8-3 (6x)	Stringer	8	lw: wnt 2nd & rdn st: sn btn	5.6
Swale Manor 7-4	East	9	h: sn led: btn st	0
Lady Patient 7-0	McIntosh	1	cl up early: sn lost pl	0
Seventa 8-0	WCarson	5	unruly s	0
Vistum 8-0	Greenaway	2	nvr trbld ldrs	0

S.P.: 9/4 STARDAO, 100/30 UpatDawn, 11/2 BeTolerant, 6 RedRum, 10 Penfort, 100/8 Seventa, 100/7 Vistum 20 Ardear, 25 SwaleManor, 33 LadyPatient. (Mrs E Smith) V Mitchell, Malton. 10 Rn
Red Rum could only stay on at his own pace to take third place inside the final furlong.

1967   **LEICESTER, Mon., Sept. 25th (Good, fast)**
NANPANTAN NURSERY H'CAP £345   1m   4.30

COONBEAM 8-11	Breasley	4	a.prom: qcknd to ld cl hme	—1
Tudor Pleasure 7-9	Maddock	5	led over 3f out: nt qckn nr fin	$\frac{1}{2}$.2
Gartree Gate 7-12‡5	AMurray	3	lw: r.o wl fnl 2f	5.3
Red Rum 8-9	DWMorris	16	h: prom & hrd rdn 2f out	$\frac{1}{2}$.4
Duo 8-5	Cook	10	gd hdwy fnl f: nvr nr to chall	2$\frac{1}{2}$.5
Fray 8-0	Barclay	15	led over 4f: wknd 2f out	5.6

Also ran:—

Ovum Avia 7-10	Cullen	14:h	Never Idle 8-7	WWilliamson	6:lw
Rich Velvet 7-3‡5	Still	7	Pike & Eel 8-5	Stansfield	12
Be Tolerant 7-4‡3	EJohnson	17	With Water 7-8‡5	Dicey	8
Soloist 7-7(2)	WCarson	2	Do Go 7-11	Letherby	9:h
Night Skite 8-10	SClayton	1	Winton Hotel 8-0	Durr	13
Sumsing 8-0	Jago	11			

S.P.: 2 WintonHotel, 6 GartreeGate, 7 COONBEAM, 10 RedRum, 100/9 Pike&Eel, NightSkite, 100/8 Sumsing, DoGo, Duo, 100/7 NeverIdle, 100/6 Fray, RichVelvet, 20 BeTolerant, 50 Others. (Mrs C Smith-Bingham) P Walwyn, Lambourn. 17 Rn   1m 38.2 (1.8 under av)
Red Rum, always prominent on the far rails, came under pressure and was beaten entering the last furlong.

1968   **DONCASTER, Wed., Mar. 27th (Good on top)**
WATERDALE (S) H'CAP (3-Y.O.) £370 (£103: £49)   7f   2.0

RED RUM 9-2	GLewis	18	lw: cl up: led 2f out: hld on wl	—1
Duo 8-10	Starkey	11	h: prom: hdwy 3f out	hd.2
Royal Arden 8-5	Connorton	7	lw: hdwy fnl 3f	5.3
Sage Rose 8-0‡7	Reavey	6	gd hdwy 3f out: ch bel dist: sn btn	1$\frac{1}{2}$.4
Golden Gal 7-13‡3	AMurray	9	prom: hdwy & ch dist: wknd	6.5
Fort Iver 8-4	ELarkin	5	lw: nrst fin	$\frac{1}{2}$.6

Also ran:—

Do Go 8-10	Etherington	3	Millie's Daughter 8-0(2)		
Sunset Fair 8-1	Barclay	16		EHide	17
Sit Tight 8-0	JWilson	10:lw	Quowonder 7-8	Parkes	2
Five Out 7-7	Bentley	8	Annaleen 7-1‡7	Coates	19
Gallinipper 8-1‡7	Gough	20	Noble Lascar 8-5	Russell	14
Mexican Mirth 7-10(6)‡7			Gayton 7-4‡3	EJohnson	1
	Graham	13	Mr Make Believe 8-0	DWhite	4
Grey Smoke 8-10(1)	Keith	12	Queen's Jewels 8-3	Lappin	15

S.P.: 11/4 RED RUM, 8 Duo, 100/9 Gallinipper, 100/8 GreySmoke, SageRose, RoyalArden, NobleLascar, 100/7 Queen'sJewels, SunsetFair, Millie'sDaughter, 100/6 SitTight, 20 DoGo, Fortiver, GoldenGal, Gayton, 33 Others. (Mr Maurice Kingsley) T Molony, Melton Mowbray. 20 Rn; bt in 1400 gns   1m 34.8 (6.8)
Red Rum, who was very fit, was in front two furlongs out and, in a driving finish, just managed to hold on.

LIVERPOOL, Sat., Mar. 30th (Good)
EARL OF SEFTON'S STKS (H'cap). (3-Y.O.) £437 (£120: £57)   1m   4.30

ALAN'S PET 7-8‡5	Eccleston	2	lw: 5th st: led bel dist: hld on wl	—1
Red Rum 8-12 (10x)	Piggott	20	prom: 3rd st: chall fr dist: r.o	s.h.2
Kemmery 7-9‡7	Hood	3	gd hdwy fnl 2f: r.o	2.3
MarkSmeaton 8-5‡3	AMurray	6	6th st: hdwy & ev ch 2f out	1.4
Wild Root 8-9	LBrown	5	lw: 7th st: hdwy & ch bel dist	nk.5
Lord Tom 8-10	Seagrave	7	h.d.w: hdwy 3f out: nt rch ldrs	2$\frac{1}{2}$.6

Also ran:—

Whangee 8-8	Russell	13	Pallant 7-10	Patton	4
Bar of Gold 8-7	EHide	10	Tudor Chip 6-13‡7	JHarris	15
Europeana 7-13	McIntosh	14	Fair Henry 7-0‡5	Still	16:lw
Ladrap 7-13	Barclay	9	In the Clear 7-0(3)‡7	Mellor	12
Queen's Route 7-10	Cullen	21	Rhondda 8-7	Henry	18
Red Pixie 9-0	Etherington	1	Pirate Prince 7-9	WJesse	11
High Cast 7-10	Maddock	8	Acton Sattalite 7-3(2)‡3		
Edward the Sixth 7-9	Sime	17		EJohnson	19

S.P.: 11/4 RedRum, 4 LordTom, 8 RedPixie,Europeana, 9 WildRoot, MarkSmeaton, 10 BarofGold, Queen'sRoute, HighCast, FairHenry, 100/9 Kemmery, 100/8 Ladrap, 100/7 Whangee,EdwardtheSixth,Rhondda, 20 ALAN'S PET & Others. (Mr A Mealor) R Barnes, Warrington. 21 Rn   1m 49 (4)
Red Rum, in the front rank all the way, put in a determined challenge in the last furlong. The penalty proved to be just too much.

THE PARADE RING
Classification of horses on looks:

gd sort = well made above average on looks
w'like = workmanlike
lw = looked very fit

bkwd = backward in condition
str = strong
swtg = sweating excessively

t = tubed
b = bandaged fore
b.hind = do. hind
H = hood or blinkers

Abbreviations

THE RUNNING

a = always
a.p = always prom.
appr = approaching
awrdd = awarded
b.b.v = broke blood vessel
bel = below
bhd = behind
bk = back
blkd = baulked
blnd = blundered
bmpd = bumped
bnd = bend
btn = beaten
c = came
cd = could
ch = chance
chal = challenge(d)
cir = circuit
cl = close
cld = claimed
clr = clear
cmftbly = comfortably
ct = caught
crse = course
dist = distance (240 yards from w.p.)
drvn = driven
dsptd = disputed
dwlt = dwelt
effrt = effort
ent = entering
ev ch = every chance
ex = extra
f = fell
fdd = faded
fin = finish
fnc = fence
fnl = final
grnd = ground
hd = head
hdd = headed
hdl = hurdle
hdwy = headway

hl = hill
hmpd = hampered
½-way = half-way
impd = improved
ins = inside
j.b = jumped badly
j.w = jumped well
l = length
lckd = lacked
ld = lead
ldr = leader
lft = left
lkd = looked
ltl = little
m = mile
mid div = mid division
n.d = no danger
n.g.t = not go through
nk = neck
no ex = no extra pace
no imp = no impression
nrr = nearer
nrst fin = nearest at finish
nt = not
nvr = never
o.d = open ditch
out = from finish
outpcd = outpaced
pckd = pecked
pl = place
pres = pressure
prog = progress
prom = prominent
p.u = pulled up
qckn = quicken
r = race
rcvr = recover
rdn = ridden
rdr = rider
ref = refused
rmntd = remounted
rm = room

rn = ran
rng = running
r.o = ran on
rspnse = response
rt = right
r.wl = ran well
s = start
s.h = short head
shld = should
shwd = showed
slt = slight
sme = some
sn = soon
spd = speed
s.s = started slowly
st = straight
stdy = steady
stdd = steadied
str = strong
strtnd = straightened
swvd = swerved
tch = touch
th = there
thro = through
thrght = throughout
tk = took
t.n.p = took no part
t.o = tailed off
trbld = troubled
uns = unseated
u.p = under pressure
uphl = uphill
v = very
w = with
wd = wide
wknd = weakened
wl = well
wnr = winner
w.r.s = whipped round start
wt = weight
wtr = water
wy = way

CHELTENHAM, Wed., Sept. 18th (Good)

1968/69

JUNIOR NOVICES' HURDLE (II) (3-Y.O.) £340 (£90: £40)   abt 2m 200y 4.30

ACASTUS 11-3	Jennings	h: led aftr 6th: hrd rdn appr last: qcknd flat	—1
Red Rum 10-10	JGifford	lw: led 2nd to 4th: ev ch appr last: one pce	5.2
Tigerlee 10-10	JKing	r.o wl fr 2 out	6.3
Baby Spot 10-10	Mould	h: nvr trbld ldrs	15.4
Certainly 10-10	Biddlecombe	prom tl wknd fr 5th	30.5
Double Diamond 10-10	Cartwright	lw: h: led to 2nd: prom to 5th: sn bhd	30.6
Rob Lad 10-10	JGuest	led 4th: hdd aftr 6th: 5th & no ch whn fell last	0
Devon Satyr 10-3‡7	RWeaver	no ch whn fell 2 out	0
From the North 10-10	BFletcher	no ch whn fell 2 out	0
Bar of Gold 10-10	RAtkins	w ldrs whn fell 6th	0

S.P.: 13/8 ACASTUS, 9/2 BarofGold, 11/2 Tigerlee, 8 RedRum, 10 Certainly, 100/8 BabySpot, 100/7 DoubleDiamond, 20 Others. (Mrs J Heath) F Walwyn, Lambourn. 10 Rn   4m 13.6 (5.4 under av)

1968/69

MARKET RASEN, Sat., Oct. 19th (Good to Soft)
HAINTON HURDLE (3-Y.O.) £272 (£72: £32)   2m   4.10

FRANCOPHILE 10-7	Broderick	lw: mstks: mde most fr 4th: hit last 2: drew clr flat	—1
Colton 10-3‡7	Greeves	jnd ldrs 5th: disp ld last 2: one pce flat	6.2
Sea Empress 10-0	GLee	prom to 5th: no hdwy aftr	8.3
Red Rum 10-7	Turnell	lw: hdwy whn mstk 6th: nt rcvr	2.4
Wakener 10-2‡5	PKavanagh	nvr nrr	5.5
Gelegnite 10-0(5)‡5	WPowell	cl up to 6th: grad wknd	7.6

Also ran:—

Vanessa 9-7‡7	Latimer	Wild Tudor 9-13(2)‡3	
Noblethorpe Lady 10-2(9)‡7	RLee		MClark (bit bkwd)
Nice Shoe 10-0	Patrick	Matanza 9-11(4)‡7	Laurie
Heather Darling 10-0	GKelly	Alcimede 9-10(3)‡7	PRussell
Little Song 9-9‡5	Holmes	Fair Henry 10-10	Glover
Gold Bloom 10-7	EAndrews	Stand Clear 10-0	Buckingham
Codswallop 10-2(2)	MGifford	Sit Tight 10-4(4)	TRyan

S.P.: 5/4 FairHenry, 5/2 RedRum, 5 FRANCOPHILE, 8 StandClear, 10 Colton, 100/6 GoldBloom, 20 Wakener, Gelegnite,Codswallop,SeaEmpress, 33 Others. (Mr J Muldoon) F Carr, Malton. 19 Rn

Red Rum looked magnificent. He moved up sharply going to the third flight from home but must have made a mistake at it, for he came out many lengths behind with his chance gone. He should be given another chance.

NOTTINGHAM, Mon., Nov. 18th (Good)
MERIT HURDLE (3-Y.O.) £837 (£230: £109)   2m   3.0

SOLONING 11-0	Beasley	hdwy fr 5th: chall & slt ld last: rdn: jst hld on	—1
Francophile 10-10	Broderick	a.prom: led aftr 2 out: w wnr last: unable qckn nr fin	nk.2
Red Rum 10-7	Cook	gd hdwy fr 6th: nt rch ldrs	3.3
Acastus 11-0	GRobinson	lw: h: prom: no hdwy fr 2 out	4.4
Pips Song 10-10	Cartwright	nvr trbld ldrs	½.5
Tambourium 11-0	RBarry	nvr nr to chall	2½.6

Also ran:—

		Cefn Mawr 10-10	EHarty
Colton 10-7‡7	Greeves	Dubious 10-10	Reid
Sea Empress 10-7	GLee	Tigerlee 10-10	JGuest
Irishman 10-10	DNicholson	Zarathon 10-10	Uttley

S.P.: 3 Francophile, 7/2 Irishman, 5 SOLONING, Acastus, 100/8 Zarathon, RedRum, 100/6 Tambourlum,CefnMawr, 20 Colton, 25 Others. (Mrs C E Thornton) F Winter, Lambourn. 13 Rn   4m 6 (5)

Red Rum put in some good late work without looking likely to take a closer hand in the proceedings.

DONCASTER, Fri., Nov. 22nd (Soft)
PLANT NOVICES' HURDLE (II) (3-Y.O.) £272 (£72: £32) abt 2m 150y 4.30

CORAL DIVER 10-10	Biddlecombe	gd sort: lw: cl up whn mstk 2nd: jnd ldrs 4th: rdn to ld btwn last 2: hit last: r.o	—1
Rare Comedy 10-10	Leech	hdwy 5th: led 2 out: sn hdd: nt qckn	4.2
Red Rum 10-10	TSMurphy	lw: a.cl up: ev ch 2 out: no ex	1½.3
It's Mustard 10-10	Uttley	hdwy 3 out: nrst fin	4.4
Flight Pool 10-7‡3	Quinn	nvr nrr	5.5
Mi Lu 10-10	Blackshaw	lw: mde most to 2 out: wknd	4.6

Also ran:—

Midsummer Willow 11-5	Hurley	Avon Bay 10-3‡7	Goulding
Colana 10-3‡7	Doyle	Clock Corner 10-10	Fenwick
The Difference 10-3‡7	Greaves	Ponticelli 10-5‡5	PJames
Slipabout 10-10	Buckley	Sutty 10-10	Stack
At Ease 10-10	Stobbs	Ardagan 10-10	Harvey
Ripatip 10-10	EAndrews	King Cotton 10-3‡7	Shaw

S.P.: 5/2 RedRum, 4 RareComedy, 9/2 CORAL DIVER, 9 FlightPool, 10 Midsummer Willow, 100/8 Slipabout,MiLu,KingCotton,Ripatip, 100/7 TheDifference,It's Mustard, 20 AvonBay,AtEase. 33 Others. (Mr B P Jenks) T Rimell, Severn Stoke. 18 Rn   4m 11 (10) S

Red Rum was fit. He was always in the front rank and held as good a chance as any at the penultimate hurdle. From then on he could find no more pace.

WETHERBY, Sat., Mar. 8th (Good to Soft)
HAREWOOD HURDLE (4-Y.O.) £340 (£90:£40)   2m   4.0

RARE COMEDY 11-5	Barrott	hdwy appr 3 out: led flat: r.o wl	—1
Avon Bay 11-3‡[7]	Goulding	jnd ldrs 4 out: led 2 out tl flat	1½.3
Francophile 11-5	Broderick	h: led appr 3rd tl hdd & wknd 2 out	6.2
Smart Fellow 11-5	Blackshaw	lw: cl up early: lost pl ½wy: r.o fin	hd.4
Mind the Paint 10-12‡[7]	Jos Scallan	prom: nt qckn fr 3 out	4.5
Red Rum 10-7‡[7]	JDoyle	a.prom: one pce fr 3 out	1.6

Also ran:—

Be Tolerant 11-0	Stack	Fair Cheer 10-7‡[7]	JThompson
Just Paddy 10-7‡[7]	Cunningham	Mycropolis 10-7‡[7]	JFoster
Psimbidium 11-0	DAtkins	Proud Word 11-0	NWilkinson
Arctic Lodge 11-0	Harvey	It's Mustard 11-5	Blair
Potheen 11-2‡[3]	PVaughan	Codswallop 10-7‡[7]	Papworth
Avonduet 10-7‡[7]	Parkins	Sutty 10-11‡[3]	MrAKemp
		Skytron 11-0	TRyan

S.P.: 11/8 Francophile, 7 SmartFellow,Potheen,It'sMustard, 10 RARE COMEDY, RedRum,ArcticLodge, 100/9 MindthePaint, 100/8 AvonBay, 100/7 BeTolerant, ProudWord, Psimbidium, 20 Others. (Mrs J M Richards) M H Easterby, Malton. 19 Rn   4m 4 (equals av)

LIVERPOOL, Thurs., Mar. 27th (Good)
LANCASHIRE HURDLE (4-Y.O.) £690 (£190: £90)   abt 2m 100y   2.30

CLEVER SCOT 11-0	BFletcher	led 2nd: mde rest: clr last	—1
Red Rum 10-7	Broderick	a.prom: chasd wnr fr 3 out: no imp	10.2
Lord Tom 11-0	WRees	h: prom: one pce fr 3 out	4.3
Steel Band 11-7	JKing	lw: prom: no hdwy fr 3 out	4.4
Surtsey 10-7	TNorman	lw: bhd: r.o wl fr 3 out	nk.5
Avon Bay 10-7‡[7]	Goulding	nvr nrr	2.6

Also ran:—

Nether Edge 11-0	REdwards	Magical Tudor 10-4‡[3]	AMarkham (h)
Caballero 10-7	DNicholson (h)	Prince des Iles 10-7	Mould
Dictora 10-7	TMurphy	Naughty Story 10-7	Stack
Alectryon 10-2‡[5]	DTHughes	Table Mountain 11-7	Biddlecombe
At Ease 11-0	TSMurphy	Mr Wrekin 10-7‡[7]	Holland

S.P.: 4 PrincedesIles, 5 TableMountain,AtEase, 9 Alectryon, 100/9 CLEVER SCOT, 100/8 NetherEdge,LordTom,RedRum,Dictora, 100/7 AvonBay,Caballero, 100/6 SteelBand, 20 Surtsey, 25 Others. (Mr H S Alper) C Davies, Chepstow. 16 Rn 3m 59.2 (14.8 under av)
Red Rum ran a cracking race, chasing the winner hard throughout. He looks sure to find a race if the ground stays right for him.

WETHERBY, Mon., Apr. 7th (Good)
BILTON HURDLE £204 (£54: £24)   2m   3.10

RED RUM 4-10-11	Broderick	a.prom: led 2 out: wnt clr last: comf	—1
New Brighton 5-12-0	BFletcher	gd hdwy fr 3 out: ev ch last: nt qckn	5.2
Duka-Duk 5-11-7	TSMurphy	jnd ldrs 7th: btn appr last	5.3
Saray 4-10-12([1])	Brogan	gd hdwy fin: promsg r	6.4
Ryebow 5-11-7	RBarry	a.cl up: nt qckn fr 2 out	1½.5
Bright Lad 5-11-0‡[7]	Lockerbie	led 3rd: hdd next: n.d fr 6th	10.6

Also ran:—

Guilder 7-11-3‡[7]	MrHMarples (h)	Man Overboard 5-11-7	GScott
Lismore Light 6-11-7‡[3]	JTurner	Purple Path 5-11-0‡[7]	JDoyle
Solwyn 9-11-3‡[7]	MrRBennett	Keifer 4-10-4‡[7]	Cunningham
Singing Well 5-11-7	Buckley	Pinacinth 4-10-6‡[5]	MGreeves
Fiery Don 6-11-10	Berry	Red Candle 5-11-7	McCarron
Petruchios Son 6-11-7‡[7]	WRedfern	Rock Hard 8-11-3‡[7]	MrSWills
Vice-President 8-11-3‡[7]	MrKClemmit	Fun at Noon 4-10-4‡[7]	MrKMcCauley
Basket 5-11-7	NWilkinson	Kelly from Foxford 5-11-7	Blackshaw

S.P.: 15/8 RED RUM, 5/2 NewBrighton, 8 Pinacinth, 10 Ryebow, 100/8 Keifer, 100/6 FieryDon,PetruchiosSon,SingingWell,Duka-Duk,Basket,Saray, 20 Bright Lad, ManOverboard,RedCandle, 33 Others. (Mrs L Brotherton) R Renton, Ripon. 22 Rn   3m 59 (5 under av)

1968/69

NOTTINGHAM, Tues., Apr. 15th (Good)
BRADMORE H'CAP HURDLE (4-Y.O.) £340 (£90: £40)   2m   2.45

RED RUM 11-5 (7x)	Broderick	led 2nd: hdd flat: qcknd to ld agn nr fin	—1
At Ease 12-0	TSMurphy	hdwy fr 6th: chall last: led flat: wknd nr fin	½.2
Kivoga 11-7	MrRTate	hdwy fr 5th: ev ch appr last: sn wknd	4.3
Nether Edge 10-12	REdwards	hdwy fr 6th: hrd rdn fr 2 out: one pce	3.4
Potheen 11-0‡3	Vaughan	nvr trbld ldrs	2.5
Cefn Mawr 10-4	EHarty	sme late hdwy: n.d	4.6

Also ran:—

Coup de Vie 9-10(1)‡5	Weaver	Stolen March 10-0	Kelleway (h)
Parrotty 10-0	Uttley	Acastus 11-4	Jennings
Pinacinth 9-11‡3	JTurner	Careful Boy 10-9	Berry
Baby Spot 10-11	Mould	Regular 10-9	Cartwright
		Tiger (FR) 10-4(1)	DNicholson

S.P.: 9/2 Kivoga, 5 RED RUM, 8 CarefulBoy, 10 Acastus,AtEase,Tiger,Nether Edge,Potheen, 100/8 BabySpot,StolenMarch, 100/7 Regular, 20 Others. (Mrs L Brotherton) R Renton, Ripon. 15 Rn   4m 11.6 (10.6)

TEESSIDE PARK, Fri., Apr. 25th (Soft, patchy)
TEESSIDE CELEBRATION H'CAP HURDLE £340 (£90: £40)   2m 176y   7.15

RED RUM 4-10-10 (5x)	Broderick	lw: hld up: hdwy 5th: str rn to ld cl hme: game	—1
Rigton Prince 8-11-8 (5x)	Stobbs	lw: hdwy 4th: led 3 out: sn rdn: no ex nr fin	nk.2
Double Port 5-10-13	RBarry	a.prom: chall 2 out: nt r.o flat	1½.3
Explicit 5-12-2 (5x)	NWilkinson	hdwy 6th: nt qckn fr 2 out	7.4
Ponda Rock 8-10-5 (5x)	Hayhurst	hdwy & ev ch whn mstk 2 out: nt rcvr	nk.5
Seafield Boy 5-9-9‡7	Goulding	lw: prom to 3 out	6.6
Midnight Moss 7-10-1(1)	Stack	led aftr 3rd to 3 out: wknd	0
Vittorio 9-10-12	JBerry	h: prom tl wknd appr 3 out	0
Roslevin 5-11-13‡7	JDoyle	led tl aftr 3rd: sn bhd	0
Kalymore 5-9-8(1)‡7	Vayro	nvr trbld ldrs	0
Natousa 7-10-6	DAtkins	h: t.o whn p.u bef 6th: farne	0

S.P.: 2 RigtonPrince, 5/2 RED RUM, 9/2 Explicit, 6 DoublePort, 100/8 Vittorio, 100/7 SeafieldBoy, 20 PondaRock, 33 Others. (Mrs L Brotherton) R Renton, Ripon. 11 Rn   4m 10.6

AYR, Tues., May 20th (Good to firm)
ORCHARDTON H'CAP HURDLE £340 (£90: £40)   2m   3.15

PAIDFOR 8-10-2	KWhite	chasd ldrs tl led appr last: qcknd flat	—1
St Antonius 8-9-12‡7	MrRGreig	h: a.prom: ev ch appr last: one pce	1½.2
Geordie Lad 4-11-11	BFletcher	lw:hdwy fr 3 out: rdn appr last: unable qckn	hd.3
Coupador 7-10-3	RReid	hdwy fr 2 out: r.o appr last	¾.4
Whispering Grace 6-11-2	Buckley	no hdwy fr 2 out	1½.5
Sea Romance 7-10-12	MrPFox	lw: prom to 5th: n.d aftr	3.6
Signor Domenico 5-9-7‡7	BJones	prom to 5th	0
Red Rum 4-11-4	Broderick	lw: bhd fr 3rd: rdn 5th: no real hdwy	0
Jamoe 6-10-10	Stack	prom to 3 out	0
At Ease 4-11-12	TSMurphy	lw: hdwy whn hit 5th: w ldrs 2 out: sn lost pl	0
Patrona 5-10-3(3)	RBarry	led: clr 3 out tl wknd qckly & hdd appr last	0
Glasserton 4-9-11‡3	HMKavanagh	p.u	0

Also ran:—

Nothing Higher 5-11-7	Leech	Blackpool Rock 6-10-12	Davenport (h)

S.P.: 5 GeordieLad,NothingHigher, 6 RedRum,AtEase, 7 WhisperingGrace, 10 Coupador,SeaRomance, 100/8 Patrona, 100/7 BlackpoolRock,Jamoe, 20 PAIDFOR, 33 Others. (Mr J R Wilson) M McCourt, Upton-on-Severn. 14 Rn

1969/70

CHELTENHAM, Thur., Sept. 18th (Good)
ANDOVERSFORD H'CAP HURDLE £510 (£135: £60)   abt 2m 200y   3.20

DUNELA 5-10-7 (7x)	Haine	hdwy fr 5th: qcknd to ld flat: r.o wl	—1
Henry the Fifth 5-10-7 (7x)	Shoemark	hdwy fr 3 out: str rn flat	2.2
Delapre Lad 6-10-9‡5	CDavies	gd hdwy fr 3 out: led appr last: wknd flat	hd.3
State Visitor 6-11-2	Pitman	r.o wl fr 2 out: nvr nr to chall	5.4
Cavalry Charge 6-10-8	DNicholson	sme late hdwy: n.d	7.5
Right Proud 5-11-4	Holley	prom tl wknd qckly fr 2 out	2.6

Also ran:—

Taftan 4-11-2‡5	Soane	Yes Yes 7-10-0	Dixon
Nimble Joe 6-10-11	EHarty (h)	Devon Piper 8-9-11‡3	Weaver
Red Rum 4-10-9	Stack	Astrojet 6-10-7 (7x)	Cowley
Elliott 7-11-3	DRHughes	Scabbard 9-10-12	Biddlecombe
Hotroy 8-11-5	GRobinson	Sea Romance 7-9-7‡7	Newson
Le Flic 8-10-8 (7x)	Cartwright	Tambo 6-10-0	TNorman
Bric-Brac 10-11-2	RAtkins	Trespassing 5-10-1	Uttley
		Dragoman 6-10-0	Thorner

S.P.: 9/2 HenrytheFifth, 6 StateVisitor,CavalryCharge, 8 Hotroy, 10 DelapreLad, Taftan, LeFlic, 100/8 DUNELA, 100/7 RightProud, Bric-Brac, 100/6 SeaRomance, RedRum, Elliot, 20 Trespassing, YesYes, 33 Others. (Mr J M Spurrier) R Hollinshead, Rugeley. 21 Rn   4m 4 (13 under av)

DONCASTER, Fri., Oct. 24th (Good, slippery)
TOWN FIELD H'CAP HURDLE £449 (£124: £59)   abt 2m 150y   3.45

DUNELA 5-11-10	Haine	hld up: hdwy 3 out: led appr last: r.o wl	—1
Explicit 5-12-0	NWilkinson	hld up: c to ld aftr 2 out: sn hdd: not qckn	3.2
Hill House 9-12-3	JEnright	w.r.s: sn rcvrd: led 5th tl aftr 2 out	8.3
Little Green Man 4-10-12	DAtkins	hit 1st: ev ch 3 out: wknd	1.4
Kingzog 6-11-10	MrGMacmillan	prom tl jmpd slowly & lost pl 4th: r.o fr 2 out	1.5
Supathene 4-10-11	BFletcher	prom: jnd ldr 3 out: wknd aftr 2 out	s.h.6
Red Rum 4-11-3‡5	JDoyle	cl up tl wknd 3 out	0
Efficacy 4-9-10‡7	Leach	led 3rd to 4th: wknd fr 3 out	0
Golden Berry 5-11-3	Stack	led to 3rd: led 4th: wknd fr 3 out	0

S.P.: 6/4 Explicit, 5 Supathene, 6 DUNELA,Kingzog, 100/8 RedRum, 100/7 HillHouse, 100/6 GoldenBerry,LittleGreenMan, 20 Efficacy. (Mr J M Spurrier) R Hollinshead, Rugeley. 9 Rn   4m 7.8 (6.8)
Red Rum ran well on his seasonal reappearance, only weakening in the last half-mile. He will be all the better for this run.

WETHERBY, Sat., Nov. 8th (Good, becoming soft)
TADCASTER H'CAP HURDLE £580 (£180: £80)   2m   3.30

JAMOE 6-10-0	Stack	a.prom: led 2 out: sn clr	—1
Oldbury Lad 8-9-11‡3	PJames	a.prom: chasd wnr fr 2 out	5.2
Potheen 4-10-4	PVaughan	hdwy 3 out: r.o flat	5.3
Proud King 4-10-1‡7 (7x)	MrMBarnes	a.prom: no hdwy fr 3 out	1½.4
Roslevin 5-9-13‡3	JTurner	h: led to 3rd: led aftr 5th tl wknd 2 out	2½.5
Kingzog 6-10-9	GGriffin	hdwy 5th: wknd fr next	3.6
Pirate Prince 4-10-10 (7x)	GLee	hdwy 5th: wknd next	0
Red Rum 4-10-5‡5	JDoyle	prom to 5th	0
Swan-Shot 6-9-7‡7	SRoss	prom to 4th	0
Avon Bay 4-10-2‡5	Greeves	nvr rchd ldrs	0
First Story 5-10-2(²)	Broderick	bit bkwd: bhd fr 5th	0
Explicit 5-11-2	McCarron	rapid hdwy to ld 3rd: hit 4th hdd aftr 5th t.o	0

S.P.: 9/4 Explicit, 3 JAMOE, 6 PiratePrince, 7 AvonBay, 9 RedRum,Kingzog, 10 FirstStory, 100/7 ProudKing,Roslevin,OldburyLad, 33 Others. (Mr J Hacking) C Crossley, Wirral. 12 Rn   3m 58.6 (1.4 under av)

1969/70

DONCASTER, Sat., Nov. 22nd (Good)
DORMER DRILL H'CAP HURDLE (4-Y.O.) £857 12s (£228 12s: £106 16s)
abt 2m 150y   3.45

RARE COMEDY 10-11	Leech	lw: a.prom: rdn 2 out: stayd on to ld nr fin	—1
At Ease 11-8	TSMurphy	h: hld up: led on bit aftr 3 out: hit last: shakn up nr fin: no ex	nk.2
Potheen 10-8	McCarron	lw: w ldrs fr 3rd: ev ch last: unable qckn	2.3
Haggis 10-3	Quinn	stdy hdwy fr 3 out: r.o fin	5.4
Tambourium 10-3	RBarry	h: prom tl wknd 2 out	2.5
Red Rum 11-0	Broderick	led tl wknd aftr 3 out	1½.6
Tiger Lad 10-0(⁵)‡⁵	GShaw	jnd ldrs 5th: wknd 2 out	0
Clock Corner 10-0	Berry	h: w ldrs to 5th	0
Be Tolerant 9-7‡⁷	MrPBrogan	h: cl up to 5th	0
Bespoke Boy 10-3	PJones	h: effrt 2 out: nt rch ldrs	0

S.P.: 5/2 Potheen, 4 AtEase, 5 BespokeBoy, 8 RARE COMEDY, Tambourium, 10 Haggis, 100/8 RedRum, 100/6 BeTolerant, 20 Others. (Mrs J M Richards) M H Easterby, Malton. 10 Rn   4m 1.8 (.8)

CATTERICK, Wed., Dec. 31st (Good)
DICK WHITTINGTON H'CAP HURDLE £340 (£90: £40)   2m   2.30

AT EASE 4-12-2	GGriffin	h: hld up: hdwy 3 out: led aftr last: r.o	—1
Red Rum 4-11-5	Stack	h: hdwy 5th: led btwn last 2: no ex flat	1.2
Sea Romance 7-10-4‡⁷	JNewson	hdwy fr 3 out: r.o	4.3
Overcheck 6-11-3	PBuckley	lw: cl up 3rd tl lost pl 3 out: stayd on fr next	2.4
Persian Valor 5-10-0	NWilkinson	mstk 3rd: jnd ldrs next: led aftr 3 out tl hdd & wknd appr last	1.5
Night Patrol 5-10-5	Watkinson	nvr nr ldrs	3.6
Brass Finisher 7-11-0‡³	PJames	led tl hdd & wknd aftr 3 out	0
Passing Strange 5-9-9‡⁵	JDoyle	cl up to 3 out	0
Sweet Forfeit 8-10-9	Broderick	h: prom to 3 out	0
Beige Etoile 6-9-11‡³	Holmes	fell 2nd	0

Also ran:—
		It's Mustard 4-10-8	
Trentuno 4-10-4	DAtkins		Blackshaw (lw)

S.P.: 5/4 AT EASE, 6 RedRum, 8 BrassFinisher, NightPatrol, 10 It'sMustard, 100/9 SeaRomance, 100/8 Trentuno, 20 Others. (Maj E M W Cliff-McCulloch) W A Stephenson, Bishop Auckland. 12 Rn
Red Rum took closer order at the fifth. He went on between the last two flights but lacked the pace of the winner on the flat. A longer trip would probably suit him better.

WETHERBY, Tues., Jan. 20th (Heavy)
TOCKWITH H'CAP HURDLE £442 (£117: £52)   2m 4f   2.30

VULMEGAN 6-10-6	Mellor	lw: hdwy 4th: led aftr 3 out: easily	—1
Huperade 6-10-7‡⁷	MrDHouston	hdwy 6th: rd 3 out: chasd wnr fr next	12.2
Red Rum 5-10-13	Stack	prom: ev ch 3 out: one pce	1.3
Rare Comedy 5-11-5	Leech	lw: hdwy 7th: btn aftr 3 out	10.4
Baby Spot 5-10-0	Haine	h: prom: no hdwy fr 3 out	1.5
Avonduet 5-9-7‡⁷	MrHMarples	led 1st tl wknd aftr 3 out	2½.6

Also ran:—
		Naughty Story 5-10-4(⁵)	
Proud King 5-10-3‡⁷	MrMBarnes		SDavenport
Lifeboat 8-10-0	Cook (h)	Treasurer 5-10-9(⁹)	MrCScott
Cosmonaut 6-9-7‡⁷	Bromfield	Hungarian 6-10-2‡⁵	JDoyle
Avon Bay 5-10-7	TSMurphy	Wing Master 6-11-8	RReid
Pure Gem 9-10-2	GLee	Harvest Gold 11-10-12‡⁷	
Cornhill 7-11-1	Glover		Papworth
Tokyo Melody 6-10-2	Patrick	Vittorio 10-10-3	Watkinson

S.P.: 6 VULMEGAN, RedRum, Huperade, 13/2 RareComedy, 7 AvonBay, Wing Master, 10 Hungarian, 100/8 PureGem, 100/7 Avonduet, Vittorio, 100/6 Cornhill, ProudKing, TokyoMelody, 25 Others. (Mr D Steward) Thomson Jones, N'mkt. 19 Rn   5m 20.6 (1.6)
Red Rum ran a sound race. He was well placed throughout but, like the second, was completely unable to cope with the winner in the straight. He, too, should soon be winning.

DONCASTER, Fri., Jan. 23rd (Soft)
JANUARY H'CAP HURDLE (II) £443 (£118: £53)   abt 2m 4f   4.30

PALM BEACH 5-10-12 Biddlecombe		hdwy 6th: rdn to ld last: r.o	—1
Escahar 6-10-0	MGifford	a.cl up: led 6th: hdd last: r.o flat	1½.2
Tambourium 5-10-3(³)	RBarry	lw: a.prom: disp ld 3 out tl wknd	2½.3
Proud Stone 5-10-0	CParker	lw: bhd tl hdwy 7th: nrst fin	6.4
Running Late 6-10-2	PVaughan	h: cl up tl wknd appr 3 out	½.5
Mid Day 7-10-1	JEnright	hdwy 5th: ev ch 2 out: wknd	1½.6

Also ran:—

Supermaster 7-12-11	GGriffin	Eagles Nest 6-10-5	GLee
Zaras Pearl 5-10-0	Huber	Red Rum 5-10-11	Stack

S.P.: 11/4 PALM BEACH, 100/30 EaglesNest, 11/2 RedRum, 7 Escahar, 15/2 Supermaster, 10 MidDay, 100/8 Tambourium,RunningLate, 100/7 ProudStone, 25 ZarasPearl. (Mr C Haynes) T Rimell, Severn Stoke. 10 Rn   4m 52.3 (2.3)

WETHERBY, Sat., Feb. 7th (Heavy)
BISHOPTHORPE H'CAP HURDLE £680 (£180: £80)   2m 4f   2.30 (2.33)

SUPERMASTER 7-12-7	GGriffin	lw: hdwy to ld appr 3 out	—1
Supathene 5-10-6	BFletcher	lw: wnt 2nd appr 3 out: w wnr last: no ex pce	½.2
Vittorio 10-10-0	Mellor	h: hdwy & effrt 3 out: stayd on	3.3
Ebony King 7-10-11	GLee	hdwy 7th: ev ch whn hit 2 out: unable qckn	½.4
Potheen 5-10-0	PVaughan	lw: led 4th tl wknd appr 3 out	8.5
Red Rum 5-10-6	REdwards	cl up tl wknd appr 3 out	5.6
Alby Hill 10-9-9(²)‡⁷	Forrestal	led to 4th: wknd appr 3 out: t.o	7

S.P.: 15/8 Supathene, 3 EbonyKing, 6 RedRum, 13/2 SUPERMASTER, 7 Vittorio, 15/2 Potheen, 33 AlbyHill. (Mrs H Waite) W A Stephenson, Bishop Auckland. 7 Rn   5m 43.2 (24.2)
Red Rum raced with the leaders until forced to give ground at the third from home.

TEESSIDE PARK, Fri., Mar. 13th (Heavy)
LONG DOG H'CAP HURDLE £340 (£90: £40)   2m 5f 104y   3.45

TEALING 6-9-13‡⁷	MrVPercival	lw: a.in tch: hdwy 3 out: r.o	—1
Tambourium 5-11-3	Broderick	h: led: hit last: sn hdd: no ex	1.2
Lone Wolf 6-11-4	GGriffin	cl up to 8th: rdn 3 out: nt qckn	5.3
Grey Coat 5-11-7	TJackson	a.prom: one pce fr 3 out	8.4
Red Rum 5-11-11	BBrogan	h: hdwy 6th: wknd fr 8th	1.5
Arctic Lad 7-11-1	Leech	prom to 7th: sn bhd	12.6
Poggi 6-9-11‡³	APotts	cl up to 5th: sn bhd: t.o	7
Vittorio 10-11-4	Watkinson	lw: h: t.o fr 5th: p.u bef 7th	0

S.P.: 7/4 LoneWolf, 9/2 Vittorio,GreyCoat, 5 Tambourium, 11/2 RedRum, 8 TEALING, 20 ArcticLad, 33 Poggi. (Mr J Cousins) J Cousins, Scotforth. 8 Rn
Red Rum made a forward move at the sixth but was done with three flights later.

CHELTENHAM, Wed., Mar. 18th (Chases; Good: Hurdles; Yielding)
GEORGE DULLER H'CAP HURDLE £1365 (£365: £165)   3m & few yds   4.50

VULMEGAN 6-10-3	Mellor	hdwy 9th: led appr last: all out	—1
All Found 8-11-5‡³	Wakley	stdy hdwy 11th: ev ch whn blkd last: r.o	nk.2
Albinella 10-10-11	Coonan	ev ch fr 11th: one pce flat	5.3
Artois 6-10-8	JKing	wl bhd to 10th: rapid hdwy 2 out: fin fast	s.h.4
Clever Scot 5-11-12	Uttley	stdy hdwy 8th: ev ch appr last: unable qckn	1.5
The Sentry 6-10-8	KWhite	ev ch 8th: one pce fr 2 out	1½.6

Also ran:—

King Cutler 7-10-12	BFletcher	Four Wishes 7-9-11‡³	BWDavies
Jacthelot 6-10-7	BRDavies	Pappa Surprise 9-9-11‡³	
Stubbs II 9-10-5	RAtkins		Weaver (h)
Brimful 7-10-4	PJones	Partlet 10-10-0	Turnell
Eloped 9-10-5(¹)	DNicholson	Vulpliant 7-9-12(⁵)‡⁷	Laurie
Turks Arrow 7-10-3‡⁷	PRussell	Esban 6-11-2	Shortt
Alaska Fort 5-10-0	DTHughes	Another 10-10-5	Thorner
Candid Camera 7-10-3(²)	Mould	Lady Upham 7-10-0	Shoemark
Stepherion 9-10-1(¹)	Pitman	Right Now 5-10-5	Cook
Ace 8-10-8	JGifford	New Liskeard 9-11-1	Cartwright
Red Rum 5-10-4(⁴)	REdwards	Master Daniel 5-10-2	Dennard
Escahar 6-10-0	MGifford	Light Reading 8-10-10	Leech

S.P.: 6 AllFound, 7 TurksArrow, 8 CleverScot, 10 Esban, 100/9 NewLiskeard,Ace, 100/8 VULMEGAN, Another,MasterDaniel,Jacthelot, 100/7 Albinella,LightReading,Artois,Eloped,AlaskaFort, 100/6 Stubbs II, 25 Others. (Mr Donald Steward) Thomson Jones, N'mkt. 29 Rn   6m 8.2 (5.8 under av)

1969/70

CHELTENHAM, Sat., Apr. 11th (Soft)
RONALD ROYDS H'CAP HURDLE (1) £540 (£147: £68)   2m 4f   1.30

IRISH SPECIAL 5-10-7 (6x)	Glover	a.prom: led last: rdn out	—1
Multigrey 7-10-4	Pitman	led to 4th: led 5th: unable qckn flat	1½.2
April the Nineteenth 8-10-8	RAtkins	lw: hdwy fr 6th: ev ch appr last: one pce	1½.3
Persian Velvet 4-10-11‡³ (10x) Greeves		hdwy fr 7th: hrd rdn appr last: one pce	½.4
Say Who You Are 6-10-2	BRDavies	led 4th tl tried rn out 5th: hdwy fr 3 out: wknd appr last	6.5
Red Rum 5-10-7	Stack	h: rn rear fr 6th	4.6
Black Justice 8-12-0	JKing	hdwy fr 5th: rdn 2 out: sn wknd	0
Austrian Monarch 6-9-9‡⁵	BJones	hdwy fr 3 out: hrd rdn 2 out: wknd qckly	0
Russian Leather 6-9-7‡⁷	KEdwards	prom to 6th	0
Footpath 8-10-5	KWhite	bhd fr 5th: t.o whn p.u bef last	0

S.P.: 5/2 SayWhoYouAre, 5 IRISH SPECIAL, 6 RedRum,PersianVelvet, 9 Multigrey, 10 RussianLeather, 100/7 ApriltheNineteenth, 100/6 BlackJustice,Footpath, 33 AustrianMonarch. (W/Cmdr J S F Hood) S Palmer, Bottesford. 10 Rn   5m 47.6

PERTH, Tues., Apr. 21st (Good)
PERTHSHIRE DRAG HUNT H'CAP HURDLE £544 (£144: £64)   3m   3.30

TABIX 5-10-12	McCarron	lw: a.cl up: led 8th: sn hdd: led 3 out: hld on wl	—1
Red Rum 5-11-2	Stack	lw: h: hdwy 8th: rdn 2 out: r.o jst faild	s.h.2
Sikeyot 5-9-13(³)‡⁷	MrRGreig	a.prom: ev ch fr 2 out: nt qckn flat	2.3
Tipperty 8-11-7	JEnright	h: hld up: hdwy 8th: ev ch 2 out: one pce flat	3.4
Ballyath 4-10-6	PEnnis	h: prom: led 9th: sn hdd: wknd fr 2 out	4.5
Fooasaboot 6-10-6‡⁵	JDoyle	nvr trbld ldrs	6.6
Slaves Dream 6-10-6	CParker	lw: cl up tl wknd 3 out	0
Wild Sunset 11-11-0	Holmes	led to 8th: sn lost pl	0
Pandorana 5-10-2(²)	MrAMactaggart	a.rear div	0
Straven 6-10-1(¹)	Fenwick	a.bhd	0

S.P.: Evens Tipperty, 6 TABIX, RedRum,Fooasaboot,Sikeyot, 8 Ballyath,Slaves Dream, 100/6 Others. (Mr W A Carrick) W Atkinson, Carlisle. 10 Rn

WETHERBY, Wed., May 6th (Firm)
CHURCH FENTON H'CAP HURDLE £442 (£117: £52)   2m   7.0

PROUD STONE 5-10-0	CParker	lw: sn prom: led appr last: kpt on	—1
Arctic Coral 5-10-0	BFletcher	hdwy 3 out: r.o wl flat	½.2
King Cup 8-10-1	Patrick	led 4th tl hdd appr last: nt qckn	2½.3
Smart Fellow 5-10-7	Blackshaw	led 3rd: sn hdd: rdn appr 2 out: nt qckn	2.4
Hialeah 4-10-3(³)	RBarry	hdwy fr 3 out: nvr nrr	2½.5
Jamoe 7-10-7	RReid	h: a.prom: one pce fr 3 out	hd.6
Shimmering Satin 6-10-12‡⁷ MrJWalton		lw: late hdwy: r.o	0
Heathers Pride 6-10-0	Glover	cl up to 3 out: wknd	0
Whispering Grace 7-10-3	PBuckley	cl up tl wknd appr 2 out	0
Avonduet 5-10-12 (7x)	PEnnis	lw: led to 3rd: wknd 5th	0
Hasty Arrow 6-10-1(⁸)‡⁷	McInerney	sn cl up: lost pl 5th	0
ProudKing 5-9-13‡⁷	MrMBarnes	prom to 5th	0
Prince of Verona 6-9-8(¹)‡⁷ MrJMerchant		prom to 4th	0
Sylvan Prince 9-10-4	Mellor	hdwy 4th: sn wknd	0
Red Rum 5-10-0	Stack	h: prom tl fell 2 out	0

Also ran:—

At Ease 5-12-5	Griffin (h)	Whistlers Image 4-9-10(¹)‡⁷ DMunro (lw)	
Trade Gap 7-10-3‡⁵	GShaw (lw)	Oldbury Lad 9-9-11‡³	PJames
Dulciana 4-10-1	Holmes	Potheen 5-9-11‡³	PBrogan(lw)

S.P.: 5 SmartFellow, 8 PROUD STONE, Potheen, 10 SylvanPrince,Whispering Grace,WhistlersImage,KingCup,RedRum, 100/9 TradeGap, 100/8 AtEase,Avonduet,ShimmeringSatin,HastyArrow, 100/7 ArcticCoral,Jamoe, 25 Others. (Mr J McGhie) G W Richards, Penrith. 21 Rn   3m 48.8 (11.2 under av)

AYR, Mon., May 18th (Firm)
MILSINGTON H'CAP HURDLE £442 (£117: £52)   3m   3.15

INDIAN STYLE 8-10-0	RReid	hdwy ½wy: slt ld 2 out: stayd on wl—1	
Tipperty 8-11-3	JEnright	h: hdwy 8th: led appr 2 out: sn hdd: rdn last: one pce	3.2
Choir Belle 6-10-4‡⁷ (6x)	MrRSmith	bhd to 8th: gd hdwy appr 2 out: unable qckn appr last	4.3
Mossdale 5-9-9(²)‡⁷	JosephScallan	h: chasd ldr to 8th: kpt on one pce fr 3 out	3.4
Sikeyot 5-9-13(³)‡⁷	MrRGreig	prom tl wknd 3 out	8.5
Red Rum 5-10-13	Stack	h: mstk 3rd: rdn appr 3 out: nt rch ldrs	1.6
Drive On Joe 9-9-7‡⁷	PRogers	h: led to 7th: grad lost pl	0
Straven 6-10-1(⁴)‡³	EPrendergast	led 7th to 2 out: wknd qckly	0
Jackanory 6-10-0	NWilkinson	prom to 5th: bhd fr 3 out	0

S.P.: 15/8 Tipperty, 11/4 ChoirBelle, 5 RedRum, 10 INDIAN STYLE, 100/8 Sikeyot,DriveonJoe,Mossdale, 25 Others. (Mr D Dippie) J Bower, Heswall. 9 Rn

NEWCASTLE, Wed., Oct. 28th (Firm)
VITTORIA NOVICES' CHASE £272 (£72: £32)   2m 120y   3.45

ROYAL EDEN 8-12-0	BBrogan	lw: led 4th: sn hdd: led 3 out: just held on	—1
Rare Comedy 5-11-9	PBroderick	lw: hdwy 8th: w wnr from 2 out: drvn flat: just failed	s.h.2
Red Rum 5-11-9	TStack	bkwd: a.p: one pace from 2 out	6.3
Mr Owen 7-12-0	JEnright	led 5th till hdd 3 out: wknd flat	3.4
Autumn Wood 6-12-0	RBarry	led to 4th: effrt 3 out: sn btn	2.5
Bright Imitation 5-11-4	JHaldane	t.o when p.u bef 9th	0

S.P.: 7/4 AutumnWood, 5/2 MrOwen, 11/4 RareComedy, 7 RedRum, 100/6 ROYAL EDEN, 25 BrightImitation. (Mr R M Whitaker) D Williams, Ferryhill, Co. Durham. 6 Rn   4m 14.4 (4.4)

Red Rum ran well but could only stay on at the one pace from the second last fence. He should be all the better for this.

DONCASTER, Fri., Nov. 6th (Firm)
TOWN MOOR NOVICES CHASE £580 (£155: £70)   2m 150y   2.0

RED RUM 5-11-9	TStack	a.p: led after 2 out, qcknd flat	—1
Orient War 7-12-5	JEnright	lw: pckd 6th: ld 8th: hit last 2 r.o	¾.2
Best View 6-11-12	PBroderick	t.o. from 4th	bad.3
Oliver's Mount 7-12-5	PBrogan	hdwy 7th: prom when f 9th	0
Treble Kay 6-11-12	JCook	ld to 8th: 2nd when blnd & f 10th	0
Noble Lad 5-11-0	PMcCarron	mstk 2nd: f 3rd	0

S.P.: 4/9 OrientWar, 10 TrebleKay, 100/8 Oliver'sMount, 100/7 RED RUM, NobleLad, 33 BestView. (Mrs L Brotherton) R Renton, Ripon. 6 Rn   4m 3 (b2)

Red Rum has always possessed ability, particularly on fast ground. Pressing the favourite in the straight, he got the upper hand after the second last and held his advantage to the line.

CHELTENHAM, Fri., Nov. 13th (Good)
BOROUGH CHASE £442 (£117: £52)   2m and a few yds   4.0

JABEG 5-11-12	JHaine	j.w: made all: easily	—1
Soloning 5-11-12	PKelleway	lw: nt j.w: ldr when mistake 2 out: nt rcvr	12.2
Red Rum 5-11-8	TStack	a.p: one pace from 2 out	½.3
Table Mountain 5-11-0	KWhite	4th and no ch when blnd badly 10th	25.4
Call Duck 6-11-3	PCowley	mistake 7th: sn bhd: t.o when p.u bef 10th	0

S.P.: 5/6 Soloning, 7/2 JABEG, 9/2 RedRum, 10 TableMountain, 50 CallDuck. (Lt-Col W Whetherly) A Turnell, Ogbourne Maisey, Marlborough, Wilts. 5 Rn 4m 7 (a7)

Red Rum kept on at the one pace from the second last fence.

1970/71

WETHERBY, Fri., Nov. 20th (Good)
W D & H O WILLS PREMIER CHASE (Qualifier) £860 (£238: £114)
2m 4f   2.45

HUPERADE 6-12-0	TSMurphy	lw: a.p: led 12th to next, hard drvn to ld flat	—1
Orient War 7-12-0	JEnright	lw: hdwy on bit apprg 12th, led 3 out to flat: rdn: r.o	nk.2
Red Rum 5-11-13	TStack	a.p. kept on wl from 3 out	2½.3
Rare Comedy 5-10-12	PBroderick	lw: led 3rd to 12th: gradually wknd	10.4
Woodbridge 6-10-10(¹)‡⁷	MrTGillam	lost tch 11th: n.d after	12.5
Eagle's Nest 6-12-0	AKavanagh	f 2nd	0
Kilpatrick 6-12-0	MDickinson	f 2nd	0
Avonduet 5-10-12	EFenwick	led to 3rd: cl up till f 12th	0
Chamtex (H) 6-11-2	DAtkins	tried to ref and f 1st	0
The Wonderloaf 7-11-7	MrJLawrence	b.d 2nd	0
Supermaster 7-12-0	BBrogan	baulked and f 1st	0
Cross-Country (H) 8-11-7			
	SDavenport	j.b. and t.o till p.u bef 4th	0

S.P.: 3 HUPERADE, 100/30 OrientWar, 13/2 Supermaster, 9 RareComedy, 100/8 Eagle'sNest,RedRum, 20 Wonderloaf, 25 Kilpatrick,Avonduet, 50 Others. (Brig J A Grant-Peterkin) W A Stephenson, Leasingthorne, Bishop Auckland, Co Durham. 12 Rn   5m 30 (a19.60).
Red Rum ran splendidly but was just outpaced by the first two over the last three fences. He will find plenty more opportunities.

SEDGEFIELD, Sat., Dec. 5th (Good)
HOPE INN CHASE £272 (£72: £32)   2m 250y   3.30

RED RUM 5-12-5	TStack	lw: a.p: rdn 3 out, r.o to ld flat	—1
Choir Belle 6-12-0	PBrogan	led 8th to flat: nt qckn	2.2
Fooasaboot 6-11-7‡⁷	MrTGillam	mistake 11th hdwy 14th: ev ch last: one pace	2½.3
Fair Vulgan 6-11-9‡³	MrJWalton	mistakes 1st and 4th: w ldrs till blnd 15th: sn wknd	20.4
Royal Eden 8-12-0‡⁷	MrRWhitaker	lw: made most to 8th: mistake 9th and 13th: sn no ch	20.5
Autumn Wood 6-12-0	RBarry	w ldrs till f 8th	0

S.P.: 4/5 RED RUM, 9/2 AutumnWood,Fooasaboot, 9 FairVulgan, 10 ChoirBelle, 20 RoyalEden. (Mrs L Brotherton) R Renton, Ripon, Yorks. 6 Rn   6m 26.20 (a2.20)
Red Rum was always handily placed. He was ridden three out and ran on gamely to take a decisive advantage on the flat.

WETHERBY, Sat., Dec. 26th (Yielding)
ROWLAND MEYRICK H'CAP CHASE £2,040 (£568: £274)   3m 100y   2.15

EXCESS 8-10-9 (5x)	SMellor	lw: w ldr till led 9th: hdd 15th: led next to 3 out: blnd 2 out-lft ch last	—1
San-Feliu 7-10-9	PBuckley	prom to 14th: stayed on from 3 out	6.2
Red Rum 5-10-8 (5x)	MGifford	lw: lost tch from 14th	8.3
Kilmogany Five 7-10-5 (5x)			
	EFenwick	led to 9th: sn lost pl	20.4
Another Guy 6-11-2	BBrogan	lw: a.p: led 15th to next: led 3 out till f last	0
Supermaster 7-11-4 (5x)	JEnright	lw: nvr going wl: bhd when f 16th	0

S.P.: 6/5 EXCESS, 5/2 Supermaster, 5 San-Feliu, 10 AnotherGuy,RedRum, 25 KilmoganyFive. (Mrs H Thomson Jones) H Thomson Jones, N'mkt. 6Rn 6m 43 (a16)
Red Rum showed prominently to the fourteenth.

AYR, Fri., Feb. 5th (Good)
GIRVAN H'CAP CHASE £442 (£117: £52)   2m 4f   2.30

RED RUM 6-11-6	TStack	chased ldr most of wy: w ldr last: sn rdn: r.o to ld flat	—1
Banderole 7-12-1	JEnright	lw: hdwy from 13th: lft in ld 3 out: rdn last: nt qckn: lame after r	½.2
Rossglass Lad 8-10-10	SHayhurst	mistake: led till blnd 3 out: n.d after	6.3
Swan-Shot 8-11-11	PMcCarron	mistake 2nd: no ch from 13th	2.4
Humbleton Manor 8-10-0	PBrogan	prom to 13th: wknd qckly	3.5
Corseal 7-12-7	BFletcher	t.o from 10th	bad.6

S.P.: 6/4 Banderole, 7/2 Swan-Shot, 4 RED RUM, 7 RossglassLad, 12 Others. (Mrs L Brotherton) R Renton, Ripon, Yorks. 6 Rn   5m 16.60 (a20.60)
Red Rum, a plucky individual, was always chasing the leader. Though apparently beaten going to the last, he gave his all to gain the upper hand.

NEWBURY, Sat., Feb. 13th (Soft)
COMPTON CHASE (5y & 6y) £445 (£120: £55)   3m   2.0

LUCKY EDGAR 6-11-2	JWoodman	nt j.w: hard rdn 9th: gd hdwy 15th led near fin	—1
Rome Express 6-11-11‡[5]	MrWShandKydd	led 15th to flat: unable qckn	½.2
Jask 6-12-2	JCook	no hdwy from 13th	15.3
Red Rum 6-12-2	TStack	bhd from 12th	12.4
Even Delight 6-12-2	TBiddlecombe	mistake 9th: t.o 10th till p.u after 13th	0
Merryville (H) 6-11-2	EHarty	bhd till b.d 16th	0
Vital Sanction 6-11-2	PKelleway	led to 14th: 2nd when f 16th	0

S.P.: 7/2 RedRum, 9/2 Jask, RomeExpress, 11/2 LUCKY EDGAR, 6 Merryville, 9 EvenDelight, 10 VitalSanction. (Mr T Brindle) R Smyth, Epsom. 7 Rn   6m 27.80 (a26.80)
Red Rum proved disappointing. He dropped right out of the race more than a mile from home and there seemed no valid excuse.

TEESSIDE PARK, Fri., Feb. 26th (Good)
FACEY ROMFORD H'CAP CHASE £340 (£90: £40)   3m 31y   2.30

SUPERMASTER 8-12-0	JEnright	lw: led 4th to 3 out: r.o wl to ld last	—1
Gyleburn 8-10-13	RBarry	lw: cl up till led 3 out: r.o flat	¾.2
Red Rum 6-11-5	TStack	cl up: ran 13th: no ch from 3 out	12.3
Castle Falls 14-10-0	AKavanagh	led to 11th: blnd 14th: wknd	30.4
Proud Chimes 11-10-55	JLeech	bhd from 10th: t.o	30.5
Tarik 9-10-6 (6x)	PBrogan	3rd when blnd and f 15th	0
Kerman 7-9-8(¹)‡[7]	PMangan	prom to 13th: no ch when blnd and u.r 2 out	0

S.P.: 6/4 Gyleburn, 9/4 SUPERMASTER, 4 RedRum, 8 Tarik, 16 Others. (Mrs H Waite) W A Stephenson, Leasingthorne, Bishop Auckland, Co Durham. 7 Rn 6m 11.60 (a5.60)
Red Rum, in trouble six fences from home, was soon fighting a losing battle.

1970/71

CHELTENHAM, Thurs., Mar. 18th (Very Heavy)
MILDMAY OF FLETE CHALLENGE CUP H'CAP CHASE £1,020 (£270: £120)
                                                    2m 4f   2.30

HOUND TOR 7-10-2	MGifford	led to 4th: blnd 5th: led 7th till blnd 2 out: mistake last: hard rdn: led cl home	—1
Loup Cervier 9-11-5	GThorner	held up: led last: hard driven: wknd flat	1½.2
Fashion House 7-10-6	BRDavies	led 5th and 6th: ev ch 12th: wknd 14th	20.3
Red Rum 6-10-3	TStack	no hdwy from 13th	1.4
Trajan 7-10-1 (4x)‡³	AMawson	blnd 6th: a bhd	6.5
Red Ruler 7-10-1	DCartwright	bhd from 11th	1.6
East Bound 7-12-7 (4x)	SBarker	4th and ev ch when f 13th	0
Arctic Feast 8-11-1	KWhite	hdwy 10th: 2nd and ev ch when f 2 out	0
Supermaster 8-12-1	JEnright	bhd from 9th: blnd 11th, p.u after 12th	0
Waveney 9-10-6	PJones	blnd 5th: bhd from 8th till p.u after 12th	0

S.P.: 5/2 ArcticFeast, 7 EastBound, 8 LoupCervier,FashionHouse,Trajan, 10 Supermaster, 13 Waveney, 14 HOUND TOR,RedRuler, 16 Red Rum. (Mr J Tilling) G Harwood, Pulborough, Sussex. 10 Rn   5m 49.50 (a46.30)
Red Rum was never near the leaders at any stage.

WETHERBY, Mon., Apr. 12th (Firm)
CROSSLEY H'CAP CHASE £442 (£117: £52)   2m 4f   2.35

CLEAR CUT 7-10-6	PMcCarron	—1
Preston Deal (II) 6-10-0	SHayhurst	5.2
Red Rum 6-10-12	TStack	2½.3
Princess Camilla 6-10-3	BFletcher	4
Avonduet 6-10-2	MrAMactaggart	5
Mr Owen 8-9-11‡³	DGoulding	6
Humbleton Manor 8-10-6(⁶)	RBarry	7
Verona Forest 8-10-13	GScott	8
Royal Eden (H) 10-10-0	GHolmes	9
Dormist 7-9-12(⁵)‡⁷	IHewartson	10

S.P.: 15/8 CLEAR CUT, 7/2 RedRum, 6 PrincessCamilla, 8 PrestonDeal, 9 Verona Forest, 10 Avonduet,MrOwen, 12 Dormist, 20 Others. (Mr J W Hemingway) W A Hall, Tadcaster, Yorks. 10 Rn   5m 17.40 (a7)

WETHERBY, Wed., May. 5th (Firm)
RIGTON H'CAP CHASE £442 (£117: £52)   3m 100y   8.0

AVONDUET 6-10-7 (7x)	MDickinson	gd hdwy after 15th: led 2 out, sn clr: rdn flat	—1
Lothian Prince 8-10-9	RBarry	a.p: led 15th: clr next hdd 2 out: wknd flat	3.2
High Lettre 10-10-3	PEnnis	bhd 14th: stayed on u.p from 16th: nrst fin	½.3
Rigton Prince 10-11-13	JEnright	hdwy 6th: ev ch 15th: stayed on wl from 3 out	hd.4
Red Rum 6-10-6	TStack	lw: prom to 14th: kept on from 3 out	hd.5
Rain Lover 8-11-7	GScott	lw: nt j.w: led to 15th: wknd from next: t.o	30.6
Beautola (H) 10-9-11‡³	DGoulding	t.o from 5th	7
China Cloed (H) 8-10-5	JHaldane	lost tch 13th: t.o	8

S.P.: 11/4 AVONDUET, 7/2 RedRum, 4 RigtonPrince, 5 RainLover, 7 Lothian Prince,HighLettre, 14 ChinaCloed, 20 Beautola. (Mr A Watson) A Watson, Skipton in Craven, Yorks. 8 Rn   6m 23.20 (b3.80)

PERTH, Thur., May, 20th (Hard)
SPITTALFIELD H'CAP CHASE £272 (£72: £32)   2m 4f   3.15

MR OWEN 8-10-4	JEnright	lw: effrt 11th: led next: sn clr: cmftbly	—1
Red Seven 11-10-4	MrAMactaggart	str: effrt 2 out: r.o: nt reach wnr	4.2
Red Rum 6-11-2	TStack	w ldr: nt qckn from 2 out	hd.3
Clyde Bridge 12-10-7	RBarry	lw: led 12th: wknd from 3 out	15.4

S.P.: 7/4 MR OWEN, 5/2 RedRum,RedSeven, 7 ClydeBridge. (Mr J Barker), W A Stephenson, Leasingthorne, Bishop Auckland, Co Durham. 4 Rn   5m 4 (a2)

1971/72

SOUTHWELL, Mon., Oct. 12th (Firm)
COLONEL R THOMPSON MEMORIAL TROPHY H'CAP CHASE

		£1,192 (£326: £153) 3m 110y 3.30	
NOM DE GUERRE 9-10-8	KWhite	lw: led to 12th: led last: drvn out	—1
Indian Yeldah 7-10-7‡³	PMorris	cl up: mistake 7th: led 2 out:	
		nt quckn apprg last	3.2
Frodo (H) 5-10-4	RChampion	swtg: led 12th to 2 out: one pace	2.3
Red Rum 6-10-12	TStack	bit bkwd: prom to 16th	25.4
The Chef 10-10-0	MGifford	swtg: no ch from 14th	4.5
Shybo 9-9-13(³)	SBuckley	bhd most of wy	2.6
The Inventor 10-11-12 (5x)	JCook	lw: held up: mistake 7th: rdn 11th:	
		sn wknd	7
Golden Crisp 9-10-11	BRDavies	swtg: no ch from ½-wy	8
S.J.H. 11-10-4(⁷)‡³	JMerchant	prom to 10th: p.u bef 3 out	0

S.P.: Evens TheInventor, 9/2 Frodo, 6 NOM DE GUERRE, 10/1 IndianYeldah, TheChef, 14 GoldenCrisp, 16 RedRum, 33 Others. (Mrs T Pilkington) David Nicholson, Stow-on-the-Wold, Gloucestershire. 9 Rn   6m 21.40 (a11.40)

KELSO, Sat., Oct. 23rd (Firm)
ANTHONY MARSHALL TROPHY H'CAP CHASE £837 (£232: £111)   3m   3.0

RED SWEENEY 7-10-7	EFenwick	a.p: effrt 4 out: dsptd ld last:	
		r.o wl flat	—1
Slaves Dream 7-10-5	BFletcher	lw: led 2f out: dsptd ld last: r.o	hd.2
Irish Rain 9-11-13	JEnright	lw: gd hdwy 15th: ev ch 2 out:	
		one pace flat	2½.3
Tarik 9-9-9‡⁵	JMcDougall	cl up 13th: one pace from 2 out	2.4
Red Rum 6-10-4	TStack	nvr better than mid div	5.5
Kippie Lodge (H) 6-11-7	DMunro	lw: led to 2 out: sn wknd	2.6
High Lettre 10-10-1	JHaldane	a.p: wknd from 3 out	7
Proud King 6-9-12‡³	MBarnes	a bhd	8
Niagrador 7-10-2(²)	PBuckley	prom to 11th	9
Count Your Pence 9-10-2(²)			
	SHayhurst	sn bhd	10
Sir Roger 5-10-6 (6x)	PEnnis	lw: f 3rd	0

S.P.: 11/4 RED SWEENEY, 7/2 SlavesDream, 4 SirRoger, 15/2 KippieLodge, 10 IrishRain, 12 RedRum,HighLettre,ProudKing,Tarik, 13 Niagrador, 20 Count YourPence. (Mr D S George) G W Richards, Penrith, Cumberland. 11 Rn 6m 10.10 (b2.90)

NEWCASTLE, Sat., Nov. 6th (Firm)
JOHN EUSTACE SMITH TROPHY H'CAP CHASE £510 (£135: £60) 3m   2.30

SLAVES DREAM 7-10-4	BFletcher	lw: j.w: made all, r.o u.p from 3 out	—1
Red Rum (H) 6-10-4	TStack	chased wnr from 11th: nt qckn	
		apprg last	4.2
Proud King 6-10-6 (6x)	MBarnes	prom 12th: went 3rd 15th: no	
		hdwy from next	20.3
Tarik 9-10-0	PBrogan	no ch from 12th	4.4
Irish Rain 9-11-12	JEnright	lw: mistake 6th: reminders 8th:	
		bhd after	1½.5
Rampsman 7-10-3	BBrogan	lost pl 10th	hd.6
Kippie Lodge 6-11-4	DMunro	prom to 12th	7

S.P.: 5/4 IrishRain, 7/2 SLAVES DREAM, 4 Rampsman, 6 KippieLodge, 16 Others. (Mrs L Carr) R Hall, Heddon-on-the-Wall, Newcastle upon Tyne, Northumberland. 7 Rn   5m 53.20 (b6.80)
Red Rum chased the winner from the eleventh but could make no impression from the second last.

1971/72

HAYDOCK PARK, Wed., Dec. 1st (Good)
SUNDEW H'CAP CHASE £911 (£249: £117)   3m   2.15

RED SWEENEY 7-10-8	EFenwick	hdwy 11th: led 2 out: r.o wl	—1
Nom De Guerre 9-10-2(¹)			
	PMcCarron	led to 11th: ev ch 3 out: no ex flat	3.2
No Other 8-12-5	BBrogan	led and hit 11th: mistake 13th: n qckn from 2 out	1½.3
Permit 8-9-7‡⁷	MrRCrank	stayed on from 15th: nvr nrr	2.4
Red Rum (H) 6-10-1	TStack	no hdwy from 13th	10.5
Supermaster (H) 8-11-8	JEnright	joined ldrs 8th: wknd 15th	5.6
Garpin 7-10-1	JBourke	hdwy 9th: wknd 14th	7
Golden Crisp 9-10-0	BFletcher	mistake 1st: a bhd	8
Two Springs 9-11-12	PBroderick	prom to 10th: p.u 15th	0
Kippie Lodge (H) 6-11-3	DMunro	f 1st	0

S.P.: 9/4 NoOther, 5 RED SWEENEY, 6 NomDeGuerre,Supermaster, 9 Two Springs, 10 RedRum, 14 KippieLodge,Permit, 16 Garpin, 20 GoldenCrisp. (Mr D S George) G W Richards, Penrith, Cumberland. 10 Rn   6m 16.60 (a2.60)
Red Rum, pushed along to keep in touch at the water, got near enough half-way down the back straight but weakened at the fourth last.

CATTERICK, Sat., Dec. 11th (Good to firm)
CHARLES VICKERY MEMORIAL CUP H'CAP CHASE £930 (£295: £120)
                                                    3m 300 y   2.0

RED RUM (H) 6-10-7	TStack	a cl up: led 3 out: drvn out	—1
Proud King 6-10-0	MBarnes	went prom 9th: stayed up u.p	1.2
Off The Cuff 6-10-11(¹)	PBuckley	mistakes: w ldr till wknd 14th: stayed on again from 3 out	8.3
Great Noise 7-10-11	PMcCarron	bit bkwd: j.w: led 5th to 13th: led 15th to 3 out: wkng when hmpd next	12.4
Shybo 9-10-0	GHolmes	t.o from 8th	12.5
Garpin 7-10-8	JBourke	led to 5th: led 13th to 15th: sn lost pl	7.6
Mr Parker 12-9-11‡³	JDoyle	t.o from 8th	7
Fortune Bay II 7-10-6	JEnright	lw: hdwy 5th: going wl when blnd and uns rdr 14th	0

S.P.: Evens FortuneBayII, 9/2 RED RUM, 5 ProudKing, 9 GreatNoise, 10 Garpin, 16 OffTheCuff, 20 Others. (Mrs L Brotherton) T Gillam, Boroughbridge, Yorks. 8 Rn   6m 23 (a2)
Red Rum led with three to go and, driven out for all he was worth held on well.

CATTERICK, Wed., Dec. 22nd (Firm)
DENBY H'CAP CHASE £340 (£90: £40)   3m 300y   1.0

FORTUNE BAY II 7-11-3 (6x)			
	JEnright	lw: held up: hdwy 13th: mistake 15th: led flat: cmftbly	—1
Nom De Guerre 9-11-0	DNicholson	lw: led to 4th: w ldr till led 3 out: no ch w wnr flat	5.2
Red Rum 6-11-0 (6x)	TStack	a.p: effort 3 out: r.o one pace	½.3
Golden Crisp (H) 9-10-3	BBrogan	led 4th to 3 out: wknd next	8.4
Chop-n-Change 9-10-7(²)	RBarry	lw: bhd from 13th	4.5
High Lettre 10-10-2	SHayhurst	bhd from 8th	2½.6
McRob 9-9-13(⁶)‡⁷	IHewartson	bhd when blnd and uns rdr 6th	0

S.P.: 4/5 FORTUNE BAY II, 7/2 NomDeGuerre, 15/2 RedRum, 10 Chop-n-Change, 20 GoldenCrisp, 33 Others. (Charlotte Lady Reay) W A Stephenson, Leasingthorne, Bishop Auckland, Co. Durham. 7 Rn   6m 24.40 (a3.40)
Red Rum, always well on terms, found the pace a little too fast from three out.

CATTERICK, Sat., Jan. 1st (Good)
ZETLAND H'CAP CHASE £551 (£177: £82)   3m 300y   1.30

RED RUM 7-10-10 (8x)	TStack	pushed along from 10th: led 2 out: sn clr	—1
Great Noise 8-10-6 (6x)	PMcCarron	lw: led 13th till 2 out: unable qckn	7.2
Kippie Lodge (H) 7-10-9‡[7]	DNolan	ldg most of way: led to 13th: sn lost pl	dist.3
Permit 9-10-7([2])	MDickinson	a t.o last	12.4

S.P.: 4/7 GreatNoise, 7/2 RED RUM, 6 Permit, 10 KippieLodge. (Mrs L Brotherton) T Gillam, Ripon. 4 Rn   6m 27.80 (a6.80)
Red Rum, pushed along virtually throughout, joined the leader at the last fence on the far side. Getting the upper hand at the second last, he drew right away under pressure.

CATTERICK, Mon., Mar. 6th (Yielding)
BUSBY H'CAP CHASE £510 (£138: £64)   3m 300y   3.45

BEST VIEW 8-10-0	DGoulding	a going wl: lft in ld 14th: easily	—1
Ideal Lady 8-10-0	JBourke	hdwy 13th: chased wnr from next: no imp	12.2
Turmo-Tang 6-10-3([2])	PEnnis	lw: led 5th to 11th: sn rdn: wknd 13th	10.3
Zaras Grove (H) 9-10-2([2])	PBuckley	led 11th: sn hdd and wknd	8.4
Red Rum 7-10-7	TStack	prom till b.d 14th	0
David French 7-10-0	DAtkins	led to 5th: led 12th till f 14th	0

S.P.: 4/5 RedRum, 9/2 Turmo-Tang, 7 ZarasGrove, 10 IdealLady, 12 BEST VIEW,DavidFrench. (Mr W A Stephenson) W A Stephenson, Leasingthorne, Bishop Auckland, Co. Durham. 6 Rn   6m 54 (a33)
Red Rum was in close touch and going as well as any but the winner when he was brought down at the fourteenth.

NOTTINGHAM, Tues., Mar. 21st (Soft)
TRENT H'CAP CHASE £442 (£117: £52)   2m 6f   4.15

NOM DE GUERRE 10-10-4	JHaine	led to 15th: hard rdn and led last all out	—1
Guiburn (H) 8-10-8	PBrogan	a.p: led 15th to last: unable qckn cl home	1.2
Red Rum 7-10-9	MGifford	a.p: hard rdn and no hdwy from 2 out	1½.3
Guiting Green 9-10-10	GThorner	a.p: no hdwy from 3 out	1½.4
Just The Job 7-10-2	WShoemark	hdwy from 14th: nvr nr to chal	¾.5
Escadale 8-10-0	FCollings	rear from 12th	12.6
Rigton Prince 11-11-11	JEnright	bhd from 16th	0
Jolly Swagman 6-10-0	JSkjoedt	bhd from 13th	0
Hard Nut 6-10-4	BBrogan	rear when f 11th	0
Welsh Blizzard 9-9-10([3])‡[7]	GWhite	a bhd: p.u bef last	0

S.P.: 5/2 NOM DE GUERRE, 5 RedRum, 6 GuitingGreen, 15/2 HardNut, 8 Just TheJob,RigtonPrince, 9 Guiburn, 25 Escadale, 33 Others. (Mrs T Pilkington) David Nicholson, Stow-on-the-Wold, Gloustershire. 10 Rn   5m 42.20

WETHERBY, Mon., Apr. 3rd (Soft)
WETHERBY H'CAP CHASE £2,385 (£660: £315)   3m 100y   3.45

BALLYSAGERT 7-11-7	JEnright	bhd: hdwy and 2nd 15th: led next: rdn flat: r.o	—1
Jomon 6-11-2	SMellor	joined ldrs 15th: kept on from next: r.o nt qckn w wnr cl home	2.2
Red Rum 7-10-1	TStack	lw: 2nd till led 11th: hdd 16th: one pace from next	1½.3
Supermaster 9-11-12	MrDBrown	prom when mistake 12th: n.c from 4 out	6.4
Petruchio's Son 9-10-10	RBarry	led till hdd 11th: mistake 14th: n.d after	25.5

S.P.: 5/4 Jomon, 2 BALLYSAGERT, 11/2 Supermaster, 9 RedRum, 20 Petruchio's Son. (Major E M W Cliff-McCulloch) W A Stephenson, Leasingthorne, Bishop Auckland, Co. Durham. 5 Rn   6m 52 (a28)

1971/72

AYR, Sat., Apr. 15th (Good)
SCOTTISH GRAND NATIONAL H'CAP CHASE £5,137 (£1,546: £748:£349)

4m 120y   2.50

QUICK REPLY 7-9-9	MBarnes	hdwy 8th: mistake 19th: led 3 out: mistake and rdr lost irons last: r.o flat —1
Slaves Dream 8-10-0	JHaldane	led to 20th: ev ch 3 out: stayed on wl 2.2
Esban 8-10-2 (4x)	JBourke	a.p: kept on u.p hd-3
Beggar's Way 8-9-13	BHannon	prom to 13th: lost pl and sn bhd: gd hdwy 21st: mistake 2 out: kept on wl from last nk.4
Red Rum 7-9-8([1])	MBlackshaw	cl up: led 20th till hdd 3 out: wknd from next 5.5
Ashville 7-9-11	SMellor	a chasing ldrs: one pace from 4 out 7.6
Red Sweeney 8-10-4([3])	BRDavies	effrt 18th: nvr troubled ldrs 7
Young Ash Leaf 8-11-9	TStack	hdwy 8th: in tch 17th, no ch from 10th 8
Irish Rain 10-10-10	JEnright	blnd 12th and 18th: wl bhd till some late hdwy 9
Sir Roger 6-9-8([1])	FBerry	bhd nvr reached ldrs 10
Rouge Autumn 8-9-11	KWhite	mid div and rdn from 17th: in tch 4 out: sn wknd 11
The Spaniard 10-11-0	RBarry	prom to 18th: gradually lost pl 12
Black Justice 10-9-8([1])	GLawson	sme hdwy 20th: wknd from 4 out 13
Kippie Lodge (H) 7-10-4	DNolan	gd hdwy 17th: wknd from 21st 14
Scarlet Letch 7-10-5	EFenwick	cl up to 18th: sn lost pl 15
Charlie H 10-10-6	JHaine	bhd most of wy: p.u after 2 out 0
Supermaster 9-11-1	DGoulding	a rear div: p.u bef 3 out 0

S.P.: 4 CharlieH, 7 SirRoger, 9 RedSweeney,RougeAutumn, 10 Esban, 11 QUICK REPLY,ScarletLetch,Ashville, 14 SlavesDream,YoungAshLeaf,TheSpaniard,Beggar'sWay, 16 IrishRain, 17 BlackJustice, 20 Supermaster, 25 KippieLodge, 33 RedRum. (Mr W Thyne) C Bell, Hawick, Roxburghshire. 17 Rn   8m 32.90 (a23.90)

MARKET RASEN, Sat., Apr. 29th (Yielding)
CHAMPAGNE H'CAP CHASE £594 (£90: £40)   3m   4.0

RAINBOW PATCH 7-10-9	SMellor	led 2nd: rdn from 3 out: jmpd lft 2 out and lft clr: fin tired —1
Shybo 10-10-0	GHolmes	led 1st to 2nd: stayed on u.p from 3 out 3.2
Bobby Corbett 7-10-9	CCandy	prom to 10th: lost pl: hdwy u.p from 3 out: no ex from next 4.3
Red Rum 7-10-4	TStack	a.p: ev ch 16th: wknd from 3 out 8.4
Beautola (H) 11-10-0	PJames	t.o from 15th 20.5
Petruchio's Son 9-10-12	RBarry	prom: ev ch 3 out:hmpd and f next 0
Solway Sands 8-10-0	PBrogan	prom when blnd and uns rdr 0

S.P.: 7/4 RedRum, 15/8 RAINBOW PATCH, 5 Petruchio'sSon, 8 SolwaySands, 12 BobbyCorbett, 25 Shybo, 33 Beautola. (Mr A Stewart) R Armytage, East Ilsley, Berks. 7 Rn   6m 38 (a29)

Red Rum raced with the two leaders most of the way but had come to the end of his tether going to the second last fence.

1972/73

CARLISLE, Sat., Sept. 30th (Hard)
WINDERMERE H'CAP CHASE £622 (£170: £80)   3m   4.0

RED RUM 7-10-13	TStack	lw: a cl up: rdn from 3 out: led flat: all out —1
Gyleburn 9-11-8	RBarry	led: hit 5th: rdn from 3 out: nt qckn flat ¾.2
Proud King 7-10-5	MBarnes	rdn from 9th: no hdwy from 3 out 3.3
Nephin Beg 10-10-9 (6x)‡[3]	PMorris	lw: prom till mistake 10th: rdn and wknd from 15th 10.4

S.P.: 11/8 Gyleburn, 9/4 ProudKing, 3 NephinBeg, 6 RED RUM. (Mr N Le Mare) D McCain, Birkdale, Lancs. 4 Rn

WETHERBY, Wed., Oct. 11th (Good)
GORDON FOSTER H'CAP CHASE £680 (£180: £80)   3m 100y   3.45

RED RUM 7-10-10 (5x)	RBarry	lw: led to 2nd: led 11th: cir from 15th: unchallenged	—1
Ballysagert 7-11-13	JEnright	bkwd: held up: went 2nd 15th: no ch w wnr	12.2
Supermaster 9-12-4 (5x)	DGoulding	led 4th to 7th: cl up till wknd qckly 15th	2½.3
Esban 8-11-12 (5x)	JBourke	led 2nd to 4th: led 7th to 11th	15.4

S.P.: 13/8 Supermaster, 2 Esban, 3 RED RUM, 10 Ballysagert. (Mr N Le Mare) D McCain, Birkdale, Lancs. 4 Rn   6m 40.40 (a17.40)
Red Rum looked magnificent. He did not settle down to his jumping in the early stages but, when he took command at the eleventh, his fencing improved and he drew clear for a very easy win.

NEWCASTLE, Wed., Oct. 25th (Firm)
SALAMANCA H'CAP CHASE £715 (£190: £85)   3m   2.45

RED RUM 7-10-11 (5x)	TStack	lw: a.p: drvn along from 9th: stayed on wl to ld cl home	—1
Ballysagert 7-11-10	JEnright	bit bkwd: j.w: held up: hdwy to ld 4 out: clr 2 out: sn rdn and wknd: ct cl home	¾.2
Jedheads 10-10-3	PBrogan	joined ldrs 7th; hit 14th: wknd from 3 out	12.3
Off The Cuff 7-10-9 (5x)	RBarry	led till hdd and wknd 4 out	12.4
Tregarron 5-10-5 (5x)	DMoorhead	lost tch 12th	0

S.P.: 2 Ballysagert, 9/4 RED RUM, 3 OffTheCuff, 6 Tregarron, 20 Jedheads. (Mr N H le Mare) D McCain, Birkdale, Southport, Lancs. 5 Rn   6m 2.25 (a3.25)
Red Rum was flat out for most of the second circuit but neither he nor his rider would give up and he stayed on gamely to take the lead close home.

HAYDOCK PARK, Fri., Nov. 3rd (Firm)
SOUTHPORT H'CAP CHASE £684 (£188: £89)   3m   2.15

RED RUM 7-11-10 (8x)	TStack	lw: a.p: led 13th: cmftbly	—1
Indian Yeldah 8-10-6	PMorris	led to 6th: kept on from 3 out: no ch w wnr	3.2
The Inventor 11-11-6	JBourke	w ldrs: hit 9th: one pace from 4 out	10.3
Fortune Bay II (H) 8-11-3	JEnright	held up: blnd 4th: ev ch when blnd badly 12th: nt rcvr	25.4
Idlewild 6-10-1 (4x)‡³	PRussell	a bhd: t.o from 6th	dist.5
Garpin 8-10-8	RREvans	led 6th to 13th: wknd 4 out: p.u bef 2 out	0

S.P.: 2 RED RUM, 4 TheInventor,FortuneBayII, 9/2 Garpin, 11 IndianYeldah, 33 Idlewild. (Mr N H le Mare) D McCain, Birkdale, Southport, Lancs. 6 Rn 6m 27.10 (a13.10)
Red Rum continues to show greatly improved form. He never put a foot wrong and, galloping on strongly from the third last fence, won unchallenged without being asked a serious question.

AYR, Mon., Nov. 13th (Good)
MAUCHLINE H'CAP CHASE £695 (£191: £90)   3m 3f 40y   1.45

RED RUM 7-11-9 (4x)	BFletcher	j.w: a.p: led appr 3 out: stayed on wl	—1
Hurricane Rock 8-11-2	RBarry	hdwy from 18th: ev ch 2 out: r.o one pace	6.2
Kildrummy 7-10-8	PBroderick	a.p: w ldr from 15th till wknd appr 3 out	2½.3
Last Phebus 9-10-11	PBrogan	led 7th till hdd and wknd appr 3 out	2½.4
Slaves Dream 8-11-6	JHaldane	bit bkwd: led to 7th: wknd from 16th	8.5
Quick Reply 7-11-6	MBarnes	bit bkwd: joined ldrs 11th: lost pl 13th: n.d after	7.6
Entre Nous 10-9-9‡⁵	LLungo	last till p.u bef 14th	0

S.P.: 11/8 RED RUM, 5 HurricaneRock, 6 QuickReply,SlavesDream,Kildrummy, 20 Others. (Mr N H le Mare) D McCain, Birkdale, Southport, Lancs. 7 Rn 6m 53.90 (a3.90)
Red Rum, still cherry-ripe, reflects credit on his trainer. This was his fifth successive victory in about six weeks. He led approaching the third last and ran on well.

1972/73

CARLISLE, Wed., Jan. 31st (Yielding)
CUMBERLAND GRAND NATIONAL TRIAL H'CAP CHASE £632 (£173: £81)

3m   2.15

BOUNTIFUL CHARLES 7-10-6‡³

	JJO'Neill	chased ldr: effrt 3 out: led last: hard rdn and r.o wl	—1
Gyleburn 10-11-9	RBarry	lw: led: qcknd appr 4 out: hdd last: r.o	1½.2
Red Rum 8-11-9	BFletcher	a.p: ev ch 3 out: stayed on towards fin	s.h.3
Master Val 6-10-2	JEnright	held up: effrt 4 out: rdn and btn 2 out	8.4

S.P.: 9/4 BOUNTIFUL CHARLES,Gyleburn, 3 MasterVal, 7/2 RedRum. (Mr J Tindall) G Cunard, Malton. 4 Rn   6m 34.50 (a23.50)
Red Rum, always well placed was sent up to challenge three out. He lost a length or so going to the last but refused to give in and was staying on strongly towards the finish. He looks an ideal National type.

HAYDOCK PARK, Wed., Feb. 7th (Soft)
HAYDOCK PARK NATIONAL TRIAL H'CAP CHASE £1,266 (£351: £168)

3m 4f   2.45

HIGHLAND SEAL 10-10-0(¹)

	RDennard	joined ldrs 12th: led 13th to 15th: led appr 2 out: r.o wl	—1
Red Rum 8-10-12	BFletcher	lw: a.p: r.o from 2 out	5.2
Gyleburn 10-10-7	RBarry	jumpd wl: made most till hdd appr 2 out: nt qckn	7.3
Proud Tarquin 10-11-2	LordOaksey	w ldrs: one pace from 3 out	5.4
Southern Lad 6-10-2	DGoulding	hdwy 16th: joined ldrs 4 out: sn rdn and wknd 3 out	10.5
Mr Wrekin 8-9-11	SHolland	bhd from 16th	4.6
Swan-Shot 10-10-10 (4x)	MBlackshaw	prom: mistake 12th: wknd qckly 18th	7
Jarcot 11-10-0(⁷)	DCartwright	rdn along from 5th: t.o from 15th	8
Well To Do 10-10-8	GThorner	reminders 8th: bhd and rdn 16th: 5th and staying on wl when blnd, uns rdr last	0

S.P.: 11/4 SouthernLad, 4 WellToDo,Gyleburn, 5 Red Rum, 7 ProudTarquin, 14 Swan-Shot, 16 MrWrekin, 25 HIGHLAND SEAL, 50 Jarcot. (Mrs J Dening) R Dening, Cullompton, Devon. 9 Rn   7m 34.40 (a14.40)
Red Rum, never far from the leaders, kept on well from two out without troubling the winner. He would have preferred better going.

HAYDOCK PARK, Sat., Mar. 3rd (Soft)
GREENALL WHITLEY H'CAP CHASE £4,985 (£1,496: £720: £332)   3m   2.55

TREGARRON 6-10-6	CTinkler	lw: j.w: led 12th r.o wl	—1
Straight Vulgan 7-10-0	JHaine	led to 6th: led 10th to 12th: 4th last: stayed on	7.2
Red Sweeney 9-10-0	JEnright	lw: joined ldrs 11th: hit 3 out: wknd flat	½.3
Red Rum 8.11.2	BFletcher	lw: joined ldrs 11th: hit 13th: one pace from 2 out	½.4
Monty's Reward 7-10-10	SATaylor	bhd till hdwy 14th: wknd 3 out	15.5
Dungarvan Jewel (H) 8-10-0	RREvans	bhd from 14th	½.6
Jomon 7-11-3	PBroderick	lw: blnd and uns rdr 3rd	0
Money Market 6-10-3	DRHughes	led 6th till blnd and f 10th	0
Royal Mark (H) 7-10-0	KWhite	lw: hdwy 10th: hit 13th: p.u bef 3 out	0
Avondhu 10-11-0	DBarrott	ev ch when f 15th	0
Even Sail 8-10-0	MGifford	lw: f 4th	0

S.P.: 5 Red Rum, 13/2 Jomon,RedSweeney, 7 TREGARRON,Avondhu,Even Sail, 8 Monty'sReward, 9 MoneyMarket, 11 RoyalMark, 20 StraightVulgan, 33 DungarvanJewel. (Mr H Blyth) K Oliver, Hawick, Roxburghshire, Scotland. 11 Rn   6m 34.70 (a20.70)
Red Rum ran a great race on ground that was against him. Looking a live danger at the second last, he then stayed on gamely at one pace to the finish. When the ground dries up, he will be winning again.

LIVERPOOL, Sat., Mar. 31st (Firm)
GRAND NATIONAL H'CAP CHASE £25,486 (£7,738: £3,794: £1,822)

4m 856y   3.15

RED RUM 8-10-5	BFletcher	lw: 13th 1st canal turn: 5th water: chased ldr from 19th: rdn 23rd: r.o wl flat: led nr fin	—1
Crisp (Aus) 10-12-0	RPitman	j.w: led 1st Bechers: wl clr from Chair: hard rdn flat: fin v tired: hdd cl home	¾.2
L'Escargot 10-12-0	TCarberry	lw: 17th water, 13th 2nd canal turn: hdwy from 3 out: nvr nrr	25.3
Spanish Steps 10-11-13	PBlacker	11th 1st canal turn: 7th water, 3rd and no ch 2nd canal turn: stayed on same pace	12.4
Rouge Autumn 9-10-0	KWhite	6th 1st canal turn, 4th water and 2nd canal turn: r.o one pace	2½.5
Hurricane Rock 9-10-0	RChampion	7th 1st canal turn: 11th water: 5th 2nd canal turn: went 3rd 3 out: sn wknd	6.6
Proud Tarquin 10-10-11	LordOaksey	16th 1st canal turn: 10th water: 7th 2nd canal turn: no hdwy	7
Prophecy 10-10-3([2])	BRDavies	18th water: 14th 2nd canal turn: nrst fin	8
Endless Folly 11-10-0	JGuest	4th 1st canal turn: 2nd water: wknd 19th: 10th 2nd canal turn	9
Black Secret 9-11-2	SBarker	led to 2nd: 3rd 1st canal turn: 8th water: 6th 2nd canal turn: no hdwy	10

Also ran:—

Petruchio's Son 10-10-5([5])	DMould	Culla Hill 9-10-7([7])	MrNBrooks
The Pooka 11-10-0	AMoore	Canharis 8-10-1	PBuckley
Great Noise 9-10-2([2])	DCartwright	Beau Parc 10-10-11	ATurnell
Green Plover 13-10-0	MrMFMorris	Rough Silk 10-10-0	TNorman
Sunny Lad 9-10-3	WSmith	Princess Camilla 8-10-4([4])	RBarry
Go-Pontinental 13-10-4([1])	JMcNaught	Rampsman 9-10-0	DMunro
Mill Door 11-10-5([5])	PCullis	Nereo (Spa) 7-10-3([3])	DukeofAlburquerque
Grey Sombero 9-10-9	WShoemark	General Symons 10-10-0	PKiely
Glenkiln 10-10-7	JJO'Neill	Highland Seal 10-10-6([6])	DNicholson
Beggar's Way 9-10-1	T Kinane		
Ashville 8-10-4([1])	JKing	Mr Vimy 10-10-2([2])	JHaine
Tarquin Bid 9-10-0	JBracken	Astbury 10-10-0	JBourke
Richeleau 9-10-0	NKernick	Fortune Bay II 9-10-3([3])	MrGSloan
Charley Winking 8-10-0	MrDScott	Swan-Shot 10-10-0	MBlackshaw
Proud Percy 10-10-0	RREvans		

S.P.: 9 RED RUM,Crisp, 11 L'Escargot, 14 Ashville, 16 PrincessCamilla,Spanish Steps,Canharis, 20 Prophecy,HighlandSeal, 22 ProudTarquin,BlackSecret, 25 SunnyLad,GreySombrero, 33 Beggar'sWay,GeneralSymons,Glenkiln, 40 Rouge Autumn, 50 Astbury,GreatNoise,Petruchio'sSon,Richeleau, 66 Nereo,Fortune BayII,RoughSilk, 100 Others. (Mr N le Mare) D McCain, Birkdale, Southport, Lancs. 38 Rn   9m 1.90 (b29.10)

Red Rum set off on the daunting task of chasing Crisp going to Becher's the last time round. Ridden along, he jumped the remaining fences with precision but came to the last still all of ten lengths behind the leader. With victory in sight as he came to the elbow, he never gave up running and inching back the ground forced his head in front in the last forty yards. An indomitable and plucky win.

Crisp (Aus), flicking over these enormous fences like hurdles, pulled his way into a twenty-length lead after jumping the water. Sailing down to Becher's he actually increased his lead and, turning for the long haul home after Valentine's, looked to have an unassailable advantage. He started to tire at the second from home but was still at least ten lengths clear at the last. Then, suddenly Crisp the flying rocket, became painful flesh and blood with air-starved lungs and limbs like stone. Rolling about, out on his feet, he started to hang towards the dolls guarding the Chair and it was all Pitman could do to wrench him back on to the racecourse. Though by now he appeared to be standing still and looked certain to be caught, it was only in the last few agonizing yards of the interminable run-in that the dogged Red Rum finally cut down perhaps the greatest Aintree hero of them all.

1973/74

PERTH, Wed., Sept. 26th (Firm)
PERTHSHIRE CHALLENGE CUP H'CAP CHASE £576 (£157: £73)   3m   3.0
PROUD STONE 8-11-5 (4x)   RBarry   w ldr: dsptd ld 3 out till hdd flat:
                                       fin 2nd: 1½l: awrdd r)   —1
Red Rum 8-12-4   BFletcher   lw: a going wl: dsptd ld 3 out:
                                      led flat: fin 1st: disqualified and   2
Semigale 6-10-7‡   SPTaylor   hdwy 11th: wknd 4 out   25.3
Saggart's Choice 10-10-9 TStack   led: hmpd appr 12th: sn hdd:
                                     lost pl   20.4
Treble Kay 9-10-5   SNattriss lw: in tch when slipped up bend   0
S.P.: 10/11 PROUD STONE, 7/2 TrebleKay, 4 RedRum, 11/2 Semigale, 10
Saggart'sChoice. (Mr J McGhie) G W Richards, Greystoke, Penrith, Cumberland.
5 Rn

CARLISLE, Sat., Sept. 29th (Firm)
WINDERMERE H'CAP CHASE £405 (£108: £49)   3m   3.45
RED RUM 8-12-4   BFletcher   lw: hdwy 11th: left in ld 12th:
                                      clr 3 out   —1
James Jacques 7-11-3   RBarry   joined ldrs 8th: ev ch 14th: rdn and
                                     nt qckn 3 out   15.2
Canharis 8-11-3   PBuckley   lw: led to 11th: wknd 14th   15.3
David French 8-10-0   CTinkler   bkwd: cl up to 12th: sn wl bhd   dist.4
Meridian II 6-10-7(¹⁴)‡⁷
                          CaptHBaillie bit bkwd: hdwy 7th: led 11th till
                                        blnd and uns rdr next   0
S.P.: 8/13 RED RUM, 4 Canharis, 5 MeridianII, 6 JamesJacques, 20 DavidFrench.
(Mr N Le Mare) D McCain, Birkdale, Southport, Lancs. 5 Rn   6m 23.40 (a12.40)

AYR, Sat., Oct. 13th (Good to firm)
JOAN MACKAY H'CAP CHASE £1,551 (£463: £221: £100)   3m 110y   3.15
RED RUM 8-12-4   BFletcher   lw: a.p. led 3 out: hit last: rdn r.o.
                                      flat   —1
Straight Vulgan 7-10-6   RBarry   cl up: led 14th to 3 out: ch flat:
                                     no ex   1.2
Tregarron 6-11-9   CTinkler   j.w: hdwy ½-wy: ev ch 4 out:
                                     wknd next: better for r   10.3
Treble Kay 9-10-5   SNattriss led to 14th: wknd qckly appr 3   2.4
Tartan Ace 6-10-6   TStack   sme hdwy 15th: nvr trbld ldrs   4.5
Scout 7-10-11   DBrown   prom till lost pl ½-wy   15.6
Hurricane Rock 9-10-11   GDartnall a bhd   7
James Jacques 7-10-10   BBrogan   prom: mistakes: wknd qckly 14th:
                                     p.u bef 3 out   0
S.P.: 10/11 RED RUM, 9/2 StraightVulgan, 5 TartanAce, 8 HurricaneRock,
9 Tregarron, 14 JamesJacques, 16 TrebleKay, 20 Scout. (Mr N Le Mare) D McCain,
Birkdale, Southport, Lancashire. 8 Rn   6m 1.50 (b7.50)
Red Rum looked magnificent. Always well to the fore, he led three out and,
despite making a mess of the last, showed his great courage to quicken again on
the flat. He knocked more than seven seconds off the track record, which makes
this a fantastic performance as horses which run well in—let alone win—a
National are still being rested at this stage of the season. The only drawback with
this truly great horse is the fact that he needs this fast ground to be seen at his
best.

NEWCASTLE, Wed., Oct. 31st (Firm)
JOHN EUSTACE SMITH TROPHY H'CAP CHASE £860 (£238: £114)   3m   2.0
RED RUM 8-12-1   BFletcher   lw: a.p led 3 out: clr when hit last   —1
San-Feliu 10-10-8 (6x)   PBuckley   in tch: effrt 11th: wknd appr 15th:
                                     r.o again 2 out   4.2
Scarba 8-10-5 (10x)‡⁵   MrHBarclay a.p: ev ch 4 out: one pace next   ½.3
Off The Cuff 8-10-0   MBarnes   led till hdd and wknd qckly 3
                                     out   10.4
Even Keel 11-11-7   BBrogan   reluctant to r: hdwy 5th: dropped
                                     out 11th: sn t.o: r.o. agair 3 out   4.5
Ballysagert 8-11-11   TStack   lost tch 13th: p.u lame after 4
                                     out   0
Nuits St Georges 7-10-9   RBarry   in tch till p.u lame appr 11th   0
S.P.: 13/8 RED RUM, 3 San-Feliu, 13/2 Ballysagert, 6 NuitsStGeorges, 9 Scarba,
12 EvenKeel, 25 OffTheCuff. (Mr N Le Mare) D McCain, Birkdale, Southport,
Lancs. 7 Rn   6m 6 (a10)
Red Rum, always going nicely, was sent on three out and soon had the race
sewn up. This game performer, who looked a real picture will just not give in.

DONCASTER, Sat., Nov. 10th (Good)
DONCASTER PATTERN CHASE £1,763 (£422)   3m 2f   1.0

CRISP (Aus) 10-11-10	RPitman	lw: made all: hit 8th: qcknd and went clr 4 out: eased flat	—1
Red Rum 8-11-10	BFletcher	lw: ev ch 15th: no imp	8.2

S.P.: 4/11 CRISP, 5/2 RedRum. (Sir Chester Manifold) F Winter, Lambourn.
2 Rn   6m 32.90 (a10.90)
Red Rum ran a gallant race, jumping with the winner until the latter started to stretch out in the last three quarters of a mile. He was then outclassed.

NEWBURY, Sat., Nov. 24th (Good)
HENNESSY COGNAC GOLD CUP H'CAP CHASE £7,435 (£2,260: £1,110:
                                    £535)   3m 2f 82y   2.5

RED CANDLE 9-10-4	JFox	stdy hdwy 16th: led 2 out and last: led last strides	—1
Red Rum 8-11-4	BFletcher	led 18th and 19th: led flat: r.o wl	s.h.2
Anthony Watt 7-11-0	MDickinson	dropped rear 17th: gd hdwy 2 out: r.o	6.3
Cuckolder 8-10-1	ATurnell	lw: ev ch 18th: mistake 2 out: unable qckn	$\frac{1}{2}$.4
Nereo (Spa) 7-10-0	VSoane	hdwy 16th: ev ch 17th: one pace	6.5
Spanish Steps 10-11-10	PBlacker	ev ch 17th: no hdwy 18th	2$\frac{1}{2}$.6
Prairie Dog 9-10-2	ABranford	prom to 17th	7
Roman Holiday 9-10-7 (7x)	JKing	led to 3rd:chased ldr 4th till wknd 17th	8
Charlie Potheen 8-12-4	RBarry	mistake 11th: led 4th to 17th	9
Bighorn 9-11-0	DCartwright	bhd till b.d 13th	0
Great Haven (H) 8-10-0	JGlover	bhd till f 13th	0

S.P.: 9/2 CharliePotheen, 6 SpanishSteps,Nereo,AnthonyWatt, 15/2 Cuckolder, 8 RedRum, 9 Bighorn, 12 RED CANDLE, 14 PrairieDog, 18 RomanHoliday, 25 GreatHaven. (Mrs C O'Shea) G Vallance, Bishops Cannings, Devizes, Wilts.
11 Rn   6m 37.80 (a2.80)
Red Rum jumped his way to the front four out and battled on dourly when Red Candle headed him two fences later. His tenacity got him in front again late on the run-in but weight told close home. A very game performance.

CATTERICK, Wed., Feb. 20th (Soft)
BRETTANBY H'CAP CHASE £939 (£254: £117)   3m 300y   3.45

RED RUM 9-12-7	BFletcher	lw: hdwy 13th: chal 3 out: lft in ld last: stayed on wl	—1
Fanatic 7-10-0	PBuckley	prom: led 12th: hard drvn and blnd badly last: nt rcvr	8.2
Wing Master 10-10-0	DGoulding	blnd 13th: sn wl bhd: stayed on 2 out	12.3
Huperade 10-11-0	RBarry	lost tch 12th: blnd 14th	$\frac{3}{4}$.4
Tregarron 7-10-8	CTinkler	prom: ev ch when f 3 out	0
Ernie Wiltshire 8-10-0	JJO'Neill	in tch when f 9th	0
Saggart's Choice 11-10-0	Blackshaw	led to 12th: p.u bef next	0

S.P.: 11/4 ErnieWiltshire, 3 RED RUM, 4 Tregarron, 13/2 Fanatic, 15/2 Wing Master, 10 Huperade, 33 Saggart'sChoice. (Mr N le Mare) D McCain, Birkdale, Southport, Lancs. 7 Rn   7m 4.30 (a43.40)
Red Rum began to move up with a circuit to go. He challenged three out and, when the leader took the last by the roots, went on and galloped clear in his relentless fashion.

1973/74

HAYDOCK PARK, Sat., Mar. 2nd (Good to soft)
GREENALL WHITLEY H'CAP CHASE £4,638 (£1,389: £667: £306)   3m   2.0
GLANFORD BRIGG 8-10-7

	SHolland	j.w: made all: clr from 5th: easily	—1
Money Market 7-10-9	JKing	a.p: blnd 11th: chased wnr from 2 out: no imp	25.2
Vultown 9-11-2	DMould	lw: joined ldrs 11th: rdn and wknd appr 3 out	8.3
Noble Hero 7-10-0	MGifford	bhd till sme hdwy 2 out: nrst fin	¾.4
Rouge Autumn 10-10-3(³)	WSmith	sn cl up: behind from 7th	4.5
The Leap 9-10-5	MrSParkyn	j lft: in touch: one pace from 14th	½.6
Wing Master 10-10-0	RREvans	nvr went pace	7
Tregarron 7-10-8	CTinkler	lw: bhd and rdn 10th: n.d	8
Gyleburn 11-10-12	RBarry	bhd from 10th	0
Colley Mill 11-10-12	DCartwright	blnd 3rd: no ch from 13th	0
Red Rum 9-12-7	BFletcher	lw: hmpd and u.r after 1st	0
Tartan Ace 7-11-11	TStack	blnd and u.r 1st	0

S.P.: 4 GLANFORD BRIGG, 9/2 Tregarron, 5 RedRum, 6 Vultown, 7 TartanAce, 11 TheLeap, 14 Gyleburn,MoneyMarket, 20 ColleyMill,WingMaster,Rouge Autumn, 33 NobleHero. (Mr P Harper) J Hardy, Staunton, Notts. 12 Rn   6m 23.30 (a9.30)

Red Rum jumped the first fence perfectly but just afterwards another horse cannoned into him, giving Fletcher no chance of remaining in the saddle. He looked in great shape before the race and must have a good chance of landing his second National.

LIVERPOOL, Sat., Mar. 30th (Good)
GRAND NATIONAL H'CAP CHASE £25,102 (£7,620: £3,735: £1,792)

		4m 856 y	3.15
RED RUM 9-12-0	BFletcher	l.w: 10th water: led 2nd Bechers: blnd 26th: shaken up 2 out: easily	—1
L'Escargot (H) 11-11-13	TCarberry	lw: 6th 1st Canal turn: 5th water: 5th 2nd Canal turn: ev ch 2 out: one pace	7.2
Charles Dickens 10-10-0	ATurnell	2nd 1st Canal turn, led 10th: hmpd 13th: hmpd Chair: 2nd water: led 17th to 2nd Bechers: ev ch 3 out: r.o wl flat	s.h.3
Spanish Steps 11-11-9	WSmith	lw: 10th 1st Canal turn: 6th water and 2nd Canal turn: hard rdn 4 out: one pace	8.4
Rough Silk 11-10-0	MMorris	dsptd ld 2nd to 6th: 3rd 1st Canal turn: blnd Chair: 7th water 2nd Canal turn: one pace	7.5
Vulgan Town 8-10-8	JHaine	lw: 5th 1st Canal turn: 3rd water: dsptd ld 17th till 2nd Canal turn: wknd Valentines	7.6
Rouge Autumn 10-10-0	KWhite	11th 1st Canal turn: 14th water: 13th 2nd Canal turn: one pace	7
Nereo (Spa) 8-10-6	DukeofAlburquerque	12th 1st Canal turn: 16th water: hdwy 3 out: one pace	8
San-Feliu 11-10-3(²)	PBuckley	8th water: 9th 2nd Canal turn: r.o	9
Norwegian Flag 8-10-0	JBourke	11th water: one pace	10
Scout 8-10-0	TStack	lw: 8th 1st Canal turn: 12th water: 3rd 2nd Canal turn: ran 4 out: wknd 2 out	11
Quintus 8-10-0	GThorner	23rd water: a bhd	12
Dunno 10-10-11	MrNMitchell	20th water: 10th 2nd Canal turn	13
Tubs VI 11-10-6(⁶)	VO'Brien	26th water	14
Escari 8-10-2(²)	PBlack	15th water: sn bhd	15
Sunny Lad 10-10-4	DCartwright	led 6th to 10th, 4th water: 11th 2nd Canal turn	16
Princess Camilla 9-11-4	MBlackshaw	17th water:12th 2nd Canal turn	17
Royal Relief 10-11-6	LordOaksey	f 1st	0
Huperade 10-10-12	MrJCarden	f 1st Canal turn	0
Straight Vulgan 8-10-8	RBarry	4th 1st Canal turn: 9th water: prom when f 18th	0
Rough House 8-10-6	MrJBurke	f 1st Canal turn	0
Francophile 9-10-5(³)	RPitman	19th water, ref 28th	0
Glenkiln 11-10-2	RCrank	7th 1st canal turn: 13th water: f 19th	0
The Tunku 8-10-1	RREvans	28th water: p.u 18th	0

Also ran:—

Deblins Green 11-10-0 NWakley
Beau Bob (H) 11-10-0 JGlover
Estoile 10-10-0 RHyett
Mill Door 12-10-2([2]) JMcNaught
Culla Hill 10-10-8([8]) MrNBrookes
Go-Pontinental 14-10-0 JSuthern
Shaneman 9-10-2 SHannon
Argent 10-11-10 RCoonan
Sixer 10-10-0 MSaleman

Karacola 9-10-0 CAstbury
Roman Holiday 10-10-7 JKing
Bahia Dora 9-10-2 JGuest
Stephen's Society 8-11-5([9])
MrCCollins
Pearl of Montreal 11-10-0 TKinane
Astbury 11-10-0 MrWJenks
Wolverhampton 7-10-0 RQuinn
Cloudsmere 10-10-4([4]) PKelleway
Beggar's Way 10-10-2 VSoane

S.P.: 7 Scout, 17/2 L'Escargot, 11 RED RUM, 14 RoughHouse, 15 SpanishSteps, StraightVulgan, 16 Francophile, 18 RoyalRelief, 20 SunnyLad, 22 San-Feliu, TubsVI, 25 DeblinsGreen,Wolverhampton, 28 PrincessCamilla,RougeAutumn, 33 Quintus, 35 VulganTown, 40 Stephen'sSociety, 50 Argent,Glenkiln,Norwegian Flag,Shaneman,CharlesDickens,PearlofMontreal, 66 RomanHoliday,Sixer,Astbury,Estoile,Escari,Beggar'sWay,RoughSilk, 100 Others. (Mr N le Mare) D McCain, Birkdale, Southport, Lancs. 42 Rn   9m 20.30 (a2.30)

Red Rum, a tough, relentless galloper and a much improved chaser made this look incredibly easy. Very much at home on the fast surface, he was going so easily that his rider had to let him hit the front approaching Becher's the last time round. Cruising in the lead coming on to the racecourse, he quickened appreciably and, with his race won long before the elbow, his rider was able to salute the crowd and then ease him back before the post. This was a fantastic performance and Red Rum, whose win last year was rather overshadowed by the gallant efforts of the second, now dominates the Aintree scene as a figure of heroic proportions in his own right. Such dramatic improvement reflects the highest credit on his trainer.

AYR, Sat., Apr. 20th (Firm)
SCOTTISH GRAND NATIONAL H'CAP CHASE £7,922 (£2,396: £1,168: £554)
4m 120y   2.55

RED RUM 9-11-13 (6x)	BFletcher	lw: held up:hdwy 19th: led appr last: r.o wl	—1
Proud Tarquin (H) 11-10-7 (6x)	LordOaksey	a.p: led 18th: hit 3 out: hdd appr last: no ex flat	4.2
Kildagin 10-9-7	JSuthern	lw: hdwy 14th: ev ch 3 out: stayed on wl	nk.3
Canharis 9-10-3 (4x)	PBuckley	led: hit 6th and 15th: hdd 18th: r.o one pace	4.4
Quick Reply 9-9-9([2])	MBarnes	hdwy 21st: no ex from 3 out	2½.5
Dicasee 8-9-12([5])	MGifford	lw: prom: no hdwy 21st	4.6
Moonlight Escapade 8-10-11 (4x)	DCartwright	lw: bhd: hdwy 17th: n.d	7
Tee-Cee-Bee 8-10-12([7])	MrGMacmillan	bhd:hdwy 21st: n.d	8
Deblin's Green 11-9-13([6])	NWakley	prom to 14th	9
Corrie Burn 8-10-8	MDickinson	prom to 12th	10
Ernie Wiltshire 8-9-12([5])	MrRLamb	hdwy 17th: sn prom: rdn and wknd 21st	11
Lampoon (H) 10-9-11([1])	GHolmes	prom to 18th	12
Francophile 9-9-8([1])	GThorner	in tch 17th: sn lost pl: t.o	13
Pattered 8-9-13	KBWhite	lw: prom till uns rdr 15th	0
Scout 8-9-13([6])	TStack	bhd: t.o when p.u bef 3 out	0
Noble Neptune 8-10-3	VSoane	prom to 20th: wknd: p.u bef 3 out	0
Rainbow Patch (H) 9-10-0([7])	JGlover	prom to 23rd:wknd qckly: p.u bef last	0

S.P.: 11/8 RED RUM, 6 Tee-Cee-Bee, 11 Scout,MoonlightEscapade, 12 Pattered, 14 NobleNeptune, 16 Canharis,ProudTarquin,QuickReply,Francophile, 20 Kildagin, RainbowPatch,Deblin'sGreen, 25 CorrieBurn, 33 Others. (Mr N le Mare) D McCain, Southport, Lancs. 17 Rn   8m 8.60 (b0.40)

Analysis of Races run and Stakes won (this excludes place money

Under Jockey Club Rules

Age	Starts	1st	2nd	3rd	Stakes
2	8	1½	0	2	600
3	2	1	1	0	492
	10	2½	1	2	£1,192

Under National Hunt Rules

Age	Starts	1st	2nd	3rd	Stakes
3–4	10	3	2	2	884
4–5	14	0	2	1	—
5–6	13	3	0	7	1,294
6–7	12	2	1	3	1,481
7–8	9	6	1	1	28,882
8–9	10	6	3	0	36,779
	68	20	9	14	£69,320

Red Rum's pedigree

QUORUM (gr. 1954)
- Vilmorin
  - Gold Bridge
    - Swynford or Golden Boss
    - Flying Diadem
  - Queen of the Meadows
    - Fairway
    - Queen of the Blues
- Akimbo
  - Bois Roussel
    - Vatout
    - Plucky Liege
  - Bulolo
    - Noble Star
    - Pussy Willow

MARED (b. 1958)
- Magic Red
  - Link Boy
    - Pharos
    - Market Girl
  - Infra Red
    - Ethnarch
    - Black Ray
- Quinta
  - Anwar
    - Umidwar
    - Stafaralla
  - Batika
    - Blenheim
    - Brise Bise (25)

The progeny of Mared

MARED: bred by S. J. Parr. Won 1 race, £202, at 3 years.
1963—Neared, b.f. by Neron. Unraced.
1964—Quintula, b.f. by Neron. Sent to Germany; unraced.
1965—RED RUM, b.g. by Quorum. Won 2½ flat races, £971, at 2 and 3 years, and 3 hurdle races and 17 steeplechases, total £69,427, from 4 to 9 years, including Grand National Chase, Liverpool (twice) and Scottish Grand National Handicap Chase, Ayr; second in Hennessy Cognac Gold Cup, Newbury.
1967—b.c. by Typhoon. Sent to Italy.
1968—OUR RICHARD, b.c. by Our Babu. Won 1 race, £603, at 3 years.
1969—b.f. by Fray Bentos.
1970—Fraymar, br.f. by Fray Bentos. Unraced.
1971—b.c. by Fray Bentos.
1972—b.f. by Fray Bentos.
1973—b.f. by Fray Bentos.